MOUS *Essentials*

PowerPoint® 2000

LINDA BIRD

Prentice Hall

Upper Saddle River, New Jersey

MOUS Essentials: PowerPoint® 2000

Trademark Acknowledgments

Editor-in-Chief:
Mickey Cox

Acquisitions Editor:
Lucinda Gatch

Assistant Editor:
Jennifer Stagman

Managing Editor:
Monica Stipanov

Technical Editor:
Georgena Harrison

Editorial Assistant:
Mary Toepfer

Director of Strategic Marketing:
Nancy Evans

Marketing Manager:
Kris King

AVP/Director of Production & Manufacturing:
Michael Weinstein

Manager, Production:
Gail Steier de Acevedo

Project Manager:
Tim Tate

Manufacturing Buyer:
Natacha St. Hill Moore

Associate Director, Manufacturing:
Vincent Scelta

Book Design:
Louisa Klucznik/Graphic World Inc.

Cover Design:
Pisaza Design Studio, Ltd.

Composition:
Gillian Hall, The Aardvark Group

About the Authors

Linda Bird specializes in corporate training and support through Software Solutions, her own company. She has successfully trained users representing more than 75 businesses, including several Fortune 500 companies, custom designing many of her training materials. Her clients include Appalachian Electric Power Co., Goodyear, Pillsbury, Rockwell, and Shell Chemical. Her background also includes teaching at Averett College and overseeing computer training for a business training organization.

Linda has written numerous books on PowerPoint, Word, Excel, Access, and Windows. Additionally, she has written almost 20 instructor's manuals and contributed to books on desktop application programs. She has also penned more than 125 magazine articles and authors monthly how-to columns for Smart Computing magazine.

Linda, a graduate of the University of Wisconsin, lives in Gallipolis, Ohio with her husband, Lonnie, and daughters, Rebecca and Sarah. Besides authoring books, Linda home schools her daughters.

Dedication

I would like to dedicate this book to my family: Lonnie, who is a published author and my best supporter; and Rebecca and Sarah, our family's future authors.

Acknowledgments

No book is ever the result of a sole person, but rather the result of a hard-working team of talented individuals. Although most of these persons work behind the scenes, I would like to publicly acknowledge their professionalism, hard work, and dedication to producing a top-quality publication.

First I'd like to thank Acquisitions Editor **Lucinda Gatch** for giving me the opportunity to be involved in the project; Managing Editor **Monica Stipanov** for her quick and valuable feedback; and Project Manager **Tim Tate** for shepherding the book through production. I also want to express my appreciation to Technical Editor **Georgena Harrison** and Copy Editor **Keith Cline** who served as a top-notch editorial team and helped to ensure the quality of the book.

I'd also like to thank the other MOUS Essentials authors for their valuable feedback, their willingness to network, and for their friendship: **Larry Metzelaar** and **Marianne Fox** (MOUS Essentials: Excel 2000), **Keith Mulbery** (MOUS Essentials: Word 2000), and **Robert Ferrett**, **Sally Preston**, and **John Preston** (MOUS Essentials: Access 2000).

Most of all, I would like to thank my family: **Lonnie**, **Rebecca**, and **Sarah**. They were my best fans and cheerleaders throughout the entire writing process.

Contents at a Glance

Table of Contents

Introduction

Essentials courseware from Prentice Hall is anchored in the practical and professional needs of all types of students. Each title in the series reflects a "learning-by-doing" approach that encourages you to grasp application-related concepts as you expand your skills through hands-on tutorials.

The *MOUS Essentials* series has an added focus—preparing you for certification as a Microsoft Office User Specialist. The Specialist designation distinguishes you from your peers as knowledgeable in using Office products, which can also make you more competitive in the job market.

The Specialist program is available for many Office 2000 applications at both Core and Expert User levels. You can learn more about the Specialist program by reviewing Appendix B, "Preparing for MOUS Certification," and by visiting the www.mous.net Web site.

How To Use This Book

You have selected a book providing a comprehensive approach to learning PowerPoint, with emphasis on skill sets designated by Microsoft as *Core* or *Expert* for purposes of certification as a Microsoft Office User Specialist. Please take a few moments to familiarize yourself with the icons used in this book and its conventions. If you have questions or comments, visit the related Prentice Hall *MOUS Essentials* Web site at www.prenhall.com/mousessentials.

Each *MOUS Essentials* text consists of modular lessons built around a series of numbered step-by-step procedures that are clear, concise, and easy to review. Brief explanations are provided at the start of each lesson and, as needed, between steps. Many lessons contain additional notes and tips.

A *MOUS Essentials* book may contain anywhere from 15–21 projects, two appendixes, and a glossary. Each project covers one area (or a few closely related areas) of application functionality, and is divided into lessons related to that topic. For example, a project on formatting text and bullets includes lessons on changing text appearance, using the Format Painter, modifying text alignment, setting tabs, adding, modifying, and removing bullets. Each lesson presents a specific task or closely related set of tasks in a manageable chunk that's easy to assimilate and retain.

Each element in a *MOUS Essentials* title is designed to maximize your learning experience. Here's a list of the *MOUS Essentials* project elements and a description of how each element can help you:

- **Required MOUS Objectives Table**   These tables are organized into three columns: Objective, Required Activity for MOUS, and Exam Level. The Objective column lists the general objectives of the project. The associated MOUS requirements for each objective are listed in the Required Activity for MOUS column. The particular exam levels of those activities—Core or Expert—are listed in the Exam Level column. Look over the objectives and MOUS requirements on the opening page of each project before you begin, and review them after completing the project to identify the main goals for each project.

- **Key Terms**   This book includes useful vocabulary words and definitions, specific to the application. Key terms introduced in each project are listed in alphabetic order on the opening page of the project. These key terms then appear in bold italic within the text and are defined during their first occurrence in the project. Definitions of key terms are also included in the glossary.

- **Why Would I Do This?**   You are studying PowerPoint to accomplish useful tasks in the real world. This brief section at the beginning of each project tells you why these tasks or procedures are important. What can you do with the knowledge? How can these application features be applied to everyday tasks?

 - **MOUS Office Core Objective Icon**   This icon indicates that a lesson or exercise relates to a specific MOUS Core-level skill. MOUS skills may be covered by a whole lesson or perhaps just a single step within a lesson. They may also be covered in an end-of-project exercise.

 - **MOUS Office Expert Objective Icon**   This icon indicates that a lesson or exercise relates to a MOUS Expert-level skill. There may be a mix of Core and Expert objectives within a project. Some objectives are both Core and Expert, as well.

- **Lessons**   Most lessons contain one or more tasks that correspond to an objective or MOUS requirement, which are listed on the opening page of the project. A lesson consists of step-by-step tutorials, associated screen captures, and the sidebar notes of the types described later. Although each lesson often builds on the preceding one, the lessons have been made as modular as possible. For example, you can skip tasks that you've already mastered and begin a later lesson, if you choose.

- **Step-by-Step Tutorials**   The lessons consist of numbered, bolded, step-by-step instructions that show you how to perform the procedures in a clear, concise, and direct manner. These hands-on tutorials, which are the "essentials" of each project, let you "learn by doing." A short paragraph may appear after a step to clarify the results of the step. Screen captures are provided after key steps so that you can compare the results on your monitor. To review the lesson, you can easily scan the bold, numbered steps.

 - **Exam Notes**   These sidebars provide information and insights on topics covered on MOUS exams. You can easily recognize them by their distinctive icon. It's well worth the effort to review these crucial notes again after completing a project.

 - **Inside Stuff**   Inside Stuff comments provide extra tips, shortcuts, and alternative ways to complete a process, as well as special hints. You may safely ignore these for the moment to focus on the main task at hand, or you may pause to learn and appreciate these tidbits.

 - **If You Have Problems...**   These short troubleshooting notes help you anticipate or solve common problems quickly and effectively. Even if you don't encounter the problem at this time, do make a mental note of it so that you know where to look when you find yourself having difficulties.

- **Summary**   This section provides a brief recap of the activities learned in the project. The summary often includes suggestions for expanding your knowledge.

 - **Checking Concepts and Terms**   This section offers optional true/false and multiple-choice questions designed to check your comprehension and to assess retention. If you need to refresh your memory, the relevant lesson number is provided after each question. For example, [L5] directs you to review Lesson 5 for the answer.

- **Skill Drill**   This section enables you to check your comprehension, evaluate your progress, and practice what you've learned. The exercises in this section build on and reinforce what you have learned in each project. Generally, the Skill Drill exercises include step-by-step instructions. A Core or Expert icon indicates whether a MOUS required activity is introduced in a Skill Drill exercise.

■ **Challenge**   This section provides exercises that expand on or relate to the skills practiced in the project. Each exercise provides a brief narrative introduction followed by instructions. Although the instructions are written in a step-by-step format, the steps are not as detailed as those in the Skill Drill section. Providing fewer specific steps, the Challenge section helps you learn to think on your own. A Core or Expert icon indicates whether a MOUS required activity is introduced in a Challenge exercise.

■ **Discovery Zone**   These exercises require advanced knowledge of project topics or application of skills from multiple lessons. Additionally, these exercises might require you to research topics in Help or on the Web to complete them. This self-directed method of learning new skills emulates real-world experience. A Core or Expert icon indicates whether a MOUS required activity is introduced in a Discovery Zone exercise.

■ **PinPoint Assessment**   Each project ends with a reminder to use MOUS PinPoint training and testing software to supplement the projects in the book. The software aids you in your preparation for taking and passing the MOUS exams. A thorough explanation of how to use the PinPoint software is provided in Appendix A, "Using the MOUS PinPoint 2000 Training and Testing Software."

Typeface Conventions Used in this Book

We have used the following conventions throughout this book so that certain items stand out from the rest of the text:

■ Key terms appear in **_bold italic_** the first time they are defined.

■ Monospace type appears frequently and looks `like this`. It is used to indicate 1) text that you are instructed to key in; 2) text that appears on screen as warnings, confirmations, or general information; 3) the name of a file to be used in a lesson or exercise; and 4) text from a dialog box that is referenced within a sentence, when that sentence might appear awkward if the dialog box text were not set off.

■ Hotkeys are indicated by underline. Hotkeys are the underlined letters in menus, toolbars, and dialog boxes that activate commands and options, and are a quick way to choose frequently used commands and options. Hot keys look like this: File, Save.

How To Use Student Data Files on the CD-ROM

The CD-ROM accompanying this book contains PinPoint as well as all the data files for you to use as you work through the step-by-step tutorials within projects and the Skill Drill, Challenge, and Discovery Zone exercises provided at the end of each project. The CD contains separate parallel folders for each project.

The names of the student data files correspond to the filenames called for in the textbook. Each filename includes seven characters—two letters indicating the application, a dash, two digits indicating the project number, and two digits indicating the file number within the project. For example, the first file used in PowerPoint Project 2 is named pp-0201. The third file in PowerPoint Project 14 is named pp-1403. The Word document named **pp-stufiles.doc** on the companion Web site (www.prenhall.com/mousessentials) provides a complete listing of data files by project, including the corresponding names used to save each file.

Refer to the readme file on the CD for instruction on how to use your CD-ROM.

Supplements

Instructors get extra support for this text in the following supplements:

- *Instructor's Resource CD-ROM* —The Instructor's Resource CD-ROM includes the entire Instructor's Manual for each application in Microsoft Word format and also contains screen shots that correspond to the solutions for the lessons in the book. A computerized testbank is included to create tests, maintain student records, and to provide online practice testing. Student data files and completed solutions files are also on the CD-ROM. PowerPoint slides, which elaborate on each project, are also included.

- *Companion Web Site (www.prenhall.com/mousessentials)* — For both students and instructors, the companion Web site includes all the ancillary material to accompany the MOUS Essentials series. Students can also access the Interactive Study Guide online, allowing them to evaluate their understanding of the key concepts of each application with instant feedback on their results. Instructors will find the data and solutions files, Instructor's Manual, and PowerPoint slides for each application.

Microsoft PowerPoint 2000 MOUS Core and Expert User Skills

Each MOUS exam involves a list of required tasks you may be asked to perform. This list of possible tasks is categorized by skill area. The following tables list the skill areas and where their required tasks can be found in this book. Table A contains the Core-level tasks. Table B contains the Expert-level tasks.

 **Table A Microsoft PowerPoint 2000 Core MOUS Skills**

Skill Set	Required Activity for MOUS	Project	Lesson(s)	Page(s)
Creating a presentation				
	Delete slides	3	2	58
	Create a specified type of slide	3	2	58
	Create a presentation from a template and/or a wizard	2	1–2	28–31
	Navigate among different views (Slide, Outline, Sorter, Tri-pane)	2	3–4	34–38
	Create a new presentation from existing slides	12	4	289
	Copy a slide from one presentation into another	3	5	66
	Insert headers and footers	6	6	137
	Create a blank presentation	1	2	144
	Create a presentation using the AutoContent Wizard	2	2	31
	Send a presentation via e-mail	14	5	345
Modifying a presentation				
	Change the order of slides using Slide Sorter view	3	3	62
	Find and replace text	9	3	207
	Change the layout for one or more slides	3	2	58
	Change slide layout (Modify the Slide Master)	6	5	135
	Modify slide sequence in the outline pane	3	3	62
	Apply a design template	6	1	124
Working with text				
	Check spelling	3	6	68
	Change and replace text fonts (individual slide and entire presentation)	4 1	1 2	78 144
	Enter text in Tri-pane view	3	4	63
	Import text from Word	12	1	280
	Change the text alignment	4	3	83
	Create a text box for entering text	11	1	249
	Use the Wrap Text in TextBox feature	11	1	249
	Use the Office Clipboard	12	8	300
	Use the Format Painter	4	2	81
	Promote and demote text in Slide and Outline panes	3	4	63
Working with visual elements				
	Add a picture from the ClipArt Gallery	10	1–2	224–228
	Add and group shapes using WordArt or the Drawing toolbar	11	1, 3, 7	249, 256, 270

Core Level MOUS Skills (continued)

Skill Set	Required Activity for MOUS	Project	Lesson(s)	Page(s)
Working with visual elements (continued)	Apply formatting	11	4–6	261–267
	Place text inside a shape using a text box	11	2	252
	Scale and size an object including ClipArt	10	2	228
		2	3	34
	Create tables within PowerPoint	12	3	285
	Rotate and fill an object	11	3–4	256–261
Customizing a presentation	Add AutoNumber bullets	4	6	91
	Add speaker notes	5	1	102
	Add graphical bullets	4	4–5	87–89
	Add slide transitions	8	1	178
	Animate text and objects	8	2–3	182–183
Creating output	Preview presentation in black and white	2	5	41
		8	3	183
	Print slides in a variety of formats	2	5	41
		8	5	188
	Print audience handouts	5	2	106
	Print speaker notes in a specified format	5	2	106
Delivering a presentation	Start a slide show on any slide	2	5	41
	Use on screen navigation tools	2	5–6	41–43
	Print a slide as an overhead transparency	5	6	114
	Use the pen during a presentation	8	5	188
Managing files	Save changes to a presentation	2	7	44
	Save as a new presentation	2	3	34
	Publish a presentation to the Web	14	4	343
	Use Office Assistant	1	5	13
		12	5	291
		5	2	106
	Insert hyperlink	13	3–4, 7	319–321, 328

Table B Microsoft PowerPoint 2000 Expert MOUS Skills

Skill Set	Required Activity for MOUS	Project	Lesson(s)	Page(s)
Creating a presentation				
	Automatically create a summary slide	9	6	214
	Automatically create an agenda slide	9	6	214
	Design a template	6	1	124
	Format presentations for the Web	14	2	339
Modifying a presentation				
	Change tab formatting	4	3	83
	Use the Wrap Text in AutoShape feature	11	2	252
	Apply a template from another presentation	6	2	127
	Customize a color scheme	6	3	130
	Apply animation effects	7	6	163
		8	3	183
	Create a custom background	6	4	132
	Add animated GIFs	10	6	238
	Add links to slides within the presentation	13	1, 3–5	314, 319–323
	Customize clip art and other objects (resize, scale, and so on)	10	3	231
		11	3, 7	256,270
	Add a presentation within a presentation	12	4	289
		13	1	314
	Add an action button	13	5	323
	Hide slides	8	1	178
	Set automatic slide timings	8	4	186
Working with visual elements				
	Add textured backgrounds	6	4	132
	Apply diagonal borders to a table	12	3	285
Using data from other sources				
	Export an outline to Word	12	9	303
	Add a table (from Word)	12	6	295
	Insert an Excel chart	12	5	291
	Add sound	10	4	233
	Add video	10	5	236
Creating output				
	Save slide as a graphic	2	7	44
	Generate meeting notes	8	6	171
	Change output format (page setup)	5	6	114
	Export to 35mm slides	5	7	115
Delivering a presentation				
	Save presentation for use on another computer (Pack and Go)	14	1	337
	Electronically incorporate meeting feedback	8	6	191
	View a presentation on the Web	14	3	341

Expert Level MOUS Skills (continued)

Skill Set	Required Activity for MOUS	Project	Lesson(s)	Page(s)
Managing files				
	Save embedded fonts in presentation	2	7	44
	Save HTML to a specific target browser	14	4	343
Working with PowerPoint				
	Customize the toolbar	15	1, 3	358, 365
	Create a toolbar	15	2	362
Collaborating with workgroups				
	Subscribe to a presentation	14	6	347
	View a presentation on the Web	14	3	341
	Use NetMeeting to schedule a broadcast	14	6	347
	Use NetShow to deliver a broadcast	14	6	347
Working with charts and tables (objectives moved from Proficient level)				
	Build a chart or graph	7	2	148
	Modify charts or graphs	7	3–5	152–159
	Build an organization chart	7	7	164
	Modify an organization chart	7	8	167
	Modify PowerPoint tables	12	3	285

Project 1

Getting Started with PowerPoint 2000

Key terms introduced in this project include

- AutoLayouts
- editing mode
- electronic slide show
- full menu
- hyperlink
- keywords
- Navigation pane

- Normal view
- Notes pane
- Office Assistant
- Outline pane
- personalized menus and toolbars
- placeholders
- presentation

- presentation graphics program
- Random Access Memory (RAM)
- ScreenTip
- short menu
- shortcut menu
- Slide pane

Objectives	Required Activity for MOUS	Exam Level
➤ Start PowerPoint		
➤ Create a Blank Presentation	Create a Blank Presentation	Core
➤ Explore the PowerPoint Window		
➤ Work with Toolbars and Menus		
➤ Use the Office Assistant	Use Office Assistant	Core
➤ Close Your Presentation and Exit PowerPoint		

Why Would I Do This?

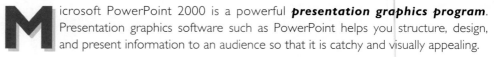

icrosoft PowerPoint 2000 is a powerful **presentation graphics program**. Presentation graphics software such as PowerPoint helps you structure, design, and present information to an audience so that it is catchy and visually appealing.

A **presentation** is simply a series of slides that contain visual information that you can use to persuade an audience. Using PowerPoint, you can effectively and efficiently create professional-looking handouts, overheads, charts, and so on. Whether you are developing a marketing plan, reporting progress on a project, or just conducting a meeting, PowerPoint can help you quickly create powerful presentations. And after you initially develop a presentation, you can jazz it up by adding and modifying text, charts, clip art, and drawn objects.

You can deliver PowerPoint presentations in various ways—by using printed handouts, 35mm slides, or overhead transparencies. Probably the most popular way to show a presentation, however, is to display it as an **electronic slide show**. An electronic slide show is a predetermined list of slides displayed sequentially. You can show the list on you computer's screen or by connecting your system to an overhead projector to cast the image from your computer onto a large screen. As you learn PowerPoint, you'll probably think of many ways that you can use the program to communicate information effectively to others.

In this project, you get a jump-start on working with PowerPoint. You learn the basics of starting PowerPoint and of creating a new presentation. You also see how to find help by using the **Office Assistant**, PowerPoint's online Help system, so that you can learn the program quickly and easily.

It's easy to communicate effectively when you use PowerPoint presentations. So grab your mouse and let's get going!

Lesson 1: Starting PowerPoint

Most people like choices. Luckily, Microsoft offers you a variety of methods that you can use to start PowerPoint. One of the easiest methods to use is to click the Windows Start button, and then choose Microsoft PowerPoint from the Programs menu. In this lesson, you start PowerPoint by using this method.

To Start PowerPoint

1 **Move the mouse pointer to the Start button at the left edge of the Windows taskbar, and then click the left mouse button.**
The Start button's pop-up menu displays (see Figure 1.1).

2 **Move the mouse pointer to the Programs menu item.**
A listing of available programs displays. Don't panic if the ones shown on your system don't match those on other computers, however. The exact programs listed just reflect the ones installed on each individual system.

 If You Have Problems...
If you don't see Microsoft PowerPoint on the Programs submenu, move the mouse pointer over the Microsoft Office folder. Then, click the PowerPoint icon from the Microsoft Office submenu.

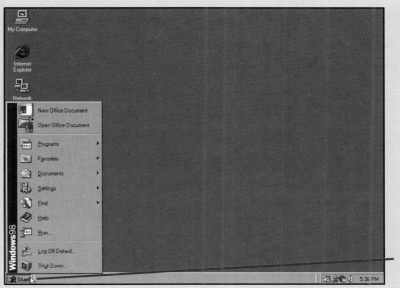

Figure 1.1
You can launch PowerPoint by using the Windows Start button.

Click here to display the Start menu

③ Move the mouse pointer to Microsoft PowerPoint, and then click the left mouse button.

PowerPoint is loaded into the computer's working area—***Random Access Memory (RAM)***—and displays on your screen (see Figure 1.2). Random Access Memory is the temporary storage space that a computer uses for programs that it's currently working on.

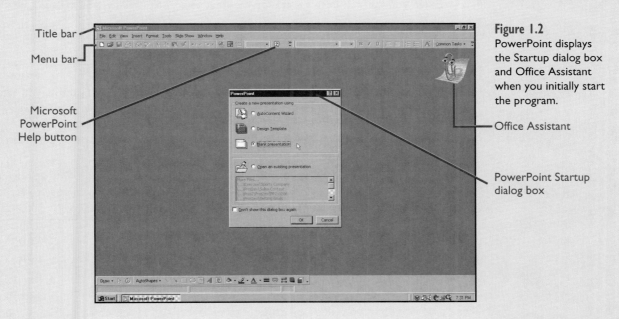

Title bar

Menu bar

Microsoft PowerPoint Help button

Figure 1.2
PowerPoint displays the Startup dialog box and Office Assistant when you initially start the program.

Office Assistant

PowerPoint Startup dialog box

As you scan the PowerPoint window, you probably notice that many screen components are similar to other Windows programs. For example, the menu bar, title bar, and toolbars look similar to other programs that you may have used. (If you're not sure where PowerPoint's commands and features are located, don't worry—you will take a tour of the PowerPoint application window shortly.)

continues ▶

To Start PowerPoint   (continued)

Additionally, PowerPoint displays a Startup dialog box designed to help you quickly create presentations. And unless the feature has been turned off, usually the Office Assistant appears onscreen as well.

 If You Have Problems...
Don't worry if the Office Assistant doesn't display on your screen; most likely, a previous user turned off the Assistant. Later in this project, you learn how to turn the Assistant's display on and off. And don't be concerned if the Office Assistant on your computer appears different from the one shown in this book's figures. Although the default Office Assistant looks like an animated paper clip, it's possible that another user has chosen a different "look." For example, you can use an animated dot, a robot, or even a genius!

 If You Have Problems...
If the Startup dialog box doesn't show when you initially launch PowerPoint, most likely it was turned off during a previous work session. To change the settings so that it shows the next time, you start PowerPoint, choose Tools, Options; then click the View tab. Check the box for Startup dialog; then click OK.

④ Make sure that your screen matches the one shown in Figure 1.2, and that the PowerPoint Startup dialog box is displayed.
Leave your screen in this state for the next exercise, in which you create a new blank presentation.

Inside Stuff: Starting PowerPoint
If a shortcut icon for PowerPoint is displayed on your Windows desktop, you can start PowerPoint by double-clicking it. You can also right-click the icon to display a ***shortcut menu***, which is a list of context-sensitive commands that you display by right-clicking an object. After the shortcut menu is displayed, choose Open from the displayed menu to start PowerPoint.

Many systems are also set up to automatically display the Microsoft Office Shortcut Bar on the Windows desktop. This bar contains buttons that you can use to launch Microsoft Office programs, including PowerPoint.

 ## Lesson 2: Creating a Blank Presentation

Now that you've launched PowerPoint, the stage is set for creating your first presentation! The PowerPoint Startup dialog box provides three options for quickly creating any new presentation: using the AutoContent Wizard, using a design template, or starting completely from scratch by using a blank presentation.

This lesson focuses on creating a new presentation from the ground up. (In Project 2, "Creating Presentations," you learn how to use a template or the AutoContent Wizard to speed up the process.) Try creating a blank presentation from scratch now.

To Create a Blank Presentation

1 **In the PowerPoint Startup dialog box that is still open from Lesson 1, click the Blank presentation option button; then choose OK.**

> ### If You Have Problems...
> Don't despair if you accidentally closed PowerPoint's Startup dialog box or if it didn't display when you launched PowerPoint. Just choose File, New from the menu to display the New Presentation dialog box. On the General tab, click the Blank Presentation icon; then choose OK. Continue with Step 2 of the tutorial.

The New Slide dialog box displays with 24 predefined layout options called **AutoLayouts** (see Figure 1.3). Each AutoLayout includes **placeholders**, which are areas on a slide that can accept different types of objects, such as graphics and text. For example, the Title Slide AutoLayout contains areas for the slide's title and subtitle. Using the AutoLayouts takes considerably less time than individually defining the format for each slide.

Selected AutoLayout →

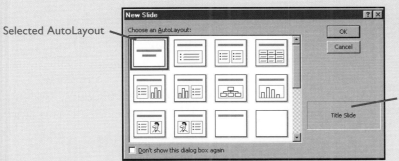

Figure 1.3
You can quickly create a slide for your presentation with preset formatting.

Name of selected AutoLayout

2 **Single-click on several of the AutoLayouts.**
A darkened border appears around the border of an AutoLayout when you select it. Also notice that the name of each AutoLayout displays in the lower-right corner of the New Slide dialog box when you click the associated AutoLayout.

3 **After you have finished experimenting, click on the Title Slide AutoLayout; then choose OK.**
Your first presentation slide displays on your desktop in **Normal view**. This tripane view includes a Slide pane, an Outline pane, and a Notes pane (see Figure 1.4). Each of the three panes represents a way to work with your presentation. You use the **Slide pane** to see how each slide appears and to add text, graphics, and other objects to the slide. In contrast, you use the **Outline pane** to organize the content of the entire presentation and to get a feel for the overall flow. Finally, you use the **Notes pane** to develop speaker notes. For now, you use only the Slide pane to enter your text.

As you develop your presentation, you will probably use the Normal view to enter text and graphics, as well as to quickly scan the presentation's entire flow and content. Because of this versatility, Normal view is a handy all-purpose view.

continues ▶

To Create a Blank Presentation   (continued)

Figure 1.4
Your first slide is
displayed in
PowerPoint's
Normal—or
tri-pane—view.

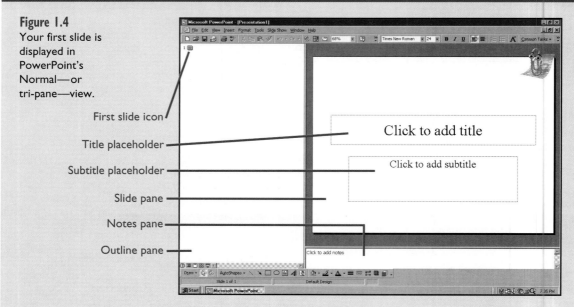

First slide icon
Title placeholder
Subtitle placeholder
Slide pane
Notes pane
Outline pane

④ In the Slide pane, click in the title placeholder (the upper placeholder). (If you're unsure where the title placeholder is located, refer to Figure 1.4.)

The title placeholder is activated in **editing mode** and appears with a rope-like border. When a placeholder is in editing mode, it just means that you can enter or edit text in the placeholder.

⑤ Type Training Proposal.

Your text is entered in the title placeholder. Don't panic if you make a mistake as you enter the text. You can make corrections as you do in a word processing program—just press Del or ⬅Backspace.

⑥ Click in the subtitle placeholder (the lower placeholder); then type By, followed by your name.

Notice that the text you enter on the slide is simultaneously displayed by the first slide icon in the Outline pane. This helps you see how the text you enter relates to the rest of the presentation when you develop multiple-slide presentations.

 If You Have Problems...

If a red squiggly line appears beneath a word (such as your name), don't worry. PowerPoint flags possible typos or misspellings with the red line so that you can correct them. In this case, PowerPoint just doesn't recognize your name—you can safely ignore the red line.

⑦ Click in the Slide pane outside of the subtitle placeholder.

The placeholder is deselected and is no longer in editing mode.

Congratulations! You just developed your first presentation. To build the presentation further, you could add more slides and text. For now, though, leave the presentation in its present state so that you can "take a tour" of PowerPoint's application window.

Inside Stuff: **Entering Text**

When you initially display a Title (or Bulleted List) slide, you don't have to click in a placeholder to enter text. Instead, just start typing; the upper placeholder is automatically activated in editing mode. To move the insertion point to the next placeholder, press and hold down Ctrl, and then press ↵Enter. Release both keys.

Lesson 3: Exploring the PowerPoint Window

Now that you've started PowerPoint and created a simple presentation from scratch, it's time to become familiar with the PowerPoint application window, or screen. Even if you've worked with previous versions of PowerPoint or other Windows software, you will find some changes in PowerPoint 2000. Come along as we take you on a tour...

To Explore the PowerPoint Window

1 **Compare the location of the screen components listed in Figure 1.5 with those on your computer.**

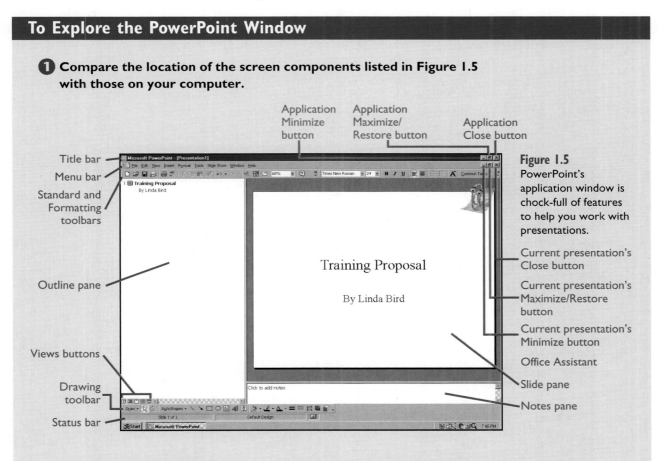

Figure 1.5
PowerPoint's application window is chock-full of features to help you work with presentations.

The title bar, located at the very top of the window, includes the Application Minimize, Maximize/Restore, and Close buttons. The menu bar includes the main menu commands, as well as the current presentation's Minimize, Maximize/Restore, and Close buttons.

The Standard and Formatting toolbars are represented by the row of buttons beneath the menu bar. The Drawing toolbar is displayed at the bottom of the screen; it includes buttons for drawing objects on your slide. (You will see in a minute how to use the toolbar buttons.)

continues ▶

To Explore the PowerPoint Window (continued)

 If You Have Problems...
If your toolbars don't look like those shown in Figure 1.5, another user probably customized their appearance—perhaps without even realizing it! That's because PowerPoint adapts to the way you work by placing the most frequently used commands on the toolbars and menus. Later in this project, you learn how to reset your toolbars and menu commands so that they match those shown in the book.

The main part of the application window is reserved for the presentation itself. Currently, the presentation is shown in Normal view, which was discussed in the preceding lesson. (You see how to switch to other PowerPoint views in Project 2.)

Now, try working with PowerPoint's toolbar buttons.

2 **Rest your mouse pointer over each of the toolbar buttons on the Standard, Formatting, and Drawing toolbars.**
As you rest your mouse pointer over each button, a *ScreenTip* displays, naming the button (see Figure 1.6). Therefore, ScreenTips are a handy way to become familiar with the toolbar buttons.

Figure 1.6
You can display a ScreenTip to find out a button's function.

Standard and Formatting toolbars share one row

ScreenTip

Drawing toolbar

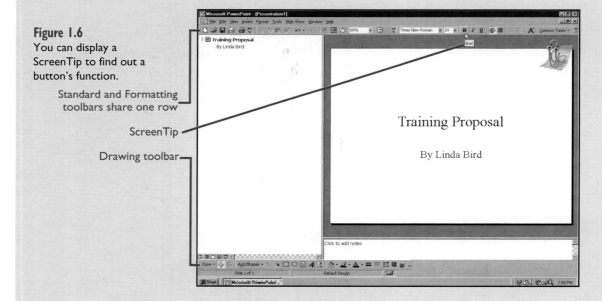

 If You Have Problems...
If the ScreenTips don't show, it's possible that their display has been turned off. Choose **T**ools, **C**ustomize; then click the **O**ptions tab. Check the box for Show Screen**T**ips on toolbars and click Close.

Try expanding the information you can view about a toolbar button. To expand a ScreenTip, you first press ⬆Shift + F1, which activates the What's This? pointer. You can then use this pointer to click the button (or other screen component) that you want to research. Try using ScreenTips now.

3 **Press** ⟨◆Shift⟩ **+** ⟨F1⟩**; then click the Save button on the Standard toolbar.**
PowerPoint displays a ScreenTip that displays information about the Save button.
(If you want, activate ScreenTips for other toolbar buttons and screen compo-
nents. When you finish experimenting, proceed with the tutorial.)

Now, take a look at how the toolbars are laid out in the application window.
PowerPoint 2000 differs from previous versions of the program because both the
Standard and the Formatting toolbars share the same row. Although this saves
space, many of the available buttons don't display. However, you can quickly access the buttons you need by clicking the More Buttons feature at the right end
of each toolbar. Try using this new toolbar setup now.

4 **If necessary, click in the Slide pane to clear the ScreenTip you dis-**
played in the preceding step.

5 **Click the More Buttons button on the Formatting toolbar (located at**
the far right side of the toolbars).
PowerPoint displays a drop-down palette of toolbar buttons included on the default Formatting toolbar (see Figure 1.7). When you click a button on this palette,
it executes the command and also places the button on the Formatting toolbar
for future use. For example, if you typically use the Text Shadow button, which
isn't included on the default setup for the Formatting toolbar, you can choose it
from the palette.

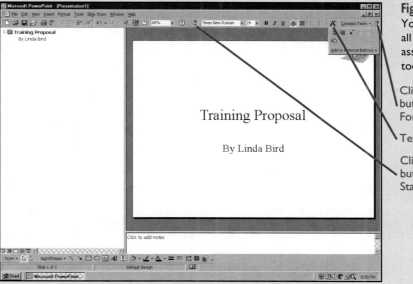

Figure 1.7
You can quickly access
all the buttons
associated with a
toolbar.

Click here to see more
buttons on the
Formatting toolbar

Text Shadow button

Click here to see more
buttons on the
Standard toolbar

6 **Click the Text Shadow button on the Formatting toolbar's More**
Buttons palette.
The Text Shadow button is displayed on the Formatting toolbar. Additionally, if
you had text selected, the Text Shadow effect would have been applied to it.

continues ▶

To Explore the PowerPoint Window   (continued)

Now, take a look at the menu commands in PowerPoint. As in other Windows programs, you execute a command by clicking a command on the menu bar; then by clicking the command you want from the submenu. PowerPoint 2000, however, gives you the option of using either short or full menus. The **short menu**, true to its name, displays an abbreviated list of commonly used commands. The **full menu** includes all of PowerPoint's commands. Try using this new menu setup now.

7 **Click the Insert menu on the menu bar; then rest the mouse pointer over the word Insert until a full menu of choices displays.**

The short menu displays first, showing a list of the most commonly used commands. When you rest the mouse pointer momentarily over the menu command, however, the full menu displays (see Figure 1.8).

Figure 1.8
The short menu displays initially when you choose a command. But PowerPoint provides quick access to the full menus when you momentarily rest your pointer over the command.

 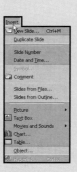

 If You Have Problems...
If the menus on your computer don't appear exactly like those shown in the book, don't worry. PowerPoint 2000 includes adaptable, or personalized, menus. This just means that the program shows the commands at the top of each pull-down menu that you use the most frequently. Because the program automatically customizes the menus to the way you work, it's likely that your menus will display slightly different commands from those shown in the figures.

Inside Stuff: Working with Menus
There are a couple of alternative methods of displaying the long menus. First, you can rest your mouse pointer on the double down-arrows at the bottom of the pull-down menu. Second, you can double-click a main menu command to quickly display the full menu associated with it.

---

8 **Click outside the pull-down menu to close it, without choosing any commands.**

Leave PowerPoint running for the next tutorial, in which you learn to work with toolbars.

Lesson 4: Working with Toolbars and Menus

By now, you should be feeling more comfortable with using ScreenTips to display information about toolbar buttons, and with displaying short and full menus. In this lesson, you expand your knowledge as you work with PowerPoint's Common Tasks button and learn to customize toolbars.

To Work with Toolbars and Menus

1 **Make sure that PowerPoint is running and your new presentation displays in Normal view.**

Now you're ready to display the Common Tasks menu. True to its name, this menu includes frequently used commands, such as adding a new slide. Try displaying this menu now.

2 **Click the Common Tasks button on the far right side of the Formatting toolbar.**

The Common Tasks menu displays, showing a list of three frequently used tasks (see Figure 1.9).

Figure 1.9
Click the Common Tasks button for quick access to these commands.

3 **Click outside of the Common Tasks menu to close it, without choosing any of the commands.**

Now, turn your attention to the *personalized menus and toolbars* included in PowerPoint. PowerPoint's capability to adapt to an individual's work habits by automatically changing the display of menus and toolbar buttons is advantageous because the commands shown are those you use the most. To ensure that your screens display the same way as the figures shown in this book, the personalized menus are turned off, and the Standard and Formatting toolbars are separated to keep all the buttons handy.

4 **Choose Tools, Customize from the menu; then click the Options tab.**

The Options page of the Customize dialog box displays (see Figure 1.10). You use this dialog box to control how PowerPoint's adaptable menus and toolbars work. For example, you can change the settings so that only the full menus show, or you can separate the Standard and Formatting toolbars.

Uncheck this box to separate the toolbars

Uncheck this box to turn off personalized menus

Click here to reset your toolbars and menus

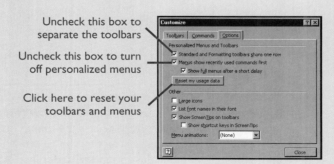

Figure 1.10
You can control the way your toolbars and menus operate.

continues ▶

To Work with Toolbars and Menus   (continued)

First, erase the record of which commands you (or another person) used in PowerPoint. When you do this, PowerPoint reverts back to the original toolbar and menu commands.

5 **Click the Reset my usage data button.**
PowerPoint (or the Office Assistant) displays a message, warning you that resetting usage data will erase the record of commands you used.

6 **Click Yes to confirm your action.**

7 **Uncheck the following boxes: Standard and Formatting toolbars share one row and Menus show recently used commands first.**
Turning off these options separates your Standard and Formatting toolbars. It also ensures that PowerPoint's full menus display.

8 **In the Customize dialog box, click Close.**
The Standard and Formatting toolbars appear on separate rows (see Figure 1.11) and all the buttons associated with each toolbar display. Because all the figures in this book are shown using this toolbar layout, it's a good idea to leave your screen this way as well.

Figure 1.11
Separate the Standard and Formatting toolbars for quick access to all their buttons.

Standard toolbar

Formatting toolbar

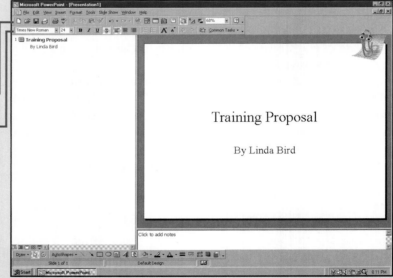

Leave your presentation open for the next lesson, in which you learn how to use the Office Assistant to get help.

 Inside Stuff: **Using Keyboard Shortcuts to Open Menus**
If you're a keyboard fan, you'll be glad to know that you don't have to use the mouse every time you want to access the menus. Instead, press Alt and the menu command's underlined letter to open the pull-down menu. To choose a command on the pull-down menu, just press the underlined letter associated with the command. For example, you can press Alt + I to open the Insert menu; then press H to choose the Chart command on the Insert menu.

Lesson 5: Using the Office Assistant

Have you ever wished for a personal computer trainer—someone to personally guide you through a new software program? Fortunately, PowerPoint 2000 includes an electronic version of such a person—the Office Assistant. Although not a full-blown substitute for a personal computer trainer, the Office Assistant can bring up a list of subjects related to a question you type.

You can choose Help, Microsoft PowerPoint Help to display the Office Assistant. Alternatively, you can click the Microsoft PowerPoint Help button on the Standard toolbar or just press F1. Once the Office Assistant is displayed, you can easily bring up context-sensitive help. Try using this handy feature now.

To Get Help

1 Choose Help, Microsoft PowerPoint Help.

Alternatively, click the Microsoft PowerPoint Help button. No matter which method you choose, the Office Assistant displays a message balloon. You can enter a question in the text box area of the balloon and then have the Office Assistant find all the information related to your inquiry (see Figure 1.12). This balloon also sometimes includes a list of Help topics related to whatever features you used most recently. (If the Office Assistant is already displayed on your screen, just single-click it to display the balloon.)

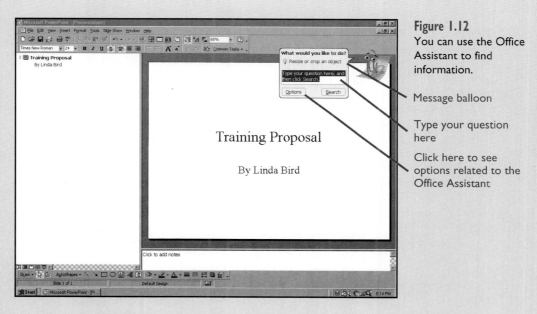

Figure 1.12
You can use the Office Assistant to find information.

Message balloon

Type your question here

Click here to see options related to the Office Assistant

2 In the text box area, type How do I reset my toolbars? **and click Search.**

A list of related topics displays (see Figure 1.13). You can click the topic you want to display help about or you can click the See more... button to view additional topics.

continues ▶

To Get Help (continued)

Figure 1.13
The Office Assistant answers your question by displaying related topics.

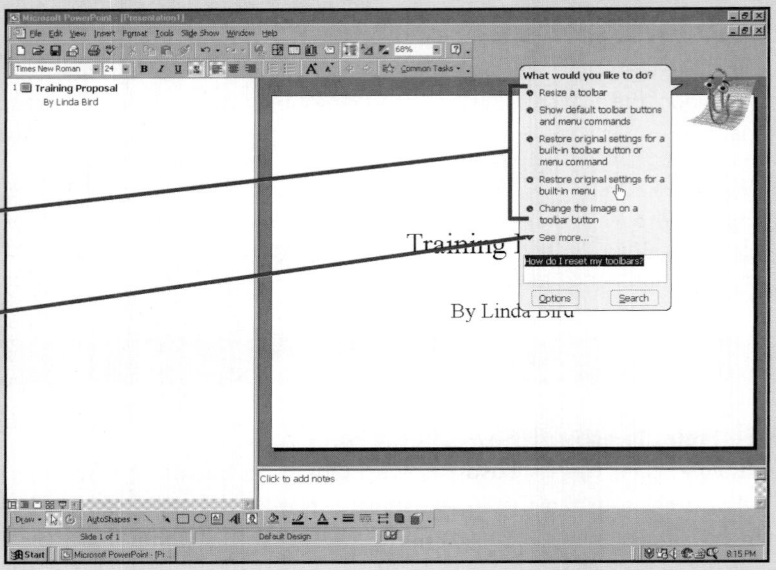

List of topics produced by the search

Click here to see additional topics

3 **From the list, click** `Restore original settings for a built-in toolbar button or menu command.`
The Microsoft PowerPoint Help window for this topic displays (see Figure 1.14). Don't be concerned that the Help window displays on top of your PowerPoint application window and that the screen looks a bit cluttered. When you eventually close the Help window, PowerPoint will display your presentation in the Normal view again. If the Office Assistant displays on top of the Help window, just drag the Assistant to another location.

Figure 1.14
The PowerPoint Help window gives you step-by-step instructions.

Help window

Hyperlink

Office Assistant

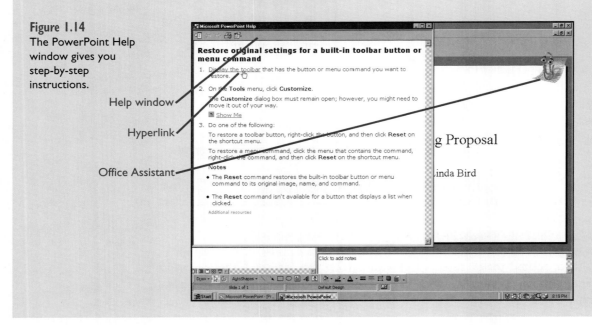

You can read the information included in the topic or view related topics. You can also click a **_hyperlink_** in the dialog box. Hyperlink text is underlined and shown in a contrasting color, and a special "helping hand" pointer displays whenever you move the mouse pointer over the hyperlink text. You can click a hyperlink to display related information. Try using a hyperlink now.

❹ Move your mouse pointer over the `Display the toolbar` hyperlink in the Help window until the hand pointer displays; then click.

The PowerPoint Help window displays information related to the hyperlink—in this case, how to show or hide a toolbar (see Figure 1.15).

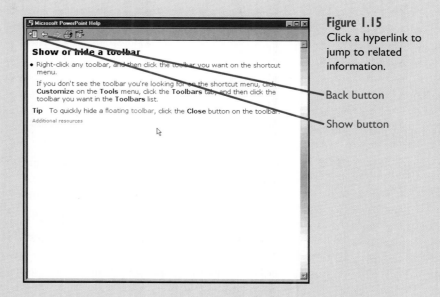

Figure 1.15
Click a hyperlink to jump to related information.

Back button

Show button

Now, try returning to the preceding screen by using the Back button that displays in the PowerPoint Help window.

❺ Click the Back button in the PowerPoint Help window.

The preceding Help screen displays. Notice that the Forward button is now activated. As you probably guessed, you can easily scroll between Help topics just by using the Forward and Back buttons.

Now, see how to access PowerPoint's Help Contents and Index pages.

❻ Click the Show button in the PowerPoint Help window.

PowerPoint splits the Help window into two panes so that you can access Help in alternative ways (see Figure 1.16). The left pane is called the **_Navigation pane_** because it helps you navigate through various subjects by topic or keyword. For example, instead of asking questions of the Office Assistant, you can find the information topically on the <u>C</u>ontents page—much as you would use a book's table of contents. You can also use PowerPoint's alphabetic listing of topics found on the <u>I</u>ndex page. To display the <u>C</u>ontents or <u>I</u>ndex pages, just click the associated tab.

continues ▶

To Get Help   (continued)

Figure 1.16
Tired of the Office Assistant? Try using the <u>C</u>ontents or <u>I</u>ndex pages instead.

<u>C</u>ontents tab
<u>I</u>ndex tab
Navigation pane

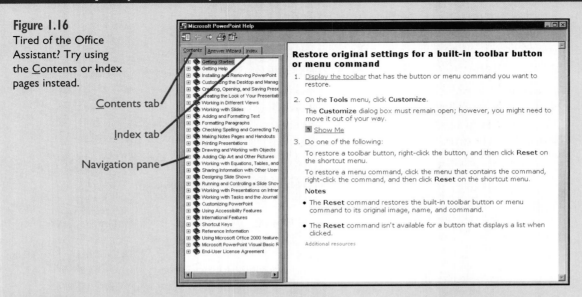

Now, you're ready to use the <u>C</u>ontents page to find information. This page shows subjects topically—just like a book's table of contents. A book icon represents each topic; you can double-click the icon to display subtopics related to the main topic. Try using the <u>C</u>ontents page now.

❼ Click the <u>C</u>ontents tab to display it; then double-click the Getting Help book icon.

A list of subtopics appears, as shown in Figure 1.17. Don't worry if you can't view the entire name of a subtopic because you can rest your mouse pointer over the topic until the full name displays. When you find the topic you want, click its icon to see information about the topic.

Figure 1.17
A listing of subtopics is only a double-click away.

Main topic
Subtopics

Choose this subtopic

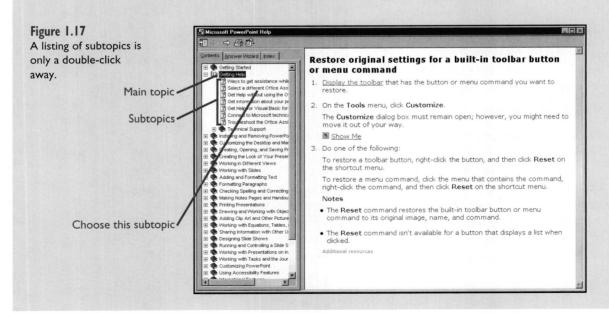

⑧ Rest your mouse pointer over the `Select a different Office Assistant` subtopic until the full name of the topic appears and click.

The information related to the topic displays in the right pane of the Help window (see Figure 1.18). (If you want, spend a minute or two clicking on other topics on the Contents page and reading the associated information. You can also practice closing an open book icon by double-clicking it.)

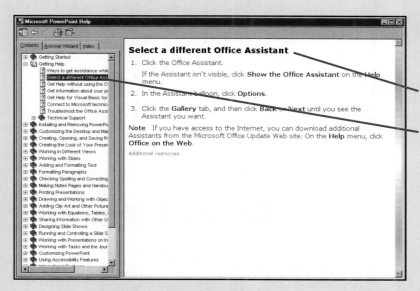

Figure 1.18
Click a subtopic to see related information.

Information related to the chosen subtopic

Selected subtopic

Now, try using the Index, which includes an alphabetic list of topics, or **keywords**, that you can use to find all related topics. For example, if you enter the keyword **Print**, PowerPoint may find more than 40 topics related to the word, and then display them in the Help window. You can click a topic to select it and display its associated Help screen.

⑨ Click the Index tab; then click in the Type keywords text box and enter `Save`. Choose Search.

A list of topics related to the keyword displays in the `Choose a topic` section of the dialog box, as shown in Figure 1.19.

You can click a topic on the `Choose a topic` list to see related information in the right pane. Try using this feature now.

⑩ In the `Choose a topic` list, click `Troubleshoot saving a presentation`.

Information about the topic displays in the right pane of the Help window (see Figure 1.20).

To redisplay a single pane in the PowerPoint Help window, you can click the Hide button. To completely close the PowerPoint Help window, click its Close button in the upper-right corner of the window.

⑪ Click the Hide button to close the Navigation pane. (If you're unsure where the Hide button is located, refer to Figure 1.20.)

continues ▶

To Get Help   (continued)

Figure 1.19
You can find all topics related to a keyword you type.

Keyword

Related topics

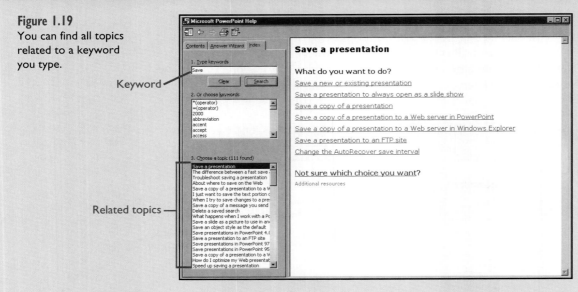

Figure 1.20
Click a topic to see related information.

Hide button

Close button

Related information

Selected topic

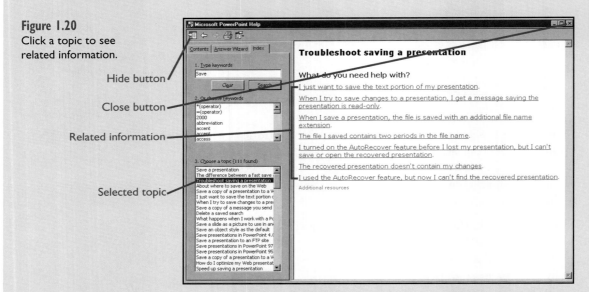

12 **Close the PowerPoint Help window by clicking its Close button (refer to Figure 1.20).**

The PowerPoint Help window closes and your presentation redisplays in Normal view. Keep the presentation open for the next lesson, in which you learn how to exit PowerPoint.

Inside Stuff: **Finding Help on the Web**

If you're like most users, you'll probably rely heavily on PowerPoint's built-in Help system to find ways to work more effectively with the program. If you absolutely can't find the information you need within PowerPoint, however, you have another option: You can tap into the resources available on the World Wide Web. Assuming that you have Internet access, you can choose <u>H</u>elp, Office on the <u>W</u>eb. Perform whatever steps you usually do to connect to the Web (such as entering your password). PowerPoint automatically displays Microsoft's Web site for PowerPoint. After you're connected to the Web, you can use hyperlinks to move between Web sites. After you have finished cruising the Web, click the Close button to disconnect from the Web and redisplay PowerPoint.

Lesson 6: Closing Your Presentation and Exiting PowerPoint

Now you're ready to close your presentation and exit PowerPoint. Closing a presentation and clearing it from memory is similar to clearing your desk at school or work to make room for another project. And if closing a presentation is similar to clearing off your desk, exiting the entire program is like leaving your office.

Remember: Any presentation exists only in RAM until you save it, and the presentation you created in this lesson is no exception. Unless you save the presentation to a permanent storage location, such as a disk or drive, closing it also permanently clears it from your computer. Because of this, you typically should save most presentations before closing them. However, because you won't need the presentation you created in Lesson 2, you learn how to clear this presentation without saving it.

This lesson also covers how to properly exit the PowerPoint program. You can exit PowerPoint in a couple of ways: by clicking the Application Close button or choosing <u>F</u>ile, E<u>x</u>it from the menu. Try closing your presentation and exiting PowerPoint now.

To Close Your Presentation and Exit PowerPoint

❶ Choose <u>F</u>ile, <u>C</u>lose.
PowerPoint displays a message asking whether you want to save the presentation (see Figure 1.21). Any time you make changes to a presentation and then attempt to close it without saving your revisions, PowerPoint displays this message.

X ***If You Have Problems...***
The exact appearance of the message that displays depends on whether the Office Assistant is shown. If the Assistant is displayed, the message appears in the Assistant's balloon. If not, the message instead appears in a message box.

❷ Choose <u>N</u>o.
PowerPoint clears the presentation from memory. Now you are ready to exit the program.

❸ Click the Application Close button.
Alternatively, you can choose <u>F</u>ile, E<u>x</u>it from the menu. The PowerPoint program closes and the Windows desktop (or another open application) redisplays.

continues ▶

To Close Your Presentation and Exit PowerPoint (continued)

Figure 1.21
PowerPoint always asks whether you want to keep unsaved changes.

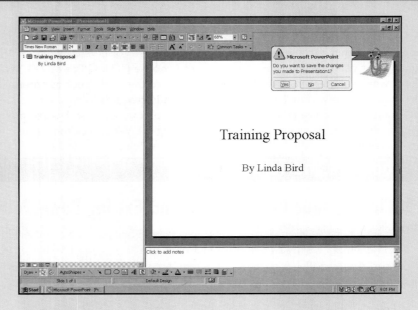

It's also important to properly exit Windows before turning off the computer. The best way to do this is to use (ironically enough) Windows' Start button. (Be sure that you close all other open applications before proceeding. If you don't know whether another program is running, see your instructor for help.)

4 **Click the Start button, and then choose Sh_u_t Down from the menu.**
The Shut Down Windows dialog box displays. You use this dialog box to control how to shut down or restart Windows.

5 **Make sure that the _S_hut down option button is chosen, and then click OK.**
Windows closes temporary files and clears them from memory. This process generally takes a few seconds, so be patient during the process. It's important to wait until Windows indicates that you can turn off the computer.

6 **Wait until the It's now safe to turn off your computer message displays (or ask your instructor whether Windows has cleared).**
After you receive confirmation, you can turn off your computer.

7 **Turn off your computer's main unit, monitor, and any other hardware (such as speakers or a printer).**

Summary

Congratulations! In this project, you learned the basics of starting PowerPoint and creating a new, blank presentation. You also became familiar with the PowerPoint window and navigated the program's toolbars and menus. You acquired skills for researching Help topics by using the Office Assistant. Finally, you learned how to properly exit PowerPoint and shut down Windows.

To expand on your knowledge, spend a few minutes exploring Help on these topics. Additionally, complete some of the Skill Drill, Challenge, and Discovery Zone exercises.

Checking Concepts and Terms

True/False

For each of the following, check *T* or *F* to indicate whether the statement is true or false.

__T __F   **1.** You can get help by using PowerPoint's Window Assistant. [L5]

__T __F   **2.** Closing a presentation and exiting PowerPoint are the same. [L6]

__T __F   **3.** If power is interrupted to your computer, you lose everything in Random Access Memory (RAM). [L6]

__T __F   **4.** By default, PowerPoint includes both short and full menus for each menu command. [L4]

__T __F   **5.** By default, PowerPoint menus and toolbars change which commands display automatically to reflect the ones you use the most frequently. [L4]

Multiple Choice

Circle the letter of the correct answer for each of the following.

1. PowerPoint's Normal view includes the _____ component. [L2]

   a. Slide pane

   b. Outline pane

   c. Notes pane

   d. all of the above

2. You can develop a presentation in PowerPoint by _____. [L2]

   a. creating a new one completely from scratch

   b. using the AutoContent Wizard

   c. using a template

   d. any of the above

3. Which of the following is true regarding PowerPoint's menus? [L3–4]

   a. They adapt to the user's work habits by displaying the most commonly used commands near the top.

   b. You must use the mouse to access their commands.

   c. By default, the long, or full, menus display first.

   d. all of the above

4. Which of the following is true regarding PowerPoint's toolbars? [L4]

   a. You cannot change which buttons display unless you reinstall PowerPoint.

   b. By default, the Standard and Formatting toolbars appear on the same row.

   c. You cannot display the toolbars and the Office Assistant at the same time.

   d. All toolbars appear at the top of the PowerPoint application window.

5. To exit PowerPoint, _____. [L6]

   a. simply turn off the computer

   b. choose File, Close

   c. click the Application Close button

   d. press Esc

Screen ID

Identify each of the items shown in Figures 1.22 and 1.23.

Figure 1.22

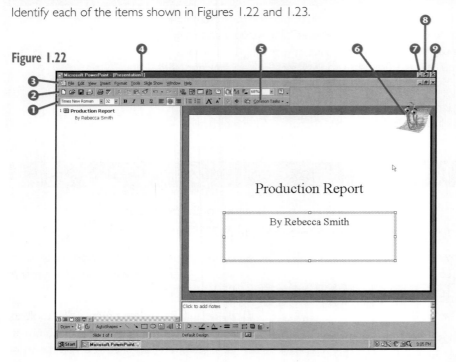

1. _____   4. _____   7. _____

2. _____   5. _____   8. _____

3. _____   6. _____   9. _____

Figure 1.23

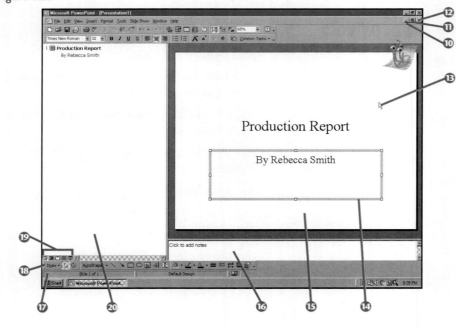

10. _____   14. _____   18. _____

11. _____   15. _____   19. _____

12. _____   16. _____   20. _____

13. _____   17. _____

A Presentation Close button

B Formatting toolbar

C Title bar

D Standard toolbar

E Office Assistant

F Notes pane

G Slide icon

H Menu bar

I Application Minimize button

J Presentation Minimize button

K Common Tasks button

L Application Close button

M Outline pane

N Mouse pointer

O Slide pane

P Application Maximize/Restore button

Q Subtitle placeholder

R Status bar

S Presentation Maximize/Restore button

T View buttons

U Drawing toolbar

Skill Drill

Skill Drill exercises reinforce project skills. Each skill that is reinforced is the same, or nearly the same, as a skill presented in the project. Detailed instructions are provided in a step-by-step format.

1. Creating a New Blank Presentation

You need to quickly produce a flyer for a company picnic. Because it's quick and easy to create a presentation in PowerPoint, you decide to use the program to make the flyer. [L2]

1. Start PowerPoint. In the Startup dialog box, choose Blank Presentation, and then choose OK.

2. Make sure the Title Slide AutoLayout is chosen in the New Slide dialog box (the first AutoLayout on the top row). Click OK to create a blank slide using this type of AutoLayout.

3. In the Slide pane, click in the title placeholder. Type **Company Picnic!**.

4. Click in the subtitle placeholder. Type **Raccoon Creek Park**. Press (Enter) to move the insertion point to the next line. Type **April 17** and press (Enter). Type **5:00 p.m.-9:00 p.m.**

5. Click outside of the placeholders. Leave the presentation open and PowerPoint running for the next exercise.

2. Exploring the PowerPoint Application Window

Your computer instructor has hired you part-time to assist other students during an open lab. You're new to PowerPoint, however, and are worried that you won't remember the toolbar buttons' functions. To brush up on the program's commands, you spend a few minutes using ScreenTips. [L3]

1. In the open PowerPoint window, rest your mouse pointer over each toolbar button on the Standard, Formatting, and Drawing toolbars until a ScreenTip displays. Note the name of each button.

2. Click the Common Tasks button on the Formatting toolbar. Write down the name of the three commands listed. Click in the Slide pane area to close the toolbar without activating any commands.

3. Locate the More Buttons button on the Standard and Formatting toolbars. Click the button to see what buttons (or commands) are shown on the palette. Click in the Slide pane area to close the palette without activating any commands.

4. Press (Shift) + (F1) to activate the What's This? pointer. Click on the New button on the Standard toolbar. Read the ScreenTip associated with the button. Repeat the process for at least five other buttons.

5. Choose File, Close, and then click No to close the presentation without saving it. Leave PowerPoint running if you plan to complete the next exercise.

3. Using the Office Assistant

You stay late one night at the office to learn a few new features in PowerPoint. To use your time efficiently, you decide to use PowerPoint's Office Assistant to find the information you need. [L5]

1. In the open PowerPoint screen, choose Help, Show the Office Assistant to display the Office Assistant (if necessary).

2. In the Assistant's bubble, type **How do I create a presentation?** Click Search.

3. Click Create a new presentation on the list of topics displayed in the Assistant's bubble.

4. Read the information displayed in the Microsoft PowerPoint Help window. When you finish, close the Help window.

5. Display the Assistant, if necessary. Click the Assistant to display the balloon.

6. Type **How can I get help?** in the text box area, and then choose Search.

7. Click the **Ways to get assistance while you work** option button. (If you want, click the hyperlinks listed in the Help window. Click <u>B</u>ack to move to the preceding screen.)

8. After you have finished reading the information, close the Help window. Leave PowerPoint open if you plan to complete the Challenge or Discovery Zone exercises.

Challenge

Challenge exercises expand on or are somewhat related to skills presented in the lessons. Each exercise provides a brief narrative introduction, followed by instructions in a numbered-step format that are not as detailed as those in the Skill Drill section.

I. Researching Help Topics with the Office Assistant

One of the Help Desk employees for your company is on vacation, and you've been asked to cover for him. To answer questions that some of your coworkers ask about PowerPoint, you rely on the Office Assistant. [L5]

I. Choose <u>H</u>elp, Show the <u>O</u>ffice Assistant to display the Office Assistant (if necessary). Then, use the Assistant to research the following topics:

- How to create a new presentation
- How to print a presentation
- How to save a presentation
- How to open an existing presentation
- Which AutoLayouts are available in PowerPoint
- How to format text with bold or italic
- What views are available in PowerPoint
- How to create speaker notes
- How to insert clip art on a slide

2. Write down the steps to performing at least two of these actions, and then try out the steps in PowerPoint.

3. Explain verbally to another user the steps involved in performing two other actions you researched. If possible, have the user complete the steps on a computer as you "talk" him or her through the actions. Leave PowerPoint running if you plan to complete the next exercise.

2. Creating and Printing New Presentations

Your boss wants you to create some motivational and safety flyers to post around your building. To quickly create the flyers, you decide to develop a series of one-slide presentations in PowerPoint. [L2, 5]

I. If necessary, use the Office Assistant to brush up on how to create a new blank presentation. Then, use Help to find out how to print a presentation slide.

2. Create a new blank presentation. Choose the Title Slide AutoLayout for the first (and only) slide. Enter **Don't Forget!** in the slide's title placeholder. Then type **Safety is our #1 priority!** in the subtitle placeholder. Print the slide, and then close the presentation without saving it.

3. Using the preceding step as a guide, create another flyer. Enter **If You Don't Know . . . Ask!** in the title placeholder. Print the slide, and then close the presentation without saving it.

4. Create a third flyer. In the title placeholder enter **We're Part of the Same Team!** Print the slide, and then close the presentation without saving it. Leave PowerPoint running if you plan to complete the next exercise.

3. Creating and Printing a New Presentation

You work for the registrar's office at a local college. To get ready for fall registration, your boss wants you to develop signs to help direct students to the various college departments. [L2]

1. Create a new blank presentation. Choose the Title Slide AutoLayout for the first (and only) slide. Enter **Accounting Department** in the slide's title placeholder. Type **Room 100** in the subtitle placeholder. Print the slide, and then close the presentation without saving it.

2. Using the preceding step, create a slide for each of the following departments. Print each slide, and then close the presentation without saving it.

Enter in Title Placeholder	Enter in Subtitle Placeholder
Business Department	**Room 112**
Computer Science Department	**Room 120**
Drafting Department	**Room 125**
Industrial Technology Department	**Room 132**
Nursing Department	**Room 145**
Production Control Department	**Room 154**

Leave PowerPoint running if you plan to complete the Discovery Zone exercises.

Discovery Zone

Discovery Zone exercises require advanced knowledge of topics presented in *MOUS Essentials* lessons, the application of skills from multiple lessons, or self-directed learning of new skills.

1. Creating Presentations

As you worked with PowerPoint in this project, you probably thought of several presentations that you want to create using the program. Use the knowledge you gained to develop and print at least three single-slide presentations. Base each presentation on the Title Slide AutoLayout. Create one of each of the following types of presentation:

- A presentation to use in a business setting
- A presentation to promote an upcoming event
- A sign to direct people to a certain location in your business

If you forget how to perform a particular action in PowerPoint, use the Office Assistant to brush up on the concepts. Print each presentation, and then close it. Leave PowerPoint running if you plan to complete the next exercise. [L2, 5]

2. Getting Help Using the Office Assistant and on the Web

The World Wide Web includes tremendous resources and information related to working with PowerPoint. You're writing a paper for your Computer Science class on PowerPoint 2000 and you exhausted the Help information included in the program. To obtain more data, you decide to get some help from Microsoft's Web sites.

1. Make sure that you have Web access and that your equipment is set up to connect to the Web. (If you have questions, see your instructor.)

2. Choose <u>H</u>elp, Office on the <u>W</u>eb. Complete whatever steps are necessary on your system to connect to the Web.

3. Explore Microsoft's Web sites for PowerPoint. If you're having trouble locating the correct site, try entering **www.microsoft.com** to access Microsoft's home page.

4. Research and write down at least five tips and tricks for working with PowerPoint that you didn't know.

5. Disconnect from the Web; then try out the new tips in PowerPoint 2000.

6. Share the information you learned with at least one other person in your class. If you want, write a short paper on what you learned.

Now think of three more topics in PowerPoint you want to know more about. Research all the information about the topics that you can by using the Office Assistant. Write down what you learn. Next, connect to the World Wide Web to find out supporting data for your topics. If necessary, go to Microsoft's home page to find hyperlinks to PowerPoint. If you are familiar with performing a search on the Web, you can also look for other PowerPoint Web sites.

Organize the information you find in outline form and share the information with at least one other person. If you are particularly ambitious, create a presentation that includes the information you found. (*Hint:* You add new slides to a presentation by choosing <u>N</u>ew Slide from the <u>C</u>ommon Tasks palette. You'll probably want to add slides based on the Bulleted List AutoLayout.) Print the presentation, and then close it without saving it. Exit PowerPoint and close Windows. [L5]

PinPoint Assessment

You have completed this project and its associated lessons, and have had an opportunity to assess your skills through the end-of-project questions and exercises. Now use the PinPoint software Evaluation Mode to further assess your comprehension of the specific exam activities you have just learned. You can also use the PinPoint Trainer Mode and the Show Me tutorials to practice these exam activities.

Project 2

Creating Presentations

Key terms introduced in this project include

- AutoContent Wizard
- clip art
- context sensitive
- footer area
- grayscale
- keyboard shortcuts
- output
- pop-up menu
- views
- pure black and white
- templates (design templates)
- thumbnail
- wizards

Objectives	Required Activity for MOUS	Exam Level
➤ Using a Template to Create a Presentation	Create a presentation from a template and/or a wizard	Core
➤ Creating a Presentation Using the AutoContent Wizard	Create a presentation from a template and/or a wizard	Core
	Create a presentation using the AutoContent Wizard	Core
➤ Navigating Among Different Views	Navigate among different views (Slide, Outline, Sorter, Tri-Pane)	Core
➤ Moving Among Slides in Normal View	Navigate among different views (Slide, Outline, Sorter, Tri-Pane)	Core
➤ Running an Electronic Slide Show	Start a slide show on any slide	Core
	Use onscreen navigation tools	Core
➤ Using the Slide Show Shortcut Keys	Use onscreen navigation tools	Core
➤ Saving Your Presentation	Save changes to a presentation	Core
	Save as a new presentation	Core
	Save slide as a graphic	Expert
	Save embedded fonts	Expert
➤ Printing a Presentation	Print slides in a variety of formats	Core

Why Would I Do This?

The more tools you have in your PowerPoint arsenal, the better equipped you are to use the program effectively. In Project 1, "Getting Started with PowerPoint 2000," you learned one tool, or method, for creating a new presentation: developing it totally from scratch. PowerPoint also includes two other ways for easily creating a new presentation: by using a template, and by relying on the AutoContent Wizard. In this project, you learn how to use these two alternative methods.

We'll also show you how to use the various perspectives, or **views**, which PowerPoint provides to work more effectively with a presentation. In this project, you learn how to switch between these views and choose the most appropriate one as you modify your presentation. You also see how to move among slides in both Normal and the Slide Show views. Finally, you learn how to save and print your presentation various ways.

Lesson 1: Using a Template to Create a Presentation

PowerPoint includes a number of predesigned **templates** (sometimes called **design templates**), upon which you can base your presentation. You can think of a template as a blueprint that PowerPoint uses to create slides. The template includes the formatting, color, and graphics necessary to create a particular "look."

Because professional graphic artists created these templates, you can use a template to create a presentation with a consistent, well-designed look. Using a template is helpful because you can concentrate on content instead of spending your time and effort on layout and design. You can choose a template when you initially create a presentation or apply one to an existing presentation. In Project 6, "Changing a Presentation's Overall Appearance," you'll learn to apply different templates to an existing presentation. For now, concentrate on developing a new presentation based on a template. Try working with templates now.

To Use a Template to Create a Presentation

1 Start PowerPoint, if necessary, and clear PowerPoint's Startup and New Slide dialog boxes.

2 Choose <u>F</u>ile, <u>N</u>ew from the menu bar.
The New Presentation dialog box displays. This dialog box, like many others in PowerPoint, includes multiple tabs. In fact, the layout of this dialog box is reminiscent of tabbed file folders in a file cabinet. To bring a dialog box page to the front, just click the associated tab.

3 Click the Design Templates tab.
The Design Templates page of the dialog box displays (Figure 2.1). You can single-click to select a template and preview it—right within the New Presentation dialog box.

4 Single-click the Blends template.
PowerPoint displays a **thumbnail**—a miniature slide that represents the selected template in the Preview area, as shown in Figure 2.2.

Click this tab to access
PowerPoint's templates

Large icons button

List button

Details button

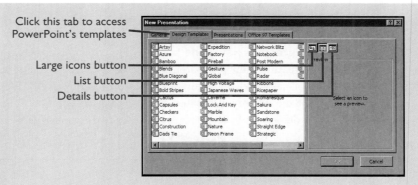

Figure 2.1
The New Presentation
dialog box gives
you access to many
templates.

Selected template

Thumbnail

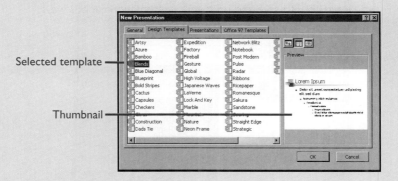

Figure 2.2
PowerPoint helps
you choose the right
template by letting you
see a preview.

 If You Have Problems...
Don't worry if the templates listed on your system look different than the
listing shown in this book. Most likely, PowerPoint is displaying the templates in either Large Icon or Details view. To make your screen resemble
that shown in Figure 2.2, click the List button in the New Presentation dialog box. Also, if you have more templates than those shown in this book,
you probably have "leftover" templates from previous versions of
PowerPoint, or ones that were customized and saved by another user on
your system. Count yourself lucky—this just means that you have more
templates from which to choose!

5 **Single-click several other templates to preview them. After you've fin-
ished experimenting, choose Factory, and then click OK.**
PowerPoint displays the New Slide dialog box, from which you can choose the
AutoLayout for your opening slide. By default, PowerPoint selects the Title Slide
AutoLayout for your initial slide. (If you need a refresher course on AutoLayouts
and placeholders, refer to Project 1, Lesson 2.)

X **If You Have Problems...**
If the Factory template isn't available on your system, choose another one.
Also, many templates are "installed on first use," which just means that
they're not installed until you attempt to use them for the first time. If the
templates you want to use need to be installed, see your instructor.

continues ▶

To Use a Template to Create a Presentation (continued)

6 **Click OK to create a new slide based on the Title Slide AutoLayout.**
PowerPoint creates a new presentation based on your selected template and displays it in Normal view (see Figure 2.3). Note that the slide includes placeholders—just as it did when you created a new blank presentation in Project 1. This presentation differs, however, because the slide background, colors, formatting, and graphics are already in place. All you have to add is the content.

✗ *If You Have Problems...*
You won't see toolbars in most of the figures in this book—unless, of course, you need to view the toolbar to understand a feature. Instead, we chose to show only the PowerPoint application window so that you could focus on PowerPoint's features.

Figure 2.3
PowerPoint's templates help you quickly create a presentation with a certain "look and feel."

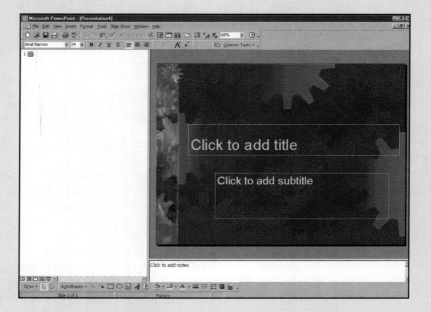

7 **Click in the title placeholder, and then type New Products.**
The text is entered in the placeholder—just like when you worked with a new blank presentation. In Project 3, "Modifying Presentations," you learn how to add additional slides to presentations that you create. For now, close this presentation without saving it so that you can learn how to use PowerPoint's Auto-Content Wizard.

8 **Choose File, Close; then choose No in the message box.**
The presentation closes without being saved. Keep PowerPoint open for the next lesson.

 ***Exam Note:* Alternative Methods of Using a Template or the AutoContent Wizard**
Although it's most common to choose a template or launch the AutoContent Wizard from the New Presentation dialog box, you can instead choose AutoContent Wizard or Design Template from PowerPoint's Startup dialog box.

Lesson 2: Creating a Presentation Using the AutoContent Wizard

Another way to create a presentation is to use the AutoContent Wizard. The **AutoContent Wizard** is a tool that helps you create presentations that include sample content as well as an underlying template. Microsoft's **wizards** are interactive tools that guide you step-by-step through a process that would otherwise be complicated or awkward—and the AutoContent Wizard is no exception. Just like other Microsoft wizards, you make choices on each page. You then click <u>N</u>ext to advance to the subsequent page, <u>B</u>ack to display the preceding page, or <u>F</u>inish to quickly complete the process. (You can also click Cancel at any time to ditch the entire process.)

You can use the AutoContent Wizard to quickly create presentations on recommending a strategy, conducting training, reporting progress, and so on. In the following tutorial, you use the AutoContent Wizard to create a presentation to recommend that your organization upgrade to Office 2000. Try using this handy tool now.

To Create a Presentation Using the AutoContent Wizard

① **Choose <u>F</u>ile, <u>N</u>ew, and then click the General tab of the New Presentation dialog box.**
PowerPoint includes an icon for the AutoContent Wizard on this page. You can quickly launch the wizard by double-clicking this icon.

② **Double-click the AutoContent Wizard icon.**
The first of five AutoContent Wizard dialog boxes displays, as shown in Figure 2.4. Notice that the chart on the left side of the dialog box helps track your progress as you create a presentation. The buttons at the bottom of the dialog box help you move between AutoContent dialog boxes (or even cancel) the wizard.

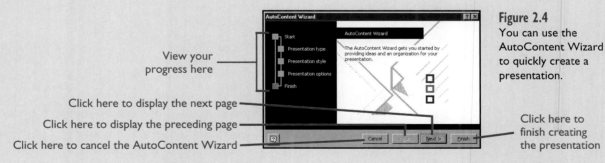

Figure 2.4
You can use the AutoContent Wizard to quickly create a presentation.

> **✕** **If You Have Problems...**
> If the Office Assistant automatically displays when you launch the AutoContent Wizard, just choose `No, don't provide help now`. After you have finished working with the AutoContent Wizard, you can clear the Assistant by right-clicking on it and choosing <u>H</u>ide.

③ **Click the <u>N</u>ext button.**
The Presentation type page of the AutoContent Wizard displays. You can use this page to determine the type of presentation that best fits your needs.

continues ▶

To Create a Presentation Using the AutoContent Wizard   (continued)

4 **Click the <u>A</u>ll button to display the entire list of predesigned presentations.**

All presentation types are shown in the list box on the right side of the dialog box (see Figure 2.5). You can limit the type of presentation listed by clicking one of the category buttons.

Figure 2.5
You can select a category, and then choose a specific presentation.

Click a category button to limit the types of presentation that display

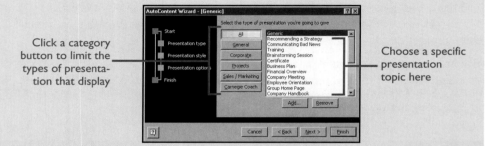

Choose a specific presentation topic here

5 **Click several of the category buttons to see what sample presentations they include. When you finish experimenting, choose the <u>P</u>rojects button.**

The presentations associated with this category display.

6 **Click Project Overview, and then choose <u>N</u>ext.**

The third AutoContent dialog box displays (see Figure 2.6).

Figure 2.6
On this page, choose the type of output you plan to use.

You can use this dialog box to choose the general type of **output** you want. If you're running a brainstorming session or meeting, for example, you can choose the On-<u>s</u>creen presentation option. In contrast, if you want to publish the presentation to the World Wide Web, choose W<u>e</u>b presentation. Because the most common use for PowerPoint is to develop onscreen presentations, this option is already selected for you.

7 **Make sure the On-<u>s</u>creen presentation option button is selected, and then choose <u>N</u>ext.**

The Presentation options page of the AutoContent Wizard dialog box displays (see Figure 2.7). You use this page to add a title to your presentation. You can also add items to the **footer area** of each slide—the place at the bottom of each slide. For example, you can add your company name or a slide number to each slide.

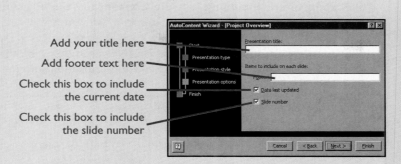

Add your title here ➤

Add footer text here ➤

Check this box to include
the current date ➤

Check this box to include
the slide number ➤

Figure 2.7
You can include footer
information on your
slides.

8 **Click in the Presentation title text box, and then type** `Upgrading to Office 2000.`

9 **Click in the Footer text box, type** `By the Information Technology Team,` **and then click Next.**

The final page of the AutoContent Wizard displays.

10 **Read the displayed information, and then choose Finish to view your presentation.**

The AutoContent Wizard creates the presentation and displays it in Normal view, as shown in Figure 2.8. As you recall from Project 1, this Tri-Pane view includes an Outline pane, a Slide pane, and a Notes pane. Additionally, the information you entered is included in the title slide. The remainder of the presentation is created as a series of slides with major topics and subtopics. These suggested topics serve as a blueprint for your presentation.

Main topic   Subtopics   Title

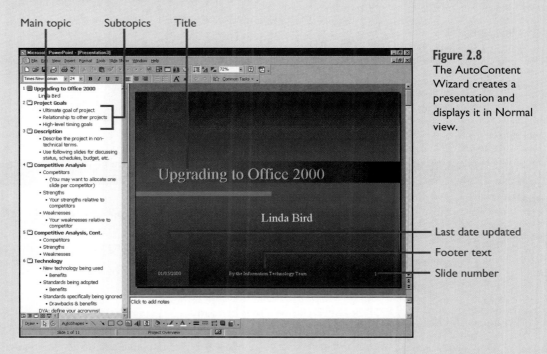

Figure 2.8
The AutoContent
Wizard creates a
presentation and
displays it in Normal
view.

Last date updated

Footer text

Slide number

Keep this presentation open for the next lesson, in which you learn how to use PowerPoint's different views.

Exam Note: **Including Sample Content in Your Presentation**
If you want to quickly create a presentation with the sample content in place, but you don't want to work through the page-by-page choices in the AutoContent Wizard, you're in luck. Just choose File, New, and then click the Presentations tab. Double-click an icon to create a new presentation with the sample content included.

 # Lesson 3: Navigating Among Different Views

After you create a presentation, you can view it in a number of different ways: Normal view, Slide view, Outline view, Slide Sorter view, Notes Page view, or as a Slide Show. So that you can quickly learn the purpose of each view, Table 2.1 describes the best uses for each.

Table 2.1 Presentation views and their uses

Use	To
Normal view	Get an overview of your entire presentation, work with the outline, notes, or individual slide elements.
Slide view	Work with one slide at a time on the entire screen, add or change text or graphics, or draw shapes.
Outline view	Work with the text in traditional outline form.
Slide Sorter view	Display miniatures (thumbnails) of all slides, including text and graphics. Use this view to change the slide order, add transitions, and set timings for electronic slide shows.
Notes Page view	Display a page in which you can create speaker notes for each slide.
Slide Show	Display your presentation as an onscreen electronic slide show.

Your presentation should currently be displayed in Normal view. You can change to a different PowerPoint view by using the View menu or clicking a view button. In this exercise, you practice by using both methods. Now, try changing the view of the presentation.

To Navigate Among Different Views

❶ In the open presentation, rest the mouse pointer on any of the view buttons (see Figure 2.9).
In a second or two, a ScreenTip displays, indicating the view button's name.

❷ Rest the mouse pointer over each of the five view buttons.
A ScreenTip identifies each button.

 ❸ Click the Outline View button.
The presentation displays as a traditional outline, with main topics and subtopics listed for each slide. The Slide and Notes panes still display, but they are greatly reduced in size (see Figure 2.10).

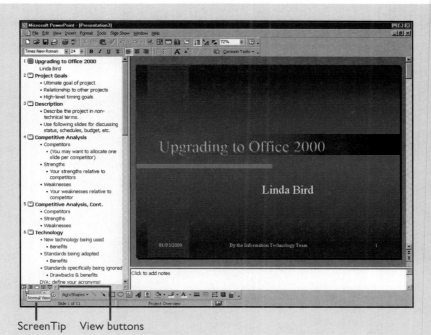

ScreenTip   View buttons

Figure 2.9
You can use the view buttons to get a different perspective on your presentation.

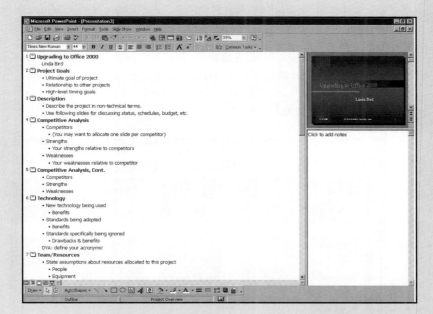

Figure 2.10
Outline view gives you an overview of your presentation's text.

④ Click the Slide View button.
The selected slide displays full-screen (see Figure 2.11). Slide view is best to use when you want to work with slide elements that might otherwise be hard to see or modify. For example, this is a good view to use to insert electronic pictures (commonly called *clip art*) or to draw pictures on the slide.

continues ▶

To Navigate Among Different Views   (continued)

Figure 2.11
Use Slide view to
work more efficiently
with individual slide
elements.

Selected slide

Outline pane

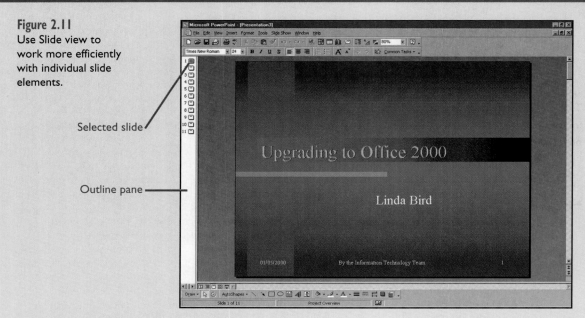

5 Click the Slide Sorter View button, or choose <u>V</u>iew, Sli<u>d</u>e Sorter from the menu.

Your presentation displays as a series of miniature slides (see Figure 2.12). The Slide Sorter view is an excellent view to use to add, delete, or rearrange slides. You can also add slide transitions and animation effects in this view by using the Slide Sorter toolbar. (You learn more about working with slide transitions and animation effects in Project 8, "Automating Electronic Slide Shows.")

Figure 2.12
You can use Slide
Sorter view to display
your presentation as
miniature slides.

Slide Sorter toolbar

Slide miniatures

Slide Sorter View button

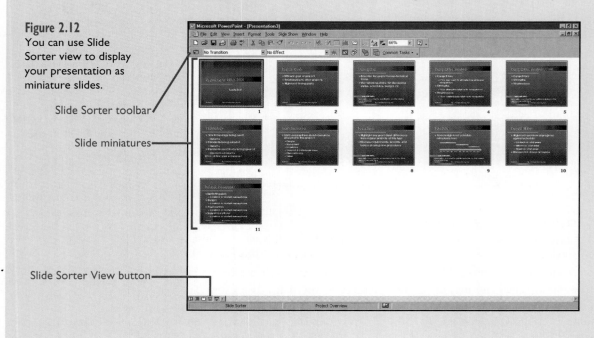

If You Have Problems...
Don't worry if your screen displays a different arrangement of slides than that shown in Figure 2.12. The number of slides displayed in Slide Sorter view depends on many factors, including monitor size.

6 **Choose View, Notes Page from the menu.**
The Notes Page view displays, as seen in Figure 2.13. This view includes a slide image, along with a notes box area. You use this view to create and print speaker notes to help remember key points. (You learn more about using the speaker notes in Project 5, "Creating Output.")

 If You Have Problems...
In Project 1, "Getting Started with PowerPoint 2000," you learned how to turn on the full menus. If you're still using the short menus, however, the Notes Page command won't initially appear when you click View. Don't worry—just double-click the View menu to display the full menu and the Notes Page command.

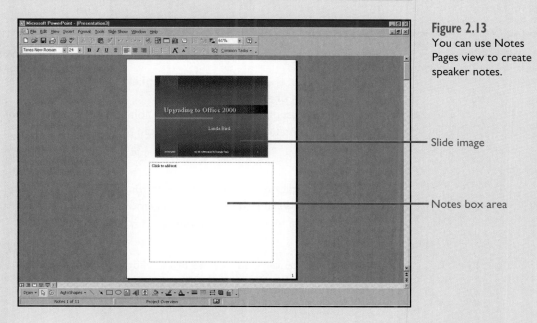

Figure 2.13
You can use Notes Pages view to create speaker notes.

Slide image

Notes box area

7 **Click the Normal View button.**
The sample presentation displays in Normal view. Remember that this view is the best all-around view for working with presentations because you can easily work in any of the three panes.

8 **Keep the presentation displayed in this view for the next lesson, in which you learn effective ways to move among slides.**

continues ▶

Exam Note: **Working with Views**

Some of PowerPoint's views can be accessed only via the view buttons; others are listed on the <u>V</u>iew menu (but don't have a corresponding view button). You can display Outline view by clicking a view button, for example, but PowerPoint doesn't list Outline view as a menu item. In contrast, you can display your presentation in Notes Page view only by using the <u>V</u>iew, Notes <u>P</u>age command. Luckily, the most popular views (such as Normal and Slide Sorter views) are accessible either way.

 ## Lesson 4: Moving Among Slides in Normal View

After you create a presentation, you need to know how to move around it efficiently. You may need to quickly move to the first or last presentation slide, for example, or "page through" the presentation slide by slide. To get you up to speed on how to move around within a presentation, we show you some efficient methods. First, you're guided through using **keyboard shortcuts**, which are simply the keys you can press on the keyboard to perform an action. Then, you learn how to perform the same actions with the mouse. As you work more and more with PowerPoint, you'll probably discover which method best complements your work habits. Try experimenting with these methods now.

To Move Among Slides in Normal View

1 **Make sure that the first slide of your presentation displays in Normal view, and then press** (PgDn).

The second presentation slide displays. You can press (PgDn) to quickly move through a presentation slide by slide; you can press (PgUp) to display the preceding slide.

2 **Press** (PgUp).

The first presentation slide displays. Try moving quickly to the end of the presentation by using a keyboard shortcut that (almost) universally displays the end of a worksheet, document, or presentation: (Ctrl)+(End).

3 **Press** (Ctrl)+(End).

The last presentation slide displays in the Slide pane. Notice that the last slide is simultaneously selected in the Outline pane. Now, try displaying the first presentation slide.

4 **Press** (Ctrl)+(Home).

The first presentation slide displays. Now that you are familiar with some common keyboard shortcuts, try your hand at performing the same actions with the mouse.

To move among slides using the mouse, you can use buttons on the vertical scrollbar in the Slide pane. For example, you can click the Next Slide or the Previous Slide buttons. Alternatively, you can drag the scroll box on the vertical scrollbar to move to the relative location within your presentation (Figure 2.14).

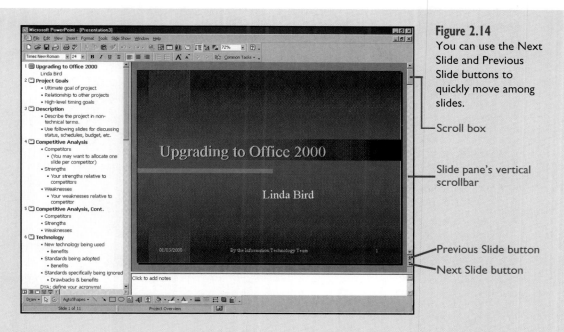

Figure 2.14
You can use the Next Slide and Previous Slide buttons to quickly move among slides.

Scroll box

Slide pane's vertical scrollbar

Previous Slide button

Next Slide button

⑤ Click the Next Slide button at the bottom of the Slide pane's vertical scrollbar (refer to Figure 2.14).

The second slide in your presentation displays.

⑥ Click the Previous Slide button at the bottom of the Slide pane's vertical scrollbar.

The first presentation slide redisplays. Now, try using the scroll box to move to a relative location in your presentation. If you want to display the fifth slide in a ten-slide presentation, for example, drag the scroll box approximately halfway down the vertical scrollbar.

⑦ Click the Slide pane's vertical scroll box, and then drag it up and down slowly.

A ScreenTip displays to the left of the scrollbar. This is a handy feature because the ScreenTip shows the slide number, total number of slides, and current slide title (see Figure 2.15). Furthermore, when you release the mouse button, the slide indicated by the ScreenTip displays.

⑧ Stop at Slide 4, Competitive Analysis, and then release the mouse button.

The slide shown in the ScreenTip becomes the active slide and is shown in Normal view. (If you see a light bulb icon, just ignore it for now—PowerPoint displays this icon when it has a suggestion on how to improve your presentation.) Now, try moving to a different slide by selecting a slide icon in the Outline pane.

continues ▶

To Move Among Slides in Normal View (continued)

Figure 2.15
The ScreenTip helps you find your location as you scroll in a presentation.

ScreenTip

Scroll box

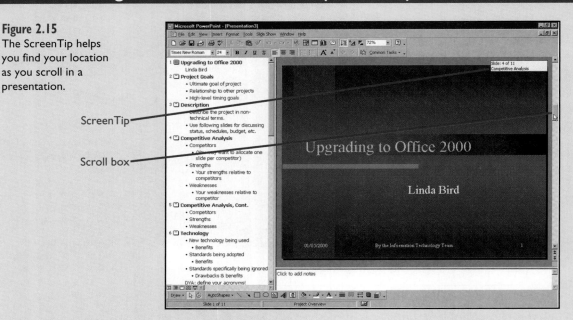

9 Move your mouse pointer over the icon for Slide 3 in the Outline pane until a four-headed arrow displays (see Figure 2.16).

Figure 2.16
You can click a slide icon in the Outline pane to quickly move to the corresponding slide.

Four-headed arrow

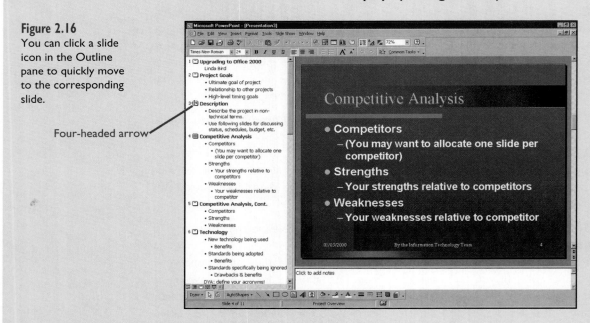

10 Click the icon for Slide 3 in the Outline pane.
The third slide is selected in the Outline pane and it displays concurrently in the Slide pane.

11 Press Ctrl+Home to display the first presentation slide. Keep your presentation open for the next exercise.

Lesson 5: Running an Electronic Slide Show

As you work with PowerPoint, you soon discover that one of the most popular and effective means of displaying a presentation is as an electronic slide show. You can run a slide show as a handy method of checking the presentation's content and flow, or to actually show the presentation to an audience on an overhead screen. You can also create an onscreen, self-running presentation for use at trade shows or on your company's intranet. In this lesson, you learn the basics of running an electronic slide show. In the next tutorial, you find out how to use shortcut keys to navigate more efficiently within the slide show.

To Run an Electronic Slide Show

1 **Make sure that Slide 1 in the open presentation is displayed in Normal view.**

2 **Click the Slide Show button (or choose View, Slide Show).**
The electronic slide show begins. Notice that the first slide displayed is the one that was active when you began the show—Slide 1. Because of this, you can start an electronic slide show from virtually any slide.

3 **Click the left mouse button.**
The next slide in the presentation displays. (If you prefer to use the keyboard, you can press ↵Enter or PgDn to advance to the next slide. Similarly, you can press ←Backspace or PgUp to move back one slide.)

Advancing through the entire slide show is easy—just keep clicking the left mouse button until a blackened screen displays. Press Esc to redisplay the presentation in the last view you used (such as Normal view). For now, however, practice some ways to jump between slides in a slide show.

For example, you can use the shortcut menu (sometimes called a *pop-up menu*) to move effectively in a slide show. Shortcut menus are displayed by right-clicking the mouse, and are *context sensitive*. Context sensitive means that the menu displays the commands related to the area of the screen that you click.

4 **Click the right mouse button.**
The slide show shortcut menu displays (see Figure 2.17). This menu includes commonly used commands that help you control a running slide show. Although you activate the shortcut menu by pressing the right mouse button, you choose commands with the left mouse button.

continues ▶

To Run an Electronic Slide Show (continued)

Figure 2.17
You can control a running slide show by using the shortcut menu.

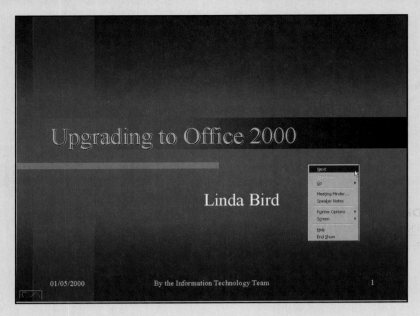

5 **Choose Previous from the shortcut menu.**
Slide 1 displays. Notice that you can also move forward in a presentation by choosing Next from the shortcut menu.

6 **Right-click the mouse to display the shortcut menu; then choose Go, Slide Navigator.**
The Slide Navigator dialog box displays. Because this dialog box shows all the slide titles, you can use it to quickly move to any slide in your presentation.

7 **Double-click Slide 7, Team/Resources.**
The presentation displays Slide 7.

8 **Right-click the mouse, and then choose End Show from the shortcut menu. (You can also end a slide show by pressing Esc.)**
PowerPoint displays the presentation in Normal view—the view you used most recently before you started the electronic slide show.

9 **Press Ctrl+Home to display the first presentation slide.**
Keep this presentation open for the next lesson, in which you learn how to use the slide show shortcut keys.

 If You Have Problems...
If the shortcut menu doesn't display when you right-click the mouse, choose Tools, Options, and then click the View tab in the Options dialog box. In the Slide show section, check the box for Popup menu on right mouse click, and then choose OK.

 Exam Note: **Starting a Slide Show on Any Slide**
You can run a slide show starting on any slide. Just display the slide in either Normal or Slide view, and then click the Slide Show button. (If you press F5 or choose View, Slide Show, however, you'll begin the slide show starting with Slide 1—no matter which slide is displayed when you launch the show.)

Lesson 6: Using the Slide Show Shortcut Keys

When you present your slide show to a live audience, it's useful to know as many ways as possible to move among your slides. For example, you may want to quickly display a slide that includes production or sales figures—even if it's not the next slide in the sequence.

In Lesson 5, you learned how to launch an electronic slide show and some basic ways to move among the slides. In this lesson, you build on that knowledge by learning keyboard shortcuts. You can use keyboard shortcuts to move between slides in a presentation or to blank out the current slide so that the audience's attention is redirected to you. Try using some of these keyboard shortcuts now.

To Use the Slide Show Shortcut Keys

1 Display the first presentation slide in Normal view, and then press F5.
F5 is a keyboard shortcut you can use to launch a slide show, beginning with the first slide. Now, try viewing the keyboard shortcuts that are available when you run a slide show.

2 Press F1.
The Slide Show Help dialog box displays, showing a list of available shortcut keys to help you get around the slide show (see Figure 2.18).

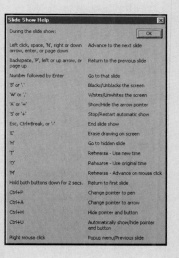

Figure 2.18
Press F1 while running a slide show to display a list of keyboard shortcuts for your slide show.

3 Click OK to close the Slide Show Help dialog box, and then press N.
The next slide displays. In a similar fashion, pressing P displays the preceding slide.

4 Press P.
PowerPoint displays the preceding slide in your electronic slide show.

You can also seamlessly display a certain slide by pressing the slide's number, followed by Enter. This method is quicker than using the Slide Navigator, and your audience doesn't see the command on screen. Try using this method to move to another slide now.

5 Press 4, and then press Enter.
The presentation displays Slide 4, Competitive Analysis.

continues ▶

To Use the Slide Show Shortcut Keys (continued)

Now, try using some of the other functions associated with keyboard shortcuts. You can use keyboard shortcuts to clear the screen, for example, so that it doesn't distract the audience during your presentation. To do this, you can press Ⓑ to blacken the screen or Ⓦ to white it out. The screen remains blank until you press Ⓑ or Ⓦ a second time to redisplay the screen. Try using this helpful feature now.

⑥ Press Ⓑ to blacken the screen, and then press Ⓑ again.

The display toggles between the screen and blackened views. (If you want, try pressing Ⓦ to white out the screen before continuing with the tutorial.)

Now, try a quick and easy way to end your slide show.

⑦ Press Esc.

The slide show ends and the presentation again displays in Normal view. Keep the presentation open for the next lesson, in which you learn to save it.

  # Lesson 7: Saving Your Presentation

So far, the presentation you developed exists only in Random Access Memory (RAM)—the working area of the computer. RAM retains its contents only as long as power is supplied to your computer. Therefore, if power is interrupted to your computer, you'll lose everything.

When you save the presentation from RAM to one of the computer's permanent storage areas (the floppy or Zip disk, the hard drive, or a network drive), however, you have a stored copy. This saved file can be opened, used, and revised at a later time.

By default PowerPoint saves files as "typical" PowerPoint presentations using the .ppt extension. However, you can also save your presentation using a variety of file formats. Table 2.2 includes a handy list of ways that you can save a presentation.

Table 2.2 Saving in alternative file formats

To Save Your Presentation As	Choose This File Format in the Save As Dialog Box
A typical PowerPoint presentation	Presentation (.ppt)
A slide as a graphic	Windows Metafile (.wmf)
A slide as a graphic for use on Web pages	GIF Graphics Interchange Format (.gif)
A slide as a graphic for use on Web pages	JPEG File Interchange Format (.jpg)
A slide as a graphic for use on Web pages	PNG Portable Network Graphics Format (.png)
A presentation outline as an outline	Outline/RTF (.rtf)
A presentation as a template	Design Template (.pot)
A presentation that will always open as a slide show	PowerPoint Show (.pps)

In this lesson, you save the sample presentation to your floppy disk—A: drive, so make sure that you have a disk in this drive before starting the tutorial.

To Save Your Presentation

1 **In the open presentation, choose File, Save As from the menu bar.**
The Save As dialog box displays (see Figure 2.19). You use this handy dialog box to indicate the name and location for your file. (Don't worry if different folders display from those shown in Figure 2.19.)

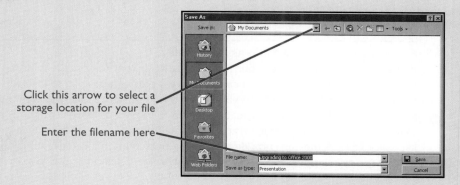

Click this arrow to select a
storage location for your file

Enter the filename here

Figure 2.19
You use the Save As dialog box when you first save a file.

2 **Click the Save in drop-down list arrow (refer to Figure 2.19).**
PowerPoint displays a list of available storage locations for your computer. This list may vary from computer to computer, depending on which drives are installed (and whether your computer is on a network).

X *If You Have Problems...*
It's possible that your instructor has another file location in mind for you to save your presentation—such as a subfolder in the My Documents folder on your hard drive. If you don't know where to save the presentation, ask your instructor.

3 **Click 3 1/2 Floppy (A:).**
The A: drive is selected as the storage location for your presentation.

4 **Move the mouse pointer in the File name text box area.**
The pointer changes to an I-beam, indicating that this is an area that can accept text. Before you can enter text, however, you must "set" the I-beam.

5 **Click in the text box area, and then drag over the default filename (Upgrading to Office 2000).**
The default filename is selected. When text is selected, you can quickly replace it just by typing in new text. As you enter the new text, the original text is replaced.

6 **Type Upgrading, and then click the Save button.**
That's all there is to it! Your presentation is saved as Upgrading on the floppy disk. Notice that the name also appears in the title bar. You now have a permanent copy of your presentation stored for later use (and you're safe from losing data to power outages, surges, and so on).

If you make changes to the presentation (either now or later), however, you should choose File, Save, or click the Save button to update the stored file.

continues ▶

To Save Your Presentation   (continued)

When you do, the presentation is automatically updated, using the same filename and location. In other words, you replace the existing file instead of creating a second copy of it.

Keep your saved presentation open for the next tutorial, in which you learn how to print it.

 Exam Note: **Saving a Slide as a Graphic**
By default PowerPoint saves your file as a "usual" PowerPoint presentation, with an extension of .ppt. However, you can also save a slide as a graphic to insert in another file (or even for use on the Web). To do this, display the slide you want to save as a graphic, and then choose File, Save As. In the Save As dialog box, choose Windows Metafile (or another graphic format) from the Save as type drop-down list. Click Save. A message box displays. If the presentation includes multiple slides, choose No to save only the displayed slide as a graphic; choose Yes to save all slides.

(After you have saved the slide as a graphic, you can insert it in a document by using the Insert, Picture, From File command.)

 Exam Note: **Saving Embedded Fonts in a Presentation**
If you want to make sure that the original fonts will display in your presentation, no matter what computer you use to run a slide show, you should save the fonts right along with the presentation. The TrueType fonts that come with Windows can be embedded in the saved presentation, although doing so increases file size. To save embedded fonts, display the Save As dialog box, and then click the Tools command. Choose Embed TrueType Fonts from the menu, and then click Save.

Lesson 8: Printing a Presentation

One common way to output, or produce, a presentation is to print it. You can print your entire presentation, including the slides and outline, in color, *grayscale*, or *pure black and white*. Grayscale includes shades of white, gray, and black. In contrast, when you choose the pure black and white option, PowerPoint converts all gray areas to black or white.

Printing an outline is particularly useful because it helps you see the overall flow and sequence of the presentation. Because the main purpose of the outline is to view the content, the printout shows only the text you entered—no graphics are shown.

You can also print the presentation as a series of slides. Of course, your slides show graphics and backgrounds as well as text. In this lesson, you learn how to preview your presentation in grayscale, and how to print outlines and slides. Try your hand at printing now.

To Print a Presentation

❶ In the open Upgrading presentation choose File, Print.
The Print dialog box displays (see Figure 2.20).

If You Have Problems...
Don't be fooled into thinking that you can display the Print dialog box by clicking the Print button on the Standard toolbar. Clicking the Print button automatically sends the current presentation to the printer with no further confirmation from you! Instead, make sure to choose File, Print from the menu so that you can access the Print dialog box.

Specify the printer here ——

Specify the number of copies here ——

Choose the print range here ——

Choose which presentation element to print here ——

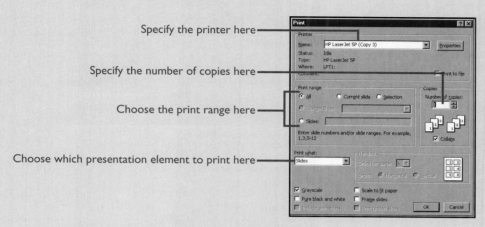

Figure 2.20
You make choices about output in the Print dialog box.

You can use this dialog box to make choices about the type of output (slides versus outline, for example), the number of copies, and the print range.

② **Click the drop-down arrow to the right of the Print what text box.**
A drop-down list displays the various ways that you can print your presentation.

③ **Select Outline View.**
Outline view is shown as the current selection in the Print what text box. Make sure that the correct settings are selected so that the entire presentation will print as an outline.

④ **In the Number of copies text box, make sure that the number of copies is set to 1.**

⑤ **In the Print range area, make sure that the All option button is selected.**

⑥ **Choose OK.**
This choice accepts the print settings and prints the outline.

You can also print your presentation as slides. However, unless you have access to a color printer, it's a good idea to see how your presentation will look in grayscale before printing it.

If you want to print only one slide (rather than the entire presentation), it's easiest to move the insertion point to the slide you want so that PowerPoint can identify it as the current slide.

With those concepts in mind, try printing a slide now.

⑦ **In the open presentation, press Ctrl+Home to move the insertion point to the first slide—the Title slide.**
Moving the insertion point to this slide makes it the current slide. Try displaying this slide in grayscale so that you can see how it will print.

continues ▶

To Print a Presentation (continued)

 8 **Click the Grayscale Preview button on the Standard toolbar.**
The slide displays in grayscale so that you can get an idea of how it will look when printed. A Slide Miniature displays in color, as shown in Figure 2.21.

Figure 2.21
You can preview the way a slide will print on a black-and-white printer.

Slide miniature

Slide shown in grayscale

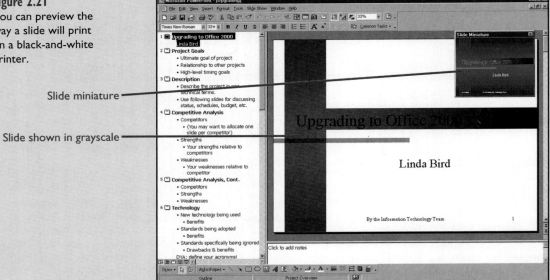

Now, change options in the Print dialog box so that the slide prints properly.

9 **Choose File, Print.**
The Print dialog box displays.

10 **In the Print range section, click the Current slide option button so that only one slide will print.**
Next, you need to confirm that you are printing slides and that they will print in grayscale—not color.

11 **Make sure that Slides displays in the Print what text box area and that the Grayscale check box is selected.**
Printing in grayscale optimizes the look of color slides for printing on black-and-white printers. (Don't make the mistake of choosing Pure black and white. This option makes your printer change all gray tones to black and white!)

12 **Click OK to print the current slide.**
This choice accepts the print settings and prints the slide.

13 **Choose File, Save, and then close the presentation.**
The changes you made to the presentation (such as modifying the print settings) are saved and the presentation is cleared from memory.

Keep PowerPoint open if you plan to complete the Skill Drill, Challenge, and Discovery Zone exercises at the end of this project. Otherwise, make sure to exit PowerPoint and shut down Windows properly before turning off your computer.

***Inside Stuff:* Printing Specific Slides**
You can also select a specific slide to print by clicking the Slides option button in the Print range area, then typing the slide number in the Slides text box. This text box also enables you to "pick and choose" slides by entering the slide numbers separated by commas. For example, entering **1,3,5,8** in the Slides text box prints only those slides. To print a range of slides, use a hyphen (rather than a comma) between the slides you want to print (such as 1–5).

Summary

You covered quite a bit of ground in this project. First, you learned two ways to create a new presentation: using a design template, and using the AutoContent Wizard. You explored PowerPoint's views and learned how to switch between them. You learned how to navigate among slides in Normal view. You also launched a slide show and used keyboard shortcuts to move around in the show. Finally, you learned how to save and print a presentation.

To expand on your knowledge, spend a few minutes exploring Help on these topics. You can also use the PinPoint CD to brush up on the concepts covered in this project. Finally, complete some of the Skill Drill, Challenge, and Discovery Zone exercises.

Checking Concepts and Terms

True/False

For each of the following, check **T** or **F** to indicate whether the statement is true or false.

___T ___F **1.** PowerPoint includes 15 different views that you can use to work with your presentation. [L3]

___T ___F **2.** You can create a new presentation based on a template. [L1]

___T ___F **3.** Outline view, Normal view, and Slide Show are just different ways of viewing the same set of slides. [L3]

___T ___F **4.** The Office Assistant Wizard creates the structure and suggested content of a presentation based on the choices you make. [L2]

___T ___F **5.** The first time you save a presentation, you must name it and indicate a file location. [L7]

Multiple Choice

Circle the letter of the correct answer for each of the following.

1. The best reason for printing a presentation as an outline is _____. [L8]

  a. to check logical flow and content

  b. to view graphics

  c. to view the colors and background used on a slide

  d. none of the above

2. To save an existing file with a new name or location, _____. [L7]

  a. click the Save button on the toolbar

  b. choose File, Save

  c. choose File, Save As

  d. choose Tools, Save As

3. To create a new presentation with sample content already in place, use the _____. [L1–2]

    a. SampleContent Wizard

    b. QuickFormat Wizard

    c. AutoContent Wizard

    d. PowerPoint Wizard

4. Which of the following statements is true? [L8]

    a. You can't print your presentation as slides—only as an outline.

    b. You must display the presentation in Slide Sorter view before opening the Print dialog box.

    c. You can print a presentation from a running slide show.

    d. You can print your presentation as slides, an outline, or notes pages.

5. Which of the following statements is true? [L1]

    a. Templates include formatting, colors, and graphics.

    b. You can base a new presentation on a template by clicking the Template button.

    c. You use the Template Wizard to create a new presentation based on a template.

    d. none of the above

Skill Drill

Skill Drill exercises reinforce project skills. Each skill reinforced is the same, or nearly the same, as a skill presented in the project. Detailed instructions are provided in a step-by-step format.

1. Using a Template to Create a Presentation

You work for a sports equipment company. Your boss wants to call a meeting to brainstorm ideas for a new product line. To remind everyone about the meeting, your boss asks you to develop a catchy flyer. You decide to create a one-slide presentation in PowerPoint, showing the appropriate information. [L1]

1. Start PowerPoint, if necessary, and then choose File, New. Click the Design Templates tab.

2. Single-click each of the templates available to preview them. Write down the names of the three templates that you like the best.

3. Click the Notebook template, and then click OK.

4. In the New Slide dialog box, make sure that the Title Slide AutoLayout is selected, and then click OK.

5. Click in the title placeholder. Enter **Brainstorming Meeting!**

6. Click in the subtitle placeholder. Enter **Conference**

Room A. Press ⏎Enter. On the second line, enter **Tuesday, 8:00 a.m.**

7. Choose View, Black and White to display your slide in grayscale.

8. Choose File, Print to display the Print dialog box.

9. Make sure that the Print range is set to All. Confirm that the Number of copies is set to **1**. Check that the Print what text box is set to **Slides**. Finally, check the Grayscale box.

10. Click OK to print a copy of your slide. Close the presentation without saving it. Leave PowerPoint running if you plan to complete additional exercises.

2. Using the AutoContent Wizard to Create a Presentation

Because you attended a PowerPoint class, everyone in your department now considers you a PowerPoint expert. For this reason, your coworkers want you to convince management to buy the "latest and greatest" computers for them. You decide to use PowerPoint to present your ideas at a staff meeting to show that purchasing new computers would be cost-effective. Because you need to prepare the presentation by tomorrow, you decide to use the

AutoContent Wizard. Then, to get a better idea of what sample content the AutoContent inserted in the presentation you created you switch between views and move between slides. [L2–6]

1. In PowerPoint, choose File, New. Click the General tab, and then double-click the AutoContent Wizard icon. Click Next to advance past the opening page of the wizard.

2. On the second page of the wizard, click All to display the entire list of presentations. Scroll down the list and choose **Selling Your Ideas**. Click Next.

3. On the third page, make sure that the On-screen presentation option is selected, and then click Next.

4. On the fourth page, enter **Improving Productivity** as the presentation title. Enter **By**, and then type *your name* in the Footer text box.

5. On the same page, make sure that the Date last updated and Slide number boxes are checked. Click Next.

6. Click Finish to create the presentation and display it in Normal view.

7. Display a ScreenTip for each of the view buttons. Click each of these view buttons: Outline View button, Slide View button, and Slide Sorter View button.

8. Display the presentation in each of the available views using the View menu. When you're finished, click the Normal View button and display the first presentation slide.

9. Now, to learn how to move effectively between presentation slides in Normal view, practice using both keyboard shortcuts and mouse commands.

10. Press (PgDn) as many times as necessary to completely advance through your presentation. Press (PgUp) three times to move back in your presentation by three slides.

11. Click one of the slide icons in the Outline pane. Notice that the corresponding slide displays simultaneously in the Slide pane. Repeat the process with other slide icons.

12. Press (Ctrl)+(Home) to display the first presentation slide. Press (Ctrl)+(End) to show the last presentation slide.

13. Drag the scroll box in the Slide pane's vertical scrollbar upward until **Slide: 4 of 5, Benefits** displays in the ScreenTip. Release the mouse button to display Slide 4.

14. Click the Next Slide button to advance to the next presentation slide. Click the Previous Slide button to show the previous slide.

15. Press (Ctrl)+(Home) to show the first presentation slide. Leave the presentation open for the next exercise, in which you run an electronic slide show.

3. Saving and Printing Your Presentation

You plan to give your presentation using a computer other than the one you developed it on. Because of this (and to have a permanent copy), you save the presentation to a disk. You also print the presentation as an outline so that you can check the flow and content. [L7–8]

1. Make sure that you have a disk in the floppy disk drive. With the presentation you developed in the previous exercises open, choose File, Save As.

2. Click the Save in drop-down list arrow, and then choose **3 1/2 Floppy (A:)** from the list.

3. Select the name in the File name text box, and then type **Our Plan for Getting New Computers** as the filename. To embed the TrueType fonts, choose Tools, Embed TrueType Fonts. Click Save.

4. Print the presentation as an outline. Choose File, Print. In the Print dialog box, click the Print what drop-down list arrow and choose Outline View. Make sure that the Number of copies is set to **1**. Click OK to print the presentation.

5. Click the Save button on the Standard toolbar to update the changes you made to the presentation.

6. Click the Slide Show button to run your presentation as an electronic slide show. Advance through the presentation by clicking the left mouse button or pressing (PgDn). Press (Esc) if necessary to end the slide show.

7. Choose File, Close to close the presentation. Leave PowerPoint running if you plan to complete the Challenge or Discovery Zone exercises. If not, exit PowerPoint and shut down Windows properly before turning off your computer.

Challenge

Challenge exercises expand on or are somewhat related to skills presented in the lessons. Each exercise provides a brief narrative introduction, followed by instructions in a numbered-step format that are not as detailed as those in the Skill Drill section.

1. Using the AutoContent Wizard

As Marketing Manager, you just found out that your boss wants you to present your new marketing plan at the upcoming annual company meeting. Because the meeting is only two days away, you decide to use the AutoContent Wizard to quickly create an onscreen presentation. [L2–8]

1. Display the New Presentation dialog box. Launch the AutoContent Wizard from this dialog box.

2. Choose the Marketing Plan as the presentation type. Create the presentation for use as an onscreen slide show. Make sure to include complete footer information, including your name in the footer area. Finally, enter **Top Sales Marketing Plan** as the presentation title. Finish creating the presentation.

3. Replace the text in the subtitle placeholder of the Title Slide with **Super Sports Equipment**.

4. View the presentation in Outline view, Slide Sorter view, and as an electronic slide show. Use both the mouse and the keyboard shortcuts to navigate among slides and views.

5. Save the presentation as **Marketing Plan for the Annual Meeting**.

6. Save the first presentation slide as a graphic (with the name **Marketing Graphic**), using Windows Metafile for the file format.

7. Print the presentation as an outline. Also print the first presentation slide as a slide (using grayscale). Close the presentation, but leave PowerPoint running if you plan to complete additional exercises.

2. Creating a New Presentation

You work for a company that deals in computer ergonomic products—products designed to help people work more comfortably and effectively at the computer. You want to create a presentation to promote your products for a sales meeting. You decide to use the AutoContent Wizard to create the basic framework and suggested slide content. [L2, 4–5, 7–8]

1. Launch the AutoContent Wizard. In the wizard, choose Product/Services Overview as the presentation type. Develop the presentation as an onscreen slide show.

2. Use **Ergonomic Products** as the presentation title, but *don't* include any footer information, the date, or the slide number. Finish creating the presentation and display it in Normal view.

3. On Slide 2, Overview, replace the bulleted points with the following text:
   - **Workstations**
   - **Keyboards**
   - **Monitors**
   - **Chairs**

4. View the presentation as an electronic slide show. Display the Slide Show Help dialog box to view the list of keyboard shortcuts available in a slide show. Clear the dialog box and practice using several of the shortcuts listed. When you finish, end the slide show.

5. Display the presentation in Normal view. Practice moving among slides in the presentation by using information in Lesson 4 as a guide.

6. Save the presentation as **Company Products** and print the presentation as an outline. When you finish, save any changes and close the presentation. Leave PowerPoint running if you plan to complete additional exercises.

3. Creating a New Presentation

You're a college student who loves working with computers and software. Unfortunately, you spent too much time playing around on the World Wide Web this term and your grades have suffered. To communicate this news to your parents, you decide to develop a presentation for them. (Because you're scared to face them in person, you plan to email them the presentation before you go home!) [L2–8]

1. In PowerPoint, display the Presentations page of the New Presentation dialog box. Click the Communicating Bad News presentation and choose OK.

2. View the presentation as a slide show to see what content is already included. Then add **By Your Loving Child** in the subtitle placeholder of the first slide.

3. Switch the presentation to Outline view. Replace the sample content with the following information:

    Slide 2, **My Situation**

    ■ **I'm failing classes this term**

    ■ **I'll be on probation next term**

    Slide 3, **How Did This Happen?**

    ■ **I love working with computers**

    ■ **I spent too much time in the computer lab (but I did learn a lot there!)**

    ■ **I got caught in the "sticky Web"!**

    Slide 4, **Alternatives Considered**

    ■ **I've talked with my advisor and professors**

    ■ **Two professors will give me incomplete grades instead of Fs**

    ■ **I can attend summer school**

4. Display the first presentation slide in Normal view, and then run the presentation as a slide show. Also practice using keyboard shortcuts to move between slides in Normal view.

5. Switch to Outline view. Explore ways to move between slides in this view. Make sure to use both keyboard shortcuts as well as the mouse. If necessary, use Help to research the methods available.

6. Switch to Notes Page view. Experiment to find out ways to move between slides in this view. Compare the methods used in Notes Page view to those used in the other PowerPoint views.

7. Save the presentation as **I promise to do better**. Print the presentation as an outline and as a series of slides.

8. Close the presentation, but leave PowerPoint running if you plan to complete additional exercises.

Discovery Zone

Discovery Zone exercises require advanced knowledge of topics presented in *MOUS Essentials* lessons, application of skills from multiple lessons, or self-directed learning of new skills.

1. Creating Presentations

You're the secretary of the University Bicycling Club. To get ready for an upcoming meeting, you develop the following presentations:

- A one-slide flyer that announces the meeting time and location. (Hint: Use a template for this flyer.)
- A presentation that introduces a speaker for the meeting. (Hint: Use the AutoContent Wizard.)
- A presentation to motivate your team of club members. (Hint: Use the AutoContent Wizard.)

Enter appropriate information in each of the presentations. Switch between each of PowerPoint's views for each presentation. If the presentation contains multiple slides, use keyboard shortcuts and the mouse to move between the slides.

Print the announcement flyer as a slide in color and in black and white (grayscale). Print the other two presentations as outlines.

Unless instructed otherwise by your teacher, close the presentations without saving them. Leave PowerPoint running if you plan to complete additional exercises. [L1–6, 8]

2. Developing a New Presentation

One of the requirements for your business class is to give a speech on a software program. Because you are familiar with PowerPoint 2000, you decide to create a PowerPoint presentation to supplement your talk.

Use the AutoContent Wizard and the Training presentation type to develop your talk. Research information on PowerPoint's main features (perhaps by using the Table of Contents of your student workbook as a guide or using Help). Replace the sample content supplied by the AutoContent Wizard with your information.

View your presentation in each of PowerPoint's available views. Also, practice moving between slides in each view. Make sure to familiarize yourself with the slide show shortcut keys, and practice starting an electronic slide show on any slide. If possible, share the presentation with at least one other user. Print the presentation as an outline. Then, unless instructed otherwise by your teacher, close the presentation without saving it. If you've finished your work session, close PowerPoint and shut down Windows before turning off your computer. [L2–8]

PinPoint Assessment

You have completed this project and its associated lessons, and have had an opportunity to assess your skills through the end-of-project questions and exercises. Now use the PinPoint software Evaluation Mode to further assess your comprehension of the specific exam activities you have just learned. You can also use the PinPoint Trainer Mode and the Show Me tutorials to practice these exam activities.

Project 3

Modifying Presentations

Key terms introduced in this project include

- clipboard
- demote
- drag-and-drop
- promote
- reverse video

Objectives	Required Activity for MOUS	Exam Level
➤ Opening an Existing Presentation	Save as new presentation	
➤ Adding and Deleting Slides and Changing Slide Layout	Delete slides	
	Create a specific type of slide	
	Change the layout for one or more slides	
➤ Changing Slide Order	Change the order of slides using Slide Sorter view	
	Modify slide sequence in the Outline pane	
➤ Adding, Demoting, and Promoting Text	Enter text in tri-pane view	
	Promote and demote text in Slide and Outline panes	
➤ Copying a Slide from One Presentation into Another	Copy a slide from one presentation into another	
➤ Selecting, Moving, and Spell Checking Text	Check spelling	

Why Would I Do This?

Creating the framework of a presentation, as you did in the previous two projects, is a good start on the road to success with PowerPoint. However, any presentation that you create with the AutoContent Wizard (or a template) is really just a springboard for further revisions. As you develop your thoughts, you'll want the flexibility of adding or removing slides and text.

Luckily, it's easy to modify an existing presentation—and in this project, we'll show you how. First, you learn how to open an existing presentation. You focus on quick methods of adding and deleting slides, changing slide order, and revising your text. You also learn how to apply a different slide layout and to spell check your presentation.

 ## Lesson 1: Opening an Existing Presentation

When you want to work with a paper file in your office, you probably get it from a file cabinet, make a copy, and then put it on your desk so that you can work on it. In the same way, opening an existing presentation in PowerPoint just creates a copy from one of the computer's storage areas and places it in memory so that you can work with it.

This is handy because it enables you to revise existing presentations instead of having to create new ones from scratch. Think of how time-consuming it would be to re-create every presentation you want to use!

After you open a file, it's also sometimes advantageous to immediately create a "clone" of the file by saving it with a new name. When you do this, you can work with the copy but still keep the original file intact. You will use this method for the tutorials in this book.

Now, try opening an existing presentation.

To Open an Existing Presentation

❶ Open PowerPoint, if necessary, and clear the Startup dialog box.

 Inside Stuff: **Opening Presentations**
You can open an existing presentation directly from the Startup dialog box. To do this, choose the **Open an existing presentation** option button, and then click OK to display the Open dialog box. However, if PowerPoint is already open, you'll probably use the File, Open command instead.

 ❷ Choose File, Open. (Alternatively, you can click the Open button on the Standard toolbar or press Ctrl+O from the keyboard.)
The Open dialog box displays, as shown in Figure 3.1. This dialog box shows the folders and files on your computer. And, just as a folder in your office might contain several documents, an electronic folder might contain several presentations.

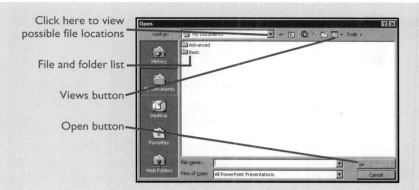

Click here to view
possible file locations

File and folder list

Views button

Open button

Figure 3.1
PowerPoint makes it
easy to find and open
presentations.

 If You Have Problems...
If the list of folders on your system doesn't match that shown in Figure 3.1,
don't worry. Because the folders on each computer can be set up to match
your work habits, it's unlikely that you'd have exactly the same ones as
those shown in the book. However, the My Documents folder is designated
(by Microsoft) as the central location to save all your work.

3 **Insert the CD-ROM disk that accompanies this book in the CD-ROM
drive of your computer, click the Look in drop-down list arrow, and select CD (D:) from the list. If necessary, double-click the Student folder.**
A list of folders displays, each containing files on the CD-ROM (see Figure 3.2).
Each folder includes the data files by project you will use to complete the tutorials in this book.

Figure 3.2
You can list the files
on any drive.

 If You Have Problems...
It's possible that your instructor has copied these data files to the hard
drive or a network drive. If you're unsure of the location of the data files
for your class, check with your instructor.

4 **Double-click the Project 3 folder.**
A listing of files you need to complete Project 3 display.

continues ▶

To Open an Existing Presentation (continued)

5 Click to select PP-0301, if necessary.
PP1-0301 displays in *reverse video*, so that you can tell that it is the file you're working with. Reverse video is just the computer's method of highlighting text on the display so that dark text is shown as bright characters on a dark background. After it has been selected, you can display information about the file.

6 With PP-0301 still selected, click the Open button.
PowerPoint opens the selected file and displays it in Normal view. To help you quickly identify which presentation is open, PowerPoint displays the presentation's name in the title bar.

Now that the file is opened in memory, you can use the Save As dialog box to copy and rename the file. This keeps the original file unaltered.

7 With the PP-0301 presentation onscreen, choose File, Save As.
The Save As dialog box displays (see Figure 3.3). In the Save As dialog box, you can enter a new name for the file and choose Save. This effectively creates a copy of the original file with a new name.

Figure 3.3
You can save an existing presentation as a new presentation.

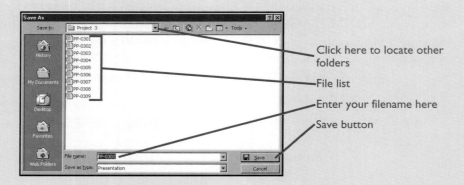

Click here to locate other folders

File list

Enter your filename here

Save button

8 In the File name text box, type Quality Computer Training, and then click the Save button.
The PP-0301 file is copied and renamed **Quality Computer Training** simultaneously. Notice that the title bar displays the new name. You'll work with this presentation in the next lesson, so leave it open.

 ## Lesson 2: Adding and Deleting Slides and Changing Slide Layout

Whether you rely on the AutoContent Wizard to create your presentations, use a template, or develop presentations from scratch, you'll want the flexibility of adding and deleting slides. To provide you with a handy reference, the following table lists the methods you can use to add or delete a slide.

Table 3.1   Adding and Deleting Slides

To	Do This
Add a slide	Choose Insert, New Slide from the menu bar.
	Click the New Slide button on the Standard toolbar.
	Press Ctrl+M.
	Click the Common Tasks button's drop-down list arrow, and then choose New Slide.
Delete a slide	In Outline and Slide Sorter views, click to select the slide, and then press Del.
	In Normal and Slide views, choose Edit, Delete Slide.

In this lesson, you add and delete slides in the Normal and Slide Sorter views because it's the easiest way to see the effect on the overall presentation. Try adding and deleting slides now.

To Add and Delete Slides and Change Slide Layout

1 **Display the Quality Computer Training presentation in Normal view, if necessary.**

2 **Click the Outline pane's vertical scrollbar down arrow until you can see Slide 6, Pricing.**

You can instantly select an entire slide by clicking the icon in the Outline pane.

3 **Move the mouse pointer over the icon for Slide 6 until a four-headed arrow displays and click.**

Slide 6 is selected, as displayed in Figure 3.4. (If a selected slide contains sub-points, they'll be selected as well.)

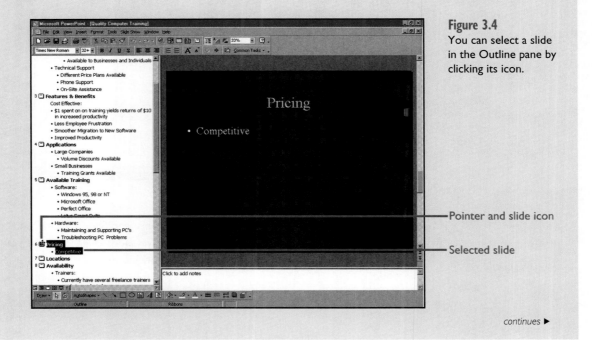

Figure 3.4
You can select a slide in the Outline pane by clicking its icon.

Pointer and slide icon

Selected slide

continues ▶

To Add and Delete Slides and Change Slide Layout (continued)

④ Press Del.

The selected slide, Slide 6, is deleted from the presentation, and the remaining slides are renumbered. You can reverse this deletion, however, by using a handy feature that PowerPoint provides to reverse your last action—Undo.

⑤ Click the Undo button on the Standard toolbar.

Slide 6 is reinserted into the presentation.

 Inside Stuff: **Using Multiple Undo**

You can reverse more than one action by clicking the Undo button as many times as is necessary to reverse your action. By default, you can reverse up to 20 actions.

You can also delete slides in Slide Sorter view. This is a good view to use when deleting, adding, or rearranging slides because you can easily see the effect of your action on the presentation as a whole.

⑥ Click the Slide Sorter View button, and then click Slide 7, Locations.

The presentation is shown in Slide Sorter view with a double border surrounding Slide 7. This indicates that it is the selected slide (see Figure 3.5).

Figure 3.5
You can select a slide in Slide Sorter view.

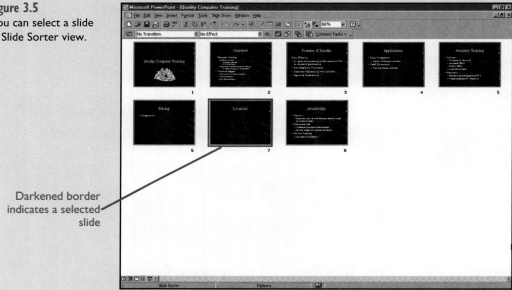

Darkened border indicates a selected slide

⑦ Press Del.

The selected slide is deleted. The black line between Slides 6 and 7 indicates that the insertion-point location is between the two slides. This is where you want to add a new slide. Luckily, you can create a specific type, or layout, for each new slide.

8 **Click the New Slide button on the Standard toolbar.**
PowerPoint displays the New Slide dialog box. As you remember from Project 1, "Getting Started with PowerPoint," you use this dialog box to select which AutoLayout you want to use for your new slide. Most AutoLayouts include placeholders, predesigned areas on the slide that accept certain types of objects. For example, the Chart AutoLayout includes a placeholder for a chart.

9 **Double-click the AutoLayout for Title Slide (the leftmost layout on the first row).**
A new slide that uses the Title Slide AutoLayout is inserted into your presentation.

Most of the time you'll stick with the AutoLayout you chose when you initially created the slide. However, if you later change your mind about how you want your slide set up, you can quickly apply a different slide layout to an existing slide. Try displaying the slide in Normal view and changing the slide layout now.

10 **Double-click Slide 7—the new slide you inserted into your presentation.**
The slide displays in Normal view. Double-clicking a slide in Slide Sorter view is a quick way to switch to Normal view. Now try changing the slide layout.

11 **Choose F_ormat, Slide L_ayout.**
The Slide Layout dialog box displays (see Figure 3.6). Notice the similarity of this dialog box to the New Slide dialog box. That's because the same slide layouts are available in each.

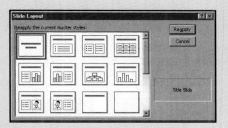

Figure 3.6
Use the Slide Layout dialog box to apply a different slide layout.

12 **Double-click the Bulleted List AutoLayout.**
The new layout is applied to the slide. Remember that you can change the slide layout for any slide on-the-fly using this method.

13 **Click the Save button to save your changes.**
Clicking Save updates the changes you made to your presentation. Keep your presentation open for the next lesson, in which you change the slide order.

 Exam Note: **Deleting (or Changing Slide Layout for) Multiple Slides**
In Outline and Slide Sorter views, you can delete several slides simultaneously. Click the first slide you want to delete, press ◆Shift), and click the last slide. All the intervening slides are selected. You can also select nonadjacent slides by pressing Ctrl) while clicking the slides you want. After you select the slides, press Del) to remove them all.

You can also quickly change the slide layout for multiple slides. In Slide Sorter view, select multiple slides by pressing Ctrl) while clicking the slides. Choose F_ormat, Slide L_ayout to display the Slide Layout dialog box. Double-click the layout that you want to apply to the selected slides.

Lesson 3: Changing Slide Order

You'll often need to rearrange the slides in your presentation to create a more logical sequence. The best view to use for reordering slides is Slide Sorter view because you immediately see the move's effect on the presentation. Here's how to move a slide in this view: First, select the slide; then drag it to the new location before releasing the mouse button. This method is sometimes referred to as *drag-and-drop*. Try shuffling your slides using this technique now.

To Change Slide Order

 1 **With the Quality Computer Training presentation open, click the Slide Sorter View button.**

This is a good view to use to rearrange slides. Before you move a slide, however, you must first select it.

 If You Have Problems...

Don't panic if the slide miniatures on your screen appear larger or smaller than those shown in the figures. The size of the slide miniatures depends on (among other things) the screen settings and monitor size.

2 **Click Slide 4, Applications, to select it.**

A double border surrounds Slide 4, indicating that it is selected.

3 **Move the mouse pointer to the middle of the selected slide, and then drag the line indicator to the space between Slides 6 and 7.**

The new location for the slide is indicated by the inserted line between Slides 6 and 7 (see Figure 3.7).

Figure 3.7
You can drag a selected slide to the new location.

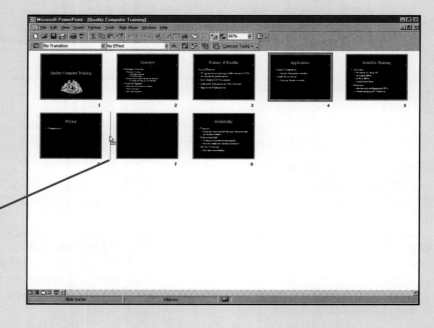

The indicator line shows the new location for the slide

4 **Release the mouse button.**
The selected slide is moved to the position between Slides 6 and 7. PowerPoint also renumbers the slides to line up with their new positions.

Now try selecting and moving multiple slides. To select more than one slide, press ⬆Shift as you click to select (or deselect) the slides. Release ⬆Shift, and then drag the group of slides to the new location.

5 **With Slide 6, Applications, still selected, press ⬆Shift while clicking Slide 5, Pricing.**
Double borders encompass both slides, indicating that you successfully selected them. You can move them to a new location by dragging, just as you did earlier in this exercise. If you drag one of the selected slides, both will move. And as before, the indicator line shows the new location for the selected slides.

6 **Move the mouse pointer to the middle of Slide 5, Pricing, and then drag the indicator line between Slides 2 and 3.**

7 **Release the mouse button to "drop" the slides into their new location.**
Both slides are moved to the specified location. Notice that PowerPoint also renumbers the presentation slides.

8 **Choose Edit, Undo Drag and Drop (or click the Undo button) to reverse the move.**
The slides are moved to their preceding location.

9 **Save your changes and keep the presentation open for the next exercise, in which you add, demote, and promote text.**

 Exam Note: **Modifying the Slide Sequence in the Outline Pane**
Although it's a bit tricky, you can select and move slides in the Outline pane as well. In the Outline pane, click a slide's icon to select it. Move the mouse pointer over the icon until a four-headed arrow displays. Drag the slide to the new location (indicated by a horizontal line), and then release the mouse button.

You can also move the slides by using Cut and Paste. Select the slide (in Slide Sorter view) or icon (in the Outline pane), and then click the Cut button. Click to set the insertion point between two slides to indicate the new location, and then choose the Paste button.

Lesson 4: Adding, Demoting, and Promoting Text

When you first create a presentation, you have only a framework for adding text and graphics. In the previous two lessons, you focused on changing the basic structure so that your presentation would flow in a more logical manner. You did this by adding, deleting, and rearranging slides. You also changed the slide layout. After the framework is in place, however, there are numerous ways to enter and modify the text itself. This lesson focuses on ways to enter, demote, and promote text in the Slide pane of the Normal view. You use the blank slide you inserted in Lesson 2 to do this. Try working with text now.

To Add, Demote, and Promote Text

 1 **Select Slide 7 in the Quality Computer Training presentation, and then click the Normal View button.**
The new blank slide is shown with placeholders for a title and a bulleted list (see Figure 3.8). The placeholders that display depend on which AutoLayout you choose. For this slide, you have title and bulleted list areas.

Figure 3.8
You can enter text in the slide's placeholders.

Placeholder for
title text

Placeholder for
bulleted text

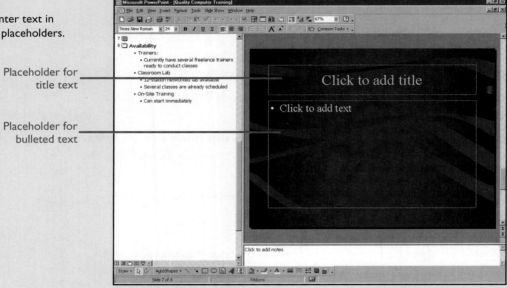

2 **Click the upper placeholder, Click to add title.**
An insertion point replaces the placeholder words, so you can enter text.

3 **Type Experienced Trainers, and then click the lower placeholder, Click to add text.**
The title is fixed in the upper placeholder and the insertion point is moved to the bulleted list area. Because this slide is based on the Bulleted List AutoLayout, you can quickly create a list with bullets. Bulleted lists are generally used when you want to emphasize each subpoint, but the order of the items is not particularly important.

4 **Type Rebecca Smithson as the first bullet point, and then press ⏎Enter.**
Rebecca Smithson is listed as the first bullet point and a second bullet is automatically created.

 If You Have Problems...
If a red squiggly line appears beneath a word (such as Smithson in this example), don't worry. PowerPoint doesn't recognize the word, and thinks that you've either misspelled or mistyped it. You can either ignore the line or right-click on the word to display a spelling shortcut menu. Choose a replacement word (or Ignore All) from the menu.

⑤ Type Sarah Jones as the second bullet point and press ⏎Enter.
Sarah Jones is entered as the second point. You can create subpoints that support or enhance your main point. One way to create subpoints is to press Tab⇄ to insert the line. Alternatively, you can click the Demote button on the Formatting toolbar.

⑥ Press Tab⇄, type Ten years corporate training experience, and then press ⏎Enter.
Pressing Tab⇄ (or clicking the Demote button) *demotes* this line—indenting it to show that it has less importance than the preceding one. Additionally, every time you press ⏎Enter, another subpoint at the same level is created.

⑦ Type Writes books for Prentice Hall as the second subpoint, and then press ⏎Enter.
You can also *promote* a line so that it is indented less. By indenting text less, you indicate its relative importance. You can do this by pressing ⬆Shift+Tab⇄ or clicking the Promote button on the Formatting toolbar.

⑧ Press ⬆Shift+Tab⇄ to *promote* the bullet on the current line, and type Lonnie Bell.
Your slide should now look similar to Figure 3.9.

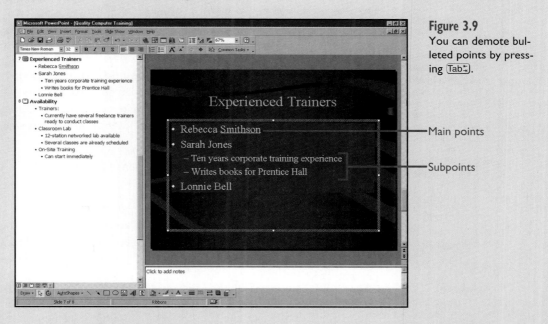

Figure 3.9
You can demote bulleted points by pressing Tab⇄.

⑨ Save the Quality Computer Training presentation.
Keep it open for the next lesson, in which you copy a slide from another presentation into this one.

Exam Note: **Promote and Demote Text in the Outline Pane**
You can also enter and edit text in the Outline pane. You position the insertion point next to the slide icon, and then type the text. You can also press Tab⇅ or ⬆Shift+Tab⇅ to demote or promote points—just like you did using the Slide pane.

 ## Lesson 5: Copying a Slide from One Presentation into Another

At times you'll have already developed a slide in one presentation that you want to use in another. For example, perhaps you have a slide that includes a chart, table, logo, or other objects that you don't want to spend time re-creating. Instead, you can just copy the slide from one presentation into another. Try using this time-saving feature now.

To Copy a Slide from One Presentation into Another

1 With the Quality Computer Training presentation open, choose View, Slide Sorter.
It's easiest to see the effects of copying and pasting slides in this view. Now open the presentation from which you'll copy a slide.

2 Press Ctrl+O.
The Open dialog box displays.

3 In the Project 3 folder in the Open dialog box, double-click PP-0302.
The PP-0302 presentation opens and displays in Slide Sorter view—the view that displayed when it was saved. (However, keep in mind that that Quality Computer Training presentation is still open in your computer's memory as well.)

4 Click Slide 2 in the PP-0302 presentation.
The slide is selected, as indicated by the darkened border. You must select a slide before copying it.

5 Choose Edit, Copy.
The selected slide is copied to the temporary storage area in the computer, called the *clipboard*. From the clipboard the slide can be copied to another presentation. Because you have finished using it, you can close the PowerPoint-0302 presentation.

6 With the PP-0302 presentation displayed, choose File, Close.
The presentation closes and the Quality Computer Training presentation redisplays. Now you can indicate where you want to insert the copied slide.

7 In the Quality Computer Training presentation, click between Slide 5 and Slide 6.
The insertion point displays between the slides, indicating the location for the copied slide (see Figure 3.10).

Figure 3.10
Click to set the insertion point between two slides.

Insertion point indicates location for copied slide

8 **Choose Edit, Paste.**

The slide is pasted from the clipboard into the Quality Computer Training presentation (see Figure 3.11).

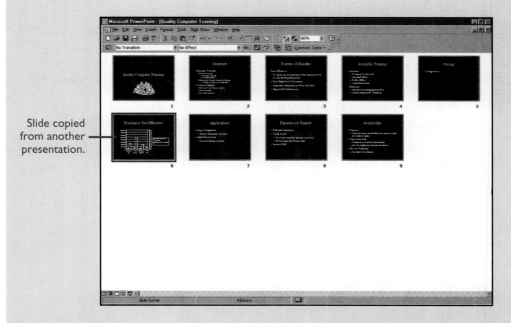

Figure 3.11
You can copy slides from one presentation into another.

Slide copied from another presentation.

9 **Save the Quality Computer Training presentation.**

Keep the presentation open for the next lesson, in which you select, move, and spell check text.

Lesson 6: Selecting, Moving, and Spell Checking Text

In addition to entering text, you can easily change the order of the presentation bullet points. The clipboard facilitates copying and moving text in the same way it facilitated copying and pasting entire slides. Before you cut or copy text, however, you must first select it. You can move text most easily in the Normal or Outline views. For this exercise, you use Outline view.

To Select, Move, and Spell Check Text

 1 **In the open Quality Computer Training presentation, click the Outline View button.**
The presentation displays in Outline view.

2 **Use the Outline pane's vertical scrollbar so that you can view Slide 4, Available Training.**

3 **On Slide 4, double-click the word Available.**
The word Available displays in reverse video to indicate that you selected it. You can move this word by cutting it, which sends it to the clipboard, and then by pasting it at another location. Try this now.

 4 **Click the Cut button on the Standard toolbar.**
The selected word is removed from the screen and sent to the clipboard. (You can also cut text by choosing Edit, Cut, or by pressing Ctrl+X from the keyboard.)

You can position your insertion point where you want to place the text, and then choose Edit, Paste. (Alternatively, you can click the Paste button or press Ctrl+V from the keyboard.)

 5 **Click the mouse to set the insertion point immediately after the word Training (on Slide 4), and then click the Paste button.**
The word is pasted at the location you indicated.

In Outline view, you can also select a subpoint and move it by using the Move Up or Move Down buttons on the Outlining toolbar. First, however, you need to display this toolbar.

 If You Have Problems...
If the Outlining toolbar is already displayed on your system, it just means that another user previously turned it on. If this is the case, proceed to Step 8.

6 **Right-click either the Standard or Formatting toolbar.**
A shortcut menu displays and shows a list of PowerPoint's toolbars (see Figure 3.12).

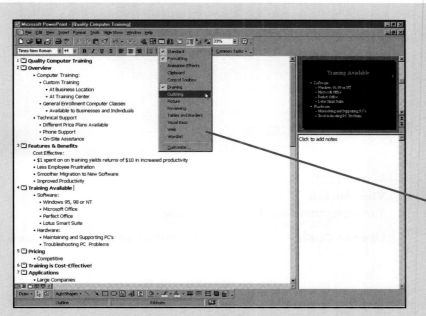

Figure 3.12
PowerPoint's toolbars are only a mouse click away.

Right-click on a visible toolbar to display this listing of available toolbars.

7 **Click Outlining on the shortcut menu.**

The Outlining toolbar displays on the left side of the Outline pane (see Figure 3.13). Now try using the Move Up and Move Down buttons to adjust the position of text on your outline.

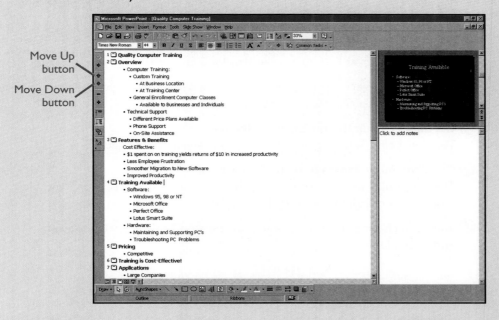

Figure 3.13
Use the Outlining toolbar buttons to work with your presentation.

8 **On Slide 4, position the mouse pointer over the bullet for the subpoint** Windows 95, 98 or NT **until it displays as a four-sided arrow, and then click.**

The entire subpoint is selected (see Figure 3.14). Now, you can use the Move Down button to position it where you want it.

continues ▶

To Select, Move, and Spell Check Text   (continued)

Figure 3.14
You can use the Move Up and Move Down buttons in Outline view.

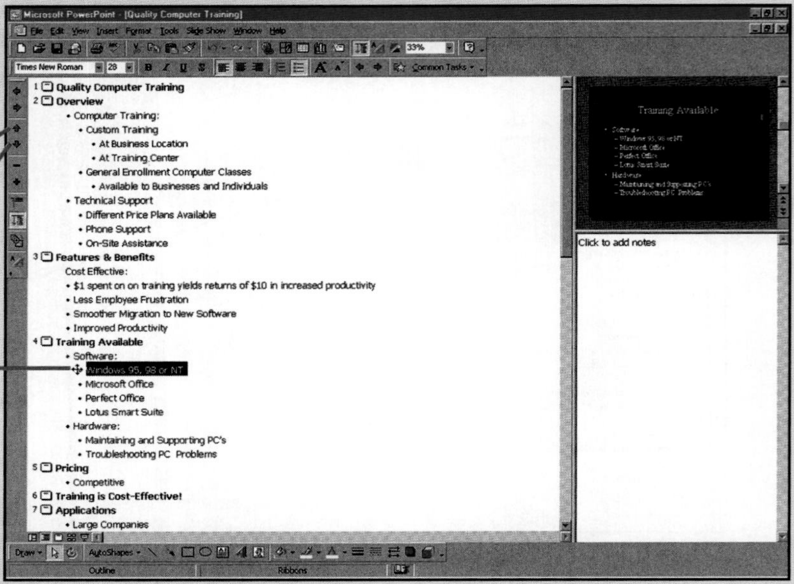

Click here to move the selected text up

Click here to move the selected text down

Click a bullet to select the associated text

⑨ **With the subpoint still selected, click the Move Down button on the Outlining toolbar.**
The subpoint moves down one line in the presentation. Likewise, you can move it up.

⑩ **Click the Move Up button on the Outlining toolbar.**
The subpoint moves back to its preceding location.

You can also select a main point, and then move it. When you select a main point, all the subpoints are automatically selected as well.

⑪ **On Slide 4, click the bullet for Software.**
The main point (Software) and all the related subpoints are selected.

⑫ **Click the Move Down button three times.**
The information about software programs is moved down three lines. Your slide should appear similar to the one shown in Figure 3.15.

⑬ **Save the changes to your Quality Computer Training presentation, and then close it.**

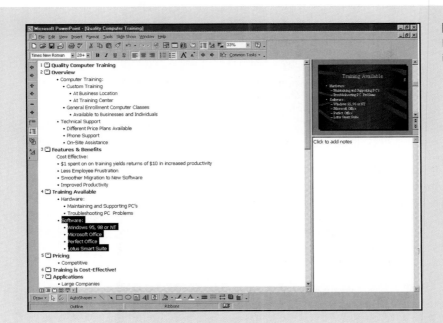

Figure 3.15
It's easy to move text in Outline view.

 Exam Note: **Checking Your Spelling**

One of the last steps before printing or giving a presentation is to make sure that it's error-free. Besides manually proofreading the presentation, you can spell check it. To do this, click the Spelling button on the Standard toolbar, or choose Tools, Spelling. PowerPoint searches your presentation for typos and misspelled words and displays them in the Spelling dialog box. You can choose Ignore to skip over the word, Change to replace it with another word, or Add to place the word in the dictionary. After PowerPoint has finished spell checking your presentation, it displays a message box. Click OK to close the message box, and you're on your way to an error-free presentation!

Summary

As you worked through this project, you refined your PowerPoint skills. First, you learned how to modify the overall structure of a presentation by adding, deleting, and reordering slides. Next you learned how to revise the content of individual slides by adding, demoting, promoting, copying, and moving text. You also learned how to apply a different slide layout and copy a slide from one presentation into another. Finally, you learned how to spell check your presentation for errors.

To expand on your knowledge, spend a few minutes exploring Help on these topics. You can also use the PinPoint CD to brush up on the concepts covered in this project. Finally, complete some of the Skill Drill, Challenge, and Discovery Zone exercises.

Checking Concepts and Terms

True/False

For each of the following, check *T* or *F* to indicate whether the statement is true or false.

__T __F **1.** Demote means to decrease the size of your text. [L4]

__T __F **2.** Slide Sorter view is the best view to use when you want to rearrange slides. [L3]

__T __F **3.** You can add a new slide to a presentation by clicking the Promote button. [L2,4]

__T __F **4.** You can copy slides from one presentation to another. [L5]

__T __F **5.** You promote a bulleted point when you click the Move Up button on the Outlining toolbar. [L4,6]

Multiple Choice

Circle the letter of the correct answer for each of the following.

1. To promote a point means to _____. [L4]

a. make the text larger

b. select a subpoint

c. indent it less

d. indent it more

2. You can delete a slide by _____. [L2]

a. clicking the Move Out button

b. showing the presentation in Slide Show view, and then pressing Esc

c. selecting a slide in Slide Sorter view, and then pressing Del

d. double-clicking a slide in Slide Sorter view

3. To add a slide, _____. [L2]

a. click the Slide Sorter View button, and then press ↵Enter

b. press PgDn in Normal view

c. click the Get a New Slide button on the Slide Sorter toolbar

d. click the New Slide button on the Standard toolbar

4. When you delete a slide, _____. [L2]

a. PowerPoint automatically renumbers the remaining presentation slides.

b. PowerPoint prompts you before removing the slide.

c. The presentation automatically displays in Normal view.

d. all of the above

5. When text is cut or copied it is sent to the _____. [L5–6]

a. Outboard

b. Office Assistant

c. clipboard

d. Explorer

Skill Drill

Skill Drill exercises reinforce project skills. Each skill reinforced is the same, or nearly the same, as a skill presented in the project. Detailed instructions are provided in a step-by-step format.

1. Opening and Resaving a Presentation

Your boss is having trouble locating a presentation that she desperately needs to conduct a new employee orientation seminar. Because you're much more familiar with computers (and PowerPoint) than your boss, she asked you to help. To quickly lay your hands on the correct file, you use the Views button in the Open dialog box. [L1]

1. In PowerPoint choose File, Open to display the Open dialog box.

2. Use the Look in drop-down list to locate the drive (and folder) where your data files are located.

3. Make sure that **PP-0301** is selected on the list. Click the Views button's drop-down list arrow (in the Open dialog box), and then choose List.

4. Click the Views button's drop-down list arrow, and then choose Details.

5. Click the Views button's drop-down list arrow, and then choose Properties.

6. Click the Views button's drop-down list arrow, and then choose Preview.

7. Repeat steps 3–6 for each of the other student data files in the folder until you locate the **PP-0303** presentation. Open the presentation and view it as a slide show.

8. Save the presentation using a different name. Choose File, Save As to display the Save As dialog box. Enter **Revision** in the File name text box, and then click Save.

9. Close the presentation. Leave PowerPoint running if you plan to complete the next exercise.

2. Saving and Modifying a Presentation

You were promoted at your company. One of your new responsibilities involves running the new employee orientation sessions. In preparation for the next orientation session, you decide to modify the overall structure of the presentation, as well as some of the text. [L1–4,6]

1. Choose File, Open to display the Open dialog box. Display the folder in which your student data files are located; then double-click **PP-0303** to open it.

2. Choose File, Save As to display the Save As dialog box. In the File name text box, type **Employee Orientation**. Click Save.

3. Click the Slide Sorter View button to display the presentation in Slide Sorter view. Click Slide 3, History of Company, and then press Del. Repeat the process to delete the (new) Slide 3, Who's Who.

4. Click Slide 6, Required Paperwork, to select it. Drag the slide to between Slide 2 and Slide 3. Release the mouse button.

5. Double-click Slide 4, Benefits Review, to display it in Normal view. Make the following changes to the text in either the Slide pane or the Outline pane:

- The fitness center has closed down, so it is no longer a benefit. Eliminate the point associated with it.

- Change the text to show that you now get 3/4 sick day per month rather than 1/2.

- Move the point for the 401(K) plan to just below the point for the two-week vacation benefit.

6 Choose Tools, Spelling to launch the spell checker. Correct any errors you find.

7 Save your changes and then close the presentation. Leave PowerPoint running if you plan to complete the next exercise.

3. Moving Text and Slides

You're a sales manager for a company and you want to present a short pep talk to your sales force about how to work with different types of people. To prepare for the talk, you revise a previously created presentation. [L1–4]

1. Open **PP-0304** and save it as **People Skills**.

2. Choose Vi̲ew, Sli̲de Sorter to display the presentation in Slide Sorter view.

3. Click Slide 3, Summary, and drag the slide to move it between Slide 1 and Slide 2.

4. With the new Slide 2, Summary, still selected, press Del to remove the slide from the presentation.

5. Click the Undo button twice to reverse the previous two actions.

6. Double-click Slide 2, Skills, to display it in Normal view.

7. Click to set your insertion point in the last line (Communication Skills). Click the Promote button on the Formatting toolbar to make the point the same level of importance as the other bulleted points.

8. Move the point for Communication Skills so that it is the first bulleted point on Slide 2.

9. Click the point for The Lion, and then click the Demote button. Repeat the process for each of the other personality types (The Beaver, The Golden Retriever, and The Otter).

10. Display the first presentation slide. Choose Fo̲rmat, Slide L̲ayout. Double-click the Title Slide AutoLayout to apply this layout to the slide.

11. Save the People Skills presentation; then close it. Leave PowerPoint running if you plan to complete the Challenge or Discovery Zone exercises.

Challenge

Challenge exercises expand on, or are somewhat related to, skills presented in the lessons. Each exercise provides a brief narrative introduction, followed by instructions in a numbered step format that are not as detailed as those in the Skill Drill section.

1. Saving and Revising an Existing Presentation

As president of the University Biking Club, you must present information to prospective members. You decide to revise an existing presentation to do this effectively. [L1, 3–4, 6]

1. In PowerPoint, open **PP-0305** and save it as **Biking Club**.

2. Display the presentation in Slide Sorter view. Move Slide 3, Officers, to between Slide 1 and Slide 2.

3. Switch to Normal view. Move the bulleted subpoint on Slide 3, Trip to watch Virginia Race of Champions, up two lines. (*Hint:* It should display immediately beneath the Coming Events main point.)

4. Add a new slide after Slide 3. Choose the Bulleted List AutoLayout for your new slide.

5. Add the following text on the newly inserted slide:

    Title placeholder: **How to Join**

    Text placeholder: **Fill out membership form**

    Fill out proof of insurance form

    Pay dues to Grace Stegall (Treasurer)

6. Spell check your presentation. Correct any errors you find.

7. Print an outline of your presentation. Save and close your Biking Club presentation. Leave PowerPoint running if you plan to complete additional exercises.

2. Saving and Modifying a Presentation

As the events coordinator for the College Horseback Riding Club, you're in charge of an upcoming horse show. To publicize the event, you decide to revise an existing presentation to show during the next club meeting. [L1–6]

1. Open **PP-0306** and save it as **Horseback Riding Club**.
2. Make the following changes to Slide 2:
   - Demote the three points listed beneath Classes.
   - Move the location (Indoor Arena) to the first line in the text placeholder so that it is the first bullet on the slide.

3. Add a slide at the end of the presentation using the Title Slide AutoLayout. Enter the following information:

   Title placeholder: **How to enter**:

   Subtitle placeholder: **Bring proof of club membership**

   Sign up for classes at entry stand

   Pay club treasurer

4. After looking over the last presentation slide, you decide that a different slide layout would display this information more clearly. Apply the Bulleted List AutoLayout to this slide.

5. Open **PP-0307**. Copy both slides from this presentation. Paste them between Slide 1 and Slide 2 in the Horseback Riding Club presentation. Close **PP-0307**.

6. Display your presentation in Normal view. Spell check your presentation and correct any errors you find.

7. Save and close your presentation. Leave PowerPoint running if you plan to complete additional exercises.

3. Working with Presentation Text

As part of one of your business classes, you're required to give a speech on a software program. Because you know PowerPoint 2000, you decide to give your talk on it. Last week, you created the basics of the presentation; today you finish it by revising the existing presentation's text. [Lessons 1–4, 6]

1. Open **PP-0308** and save it as **Business Class Speech**.
2. Using the following outline as a guide, develop the presentation (see Figure 3.16). Add and reorder slides as necessary. Also add, demote, and promote the text. Use whichever PowerPoint view (Outline, Normal, or Slide Sorter) is appropriate for the action you perform. After you have finished, view your presentation as a slide show. Don't forget to spell check the presentation.

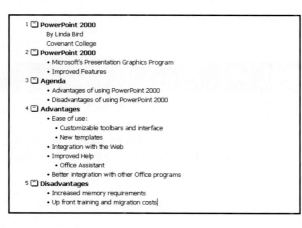

Figure 3.16
Use this outline as a guide.

3. Save the presentation; then close it. Leave PowerPoint running if you plan to complete the Discovery Zone exercises.

Discovery Zone

Discovery Zone exercises require advanced knowledge of topics presented in *MOUS Essentials* lessons, application of skills from multiple lessons, or self-directed learning of new skills.

1. Developing and Modifying Presentations

Think of two school, community, or business organizations (or clubs) with which you are currently affiliated. Develop a presentation for each one, highlighting the purpose, officers, membership requirements, upcoming events, and so on. You can use the AutoContent Wizard or a template to develop the presentations.

As necessary, add, delete, and reorder slides as you restructure your presentations. Think about which type of slide layout you want to add for each new slide. Add, demote, and promote text, using techniques covered in this project. As you develop the presentations, use whichever view (Normal, Slide Sorter, or Outline) is most appropriate. If necessary, apply a different slide layout to existing slides so that the information displays more clearly.

Spell check your presentations. If directed by your instructor, save the presentations using a name of your choice. Close the presentations, but leave PowerPoint running if you plan to complete the last Discovery Zone exercise. [L1–4,6]

2. Developing and Modifying Presentations

You're the marketing director for an office products store that primarily sells computer hardware, software, and related supplies. You're slotted to give a presentation to the local retail merchant's association about the products and services you can offer, and want to develop a whiz-bang presentation. You decide to use PowerPoint's features to do so.

Use an appropriate AutoContent Wizard to develop a presentation that highlights your store's products. Cruise the Web to glean ideas of what type of products an office products store might offer. Then replace the suggested text in your presentation with information that you find. Add, demote and promote text as needed. Add, delete, and reorder slides, using either the Outline pane or Slide Sorter view.

Insert the slide from **PP-0309** to an appropriate place in your presentation, and then close **PP-0309**. View your presentation as a slide show and make any revisions to improve the flow and content. Spell check the presentation and correct any errors.

If directed by your instructor, save the presentation using a name of your choice. Close the presentation, exit PowerPoint, and shut down your computer before turning it off. [L1–6]

PinPoint Assessment

You have completed this project and its associated lessons, and have had an opportunity to assess your skills through the end-of-project questions and exercises. Now use the PinPoint software Evaluation Mode to further assess your comprehension of the specific exam activities you have just learned. You can also use the PinPoint Trainer Mode and the Show Me tutorials to practice these exam activities.

Formatting Text and Bullets

Key terms introduced in this project include

- bullets
- character attributes
- font

- formatting
- horizontal text alignment
- palette

- points
- tab type button
- typeface

Objectives	Required Activity for MOUS	Exam Level
➤ Changing Text Appearance	Change and replace text fonts (individual slide and entire presentation)	Core
➤ Using the Format Painter	Use the Format Painter	Core
➤ Changing the Text Alignment and Setting Tabs	Change the text alignment	Core
	Change tab formatting	Expert
➤ Adding and Removing Bullets	Add graphical bullets	Core
	Add AutoNumber bullets	Core
➤ Modifying Bullets	Add graphical bullets	Core
➤ Using AutoNumber Bullets	Add AutoNumber bullets	Core

Why Would I Do This?

In the previous projects, you created and revised presentations. Most of the modifications you did involved changing the presentation's overall structure, such as rearranging slide order, or adding and deleting slides.

Now you're ready to add some pizzazz to your presentation. One way to spiff up slides is to change *formatting*, which is the way that your presentation (including text, alignment, bullets, margins, and so on) is set up to display. For example, you can change your text color, size, alignment, or overall appearance. You can also change tab spacing. After you get the text formatting just the way you want it, you can quickly copy your formatting to other text by using the Format Painter.

Finally, you can use various types of *bullets*, the markers that help delineate your ideas. Fortunately, most of the commands you need to format text and bullets are at your fingertips in the form of the Formatting toolbar (see Figure 4.1). Additionally, for more specific control over formatting, you can use commands from the Format menu. So come along and add some spice to your presentations!

Figure 4.1
The Formatting toolbar provides quick access to formatting commands.

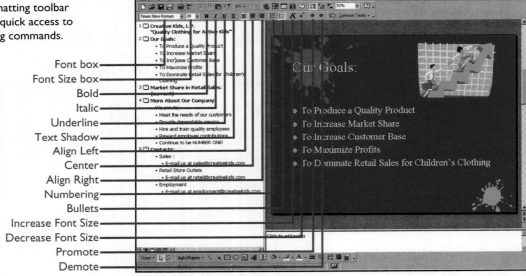

Font box
Font Size box
Bold
Italic
Underline
Text Shadow
Align Left
Center
Align Right
Numbering
Bullets
Increase Font Size
Decrease Font Size
Promote
Demote

 ## Lesson 1: Changing Text Appearance

The font, or typeface, that displays on a slide depends on the template you used to create it and the placeholder. A *font* is a collection of characters (letters, numbers, and special symbols) that have a specific appearance. Other terms for font are *typeface* and font face.

You can change the default font by adding *character attributes*, such as bold, italic, or underline. You can also modify the text's font face, size, or color. Try enhancing a presentation by formatting its text now.

To Change Text Appearance

❶ **Start PowerPoint, if necessary, and then open** PP-0401 **and save it as** Business Plan.

2 Display the first slide of the Business Plan presentation in Normal view.

3 Double-click the word `cutting`.

This selects the word so that you can change the formatting.

4 Click the Italic, Bold, and Underline buttons on the Formatting toolbar.

Italic, bold, and underline effects are added to the selected word.

 Inside Stuff: **Using Keyboard Shortcuts**

You can also add character effects by using keyboard shortcuts. For example, you can press Ctrl+B for bold, Ctrl+I for italic, and Ctrl+U for underline.

---

5 Select the text in the title placeholder, Business Plan.

Notice that the Font and Font Size boxes on the Formatting toolbar indicate that this text is currently Times New Roman 44 points (see Figure 4.2). Font size is measured in *points*, which is a unit of measurement used to designate character height. The larger the point size, the larger the text. Most slide text should be at least 18 points (or 1/4") to be readable—especially if you plan to produce transparencies or show the presentation by using an LCD panel or an overhead projector.

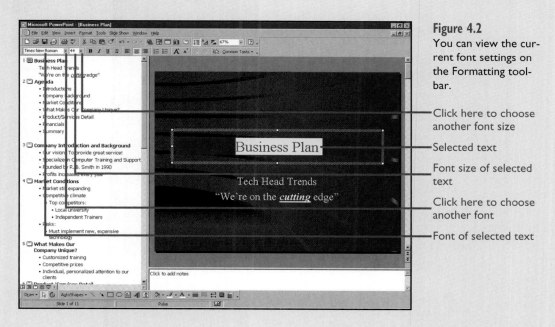

Figure 4.2
You can view the current font settings on the Formatting toolbar.

Click here to choose another font size

Selected text

Font size of selected text

Click here to choose another font

Font of selected text

Now try using the Formatting toolbar's button to change text size.

6 Click the drop-down arrow to the right of the Font Size box on the Formatting toolbar, and then click 66 to select it as the new point size.

The selected text changes to the larger point size.

Now modify the typeface's appearance.

continues ▶

To Change Text Appearance   (continued)

7 **With the title text still selected, click the Font box drop-down arrow.**
A graphical listing of fonts displays, which you can use for your presentation (see Figure 4.3). Don't panic if the fonts on your system don't match those shown in Figure 4.3. The exact fonts available depend on which programs (and printers) are installed on your system. Additionally, the most recently used fonts display at the top of the list.

Figure 4.3
PowerPoint shows you how a font looks before you select it.

Click here to display a list of fonts

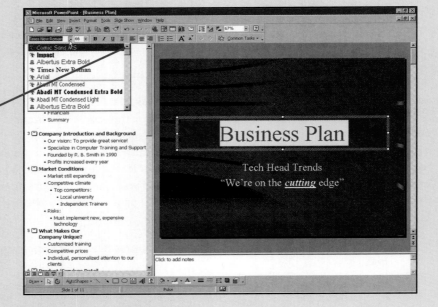

8 **Click Comic Sans MS on the list. (If Comic Sans MS is not available, select another font.)**
The new font is applied to the selected text.

Besides changing the font size and appearance, you can modify the font color. Try using the Font dialog box (rather than the toolbar) to make this change.

9 **Select the entire line, Tech Head Trends, and then choose F̲ormat, F̲ont.**
The Font dialog box displays. This dialog box includes a number of ways to format text (see Figure 4.4). Notice that some of the formatting options (such as those listed in the Effects area) are not available on the Formatting toolbar. Because of this, it's handy to know how to use this dialog box.

Figure 4.4
You can change text color in the Font dialog box.

Choose a font here

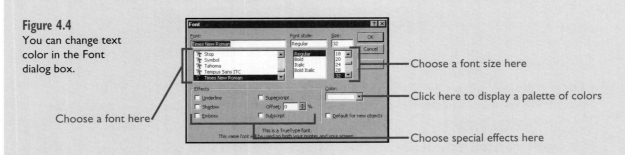

Choose a font size here

Click here to display a palette of colors

Choose special effects here

⑩ Click the _C_olor drop-down list arrow.

PowerPoint displays eight colors on a color *palette* (see Figure 4.5). The colors displayed are those most compatible with your particular template's color scheme. Just as an artist uses a palette to paint, you can pick and choose which colors you think will dress up your presentation.

Click here to display the color palette

Figure 4.5
You can choose a compatible color from the list.

⑪ Click dark orange from the color palette (the fifth from the left); then choose OK to close the Font dialog box.

Don't be surprised if the text doesn't look orange when it's selected. When text is selected (and shown in reverse video), the colors don't look the same as they do when the text isn't selected. However, you can easily see the color change just by deselecting the text.

⑫ Click anywhere else in the Slide pane to deselect the text.

When the text is deselected, you should be able to see the new font color.

⑬ Click the Save button to save your changes to the Business Plan pre-sentation.

Congratulations! You now know how to wield the basic tools for text format-ting. In the next lesson, you learn how to copy formatting by using the Format Painter, so keep the Business Plan presentation open.

 Exam Note: **Changing Font Size**

If you're in a hurry, you can change font size quickly by selecting text, and then clicking the Increase Font Size or Decrease Font Size buttons repeatedly until the font is the size you want.

Lesson 2: Using the Format Painter

If you want to use the same combination of font, color, and size throughout your presenta-tion, you don't have to laboriously create it from scratch each time. Instead you can just copy the formatting from one section of text to another. This is an efficient way to format text be-cause you can create the font and color combination you want once and then copy it.

How do you actually "paint" formatting? By using the Format Painter! Think of the text with the formatting you want to copy as a paint can. When you click the Format Painter button, you dip your paintbrush into the can. You then "paint" the formatting to other text by drag-ging over it—just as you paint a wall by dragging a paintbrush over it.

Try using this timesaving feature now.

To Use the Format Painter

1 **In your open presentation, select the Business Plan text (in the title placeholder of Slide 1).**
It's crucial to select the text from which you want to copy formatting by selecting it *before* you click the Format Painter button. Don't forget this step!

 If You Have Problems...
Make sure that the text containing the format you want to copy is selected before you click the Format Painter button. If you don't indicate the text formatting to copy, PowerPoint won't copy any formatting!

 2 **Click the Format Painter button on the Standard toolbar.**
The mouse pointer changes to the Format Painter I-beam pointer. This pointer appears, interestingly enough, as a miniature paintbrush, as shown in Figure 4.6. Now you can apply the formatting to other text.

Figure 4.6
You can quickly copy formats with the Format Painter.

Format Painter button

Format Painter pointer

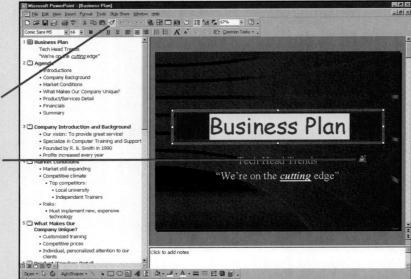

3 **Click and drag the pointer over the text for Tech Head Trends.**
The formatting styles associated with **Business Plan** are applied to **Tech Head Trends** and the Format Painter is automatically turned off.

You can keep the Format Painter feature active so that you can format multiple text sections, however—just double-click the Format Painter button.

4 **Select the word cutting in the lower placeholder, and then double-click the Format Painter button.**
The Format Painter is activated so you can copy formatting to several sections.

5 **Drag over We're in the lower placeholder, including the quotation marks immediately before the word.**
The formatting is copied to the selected word and the Format Painter is still active.

6 **Drag over the word** edge **(including the quotation marks immediately after the word) in the lower placeholder.**

The formatting is applied to the word. To turn off the Format Painter, you can click its button a second time or just press Esc.

7 **Click the Format Painter button.**

The Format Painter is turned off.

8 **To better see the formatting, click outside the lower placeholder.**

Your slide should now look similar to Figure 4.7.

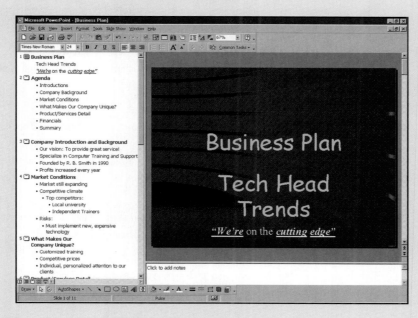

Figure 4.7
You can easily change text appearance in PowerPoint.

9 **Save your changes to the Business Plan presentation.**

Keep the presentation open for the next lesson, in which you change text alignment.

 ***Exam Note:* Copying Formatting to Another Slide**

You may be wondering if you can copy formatting to a slide other than the one that contains the original formatting. Fortunately, you can if you know the trick: Select the original text formatting that you want to copy and click the Format Painter button. Then, use the vertical scrollbar (or press a keyboard shortcut such as PgDn or PgUp)) to move to another slide before applying your formatting.

Lesson 3: Changing the Text Alignment and Setting Tabs

In addition to changing the text appearance on slides, you can change ***horizontal text alignment***, which is the way the text displays horizontally in the placeholder (or other object). The way that the text displays in a placeholder—left-justified, centered, or right-justified—depends on the template that you use. Most commonly, however, title and subtitle text is centered; bulleted list text is usually left-justified.

You can easily change text in *any* placeholder to left, center, or right alignment. The easiest way to do this is to use the alignment buttons on the Formatting toolbar. Now, try changing the alignment of text in the Business Plan presentation.

To Change the Text Alignment and Set Tabs

❶ Display the first slide of the Business Plan presentation in Normal view, if necessary.

❷ Click in the text in the title placeholder, `Business Plan`.
Notice that the Center button on the Formatting toolbar is pushed in, indicating that it is turned on. When you choose another alignment, center alignment will be turned off.

❸ Click the Align Left button on the Formatting toolbar.
The text in the placeholder becomes left-justified and the Align Left button is pushed in.

❹ Press `PgDn` twice.
Slide 3, Company Introduction and Background, now displays. This is a slide that has both title and bulleted list placeholders. You can use this slide to practice changing alignment for more than one line in a placeholder. Remember, however, that you must first select all the lines you want to format before applying a different formatting (such as alignment).

❺ Starting at the beginning of the first bulleted line, drag over all the bulleted text in the lower placeholder on Slide 3 to select it.
The text is selected.

❻ Click the Center button on the Formatting toolbar.
All the lines you selected are centered (see Figure 4.8).

Figure 4.8
You can align text within a placeholder.

Select your text and then click one of the alignment buttons

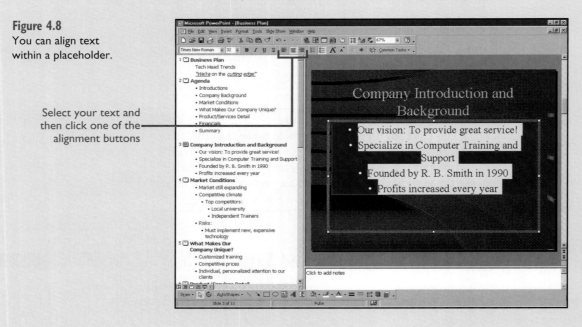

Now try setting some tabs. Just as in a word processing program, tabs in PowerPoint are used to line up text. PowerPoint includes four tab types you can use. Left tabs line up the text at the left edge of the stop; right tabs line text up at the right edge of the stop. Of course, center tabs are great for centering text under the tab stop. Finally, decimal tabs line up numbers on the decimal point and are especially handy to use when you're working with numbers.

7 **Display Slide 7, Upcoming Classes, in Normal view, and click in the lower placeholder.**

8 **Choose** **V̲iew, R̲uler.**

The ruler displays so that you can easily identify where you want to set the tabs (see Figure 4.9). Additionally, the ***tab type button*** helps you choose which type of tab you want to set. You can click on this button to cycle through the various tab choices.

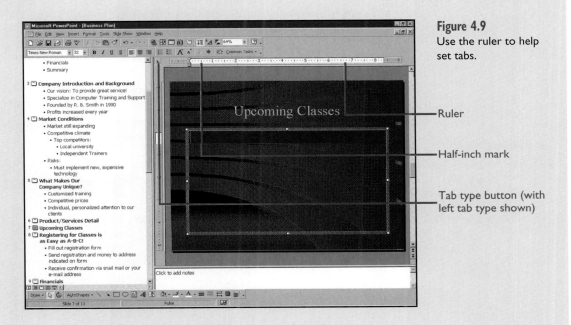

Figure 4.9
Use the ruler to help set tabs.

Ruler

Half-inch mark

Tab type button (with left tab type shown)

✖ ***If You Have Problems...***
If the tab type button appears "blank," you probably forgot to click in the placeholder to which you want to add tabs. Click in the lower placeholder on Slide 7 and you'll be ready to set tabs.

---

9 **Click the tab type button four times to see all four kinds of tabs you can set.**

When you're finished, make sure the tab type is set for a left tab (refer to Figure 4.9).

10 **With your insertion point in the lower placeholder, click the 0.5 inch mark on the ruler.**

A left tab is set where you clicked on the ruler, indicated by an *L* on the ruler at that location. Now try setting a center tab.

continues ▶

To Change the Text Alignment and Set Tabs   (continued)

11 **Click the tab type button once so that the center tab type is displayed (shown by an upside-down *T*). Click at 5 inches on the ruler.**
A center tab is placed on the ruler (see Figure 4.10). Now try using the tab stops to line up text.

> ### ❌ *If You Have Problems...*
> If you accidentally added a tab in the wrong position on the ruler, point to the tab stop and then drag it along the ruler until it's at the location you want.
>
> Alternatively, delete the stop by dragging it off the ruler into your presentation before releasing the mouse.

---

12 **Press Tab⇆ so that the insertion point lines up with the left tab stop, then type PowerPoint.**

13 **Press Tab⇆ to move the insertion point to the center tab stop position, and then type Becca University. Press ↵Enter.**
The text is lined up at the tab stops (see Figure 4.10).

Figure 4.10
Tab stops make setting up text easy.

Left tab stop

Center tab stop

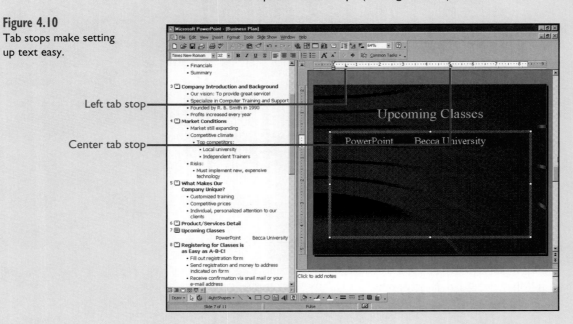

Now finish entering information on the slide.

14 **Finish entering information on your slide, using the following text as a guide:**

Word	Becca University
Outlook	Sarahson College
Excel	University of Rio Grande
Access	Buckeye Career Center

When you're finished, your slide should look similar to the one shown in Figure 4.11.

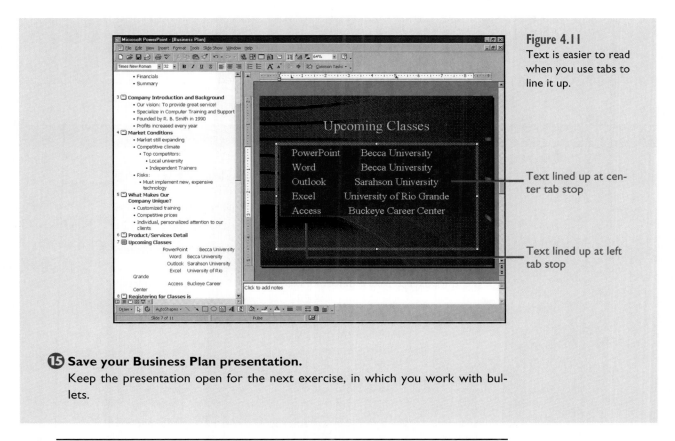

Figure 4.11
Text is easier to read when you use tabs to line it up.

Text lined up at center tab stop

Text lined up at left tab stop

 Save your Business Plan presentation.

Keep the presentation open for the next exercise, in which you work with bullets.

Exam Note: **Aligning Text**

You can also use the F̲ormat menu to change alignment. Choose F̲ormat, A̲lignment; then choose Align L̲eft, C̲enter, Align R̲ight, or J̲ustify from the submenu. (The J̲ustify command aligns text to the right and left sides of the placeholder.)

 Inside Stuff: **Lining Up Text Vertically**

If you have extra text that doesn't fit vertically within a placeholder, you can rely on PowerPoint 2000's AutoFit Text feature. This feature automatically adjusts the size of text to fit within the placeholder. However, if you want to turn off the feature, choose T̲ools, O̲ptions, and then click the Edit tab. Clear the box for A̲uto-fit text to text placeholder and then click OK.

You can also manually control line spacing by selecting the text, then choosing F̲ormat, Line S̲pacing. Indicate the number of lines in the L̲ine spacing box, and then click OK.

Lesson 4: Adding and Removing Bullets

In PowerPoint, bullets are markers that make a list of items more readable. A **bullet** is an object, such as a circle or square, which is used to set off items in a list. By default, PowerPoint displays bullets as circles, diamonds, squares, and so on. Bullets are also usually combined with indentation so that the related text wraps properly.

PowerPoint makes it easy to add bullets to a slide because it automatically includes them as part of the lower (text) placeholder on the most common type of slide—the Bulleted List AutoLayout.

Because it's easiest to make, add, and remove bulleted items in Normal view, you'll use that view for this lesson. Try working with bullets now.

To Add or Remove Bullets

1 In the open Business Plan presentation, display Slide 2, Agenda, in Normal view.
This slide contains a text placeholder with bullets. You can easily remove the bullets by selecting the associated text, and then clicking the Bullets button.

2 Position your insertion point at the beginning of the bulleted list, press ◆Shift), and then click at the end of the list.
All the bulleted text is selected. Now, you can remove the bullets.

 3 Click the Bullets button.
Bullets are removed from all the paragraphs you selected. You can also add bullets by clicking the Bullets button again.

4 With the paragraphs still selected, click the Bullets button again.
Bullets are added to the selected paragraphs.

Now, try changing the bullets to numbering. You generally use numbers rather than bullets when you want to emphasize the order or sequence of the items listed. For example, it's appropriate to use numbers if you want to show the steps involved in placing an order, maintaining a machine, or sending email. Luckily, PowerPoint makes it easy to change a bulleted list to a numbered list (and vice-versa). Just select the paragraphs, and then click the Numbering button.

 5 With the paragraphs in the text placeholder still selected, click the Numbering button.
The bullets are replaced by numbering (see Figure 4.12).

Figure 4.12
It's easy to switch from bullets to a numbered list.

Numbering button

Numbered list

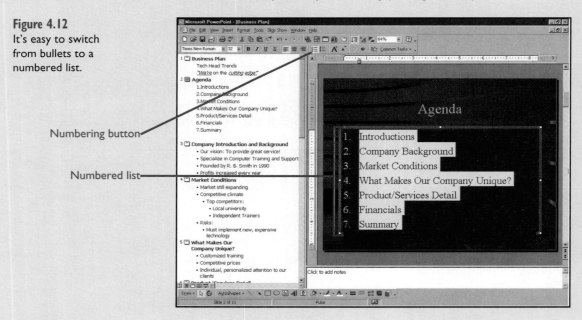

Now try reapplying bullets to your list.

⑥ With the text still selected, click the Bullets button.
The sequential numbers are replaced by bullets.

⑦ Save your Business Plan presentation.
Keep the presentation open for the next exercise, in which you modify the appearance of bullets.

Lesson 5: Modifying Bullets

The bullet's appearance is determined by each presentation's template. If you don't like the bullet's predesigned look, however, you can always change it. First, select the paragraphs with the bullets you want to change, and then choose F̲ormat, B̲ullets and Numbering from the menu bar to display the Bullets and Numbering dialog box. You can use this dialog box to change the color, size, or appearance for your bullets.

Try modifying some bullets now.

To Modify Bullets

① In the Business Plan presentation, select the bulleted list on Slide 2, if necessary.

② Choose F̲ormat, B̲ullets and Numbering; then click the Bulleted tab if necessary.
The Bullets and Numbering dialog box displays (see Figure 4.13). You use this dialog box to change the way your bullets (or numbers) appear.

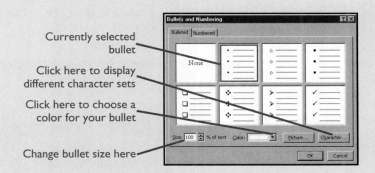

Currently selected bullet

Click here to display different character sets

Click here to choose a color for your bullet

Change bullet size here

Figure 4.13
PowerPoint offers you many ways to modify your bullets.

First, change bullet color. To do this, click the C̲olor drop-down arrow to display a palette of colors that coordinate with your template.

③ In the Bullets and Numbering dialog box, click the C̲olor drop-down arrow to display the color palette (see Figure 4.14), and then choose yellow (the rightmost box on the palette).

continues ▶

To Modify Bullets   (continued)

Figure 4.14
You can change bullet color to jazz up your presentation.

Click here to display the palette

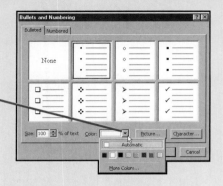

You can also use the Bullets and Numbering dialog box to change the size of your bullet relative to text. Type the bullet's percentage of the text (from 25%–400%) in the Size text box, or use the spinner arrows to change the percentage in 5% increments. Try changing the bullet size now.

4 **In the Bullets and Numbering dialog box, double-click in the Size text box.**
The current percentage (100) is selected. Once information in a text box is selected, you can just type to replace it.

5 **Type 125, and then choose OK to close the dialog box.**
The slide displays your changes. Notice that the text is still selected and displays in reverse video.

You can also use a wide variety of symbols for bullets. The Bullets and Numbering dialog box includes a number of font and character sets from which you can choose bullet symbols, or styles. Try changing the bullet style now.

6 **With the bulleted list still selected, right-click in the list to display a shortcut menu (see Figure 4.15).**

Figure 4.15
You can use the shortcut menu to open the Bullets and Numbering dialog box.

Right-click in the selected text to display this shortcut menu

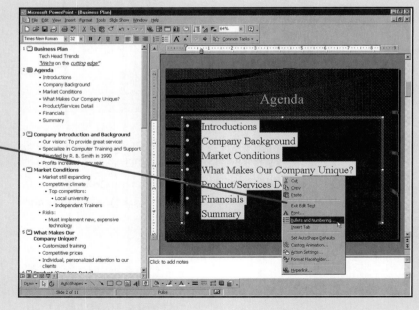

7 **Left-click on Bullets and Numbering from the shortcut menu.**
The Bullets and Numbering dialog box displays.

8 **Click the check mark style (the rightmost style on the second line), and then click OK.**
The default bullets are replaced with check marks, as shown in Figure 4.16. Customizing bullets this way helps to spice up your presentation for greater impact. Remember: The only lines for which the bullets are changed are those that you select before displaying the Bullets and Numbering dialog box.

New bullet symbols

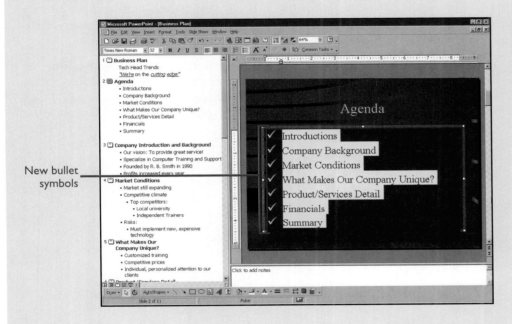

Figure 4.16
Tired of the default bullets for a slide? Choose another symbol.

9 **To better see your changes, click outside the placeholders.**

10 **Save the Business Plan presentation.**
Keep the presentation open for the next lesson, in which you explore various ways to add numbering to a slide.

Inside Stuff: **Finding More Bullet Symbols**
If you want a bigger selection of bullet symbols to use, you're in luck. On the Bulleted page of the Bullets and Numbering dialog box, click Character to display the Bullet dialog box. Click the Bullets from the drop-down list arrow, choose a character set, and then double-click the symbol you want to use.

Lesson 6: Using AutoNumber Bullets

You've already seen that you can quickly change a bulleted list to a numbered one just by selecting it and then clicking the Numbering button. Alternatively, however, you can start a numbered list when you initially create a new slide. Click in the text placeholder and then click the Numbering button before you start entering text. Every time you press the ⏎Enter key, you create a new numbered line.

You can also modify how your numbered list appears by choosing a different numbered list style in the Bullets and Numbering dialog box. Try your hand at working with AutoNumber Bullets now.

To Use AutoNumber Bullets

❶ In the Business Plan presentation, display Slide 8 in Normal view, and then select all the text in the lower placeholder.

❷ Click the Numbering button on the Formatting toolbar.
The list is formatted with numbers rather than bullets. Numbering is typically used when you want to indicate an order, process, or sequence. Now try applying a different numbering style.

❸ With the list in the lower placeholder still selected, choose Format, Bullets and Numbering, and then click the Numbered tab.
The Numbered page of the Bullets and Numbering dialog box displays (see Figure 4.17). Use this dialog box to choose a different numbering style.

Figure 4.17
PowerPoint offers a choice of numbering styles.

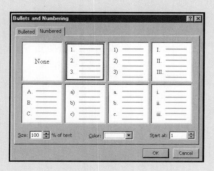

❹ Click the leftmost numbering style on the second row (A. B. C.).
Now try changing the color used for the numbers.

❺ Click the Color drop-down list and choose the light orange color from the palette (the fourth color from the left).

❻ Click OK; then click outside of the placeholders to better see your changes.
PowerPoint uses the new numbering scheme and color (see Figure 4.18).

Now try another method of adding numbering to a slide.

❼ Display Slide 10 in Normal view, and then click in the lower (text) placeholder.

❽ Press ⎵Backspace to delete the bullet, and then type 1. followed by two spaces.

❾ Type Provide excellence to customers. Press ↵Enter.
PowerPoint automatically creates a numbered list, using your formatting (a number and a period, followed by two spaces) as an example of how to set up the rest of the numbers.

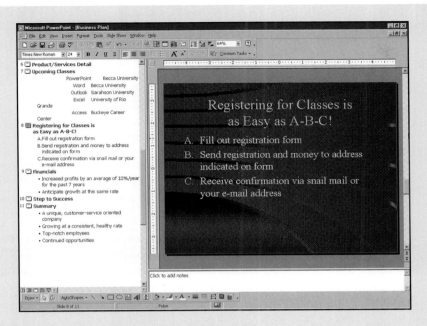

Figure 4.18
You can change the appearance of numbers on a list.

 If You Have Problems...
If PowerPoint doesn't automatically number your list, choose Tools, Options, and then click the Edit tab. Check the box for AutoFormat as you type and then click OK.

Now finish your list.

🔟 **For the second number on the list, type** `Hire top-notch employees.` **Press** ⏎Enter.
PowerPoint continues numbering your list by entering 3.

⓫ **Type** `Provide competitive rates`, **and then click outside of the place-holders.**
Your completed slide should appear similar to Figure 4.19.

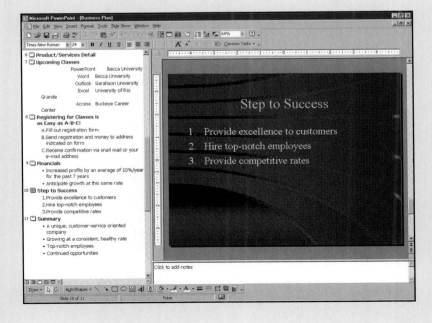

Figure 4.19
PowerPoint helps you quickly create a numbered list.

continues ▶

To Use AutoNumber Bullets (continued)

 Save and close your Business Plan presentation.
Keep PowerPoint running if you plan to complete the Skill Drill, Challenge, or Discovery Zone exercises.

Inside Stuff: **Wrapping Text**
There are times when you want to move down to the next line on a list without creating a new paragraph. To start a new line within a paragraph without a bullet (or number), press ⇧Shift+↵Enter.

Summary

In this project, you learned how to spice up your presentation by changing text appearance such as font, font size, and color. You gained efficiency by using the Format Painter to quickly apply existing formats to other sections of text. You adjusted text alignment and tabs for better appearance. Finally, you learned how to add, remove, and modify bullets and numbers.

To expand on your knowledge, spend a few minutes exploring Help on these topics. You can also use the PinPoint CD to brush up on the concepts covered in this Project. Finally, complete some of the Skill Drill, Challenge, and Discovery Zone exercises.

Checking Concepts and Terms

True/False

For each of the following, check *T* or *F* to indicate whether the statement is true or false.

__T __F **1.** You can toggle bullets on or off for selected text by clicking the Bullets button. [L4]

__T __F **2.** PowerPoint provides a variety of symbols you can use for bullets. [L5]

__T __F **3.** You can double-click the Format Painter button to keep it active. [L2]

__T __F **4.** In general, the larger the point size, the smaller the font. [L1]

__T __F **5.** PowerPoint includes left, center, decimal, and right tab types. [L3]

Multiple Choice

In the blank provided, write the letter of the correct answer for each of the following questions.

1. You can change character attributes, such as bold, italic, and underline _____. [L1]

   a. by using the Font dialog box

   b. by clicking toolbar buttons

   c. by pressing keyboard shortcuts, such as Ctrl+B for bold

   d. all of the above

2. A point is _____. [L1]

   a. a method of quickly applying formatting from one text section to another

   b. the unit of measurement typically used to designate character height

   c. a button used to promote and demote text

   d. a button used to change text alignment

3. The way text appears on a slide is determined by _____. [L1]

   a. the underlying template

   b. the placeholder

   c. formatting changes you apply

   d. all of the above

4. Which of the following is true about the Format Painter? [L2]

   a. You must first select the text that contains the formatting you want to copy.

   b. You can change text appearance only for a text placeholder (not a title placeholder).

   c. Changes are made to the underlying template.

   d. all of the above

5. Which of the following is true about bullets? [L4–5]

   a. They are usually combined with indentation so that the related text wraps properly.

   b. They can be added or removed.

   c. They can be formatted.

   d. all of the above

Screen ID

Identify each of the items shown in Figure 4.20.

Figure 4.20

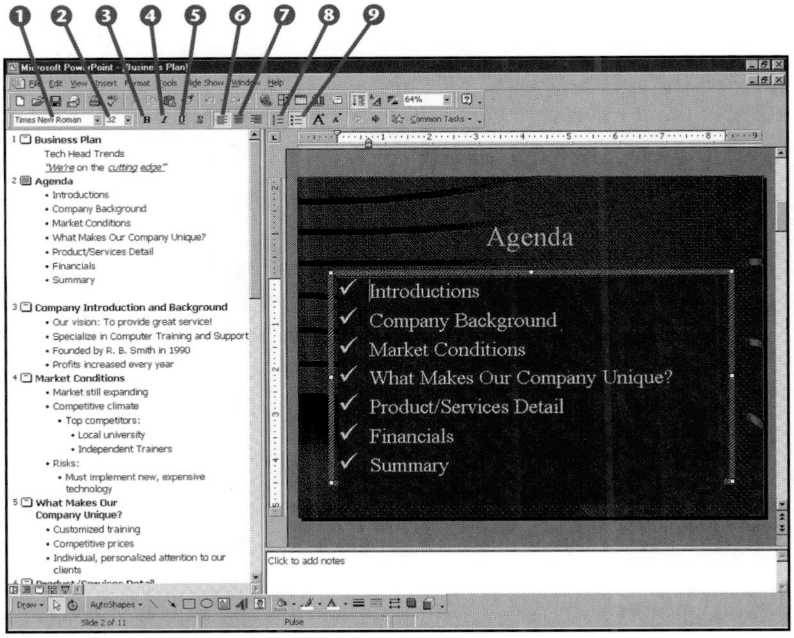

A Font Size box

B Font box

C Center button

D Italic button

E Numbering button

F Align Left button

G Bold button

H Bullets button

I Underline button

1._____   4._____   7._____

2._____   5._____   8._____

3._____   6._____   9._____

Skill Drill

Skill Drill exercises reinforce project skills. Each skill reinforced is the same, or nearly the same, as a skill presented in the project. Detailed instructions are provided in a step-by-step format.

1. Changing Text Appearance

You work for a company that conducts seminars. One of your most popular seminars is "How to Give Exciting Presentations," but frankly, you think that the publicity materials used for this seminar are not very exciting. To jazz them up, you decide to use PowerPoint's formatting features. [L1–2]

1. Open **PP-0402** and save it as **ABC Training**. Display Slide 1 of the presentation in Normal view.

2. Select the text in the title placeholder for Slide 1.

3. Click the Font drop-down list arrow and choose Impact from the list. (If this font isn't available on your system, choose another font.)

4. With the text still selected, click the Font Size drop-down list arrow and choose 48 from the list.

5. Press Ctrl+B and Ctrl+I to add bold and italic to the title text.

6. Choose Format, Font to display the Font dialog box. Click the Color drop-down list arrow and choose the red color (the second color box from the right). Click OK.

7. Click in the Slide pane to deselect your text and view your changes.

8. Double-click the word **How** in the subtitle placeholder to select it, and then click the Bold and Italic buttons on the Formatting toolbar.

9. With the word **How** still selected, double-click the Format Painter button. Drag over the remaining text in the subtitle placeholder to apply the formatting to the text.

10. Press Esc to turn off the Format Painter.

11. Save the ABC Training presentation. Keep it open for the next exercise.

2. Working with Bullets

To further modify your ABC Training presentation, you change the bullets in the presentation. Because you're not sure which bullet appearance you want, you experiment by using different bullet symbols before you finally settle on one. [L4–5]

1. Make sure that the ABC Training presentation you worked with in the preceding exercise is displayed in Normal view.

2. Display Slide 2. Select the bulleted text in the lower placeholder.

3. Click the Bullets button to remove the bullets from the slide. Then click the Bullets button again to add bullets.

4. Choose Format, Bullets and Numbering to display the Bullets and Numbering dialog box. Click the open circular bullets (the third bullet symbol on the first line), and then click OK.

5. Repeat Step 4 to apply each of the different bullet symbols shown in the Bullets and Numbering dialog box.

6. With the text in the lower placeholder still selected, display the Bullets and Numbering dialog box. Choose the square bullet symbol (the first bullet symbol on the second line).

7. In the Bullets and Numbering dialog box, click the Color drop-down list arrow and choose the red color box (the second box from the right). Choose OK.

8. Click in the Slide pane to deselect your text and view your bullets.

9. Print Slide 2 as a slide.

10. Save and close the ABC Training presentation. Leave PowerPoint running if you plan to complete additional exercises.

3. Modifying Bullets and Changing Alignment

You work part-time in a sports store near campus. To help recruit quality workers, you've put together a presentation that shows the company's commitment to their employees. To add interest to the presentation, you decide to modify bullets. You also decide to space and align the bulleted points so that they are more readable. [L3, 5]

1. Open **PP-0403** and save it as **Sports Store**.

2. Display Slide 2, Our Commitment to Employees, in Normal view. Select the text in the lower placeholder.

3. Choose F<u>o</u>rmat, Line <u>S</u>pacing to display the Line Spacing dialog box. Enter **1.25** in the <u>L</u>ine spacing box, and then click OK.

4. With the text still selected, click the Center button on the Formatting toolbar.

5. With the text still selected, choose F<u>o</u>rmat, Bullets and Numbering. Click the check mark symbol (the last symbol on the second row).

6. Click the <u>C</u>olor drop-down list arrow. Choose <u>M</u>ore Colors from the palette to display the Colors dialog box. Click a turquoise color in the dialog box, and then click OK to close the Colors dialog box.

7. Click OK to close the Bullets and Numbering dialog box, and then click in the Slide pane to deselect the text.

8. Save the Sports Store presentation; then close it. Leave PowerPoint running if you plan to complete the Challenge and Discovery Zone exercises.

Challenge

Challenge exercises expand on, or are somewhat related to, skills presented in the lessons. Each exercise provides a brief narrative introduction, followed by instructions in a numbered-step format that are not as detailed as those in the Skill Drill section.

1. Using Formatting Features

You previously created a presentation to promote your company, which sells ergonomic products. To enhance it, you use some of the formatting features PowerPoint provides. [L1–3]

1. Open **PP-0404** and save it as **Ergonomics**.

2. Display Slide 1 in Normal view, and then format the word **Ergonomics** with italic, bold, and text shadow features. Increase the point size for Ergonomics to 60 points and change the text color to orange.

3. Use the Format Painter to apply the formatting from **Ergonomics** to the word **healthy** on Slide 1.

4. Display Slide 2 and select all the bulleted text. Center the text horizontally, and then increase line spacing so that the text fills up the text placeholder.

5. Save and close the Ergonomics presentation. Leave PowerPoint running if you plan to complete additional exercises.

2. Formatting a Presentation

Because you learned PowerPoint so well, you freelance by revising presentations for various businesses. You're currently working on a production report for one of your clients. You decide to spice it up by using PowerPoint's formatting features. [L1–2, 4, 6]

1. Open **PP-0405** and save it as **Production Report**.

2. Improve the appearance of the title text on Slide 1 by changing it to another color (such as salmon) and font. Also increase the font size for the title to at least 54 points. Using the Format Painter, copy the formatting from the Slide 1 (Production Report) to the titles on Slides 2–4. (Hint: Double-click the Format Painter to keep it active.)

3. Apply italic to the subtitle text on Slide 1.

4. Change the bullet color on Slide 2 to match that of the slide title, and then change the bullets to right-pointing triangles.

5. Increase the spacing between the bullets on Slide 2 for better readability and appearance.

6. Using Slide 2 as an example, change the bullets on Slides 3–4. Increase the spacing between paragraphs, if necessary.

7. View your presentation as a slide show to see how it looks, and then print the presentation as slides and as an outline.

8. Save the Production Report presentation, and then close it. Leave PowerPoint running if you plan to complete additional exercises.

3. Using Numbering and Bullets

You're about to graduate from college, and you're handing over the responsibilities of running the student council and the Sports Club to other students. To train them in leadership skills (including giving presentations), you develop a talk. Because numbers are more appropriate than bullets to use on some of the slides, you revise your presentation to include numbers. [L4–6]

1. Open **PP-0406** and save it as **Presentation Guidelines**. Revise the presentation as follows:

   ■ Remove the bullet from Slide 3.

   ■ Change the bullets on Slide 4, Key Topic, to numbers. Also make the numbers the same size as the text (100%).

   ■ Change the color for the numbers on Slide 4 to dark blue. (Hint: Use the Numbered page of the Bullets and Numbering dialog box.)

   ■ Change the bullets on Slide 5, Goals and Problems, to drop shadow square symbols.

   ■ Change the bullets on Slide 6, Solutions and Opportunities, to a bullet of your choice.

   ■ Change the bullets on Slide 8, Close, to numbered steps. Change the color to dark blue and make the size 75% of text. (*Hint:* Use the Bullets and Numbering dialog box.)

2. Save your presentation, and then close it. Leave PowerPoint running if you plan to complete the Discovery Zone exercises.

Discovery Zone

Discovery Zone exercises require advanced knowledge of topics presented in *MOUS Essentials* lessons, application of skills from multiple lessons, or self-directed learning of new skills.

1. Changing Alignment and Spacing

You're the head of the research and development department in your company. Because you are experienced at giving presentations, your boss has asked you to give a short talk to share your tips and tricks with other employees. To enhance the presentation, you change text alignment and paragraph spacing.

Open **PP-0407** and save it as **Presenting a Technical Report**. Make the following changes to the report:

■ Left-align the bulleted text on each slide.

■ Remove Slide 2, Introduction.

■ Adjust the line spacing for the bulleted text on each slide so that the points display evenly in the placeholders.

■ Display Slide 5, Close. Delete the text **And, if applicable**. Change the remaining bullets to numbers.

■ Change the bullets on Slides 2–4 to one of the check marks from the Monotype Sorts character set. (If this character set is not available on your computer, choose another character set.)

■ View the presentation as a slide show. Print the presentation as slides and as an outline.

Save and close the presentation. Leave PowerPoint running if you plan to complete additional exercises. [L3–4]

2. Formatting Text and Bullets

As the outgoing president of the University Biking Club, you develop a presentation to help the new club officers learn how to facilitate meetings. To make the presentation more appealing, you change bullet and text appearance by using PowerPoint's formatting features.

Open **PP-0408** and save it as **Facilitating a Meeting**. Make the following changes to the presentation, using what you know about PowerPoint:

- Change the font for the Slide 1 title to **Comic Sans MS**, with 48 point text. Add shadow to the text and change the color to turquoise. Using the Format Painter, copy this formatting to the titles of the other slides in the presentation.
- On Slide 3, Opening, change the bullet symbol for the four subpoints to check marks.
- Increase the line spacing for the bulleted text on Slide 4. Change the bullets themselves to check marks.
- Modify Slide 5 and Slide 6 so that the bulleted points display similar to the bullets on Slide 4.

View the presentation as a slide show. Print the presentation as slides and as an outline. Save and close the presentation, and then exit PowerPoint. [L1–2, 5–6]

Project 5

Creating Output

Key terms introduced in this project include

- frame
- handouts
- landscape orientation
- notes box
- orientation
- portrait orientation
- slide image
- speaker notes
- toggle

Objectives	Required Activity for MOUS	Exam Level
➤ Adding Speaker Notes	Add speaker notes	Core
➤ Printing Speaker Notes and Handouts	Print audience handouts	Core
	Print speaker notes in a specified format	Core
➤ Previewing a Presentation in Black and White	Preview a presentation in black and white	Core
➤ Using Page Setup	Change output format (Page Setup)	Expert
➤ Printing Slides Using a Variety of Formats	Print slides in a variety of formats	Core
	Change output format (Page Setup)	Expert
➤ Printing a Slide as an Overhead Transparency	Print a slide as an overhead transparency	Core
	Change output format (Page Setup)	Expert
➤ Exporting to 35mm Slides	Export to 35mm slides	Expert
	Change output format (Page Setup)	Expert

Why Would I Do This?

Okay, you've spent considerable time creating and reworking that winning presentation. However, after you finally put the finishing touches on it, you probably want to tap into the various ways to output it. Outputting involves displaying, printing (or even converting to another format) the results of your hard work. Although most people think of output primarily in terms of printing a presentation, there are, in fact, a number of other ways to produce output. For example, you can create overhead transparencies, 35mm slides, and even posters.

In this project you learn the nuts and bolts for creating various forms of output. You also learn how you can preview a presentation in black and white and use the Page Setup feature to "tweak" how the presentation will display and print. Finally, you find out how to print slides using a variety of formats and how to create speaker notes and handouts.

Lesson 1: Adding Speaker Notes

Have you ever been in the middle of an important presentation, when your mind suddenly went blank? Or been asked a particularly tricky question by someone in your audience? In either case, if you had **speaker notes** to rely on, you probably got through the situation without too much trouble. Speaker notes are just what their name implies—supporting data, quotations, or illustrations that you can use when giving a presentation. Although you may have developed notes in the past by writing on a legal pad, PowerPoint includes a feature that helps you create the electronic equivalent—from right within the program.

This lesson teaches you how to quickly add speaker notes so that supporting data is right at your fingertips. Here's how it works: Each slide can have corresponding notes, which you create. You can prepare speaker notes when you initially develop your presentation or you can add them later. You can use the Notes Page view to add your notes, or use the Notes pane in Normal view. Try using both methods of preparing notes now.

To Add Speaker Notes

❶ In PowerPoint, open PP-0501 and save it as Safety Report.
Now switch to Notes Page view—a view which provides a slide image and a notes box area.

❷ Make sure that Slide 1, Safety Report, is displayed, and then choose View, Notes Page.
The current slide is shown in Notes Page view (see Figure 5.1). This view shows a small-scale version of the slide (called a **slide image**), as well as an area where you can enter your notes—the **notes box**.

You've probably noticed that the notes box area is too small to reasonably view (or enter) text. Luckily, you can enlarge the view by using the Zoom button.

❸ Click the Zoom button's drop-down list arrow and choose 75%.
The view is enlarged so that you can enter your notes (see Figure 5.2). Because the monitor size and screen settings vary from one computer to the next, don't be concerned if your screen looks slightly different from that shown in the figure.

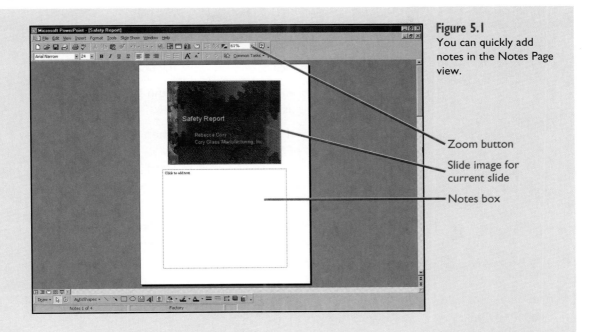

Figure 5.1
You can quickly add notes in the Notes Page view.

Zoom button

Slide image for current slide

Notes box

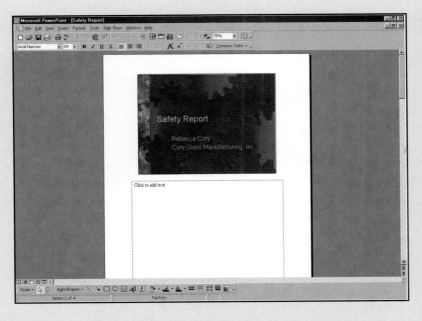

Figure 5.2
You usually need to enlarge the view to enter notes.

Now, create your speaker notes. Remember that these notes are usually used as reminders for yourself—to keep you on track and to make sure you don't forget any critical information during a presentation.

4 **Click in the notes box and type the following:**

(Make sure to play Bach's Brandenburg Concerto #5 as people arrive, and then fade it out.)

"Welcome! I'm glad to be presenting this safety report to you today. Here at Cory Glass Manufacturing we have some good news about our safety record, as well as some challenges ahead."

continues ▶

To Add Speaker Notes   (continued)

The text you typed is entered in the notes box and becomes part of the slide. Even when you switch to another view, the notes are still attached to the slide.

Another way to enter notes is to use the Notes pane in either Normal or Outline view. Try using this method now.

5 **Click the Normal View button, and then press** PgDn **to display Slide 2, Overall Status of Safety Campaign.**
This is the slide to which you want to attach some notes. By default, however, the Notes pane is so small that it's hard to see your notes. To make it easier to enter (and view) your notes, it's a good idea to first resize the Notes pane.

6 **Move your mouse pointer over the horizontal divider that separates the Notes pane and Slide pane until a two-headed resizing arrow displays (see Figure 5.3).**

Figure 5.3
Display and drag the resizing arrow to change the size of the Notes pane.

Slide pane——

Horizontal divider——

Resizing arrow——
Notes pane——

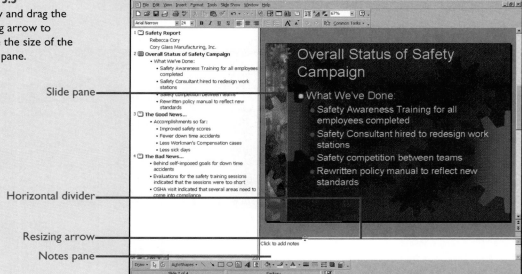

7 **Drag the resizing arrow upward until the screen is evenly split between the Slide and Notes panes, and then release the mouse button.**
The Notes and Slide panes are resized so that you can more easily see notes as you enter them (see Figure 5.4). Now try entering your notes.

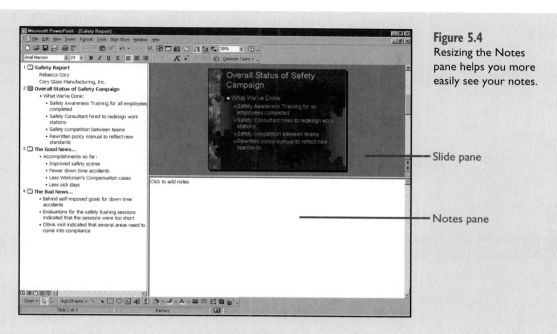

Figure 5.4
Resizing the Notes pane helps you more easily see your notes.

Slide pane

Notes pane

8 **Click in the Notes pane and enter the following text:**

Safety Awareness Training: The 1-hour mandatory program was completed by all 275 employees during the last two months.

Safety Consultant: We used Safety Engineers, Inc., from Columbus, Ohio to work closely with employees and managers. The new workstations were designed with input from our employees, and surpass OSHA, state, and local regulations.

Safety Competition: We want to thank Lauren Clark for this idea! The competition is 2 months long, and measures safety criteria (lost time accidents, sick days, etc.) for the 3 teams involved. Each member of the winning team will receive an extra 1% salary bonus. The competition is still going on, and will finish at the end of the month.

Now, resize your Slide and Notes panes back to their original sizes.

9 **Drag the horizontal divider between the Slide and Notes pane downward until each pane displays by using its original size, and then release the mouse button.**

The slide appears in Normal view. Notice that the Notes pane has a vertical scrollbar that you can use to scroll through your notes if they don't completely display in the Notes pane.

10 **Save the Safety Report presentation.**

Keep the presentation open for the next lesson, in which you print the notes.

 Exam Note: **Entering Notes During a Slide Show**

It's most common to enter and view notes in the Normal or Notes Page views. However, you can even view and enter notes during a running slide show. To do this, right-click your mouse to display the Slide Show shortcut menu, and then choose Spea_k_er Notes. View, enter, or modify the text in the Speaker Notes window that displays. After you have finished working with the notes, click the _C_lose button.

Lesson 2: Printing Speaker Notes and Handouts

Your speaker notes would be of little value if you couldn't print them for a ready reference during your presentation. Luckily, printing your notes is straightforward and relatively easy. To print the notes, choose File, Print, and then choose Notes Pages in the Print what area of the Print dialog box.

You can also print **handouts** to give to your audience. By default, PowerPoint includes options to print two, three, four, six, or nine slides per page as handouts. In contrast to the notes pages, handouts include only the slide's contents, not the accompanying notes. You print handouts the same way you print notes—by specifying the type of output you want in the Print what area of the Print dialog box.

Try printing speaker notes and handouts for your presentation now.

To Print Speaker Notes and Handouts

1 **With Slide 2 in the open Safety Report presentation displayed, choose File, Print.**
The Print dialog box displays (see Figure 5.5). You used this dialog box in Project 2, "Creating Presentations," to print slides and outlines. In this lesson, you use it to print notes and handouts.

Figure 5.5
The Print dialog box provides ready access to printing options.

Click this arrow and then choose Notes Pages or Handouts

Check this box to add a border around each slide

Check this box to print in grayscale

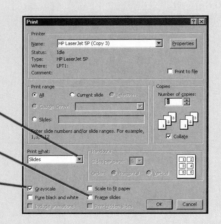

2 **Click the Print what drop-down list arrow and choose Notes Pages from the list.**
This specifies to PowerPoint that you want to print the speaker notes associated with the current presentation.

The notes generally print with a better appearance if you frame the slide image, notes box, and page. A **frame** is just a border that surrounds the slide element you choose. You can add frames by checking the Frame slides box.

3 **Check the Frame slides box, if necessary.**
You can print the current slide, print all presentation slides, or pick and choose just those that you want. You specify which slides PowerPoint should print in the Print range area of the dialog box.

4 **In the Print range area, choose the Current slide option button.**
After selecting the options you want, you're ready to print.

5 **Make sure that your printer is turned on, and then choose OK.**

The notes for your current slide print. Now, try printing audience handouts.

6 **Choose File, Print to redisplay the Print dialog box.**

7 **Click the Print what drop-down list arrow and choose Handouts from the list.**

When you choose Handouts on the list, the Handouts section of the Print dialog box becomes active (see Figure 5.6). You use this section to designate how you want to set up your handouts. For example, you can click the Slides per page drop-down list arrow and choose a different number of slides.

Choose the number of slide images per page here

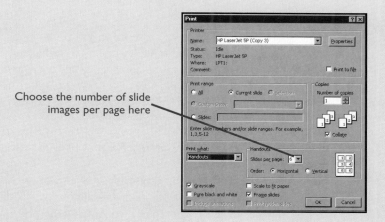

Figure 5.6
You can print handouts to give to your audience.

8 **Click the Slides per page drop-down list arrow and choose 4.**

This specifies that four slide images will print per page.

9 **Make sure that the Grayscale and Frame slides boxes are checked, and that the Print range is set to All.**

10 **Click OK to print your handouts.**

11 **Save the Safety Report presentation.**

Keep the presentation open for the next lesson, in which you learn how to preview slides in black and white.

Lesson 3: Previewing a Presentation in Black and White

Before you print a presentation, it's handy to know how the printed pages will look, especially if you're using a black-and-white printer. Additionally, you might want to show the slides on-screen in color, but print audience handouts in black and white. Previewing a presentation gives you a solid idea of how the presentation will look when printed on a non-color printer. Because of this, it saves time and toner.

To make things interesting, there are a number of options related to printing in black and white. In fact, the exact appearance of your presentation depends on which black-and-white option you choose. Here's a quick list of the ways you can vary the "look" of a black-and-white presentation:

- **Automatic**—Hides shaded background and displays only the text and graphics.
- **Grayscale**—Displays the presentation in shades of gray.

- **Light Grayscale**—Displays the presentation in light shades of gray.
- **Inverse Grayscale**—Displays and prints the presentation in reverse shades of gray, with dark tones in the original presentation appearing as light shades of gray.
- **Gray with White Fill**—Displays and prints the presentation in gray outline with white fill.
- **Black with Grayscale Fill**—Displays and prints the presentation with text and lines in black. All other elements are shown in shades of gray.
- **Black with White Fill**—Displays and prints text and line in black and white; all other elements are shown in white.
- **Black**—Displays and prints in black.
- **White**—Displays and prints in white.

After you "tweak" how the presentation looks in black and white, you can print it as slides or audience handouts. However, the way you set up the presentation to display in black and white doesn't affect the onscreen color display one iota. Furthermore, the steps for previewing the presentation are quick and easy, so come along and try your hand at them.

To Preview a Presentation in Black and White

1 Display Slide 1 in the open Safety Report presentation, and then choose View, Black and White.

The presentation displays using grayscale, or shades of black and white—just like the old-timey black-and-white televisions. Additionally, a Slide Miniature box displays to remind you how the color version of your presentation appears (see Figure 5.7).

Figure 5.7
You can preview your presentation in shades of gray.

Slide miniature

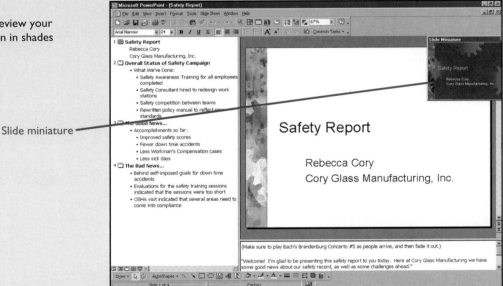

 If You Have Problems...
If the Slide Miniature box doesn't display on your computer, most likely it's been turned off by another user. Just choose View, Slide Miniature to display it.

Now try turning the black-and-white display off.

2 **Choose <u>V</u>iew, <u>B</u>lack and White.**
The presentation redisplays in color. A command that you can use to turn a feature on (and then use in the same way to turn the feature off again) is called a *toggle*. Think of toggle commands as light switches that you can turn on or off.

Now try an alternative method of displaying the presentation in black and white.

3 **Click the Grayscale Preview button from the Standard toolbar.**
The presentation again displays in black and white. Now try changing the black-and-white options. You do this by using the Black and <u>W</u>hite menu options. This menu item is only available when the presentation is displayed in black and white.

4 **With the presentation displayed in black and white, right-click in the slide (but outside of the placeholders).**
A shortcut menu displays. Notice that Black and <u>W</u>hite is a command on this menu (see Figure 5.8).

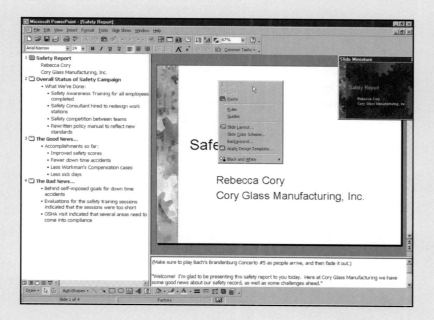

Figure 5.8
This shortcut menu includes a command you can use to adjust black-and-white settings.

X ***If You Have Problems...***
If the shortcut menu on your computer includes slightly different commands than that shown in Figure 5.8, you probably right-clicked within a placeholder. Make sure your menu matches that shown in Figure 5.8 or you will change the black-and-white settings for the placeholder rather than the entire slide.

And don't forget, a presentation must be displayed in black and white for this command to be available.

5 **Rest your mouse pointer on the Black and <u>W</u>hite command.**
A submenu displays, showing the various options (Figure 5.9).

continues

To Preview a Presentation in Black and White   (continued)

Figure 5.9
PowerPoint includes various ways to display your presentation in black and white.

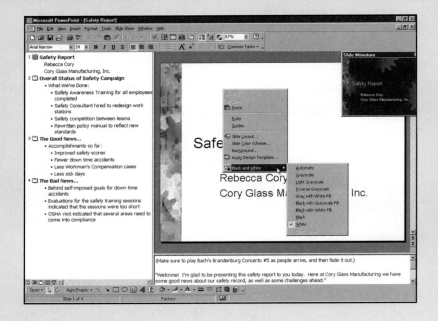

6 **Choose Light Grayscale.**

The presentation displays using the settings associated with this type of black-and-white display. Now try printing the slide in black and white.

7 **Choose File, Print.**

The Print dialog box displays. Notice that the Grayscale box is already checked so that you can print your presentation in black and white.

8 **Make sure the Grayscale box is checked, click the Current slide option button, and then choose OK.**

The slide prints in black and white. Now try switching your presentation back to a color display.

9 **Click the Grayscale Preview button.**

The presentation is shown using the color template.

10 **Save the Safety Report presentation.**

Keep the presentation open for the next lesson, in which you use the Page Setup feature.

 ## Lesson 4: Using Page Setup

You can use PowerPoint's Page Setup feature to change the slide size or **orientation**. The orientation of a slide refers to rotation of the slide when viewing or printing it. **Landscape orientation** is the layout used where the width of the paper is greater than the height. In contrast, **portrait orientation** is the layout used where the height of the page is greater than the width (see Figure 5.10). You can change the orientation of the slides as well as that of the note pages and handouts.

Figure 5.10a
Portrait orientation.

Figure 5.10b
Landscape orientation.

In this lesson you learn how to use Page Setup to make modifications in size and orientation to your presentation slides.

To Use Page Setup

① **Make sure Slide I in the Safety Report presentation is displayed in Normal view.**

② **Choose File, Page Setup.**
The Page Setup dialog box displays (see Figure 5.11). By default the slides are sized to fill the screen when used as an electronic slide show. Try choosing a different size instead.

Change slide orientation here ———

Change slide size here ———

Change speaker notes and handout orientation here ———

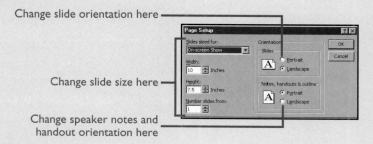

Figure 5.11
Use this dialog box to make changes to slide size or orientation.

③ **Click the Slides sized for drop-down list arrow and choose Banner, and then click OK.**
This setup automatically changes the slide size to 8 inches wide by I inch tall (Figure 5.12). Although this size might be appropriate if you want to print a slide as a banner, it doesn't work well for an onscreen show, so try making some other modifications to the slide size.

continues ▶

To Use Page Setup   (continued)

Figure 5.12
You can change slide size.

4 Choose **File, Page Setup** to redisplay the **Page Setup dialog box.**

5 Choose **Letter Paper (8.5×11 in) on the Slides sized for drop-down list.**
The width and height of the slides automatically changes to reflect the new size. (You can also change the width and height manually if you want custom-sized slides.) Before closing the Page Setup dialog box, try changing orientation.

6 **In the Orientation section of the dialog box, change the orientation of your slides to Portrait, and then click OK.**
The slides are resized and reoriented (Figure 5.13). Now try printing a slide.

Figure 5.13
You can change a slide's orientation from landscape to portrait.

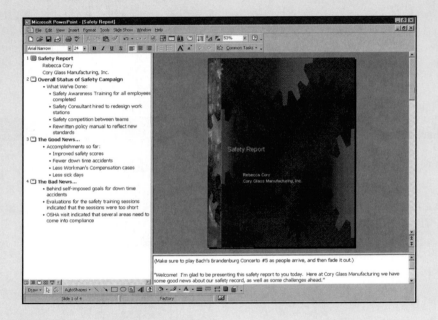

7 **With Slide 1 of your presentation displayed, choose File, Print.**

8 **Choose Current slide in the Print range section of the dialog box. (If you're printing on a black-and-white printer, also make sure Grayscale is chosen.)**

9 **Click OK.**
The slide is printed using portrait orientation. Now change the slide's orientation and size back to the original settings.

10 **In the Page Setup dialog box, size the slides for an On-screen Show. Also change the slide orientation to Landscape, then choose OK.**
The presentation displays using the default settings for a slide show.

11 **Save the Safety Report presentation.**
Keep the presentation open for the next lesson, in which you print slides using a variety of formats.

Lesson 5: Printing Slides Using a Variety of Formats

As you've seen in previous lessons, PowerPoint includes a number of ways that you can print your presentation. You can print the presentation as slides, an outline, or print the accompanying speaker notes and audience handouts. Additionally, you can change the size and orientation of the slides and print in either color or grayscale. In this lesson you explore a few more options for printing your slides.

To Print Slides Using a Variety of Formats

① **Make sure Slide 1 in the Safety Report presentation is displayed in Normal view.**

② **Choose File, Print.**
The Print dialog box displays. You can use this dialog box to indicate the number of slides you want to print, and how many copies of each you'd like.

③ **In the Print range section click the Slides option button, and then enter 1,3 in the Slides text box.**
Separating the slide numbers by commas lets you "pick and choose" which ones you want. (To pick adjacent slides, use a hyphen between the slide numbers.)

④ **Increase the Number of copies to 2 and make sure the Grayscale box is checked. Click OK.**
Two copies of Slides 1 and 3 print. Now try changing the page size and orientation to 8 1/2 × 14 inches (legal size) before printing.

⑤ **Choose File, Page Setup.**

⑥ **Select the text in the Width text box, and then type 8.5. Press Tab↹.**
The new width for your slides is set to 8 1/2 inches.

⑦ **Enter 14 in the Height text box.**
The new height (14 inches) is entered in the Height text box, and PowerPoint automatically switches the orientation to Portrait (see Figure 5.14).

The Orientation changes automatically to reflect your new slide size

Figure 5.14
You can indicate a "custom" slide size in this dialog box.

⑧ **Click OK to apply the new slide size and orientation.**
Now you're ready to print your slides. (Before you continue, make sure you have 8 1/2 × 14 inch paper in your printer.)

⑨ **Choose File, Print.**

⑩ **In the Print dialog box, enter 3-4 in the Slides text box, and then click OK.**
The slide range you indicated (Slides 3–4) is printed.

⑪ **Save your Safety Report presentation.**
Keep the presentation open for the next lesson, in which you learn how to print a slide as an overhead transparency.

Lesson 6: Printing a Slide as an Overhead Transparency

Much of the time you'll use your presentation as an onscreen slide show. If you don't have access to the equipment necessary to project the presentation electronically (or if the equipment fails), however, you'll be glad to know that you can instead create a series of overhead transparencies to use.

Most printers (of either the laser or inkjet varieties) can print transparencies. Before attempting to feed a transparency through your printer, however, make sure your model can handle this type of printing… or you'll have a gunky mess on your hands!

To Print a Slide as an Overhead Transparency

1 **In the open Safety Report presentation, display Slide 1 in Normal view.**
The presentation is still using the custom Page Setup settings you set in the preceding lesson. Try changing these settings so that you can print the presentation as an overhead transparency.

2 **Choose File, Page Setup.**
The Page Setup dialog box displays. PowerPoint includes a built-in setting you can use when you want to print overhead transparencies.

3 **Click the Slides sized for drop-down list arrow.**
An option for printing your presentation as a series of transparencies is shown (see Figure 5.15).

Figure 5.15
Set up your presentation to be printed as transparencies in this dialog box.

Choose this option

4 **Choose Overhead on the Slides sized for list.**
You can print overheads using either landscape or portrait orientation. For this exercise, you use landscape orientation.

5 **Change the orientation in the Slides section to Landscape, and then click OK.**
Now you're ready to print a slide as an overhead. (Before continuing, make sure your printer can print transparencies, and that you have a transparency master in your printer. Also make sure you load the transparency with the correct side up, following the directions on the transparency box.)

6 **Choose File, Print.**
If you are using a black-and-white printer, make sure the Grayscale box is checked. (If you want to print the slide in color and have a printer that can do so, clear the Grayscale box.)

7 **Make sure Current slide is chosen in the Print range section and that the Number of copies is set to 1. Click OK.**
The slide is printed on the transparency master.

8 **Save the Safety Report presentation, and then close it.**
Leave PowerPoint running for the next lesson, in which you export the presentation as 35mm slides.

Inside Stuff:
If you don't have a printer that can make transparencies, you can instead buy professionally produced transparencies from Genigraphics. Choose <u>F</u>ile, Sen<u>d</u> To, <u>G</u>enigraphics, and then follow the instructions in the Genigraphics Wizard.

Lesson 7: Exporting to 35mm Slides

If you need your presentation developed as a series of 35mm slides, you're in luck. A service bureau, such as Genigraphics, can prepare your PowerPoint slides as 35mm. (In fact, they can also prepare your presentation as digital color overhead transparencies, large display prints, tent cards, or posters.) In most cases, you'll find it quickest to send your presentation to Genigraphics electronically over the Internet, although you can also send them the files on a disk. Luckily, there's a Genigraphics Wizard to guide you through the process step-by-step. Try working with this built-in feature now.

To Export to 35mm Slides

1 **Open PP-0502 and save it as Certification.**

2 **Enter your name and the name of your school or organization in the subtitle placeholder.**
Before starting the Genigraphics Wizard, it's a good idea to make sure your slides are set up to be accepted by the Genigraphics service bureau. The best way to do this is to choose the 35mm option in the Page Setup dialog box.

3 **Choose <u>F</u>ile, Page Set<u>u</u>p, and then choose 35mm Slides from the <u>S</u>lides sized for drop-down list. Click OK.**

4 **Choose <u>F</u>ile, Sen<u>d</u> To, <u>G</u>enigraphics**
The Genigraphics Wizard dialog box displays (see Figure 5.16). You use this dialog box to indicate if you want Genigraphics to produce presentation, or if you need other support services.

Click here to display
Genigraphic's Web site

Click here to advance to
the next screen

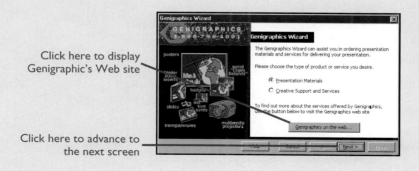

Figure 5.16
The Genigraphics service bureau can quickly produce your presentation as 35mm slides.

continues ▶

To Export to 35mm Slides (continued)

5 **Click Next to advance past the opening Genigraphics Wizard screen.**
The Product Selection page of the Genigraphics Wizard displays (see Figure 5.17). You use this page to indicate which materials you want.

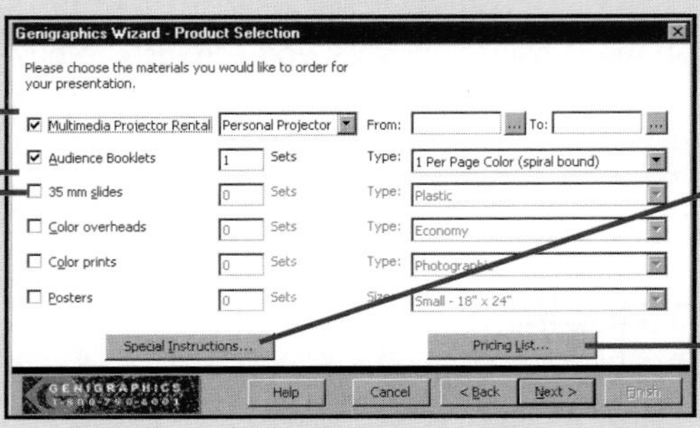

Figure 5.17
On this page, choose which items you want Genigraphics to prepare.

Clear these boxes

Check the box for 35mm slides

Click here to display a page where you can add special instructions

Click here to find out pricing information

6 **Clear the boxes for Multimedia Projector Rental and Audience Booklets (and any others that might be selected).**

7 **Check the box for 35mm slides, and then click Next.**
The Presentation Selection page of the Genigraphics Wizard displays (see Figure 5.18). This page includes options relating to which presentation you want to send and how you want to send it.

Figure 5.18
Choose how you want to send the files on this page.

Choose which presentation to send here

Choose how to send the files here

8 **Make sure Active Presentation is selected, and then choose Send via disk before clicking Next.**
The Billing Options page of the Genigraphics Wizard is shown (see Figure 5.19).

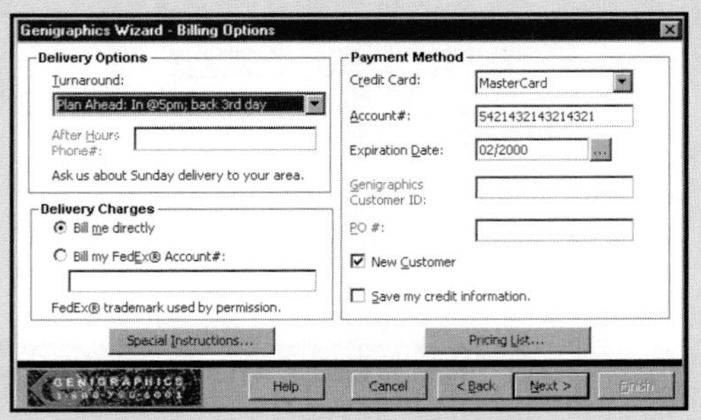

Figure 5.19
Enter turnaround time and billing information on this page.

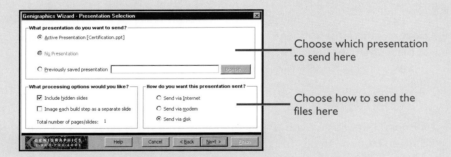

9 **Click the Turnaround drop-down list arrow and choose Plan Ahead: In @5pm, back 3rd Day.**

10 **Enter your credit card information for billing purposes, and then click Next.**

(If you don't have a credit card, just read over the remaining steps in this exercise until you think you understand them.)

11 **If prompted, enter your billing and shipping information, and then click Next.**

Your Order Summary information displays (see Figure 5.20).

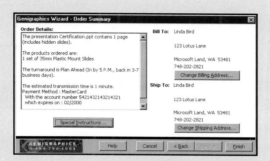

Figure 5.20
Check the information on this page for accuracy before proceeding.

12 **Read over the Order Summary page of the Genigraphics Wizard, and then click Finish.**

The Save As dialog box displays so that you can indicate where you want to save the temporary file that the Genigraphics Wizard generates. You can later send this file (via the Internet or a Zip disk) to Genigraphics. For now, just accept the default filename and location.

13 **Click Save in the Save As dialog box.**

The file is saved and the Save As dialog box closes. The Genigraphics Link dialog box displays so that you can conveniently send the file to Genigraphics (see Figure 5.21). For now, close this dialog box.

Figure 5.21
The Genigraphics Link dialog box displays when you finish using the Genigraphics Wizard.

14 **Click the Close button in the upper-right corner of the Genigraphics Link dialog box.**

If you want to send this file to Genigraphics later via the Internet, double-click the Graflink icon in the folder where your PowerPoint program files are located.

continues ▶

To Export to 35mm Slides   (continued)

15 Save and close the Certification presentation.
Keep PowerPoint running if you plan to complete the Skill Drill, Challenge, or Discovery Zone exercises.

Summary

This project focused on a variety of ways that you could output your presentation.

To expand on your knowledge, spend a few minutes exploring Help on these topics. Additionally, complete some of the Skill Drill, Challenge, and Discovery Zone exercises.

Checking Concepts and Terms

True/False

For each of the following, check *T* or *F* to indicate whether the statement is true or false.

__T __F   **1.** You can create 35mm slides by exporting your PowerPoint slides to the Genigraphics service bureau. [L7]

__T __F   **2.** Grayscale, Light Grayscale, and Inverse Grayscale are options related to previewing and printing a presentation in black and white. [L3]

__T __F   **3.** You typically use speaker notes onscreen during a running slide show because you can't print them out. [L1–2]

__T __F   **4.** You can print handouts as 2, 3, 4, 6, or 9 slides per page. [L2]

__T __F   **5.** Portrait and Landscape refer to organizations that help you convert your presentation to 35mm slides or overhead transparencies. [L4]

Multiple Choice

Circle the letter of the correct answer for each of the following.

1. Which of the following are ways that you can output a presentation? [L2, 5–7]
   a. exporting the presentation to 35mm slides
   b. printing speaker notes
   c. printing an overhead transparency
   d. all of the above

2. Using the Page Setup feature you can _____. [L4]
   a. change the orientation of speaker notes
   b. change the orientation for slides
   c. change slide size
   d. all of the above

3. When you display slides using Portrait orientation _____. [L4]
   a. the height of the slide is greater than the width
   b. the width of the slide is greater than the height
   c. speaker notes automatically use the same orientation
   d. audience handouts automatically use the same orientation

4. Speaker notes _____. [L1–2]
   a. provide supporting data or documentation during a presentation
   b. help you keep on track during a presentation

    c. help you remember quotations or anecdotes

    d. all of the above

5. The two ways to view and add speaker notes to your presentation are _____. [L2]

    a. Notes Page view and the Notes pane

    b. Handout view and Notes Page pane

    c. Speaker Notes window and Handout view

    d. Speaker pane and Normal pane

Skill Drill

Skill Drill exercises reinforce project skills. Each skill reinforced is the same, or nearly the same, as a skill presented in the project. Detailed instructions are provided in a step-by-step format.

1. Adding Speaker Notes

You're in charge of converting your company's network from Windows 95 to Windows 2000. To present your progress to management in an upcoming meeting, you prepare speaker notes. [L1]

1. Open **PP1-0503** and save it as **Upgrading to Windows 2000**.

2. Press `PgDn` twice to display Slide 3, Progress. Choose View, Notes Page.

3. Click the Zoom drop-down list arrow and choose 75% from the list to enlarge the view.

4. Click in the notes box and enter the following text:

> **Workstation conversion from Windows 95 to Windows 2000 began on time in early January. Independent contractors have been hired to help in the conversion.**
>
> **The original plan was to have trainers work with each employee within two weeks after the employee's workstation was con-**
> **verted. At this point, 68% have received training within two weeks, while the remaining 32% have been trained within three weeks.**

5. Click the Normal View button. Press `PgDn` twice to display Slide 5, Costs.

6. Type the following text in the Notes pane area of Slide 5:

> **Make sure to emphasize that no additional cost overruns are anticipated.**

7. Save the changes to your Upgrading to Windows 2000 presentation. Keep the presentation open if you plan to complete the next exercise on printing speaker notes and handouts.

2. Printing Slides, Speaker Notes, and Handouts

So that you'll have a ready reference when you give your Upgrading to Windows 2000 presentation, you print your speaker notes. You also print handouts to give to your audience. [L2]

1. In the Upgrading to Windows 2000 presentation open from the preceding exercise, display Slide 3, Progress in Normal view.

2. Choose File, Print to display the Print dialog box. Click the Print what drop-down list arrow and choose Notes Pages.

3. In the Print range section, click Current slide so that you'll only print speaker notes for Slide 3. Click OK to print your speaker notes.

4. Now print your handouts. Choose File, Print to

again display the Print dialog box. Click the Print what drop-down list arrow and choose Handouts.

5. In the Handouts section, click the Slides per page drop-down list arrow and choose 4.

6. Make sure that the Frame slides box is checked. Click OK to print your handouts.

7. Save the changes to your Upgrading to Windows 2000 presentation. Keep the presentation open if you plan to complete the next exercise.

3. Previewing and Printing Slides

Because you don't have access to a color printer, you preview your presentation slides in black and white. You also change the page setup for the slides and print them. [L3–5]

1. Display Slide 1, Project Status, of the Upgrading to Windows 2000 presentation in Normal view.

2. Choose File, Page Setup to display the Page Setup dialog box. Choose Letter Paper (8.5×11 inches) on the Slides sized for drop-down list.

3. Choose Portrait orientation for your slides, and then click OK to close the Page Setup dialog box.

4. Click the Grayscale Preview button on the Standard toolbar.

5. Right-click the slide, and then rest your mouse pointer over the Black and White menu command until the submenu displays. Choose Grayscale.

6. Display the Black and White menu command again. Choose Light Grayscale.

7. Choose File, Print to display the Print dialog box.

8. Make sure Current slide and Grayscale are both selected as options. Click OK to print the slide.

9. Save and close the Upgrading to Windows 2000 presentation. Leave PowerPoint running if you plan to complete the Challenge and Discovery Zone exercises.

Challenge

Challenge exercises expand on, or are somewhat related to, skills presented in the lessons. Each exercise provides a brief narrative introduction, followed by instructions in a numbered-step format that are not as detailed as those in the Skill Drill section.

1. Adding and Printing Speaker Notes

You're in charge of conducting new employee orientation at your company. To prepare for the meeting, you create and print speaker notes. [L1–2]

1. Open **PP-0504** and save it as **Orientation Meeting**.

2. Add the following speaker note to Slide 1:

   `Make sure to welcome new employees enthusiastically and make them feel part of the team.`

3. Add the following notes to Slide 3, History of Company:

   `Company was founded in 1990 to provide ergonomic computer equipment.`

   `Company has grown at a rate of 10% (average) per year.`

   `With increased interest in ergonomic workstation design, we anticipate continued growth.`

   `Our motto: "To make working with computers as comfortable as it is productive."`

4. Run your presentation as a slide show, starting with Slide 1. In the slide show, view your notes for both Slide 1 and Slide 3. (*Hint:* Use the Slide Show shortcut menu.)

5. Print speaker notes for your presentation and print handouts (6 slides per page).

6. Save the changes to your Orientation Meeting presentation; and then close it. Leave PowerPoint running if you plan to complete additional exercises.

2. Adding, Formatting, and Printing Speaker Notes

As sales manager of your company, you conduct training for the sales team. To motivate your salespeople, you develop a presentation for an upcoming training session. To help you remember information, you add speaker notes to the presentation. [L1–5]

1. Open **PP-0505** and save it as **Sales Team Training Session**.

2. Add the following speaker note to Slide 1, Motivating a Team:

   Make sure to have the sales awards displayed at the front of the room and to have upbeat music playing.

3. Add the following speaker note to Slide 2, Deliver an Inspirational Opening:

   "People tend to support what they help create." — Betsy Hudson

4. Format your notes. First, display Slide 2, Deliver an Inspirational Opening, in Notes Page view. Zoom to 75% to enlarge the notes box area.

5. Select the quotation, and then click the Bold button on the Formatting toolbar.

6. Select the name (**Betsy Hudson**) in the notes box, and then click the Italic button on the Formatting toolbar. Switch your presentation to Normal view.

7. Use Page Setup to change your speaker notes and handouts to landscape orientation.

8. Preview your presentation in black and white. Experiment with the various black-and-white options until you find one that displays the text and graphics clearly. Print the first presentation slide in black and white.

9. Print your speaker notes. Print handouts of your presentation (3 slides per page).

10. Save your Sales Team Training Session presentation, and then close it. Leave PowerPoint running if you plan to complete additional exercises.

3. Printing a Presentation as Transparencies and 35mm Slides

You've developed a presentation for your company that you need to give to a variety of audiences in many locations. You're concerned that you might not always have the spiffy equipment you need to display your presentation as an onscreen slide show. To make sure you can give your presentation using whatever equipment is available, you print your slides as overhead transparencies. You also send them to Genigraphics so that they can develop 35mm slides for you. [L3–7]

1. Open **PP-0506** and save it as **Creative Kids Inc**.

2. Use the Page Setup feature to configure your presentation for overhead transparencies.

3. Preview your presentation in black and white. If necessary, change the black-and-white options to better see your presentation's text and graphics.

4. Print at least one presentation slide as a black-and-white overhead transparency.

5. Use Page Setup to set up your presentation as 35mm slides. Then use the Genigraphic Wizard to prepare the presentation to be sent to Genigraphics. (*Note:* If you don't want to incur the cost of producing these materials, don't actually send the presentation to Genigraphics—just work through the steps and save the files on disk.)

6. Save the presentation, and then close it. Leave PowerPoint running if you plan to complete the Discovery Zone exercises.

Discovery Zone

Discovery Zone exercises require advanced knowledge of topics presented in *MOUS Essentials* lessons, application of skills from multiple lessons, or self-directed learning of new skills.

1. Outputting Your Presentation in a Variety of Ways

To document a recruitment talk that you are presenting to prospective members for the University Biking Club, you add speaker notes to a presentation. You also output the presentation in a variety of ways.

Open **PP-0507** and save it as **Prospective Members**. Add the following notes to the presentation:

- Slide 2: **Mention that officers are elected every September.**
- Slide 3: **Mention that Greg Schmidt, famous bicyclist, will be at the Race of Champions.**

Format the speaker note on Slide 3 as follows:

- Enlarge the font to 14 points.
- Add bold to Greg Schmidt.
- Italicize Race of Champions.

Change the orientation for your speaker notes to Landscape. Preview the presentation in black and white, and then print the speaker notes for Slide 3.

Export the slides in the presentation to Genigraphics as 35mm slides and as overhead transparencies. Finally, create a poster of the first presentation slide by sending it to Genigraphics. (*Note:* If you don't want to incur the cost of producing these materials, don't actually send the presentation to Genigraphics—just work through the steps and save the files on disk.)

Save changes to your Prospective Members presentation, and then close it. Keep PowerPoint running if you plan to complete the final exercise. [L1–7]

2. Working with the Notes Master

You're an old hand at creating and printing speaker notes. However, a friend recently told you that you could change how your notes are printed by modifying the notes master.

To find out more about using and modifying the notes master, use PowerPoint's Help. Specifically, find out the answers to the following questions:

- What is the notes master?
- What items are on the notes master?
- How can you delete, move, or resize the items on the notes master?
- Can I add a logo or other picture to a notes master?

Write down the answers to your questions. Open a presentation for which you've already developed speaker notes and modify the notes master. Print your speaker notes. Unless your instructor specifies otherwise, don't save the presentation. [L1–2]

PinPoint Assessment

You have completed this project and its associated lessons, and have had an opportunity to assess your skills through the end-of-project questions and exercises. Now use the PinPoint software Evaluation Mode to further assess your comprehension of the specific exam activities you have just learned. You can also use the PinPoint Trainer Mode and the Show Me tutorials to practice these exam activities.

Project 6

Changing a Presentation's Overall Appearance

Key terms introduced in this project include

- color scheme
- design template
- field
- gradient fills
- slide master

Objectives	Required Activity for MOUS	Exam Level
➤ Using Templates	Apply a design template	Core
	Design a template	Expert
➤ Applying a Template from Another Presentation	Apply a template from another presentation	Expert
➤ Using and Customizing Color Schemes	Customize a color scheme	Expert
➤ Changing the Slide Background	Add textured backgrounds	Expert
	Create a custom background	Expert
➤ Modifying the Slide Master	Change the slide layout (modify the slide master)	Core
➤ Inserting a Header and a Footer	Insert headers and footers	Core

Why Would I Do This?

Face it: most people respond more positively to color than they do to black and white. Consider, for example, magazine advertisements. In general, your eye is probably drawn more to a color advertisement than to a black-and-white one—which is exactly why businesses spend the big bucks to print in color.

You can use the same principle when you create PowerPoint presentations. By adding a splash of color (or even a completely different design), you can strengthen the impact of your presentation. Luckily, PowerPoint includes various built-in **design templates** and **color schemes** that you can use. Another way to use color is to change the slide background for selected (or all) slides in your presentation.

You can also quickly change the appearance of your entire presentation by making changes on the presentation's **slide master**. You use the slide master to quickly add design elements—such as date, slide number, or company logo—to all slides in your presentation.

You can combine these features to quickly and easily produce an impressive presentation, so come along and learn how.

Lesson 1: Using Templates

PowerPoint provides an extensive group of predesigned templates (also called design templates) that you can use for your presentation. A template is a "blueprint" that PowerPoint uses to create slides, including the formatting, color, and graphics necessary to create a particular "look." Because professional graphic artists created these templates, they can help you create a presentation with a consistent, well-designed look. Templates enable you to concentrate on content rather than on layout and design.

In Project 2, "Creating Presentations," you learned how to choose a template when you initially created a presentation. In this project, "Changing a Presentation's Overall Appearance," you learn how to modify templates for an existing presentation. This is handy if you've already developed a presentation, but aren't entirely satisfied with the design. You can just apply different templates until you find one you like. Try working with templates now.

To Use Templates

❶ **Start PowerPoint, if necessary, and close the PowerPoint startup dialog box.**

❷ **Choose File, New, and then click the Design Templates tab.**
The Design Templates page of the New Presentation dialog box displays, as shown in Figure 6.1. You can choose a design template on this page.

Figure 6.1
You can choose from a variety of built-in templates.

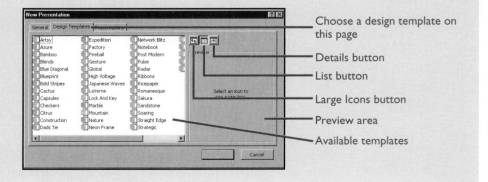

Choose a design template on this page

Details button

List button

Large Icons button

Preview area

Available templates

If You Have Problems...
If your templates display differently from that shown in Figure 6.1, don't worry. Your system probably is showing the files in Large Icons or Details view rather than List view. Just click the List button to display the templates as shown.

Additionally, some of PowerPoint's templates are only installed when you try to use them the first time. Instead of displaying a thumbnail of the template in the Preview section of the Apply Design Template dialog box, a message shows, stating that you can click OK to install the selected template. Make sure you have the Office 2000 CD-ROM in the drive, and then click OK.

❸ Click the Capsules template icon.
The preview area displays an example of the selected template. (If you want, single-click several templates to preview them, and then proceed with the tutorial.)

❹ Choose the Blueprint template, and then click OK.
The New Slide dialog box displays so that you can select an AutoLayout for your first slide.

❺ Select the Title Slide AutoLayout, if necessary, and then choose OK.
A title slide using the Blueprint template is created. Additionally, all slides you add to this presentation will automatically use the Blueprint template.

❻ In the title placeholder, type your company name, and then enter your own name in the subtitle area.
You created a presentation based on a specific template. However, you can also change templates *after* you initially create the presentation. Try your hand at applying different design templates to your presentation now.

❼ Choose F̲ormat, Apply Design Template. (Alternatively, you can right-click on the slide to display a shortcut menu, and then choose Appl̲y Design Template.)
The Apply Design Template dialog box displays with a list of all available templates (see Figure 6.2). Notice that this is the same list of templates that you saw in the New Presentation dialog box. Furthermore, you can preview a template by clicking it, just as you did earlier in this lesson.

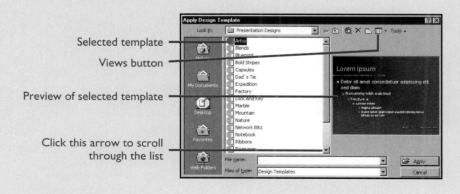

Figure 6.2
You can change templates at any time.

continues ▶

To Use Templates (continued)

 If You Have Problems...
If your Apply Design Template dialog box doesn't look like the one shown in Figure 6.2, a different view probably displays. Click the Views button drop-down list arrow, and then choose Pre_v_iew from the list.

8 **Click the Network Blitz template.**
The Network Blitz template is shown in the Preview area of the dialog box. This gives you a chance to see if you want a particular template.

9 **Choose Apply.**
The new template design is applied to the presentation (see Figure 6.3). Notice that the background, fonts, colors, and text alignment are all affected by the template you choose.

Figure 6.3
You can change design templates for a different appearance.

10 **Repeat steps 7–9 to apply other templates to your presentation. When you finish, close the presentation without saving it.**
Keep PowerPoint open for the next lesson, in which you work with color schemes.

 Exam Note: Designing a Custom Template
If you are artistically inclined (or just want to create a custom look for your presentations), you can also design your own template. To create a custom template, change any feature of a slide—color, font style, or graphics—in a presentation. Choose _F_ile, Save _A_s, and then enter a name for your new template. Choose Design Template from the Save as _t_ype drop-down list, so that it will be saved as a template and not a file. Click _S_ave, and you have a new, custom-designed template!

Lesson 2: Applying a Template from Another Presentation

Tired of using the built-in templates PowerPoint provides? If so, you can create a custom template, and then apply it to another presentation. For example, imagine you design a presentation that includes your company's corporate colors and logo. You can save this presentation as a template and then apply it to other existing or new presentations. This helps create a consistent "look" for your presentations. Try creating a custom template and applying it to a presentation now.

To Apply a Template from Another Presentation

1 In PowerPoint open PP-0601 and save it as Corporate.
This presentation will serve as the basis for your custom-designed template. A number of design elements have already been changed for this presentation. Before you save the presentation as a template, you'll make additional modifications to its design.

2 Choose Format, Background.
The Background dialog box displays (see Figure 6.4). You can use this dialog box to change the background color for all presentation slides.

Click this arrow to view background colors

Figure 6.4
You can change a slide's background.

3 Click the drop-down list arrow in the Background dialog box.
A palette of colors that coordinate with the template display.

4 Choose the third color box from the left on the top row (dark gray), and then choose Apply to All.
The background color is changed to gray (from green) for all slides (see Figure 6.5). Now try changing the font used in your presentation.

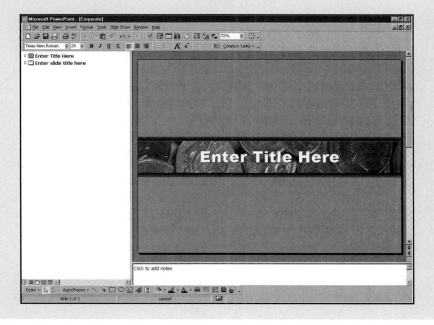

Figure 6.5
The new background color is applied to all slides.

continues ▶

To Apply a Template from Another Presentation   (continued)

5 Select the text in the title placeholder on Slide 1, and then choose Comic Sans MS from the Font drop-down list. (If this font isn't available on your system, choose another.)

Changes you make to the slide's formatting (and content) can be saved as a template.

6 Choose File, Save As.

The Save As dialog box displays. You usually use this dialog box to save your slides as a presentation. But you can also save your formatting, design, and even content as a template.

7 Click the Save as type drop-down list arrow, and then choose Design Template from the list.

PowerPoint automatically saves any templates in Office's Template folder (see Figure 6.6). This is handy because all custom templates you create are placed in this folder, where they're available whenever you create a new presentation.

Figure 6.6
Use the Save As dialog box to save a presentation as a template.

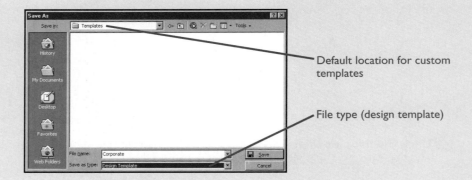

Default location for custom templates

File type (design template)

8 Enter Money in the File name text box, and then click Save.

The presentation is saved as a template. Now close the presentation and apply this custom template to a blank presentation.

9 Close the presentation.

10 Create a new, blank presentation. Use a Title AutoLayout for the first slide.

11 Enter your name in the title placeholder of the slide.

Now you're set up to apply your custom template to this presentation.

12 With your new presentation displayed in Normal view, choose Format, Apply Design Template.

The Apply Design Template dialog box displays. Notice that your new, custom template appears on the template list (see Figure 6.7).

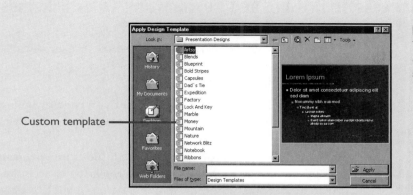

Figure 6.7
You can apply your custom template to any presentation.

Custom template

13 **Double-click the Money template on the list.**
Your custom template is applied to the open presentation (see Figure 6.8).

Figure 6.8
Applying a custom template is a snap.

14 **Close the presentation without saving it.**
Leave PowerPoint running if you plan to complete additional exercises.

 Inside Stuff: **Adding a Template to the AutoContent Wizard**
You can base a new presentation on a custom template by choosing File, New, and then clicking the General tab. Double-click your custom template.

You can also save custom-designed templates to the AutoContent Wizard so that they're available each time you launch the wizard. Choose File, New, to display the New Presentation dialog box, then click the General tab. Double-click the AutoContent Wizard and advance to the second page. Choose in which category you would like to save the template, and then choose Add. Double-click the template you want in the Select Presentation Template dialog box. Click Finish.

Lesson 3: Using and Customizing Color Schemes

A *color scheme* is the underlying set of eight coordinated colors used by each template. PowerPoint's templates include color schemes to ensure that any new objects you create (or recolor) match those already in place. Knowing a little about color schemes is useful for three reasons:

- **It helps ensure that text or objects that you recolor will match the underlying scheme.** For example, when you change font color, the colors displayed on the top row of the palette are from the underlying color scheme.

- **You can change the color scheme for all slides in a presentation.** Why? Well suppose that you're planning to do a presentation on the road, and the LCD or computer screen doesn't have the same contrast as your office computer. Being able to change the color scheme can create a better contrast and literally save your presentation (or job)!

  You may also have similar presentations, but have added customized slides for different audiences—one set for sales, one for marketing, one for advertising, and so on. By keeping the template the same, but changing the color scheme used for each audience, you can instantly tell whether you are running the correct version of your presentation.

- **You can change the color scheme for just one slide to emphasize certain information.** For example, you can highlight a new proposal or agenda. Changing color schemes for the slide that introduces the proposal is a subtle, but effective attention-grabber.

To Work with Color Schemes

Try customizing the color scheme of an existing presentation now.

1 Open **PP-0602** and save it as **Hickory**.

2 Display the presentation in Slide Sorter view so that the new color schemes are easier to see.
Color schemes are most commonly applied in Normal, Slide, or Slide Sorter views so that you can quickly see the result.

3 Choose F**o**rmat, Slide **C**olor Scheme.
The Color Scheme dialog box displays, as shown in Figure 6.9. (When you work in Normal view, you can also open this dialog box by right-clicking in the Slide pane and choosing Slide **C**olor Scheme from the shortcut menu.)

Figure 6.9
You can quickly change color schemes.

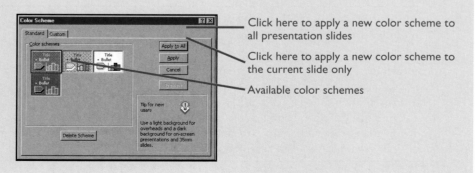

Click here to apply a new color scheme to all presentation slides

Click here to apply a new color scheme to the current slide only

Available color schemes

In general, you should select a scheme with a light background and dark text for overheads. Select a dark background with light text for onscreen display and 35mm slides. Try selecting a color scheme for onscreen display now.

4 **Select the dark maroon color scheme on the second row, and then choose Apply to All.**

The presentation is shown with the dark maroon color scheme applied to all slides. If you were to choose Apply, the color scheme for only the displayed slide would change. Try changing color scheme for just one slide now.

5 **In Slide Sorter view, click Slide 1, Hickory Grove Foods.**

You must select a slide before you can change its color scheme.

6 **Choose Format, Slide Color Scheme.**

The Color Scheme dialog box redisplays.

7 **In the Color Scheme dialog box, choose the bright blue color scheme on the first row, and then choose Apply.**

The selected color scheme is applied only to the selected slide (see Figure 6.10). Notice that the slide elements—such as the graphics and font style—remain consistent on all slides (because they are created by the underlying template), but that the color combinations differ.

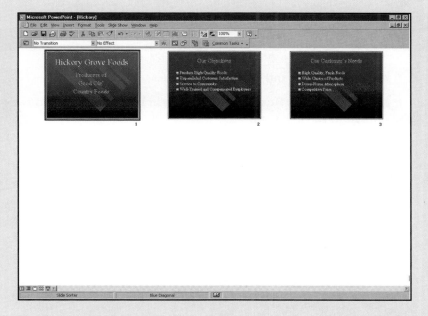

Figure 6.10
You can vary the color scheme by slide.

X *If You Have Problems...*

Make sure that you choose Apply rather than Apply to All to change the color scheme for only the current slide.

---

8 **Save the Hickory presentation, and then close it.**

Keep PowerPoint open for the next exercise, in which you change background color.

Exam Note: **Creating Custom Color Schemes**

If you like the overall color scheme, but want to change color for one screen element, click the Custom tab in the Color Scheme dialog box to display the colors that make up the scheme. Click the $\underline{S}$cheme color you want to change, and then click the Change C$\underline{o}$lor button. Choose a color in the Color dialog box, and then choose OK. You can choose $\underline{A}$pply to use the modified color scheme on the currently displayed slide, or choose Apply $\underline{t}$o All to use it on all presentation slides.

To save your changes as a new scheme, make your changes on the Custom page of the Color Scheme dialog box, and then choose A$\underline{d}$d as Standard Scheme.

 # Lesson 4: Changing the Slide Background

Want to make your presentation unique and grab your audience's attention? Just spiff up your slide background by adding shadow effects, textures, and patterns. Customizing the slide background differs from changing the entire color scheme of eight colors because you modify only the slide's background.

One of the most popular effects is to apply a textured fill to the presentation's background; but other types of customization, such as adding **gradient fills** (colors that fade from one color to another) and patterns, are also available. Try customizing the background for your slides now.

To Change the Slide Background

1 **Open PP1-0603 and save it as** `Appalachian Logging Company`.

2 **Display Slide 1, Business Overview, in Normal view, and then choose F$\underline{o}$rmat, Bac$\underline{k}$ground.**

The Background dialog box displays (see Figure 6.11). In Lesson 2 you used this dialog box briefly to customize a template. Now you'll get a chance to work more completely with the feature.

Figure 6.11
You can choose a new background for your presentation.

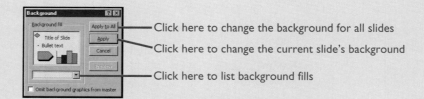

Click here to change the background for all slides

Click here to change the current slide's background

Click here to list background fills

3 **In the $\underline{B}$ackground fill section of the dialog box, click the drop-down list arrow, and then choose $\underline{F}$ill Effects.**

The Fill Effects dialog box displays (see Figure 6.12). You can use this dialog box to choose a variety of background styles.

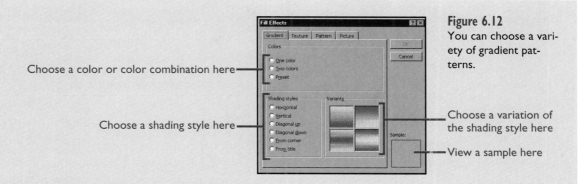

Figure 6.12
You can choose a variety of gradient patterns.

Choose a color or color combination here

Choose a shading style here

Choose a variation of the shading style here

View a sample here

4 **Click the Gradient tab, if necessary, and then click the P̲reset option button (in the Colors section).**
PowerPoint displays a preset color combination (Early Sunset). Now, explore other preset color combinations you can use for your slide's background.

5 **Click the P̲reset colors drop-down list arrow, and choose Ocean from the list.**
The Ocean color combination displays in the Sample area (see Figure 6.13). The Sample area gives you an idea of the way that the color combination will look when you apply it to your slide's background. You can further modify the color combination by choosing a shading style and variant.

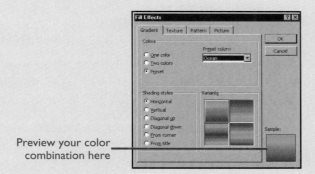

Figure 6.13
You can modify the way a color combination appears.

Preview your color combination here

6 **In the Shading styles section, click the Fro̲m title option button.**
The effect displays in the Sample section of the dialog box. Apply the fill effect to your slide's background.

7 **Choose OK in the Fill Effects dialog box, and then choose Apply t̲o All in the Background dialog box.**
The new background style is applied to your slides.

PowerPoint also provides a number of textures that you can use for a slide's background. Take a look at these textures now.

8 **Right-click in the Slide pane area (but not within a placeholder) on Slide 1 to display the shortcut menu, and then choose Bac̲kground.**
The Background dialog box displays.

continues ▶

To Change the Slide Background   (continued)

> ### ✖ If You Have Problems...
> Make sure to right-click on the background area of your slide (and not in a placeholder) so that the correct shortcut menu displays.

9 **Choose <u>F</u>ill Effects from the drop-down list of available backgrounds.**

10 **In the Fill Effects dialog box, click the Texture tab.**
The Texture page displays with a number of natural-looking backgrounds, such as wood and stone, as shown in Figure 6.14. (If you want, click several of the textures to preview them before proceeding with the exercise.)

Figure 6.14
You can choose a texture for your slide background.

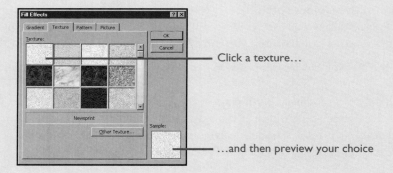

Click a texture...

...and then preview your choice

11 **Scroll down the list of textures, choose Oak (the third box in the bottom row), and click OK to close the Fill Effects dialog box.**

12 **Choose Apply <u>t</u>o All in the Background dialog box.**
The textured wood background is applied to your presentation slides (see Figure 6.15).

Figure 6.15
When appropriate, you can apply different textures to a slide's background.

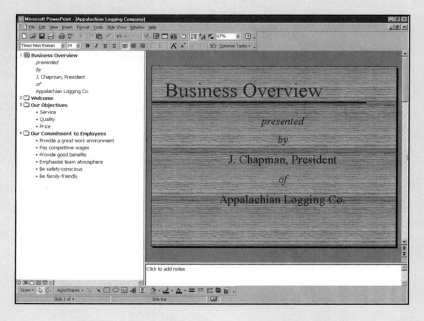

13 **Save the Appalachian Logging Company presentation, and then close it.**
Keep PowerPoint open for the next exercise, in which you work with *slide masters*.

Lesson 5: Modifying the Slide Master

Every presentation that you create automatically includes a slide master. The **slide master** is a framework slide that controls the way your presentation slides will look by governing characteristics such as font, background color, shadowing, and bullet style. When you want to make a global change to all of your slides, you don't have to change each slide individually. Instead, just make the change on the slide master and PowerPoint automatically updates all existing slides.

You can modify the slide master so that it places objects such as dates, names, page numbers, or logos on each presentation slide. For example, you can place your company's logo on the slide master so that it appears on all slides in the presentation. Furthermore, any new slides you add automatically include the changes.

Try making changes to a slide master now.

To Modify the Slide Master

1 **Open PP-0604 and save it as Star Manufacturing.**

2 **Choose View, Master, Slide Master.**
The master slide for the presentation displays (see Figure 6.16). The master contains a title object and a body object that you can use to specify the default format for the title and body text. You can also add other objects to the slide master (such as the date or a page number) to be included on all slides. Additionally, a Slide Miniature box displays, so that you can see the effect of changes to the master on one of your presentation slides. Finally, the Master toolbar displays. You can use this toolbar to quickly close the slide Master and display the presentation in Normal view again.

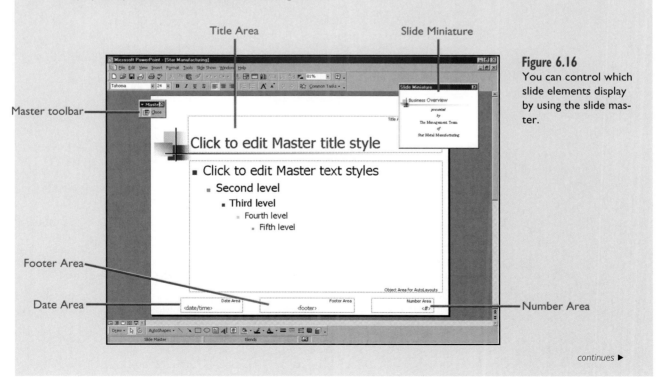

Figure 6.16
You can control which slide elements display by using the slide master.

continues ▶

To Modify the Slide Master (continued)

 If You Have Problems...
If a Slide Miniature doesn't display automatically, choose <u>V</u>iew, Slide
M<u>i</u>niature. Alternatively, click the Slide Miniature button on the Master
toolbar.

If the Master toolbar doesn't display, choose <u>V</u>iew, <u>T</u>oolbars, Master.
When you close the slide master, this toolbar automatically closes.

3 Click the object titled `Click to edit Master title style.`
The Title Area is selected, as indicated by the thickened border. Try changing the
formatting for this area—a change that will affect all title placeholders in your
presentation.

 4 Click the Italic button in the Formatting toolbar.
Italic is added to the Title Area text. Notice that the italic is also added to the
title displayed in the Slide Miniature. Because you made the change on the slide
master rather than on an individual slide, it affects all the presentation slides.

Now try making additional changes.

 **5 With the insertion point still positioned in the title placeholder, click
the Increase Font Size button twice.**
The size of the text in this placeholder increases. Again, this change will globally
affect all slides because you're changing the slide master.

**6 With the slide master still displayed, click by the first bullet level in the
lower (text) placeholder. (Click to edit Master text styles.)**
You place your insertion point in the line (or paragraph) for which you want to
change formatting.

7 Choose F<u>o</u>rmat, <u>B</u>ullets and Numbering.
The Bullets and Numbering dialog box displays (see Figure 6.17). You choose
bullet (and numbering) styles in this dialog box.

Figure 6.17
Choose another bullet
style in this dialog box.

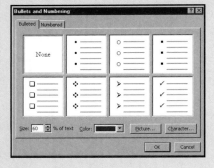

**8 Double-click the check mark style (the fourth style on the second
row).**
The style is used for the first bullet level. Now take a look at how your changes
appear in the presentation.

9 **Choose <u>V</u>iew, <u>N</u>ormal.**
The presentation displays in Normal view.

10 **Scroll through your presentation to see the changes.**

11 **Save the Star Manufacturing presentation.**
Keep it open for the next lesson, in which you insert header and footer information.

Inside Stuff: Four Masters to Choose From
Although you'll work the most often with the slide master, PowerPoint actually includes four different masters, each affecting a different part of your presentation. The title master controls which elements display on the title slide. The notes master dictates the formatting and layout for your printed notes. Finally, the handout master manages the layout for your audience handouts. You can display and revise these masters by choosing them on the <u>V</u>iew, <u>M</u>aster submenu.

Lesson 6: Inserting a Header and a Footer

Using the slide master, you can include information—such as your name, department, or company name—in the Footer, Date, and Number Areas of the slide master. You insert the information in a ***field***, areas used especially for data that might change in a document. Try creating a header and footer now.

To Insert a Header and a Footer

1 **Make sure Slide 1 of the Star Manufacturing presentation you worked with in the preceding lesson is displayed in Normal view.**
To quickly display the slide master, you can press (◆Shift) while clicking Slide View button. When you finish making changes, click the Slide View (or Normal View) button to close the slide master.

2 **Hold down (◆Shift), and then click the Slide View button.**
The slide master redisplays.

3 **On your slide master, click the <footer> field in the Footer Area object.**
The Footer Area is selected (see Figure 6.18).

continues ▶

To Insert a Header and a Footer (continued)

Figure 6.18
You can add text or
slide numbers to your
presentation.

Master toolbar with
Close button

Footer Area

Field

Date Area

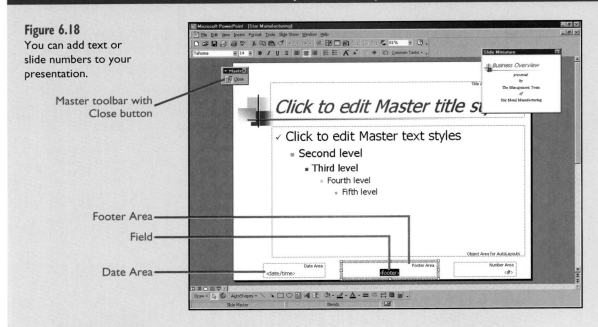

4 **In the <footer> field, enter** `Prepared by Sarah Jones.`
The text is inserted in the Footer field so that it will appear on each presentation
slide.

You can also add the current date to your slides. You do this by clicking the
<date/time> field within the Date Area box.

5 **Click the <date/time> field in the Date Area box, and then choose
Insert, Date and Time.**
The Date and Time dialog box displays so that you can choose a date format
(see Figure 6.19). You can also choose to update the date automatically whenever the presentation is opened, saved, or printed.

Figure 6.19
You can easily add a
date to your slides.

Choose a format here

Check this box to auto-
matically update the date

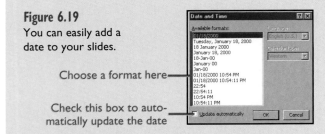

6 **In the Date and Time dialog box, check the Update automatically
check box, and then click OK.**
The current date is added to the Date Area on your slide master.

Now, switch back to Normal view so that you can see the change on your presentation slides. You can do this by choosing View, Normal, or by clicking the
Normal View button. Alternatively, you can click the Close button on the Master
toolbar.

7 **Click the Close button on the Master toolbar (refer to Figure 6.18, if necessary).**

The changes you made on the slide master globally affect all slides (see Figure 6.20).

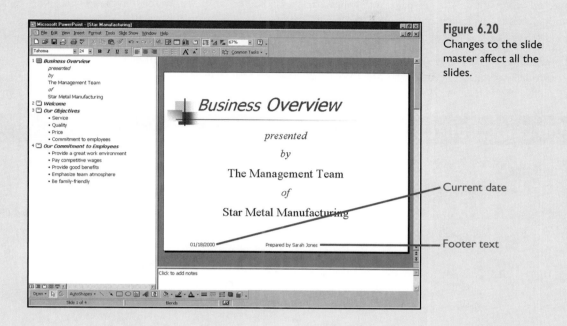

Figure 6.20
Changes to the slide master affect all the slides.

Current date

Footer text

8 **Press F5.**

Your presentation displays as an electronic slide show so that you can better view your changes.

9 **Advance through the presentation until it again displays in Normal view.**

10 **Save and close the Star Manufacturing presentation.**

Keep PowerPoint open if you plan to complete the exercises at the end of this project.

If you've finished your work session, exit PowerPoint and shut down Windows before turning off your computer. Otherwise, complete the exercises at the end of this project.

 Exam Note: Inserting Headers and Footers

Instead of using the slide master to add footer information to your slides, you can choose View, Header and Footer to display the Header and Footer dialog box. On the Slide page, enter information in the Footer text box.

You can also add header (or footer) information to your notes pages. Display the Notes and Handouts page of the Header and Footer dialog box. Enter information in the Header and Footer text boxes, and then click Apply to All.

Summary

In this project, you learned how to dip into PowerPoint's bag of tricks to develop a colorful, eye-catching presentation. You learned how to choose a design template when initially creating a presentation as well as how to apply templates to existing presentations. You experimented with various color schemes and slide backgrounds. You also customized templates, color schemes, and slide backgrounds. Finally, you learned how to modify the slide master and add header and footer information.

To expand on your knowledge, spend a few minutes exploring Help on these topics. Additionally, complete some of the Skill Drill, Challenge, and Discovery Zone exercises.

Checking Concepts and Terms

True/False

For each of the following, circle *T* or *F* to indicate whether the statement is true or false.

__T __F   **1.** You can use natural-looking textures, such as wood grain, for a slide's background. [L4]

__T __F   **2.** Changes to the slide master, such as formatting placeholder text, apply only to the current slide. [L5–6]

__T __F   **3.** A footer is used to add information at the bottom of each slide. [L6]

__T __F   **4.** Choosing the template design before building your presentation is usually best because you can't apply another template later. [L1–2]

__T __F   **5.** A color scheme consists of 32 coordinated colors. [L3]

Multiple Choice

Circle the letter of the correct answer for each of the following.

1. A good reason for changing color schemes is _____. [L3]

   a. to change display contrast when using your presentation as an electronic slide show

   b. to emphasize a particular slide

   c. to keep track of similar, yet slightly different presentations that you created for different audiences

   d. all of the above

2. Design templates _____. [L1]

   a. are the same as a presentation's slide master

   b. are a "blueprint" that PowerPoint uses to determine the overall look of a presentation

   c. can't be changed once selected

   d. none of the above

3. Which dialog box do you use to save a custom template? [L1–2]

   a. Apply Design Template

   b. Save a Template

   c. Save As

   d. none of the above

4. You can _____ by using the slide master. [L5–6]

   a. add Footer Area text

   b. change the font used for a placeholder

   c. add the current date to each slide

   d. all of the above

5. Changes made to a presentation's slide master affect _____. [L5–6]

   a. only the displayed slide

   b. all presentation slides

   c. all open presentations

   d. all presentations on your hard or network drive

Skill Drill

Skill Drill exercises reinforce project skills. Each skill reinforced is the same, or nearly the same, as a skill presented in the project. Detailed instructions are provided in a step-by-step format.

I. Learning about Color Schemes and Templates

As a middle manager for a company, you frequently give presentations. To learn more about working with color schemes and templates, you use the Help feature. [L1–2]

1. In PowerPoint make sure the Office Assistant is turned off, then choose Help, Microsoft PowerPoint Help. (If necessary, click the Show button to split the Help window into two panes.)

2. Click the Contents tab, and then double-click Creating the Look of Your Presentation to display a list of subtopics. Double-click the Using Templates icon.

3. Click each of the Using Templates subtopics listed. Take notes on what you learn.

4. Double-click the Working with Color Schemes icon (within the Creating the Look of Your Presentation topic) to display a list of subtopics. Click each of the subtopics listed.

5. With the Working with Color Schemes icon still selected, click the Print button at the top of the Help window. Choose the **Print the selected heading and all subtopics** option button, and then click OK.

6. Close the Help window. Using your notes and the printed pages as a guide, try each of the commands related to working with templates and color schemes.

7. Share what you learn with at least one other person. Alternatively, develop PowerPoint presentation that covers the various ways to use templates and color schemes. Leave PowerPoint running if you plan to complete additional exercises.

2. Using Templates, Slide Masters, and Color Schemes to Revise a Presentation

Your boss asked you to revise a presentation that she previously created. Furthermore, she wants you to add some elements to jazz it up a bit. To do this, you decide to apply a different design template and color scheme. You also add clip art and text to the slide master. [L1–3, 5, 6]

1. Open **PP-0605** and save it as **Company Overview**. Display Slide 1 of the presentation in Normal view.

2. Choose Format, Apply Design Template to view the Apply Design Template dialog box. See how the presentation looks by clicking the following templates to preview them:

   - Blends
   - Blueprint
   - Dad's Tie
   - Expedition
   - Factory
   - Marble
   - Nature
   - Network Blitz

3. Click the Ribbons template, and then choose Apply.

4. Choose Format, Slide Color Scheme to display the Color Scheme dialog box. Click the leftmost color scheme on the second row (blue), and then choose Apply to All.

5. Display the slide master by pressing (⬆Shift) while clicking the Slide View button. Enter **Report developed by B. Cory** in the <footer> field.

6. With the slide master still displayed, click the Insert Clip Art button on the Drawing toolbar. In the Insert ClipArt dialog box, click **Business**. When the Business clips display, click the second clip art image on the second row (or another appropriate image), and then choose Insert clip.

7. Close the Insert ClipArt dialog box. Resize the clip art image to approximately one-quarter of its original size, and then move it to the upper-left corner of the slide. Click the Close button on the Master toolbar.

8. View your presentation as a slide show to confirm that the changes you made to the slide master display on each slide.

9. Save and then close the presentation. Leave PowerPoint running if you plan to complete the remaining exercises.

3. Working with Design Templates

As president of the University Biking Club, you're preparing for an upcoming meeting. To choose the best design template for your presentation, you preview several before choosing one. You also change the color scheme. [L1–2]

1. Open **PP1-0606** and save it as **Biking Club Meeting**. Display Slide 1 of the presentation in Normal view.

2. Choose Format, Apply Design Template to view the Apply Design Template dialog box. See how the presentation looks by clicking the following templates to preview them:

- Artsy
- Blends
- Capsule
- Dad's Tie
- Expedition
- Marble
- Mountain
- Nature
- Ricepaper
- Strategic

3. Click the Soaring template, and then choose Apply.

4. Choose Format, Slide Color Scheme to display the Color Scheme dialog box. Click the second color scheme on the top row, and then choose Apply to All.

5. Right-click on your slide, and then choose Slide Color Scheme to redisplay the Color Scheme dialog box. Choose the leftmost color scheme on the second row (green), and then choose Apply.

6. View your presentation as a slide show to see your changes.

7. Save your presentation, and then close it. Leave PowerPoint running if you plan to complete additional exercises.

Challenge

Challenge exercises expand on, or are somewhat related to, skills presented in the lessons. Each exercise provides a brief narrative introduction, followed by instructions in a numbered-step format that are not as detailed as those in the Skill Drill section.

1. Finding Out About Notes and Slide Masters

Although you know the basics of working with a presentation's slide master, you want to learn more and to make modifications to your presentation's notes master. To find out how to do so, you use the Help feature. [L4]

1. In PowerPoint, make sure the Office Assistant is turned off, then choose Help, Microsoft PowerPoint Help. Click the Show button, if necessary, to split the Help window into two panes.

2. Click the Index tab to display the Index page. Enter **notes** in the Type keywords text box so that **notes_master** appears, and then click Search.

3. View the items shown on the Choose a topic list that pertain to the notes master and slide master. Make sure **Ways to design and give your presentation** is the last topic viewed.

4. Click the Contents tab to display the Contents page. Double-click the Using the Slide Master icon to display subtopics. Print the topics (or take complete notes).

5. Practice creating notes masters and revising slide masters using the Help information. Then create a presentation that covers the information and share it with at least one other user. Leave PowerPoint running if you plan to complete additional exercises.

2. Working with a Title Master

To make elements appear more uniform on your biking club presentation, you decide to modify the title master. [L5–6]

1. Open **PP-0607** and save it as **Upcoming Meeting**.

2. Display the title master. Make the title placeholder text italic, 40-point, Comic Sans font. Also make the text red.

3. Add the current date in the Date Area, using the format of your choice. Indicate that you want the date to be updated automatically.

4. In the <footer> field, add the text **May Meeting**, and then press ⤶Enter. Add the slide number in the Footer Area below the May Meeting text.

5. Close the title master to view your changes.

6. Save the Upcoming Meeting presentation, and then close it. Leave PowerPoint running if you plan to complete additional exercises.

3. Revising the Slide Master

You're developing a talk for your company's annual meeting. You modify the slide master so that the elements (such as your company's logo) appear on all slides. [L5–6]

1. Open **PP-0608** and save it as **Tech Head Trends**.

2. Move to Slide 2, and then display the slide master. Make the following revisions to the master:

   ■ Change the first-level bullet style to large open squares.

   ■ Format the text in the title placeholder as italic.

   ■ Format the text for the bulleted points without italic.

   ■ Draw a red filled circle in the upper-right corner of the slide master with the initials **THT** in the middle of the circle. (*Hint:* Use your Oval drawing tools. If necessary, use Help to find out how to add text to drawn objects.)

3. Close the slide master and view your changes. Make any necessary revisions.

4. Print, save, and close your Tech Head Trends presentation. Leave PowerPoint running if you plan to complete additional exercises.

Discovery Zone

Discovery Zone exercises require advanced knowledge of topics presented in *MOUS Essentials* lessons, application of skills from multiple lessons, or self-directed learning of new skills.

1. Combining PowerPoint Features

As sales manager for a mass-market kitchen cabinet factory, you develop and give a large number of presentations. Determine which PowerPoint feature you would use for each of the following situations.

- You want to display your company's logo on each presentation slide.
- You want to change the overall design and "look" of your presentation.
- You want to add a textured effect to the background of your presentation slides.
- You want to use the same design template for your presentation, but need more contrast for an onscreen display.
- You want to insert the date at the bottom of each presentation slide.
- You want to add header information at the top of your printed speaker notes and audience handouts.

Use Help to research how to use each feature. Next develop a sample presentation (using the AutoContent Wizard, if you want) and practice using each feature until you are confident that you can perform the steps automatically. Close your sample presentation without saving it. Leave PowerPoint running if you plan to complete the final exercise. [L1–6]

2. Using and Creating Templates

You assist the president of a large tooling manufacturer. Because you have a strong knowledge of PowerPoint, he's asked you to help him develop a custom template for your company, and then add it to the AutoContent Wizard.

Develop a new, blank presentation. Modify and format the presentation using what you know about design templates, color schemes, slide backgrounds, and slide masters.

Save the presentation as a template, using a name of your choice. Then add the template to the AutoContent Wizard so that it displays each time you launch the wizard.

Create a new presentation based on the template. (*Hint:* Use the File, New command.) Also create a presentation (based on your custom template) using the AutoContent Wizard. After you've finished, close all open presentations and exit PowerPoint. [L1–2]

PinPoint Assessment

You have completed this project and its associated lessons, and have had an opportunity to assess your skills through the end-of-project questions and exercises. Now use the PinPoint software Evaluation Mode to further assess your comprehension of the specific exam activities you have just learned. You can also use the PinPoint Trainer Mode and the Show Me tutorials to practice these exam activities.

Project 7

Working with Charts

Key terms introduced in this project include

- activating
- animating
- cell
- cell pointer
- chart
- chart subtypes
- data charts
- data series
- datasheet
- default
- embedded object
- icon bar
- object
- organization chart
- parent box
- peripheral program
- selecting

Objectives	Required Activity for MOUS	Exam Level
➤ Selecting an Appropriate Chart Type		
➤ Creating a Data Chart	Build a chart or graph	Expert
➤ Editing Chart Data	Modify charts or graphs	Expert
➤ Resizing, Moving, and Changing Chart Types	Modify charts or graphs	Expert
➤ Choosing a Chart Subtype and Formatting a Chart	Modify charts or graphs	Expert
➤ Adding Animation to a Chart	Apply animation effects	Expert
	Animate text and objects	Expert
➤ Building an Organization Chart	Build an organization chart	Expert
➤ Modifying an Organization Chart	Modify an organization chart	Expert

Why Would I Do This?

Have you ever longed for a way to convey complicated data in a clear, concise manner to business clients, stockholders, or colleagues? One of the best ways to do this is to present your data as a PowerPoint data chart. A **data chart** is just a pictorial representation of numerical data.

Charts, or graphs as they are sometimes called, are powerful tools in a presentation, because a well-presented chart usually convinces more people than endless words or explanations. Business users want to know the bottom line—so use PowerPoint's capability to create data charts to your advantage. For example, Figure 7.1 shows information as text. Figure 7.2 shows the same information graphically as a data chart. By the end of this project, you'll learn how to change dull, hard-to-understand statistics into colorful, appealing charts such as that in Figure 7.2.

Figure 7.1
Dull text?

Record Sales, Inc.

	1st Qtr	2nd Qtr	3rd Qtr	4th Qtr
Madison	20.4	27.4	55	20.4
Chicago	30.6	38.6	34.6	31.6
Columbus	45.9	46.9	45	43.9
Indianapolis	36	38	28	40

Figure 7.2
Use a chart!

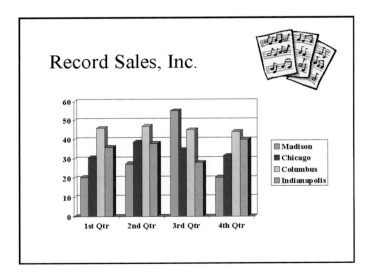

Record Sales, Inc.

You enter and revise the information in the data chart using the datasheet. You can also modify the chart using buttons on Microsoft Graph's toolbar.

Before you begin, however, it's important to know which type of chart to use for your data. In the first lesson, you explore the various chart types and learn when to use each.

Lesson 1: Selecting an Appropriate Chart Type

You can select from several standard chart types to present your data clearly and effectively. Additionally, each chart type includes several **chart subtypes**—variations on the main chart types. As you develop your presentation, make sure that you set up your data by using the best chart type for the information you're trying to convey. Because the most commonly used chart types are line, bar, column, pie, and organization, you learn how to use these. Table 7.1 lists all the chart types used in PowerPoint, so you'll have a handy reference as you expand your charting skills.

Table 7.1 PowerPoint chart types

Button	Chart Type	Main Use	Example
	Column chart	Shows data changes over time or illustrates a comparison of items. The values are organized vertically, and categories are shown horizontally to emphasize variation over time.	Sales by quarter for the year
	Bar chart	Shows comparison of individual items. Categories are arranged vertically and values are arranged horizontally, placing more emphasis on categories than values.	Sales by region, with region on the vertical axis and sales on the horizontal axis
	Line chart	Shows trends in data at equal intervals.	Monthly production over a twelve-month tperiod
	Pie chart	Illustrates the relationship of parts to the whole. Pie charts can show only one data series.	Market share held by your company versus the competitor
	(XY) Scatter chart	Shows the relationship between values in several chart series.	The relationship between quantity and price
	Area chart	Shows the magnitude of change over time.	Cumulative sales from several divisions

continues ▶

Table 7.1   PowerPoint chart types (continued)

Button	Chart Type	Main Use	Example
	Doughnut chart	Similar to a pie chart because it shows the relationship of parts to the whole. However, it can show more than one data series, each "ring" representing a series.	Expenses broken down by category for several departments
	Radar chart	Shows frequencies of changes in data relative to each other and to a center point.	Analysis of how well several products did in comparison with each other
	Surface chart	Shows where the result of combining two sets of data produces the greatest overall value.	A chart showing the greatest combination of cold and wind (wind chill)
	Bubble chart	Shows data similar to a scatter chart, but also shows (by size of the bubble) the result of the data.	A chart showing the effect of temperature and humidity on soda sales
	Stock chart	Shows high, low, and closing values	A chart that shows the performance for your company's stock
	Cylinder, Cone, and Pyramid charts	Shows data similar to that in bar and column charts, but displays it as cylinders, cones, or pyramids.	A chart using pyramids to graphically show the height of mountains

In addition to the chart types listed in Table 7.1, PowerPoint can produce **organization charts**, which show how your business is structured. (You learn how to create and modify organization charts in Lessons 7–8.) For now, you'll focus on the basics of creating a data chart.

 ## Lesson 2: Creating a Data Chart

PowerPoint has the capability to create different types of data charts so that you can illustrate your points effectively. Data charts are just charts that include numeric data (as opposed to organization charts, which show how an organization is set up).

PowerPoint uses Microsoft Graph, a **peripheral program**, to create data charts. Peripheral programs are started every time you access a feature within the main program and place an **object** (such as a chart) on a slide. You can think of the object as being a doorway that leads to the peripheral program, giving you access to its features and commands. PowerPoint shares Microsoft Graph with other Office programs. This makes chart development more uniform and efficient when working with PowerPoint and the various Office products.

You can use a couple of different methods to launch Microsoft Graph and insert a chart on a slide. You can use a chart placeholder on an existing or new slide, or you can use the Insert Chart button on the Standard toolbar. After you start Microsoft Graph, a datasheet displays so that you can enter your information. A **datasheet** is a grid of columns and rows that enables you to enter numeric data into a PowerPoint chart. The intersection of a column and row where you can enter information is called a **cell**. Cells are always named by the column heading, followed by the row number (such as A1). If you're familiar with Excel, you'll feel right at home using a datasheet because it is set up like a mini-worksheet.

When you finish entering your data in the datasheet, you close the peripheral program and your chart is embedded as an object on your slide. An **embedded object** is an item created by one program, but inserted into a document created by another program. In this case, a chart object (created by Microsoft Graph) is placed on a PowerPoint slide.

Now that you know the essentials and terminology associated with data charts, try creating one.

To Create a Data Chart

❶ Start PowerPoint, if necessary, and then open PP-0701 and save it as Bell Manufacturing.
You can create a data chart in Slide or Normal view, but it's easier to see the chart in Slide view, so make sure the presentation is displayed using it.

❷ Display Slide 1, Financial Review, in Slide view, and then click the New Slide button on the Standard toolbar.
The New Slide dialog box displays. As you probably remember from earlier projects, you can choose one of 24 AutoLayouts to quickly produce a slide with preset formatting. Three of the AutoLayouts include a chart placeholder, which makes them easy to use to create a chart. For this lesson you'll use the AutoLayout with the largest chart placeholder.

❸ Single-click the Chart AutoLayout (the fourth AutoLayout from the left, on the second row).
The Chart AutoLayout is selected. This AutoLayout includes placeholders for a title and the chart object (see Figure 7.3).

Chart AutoLayout ———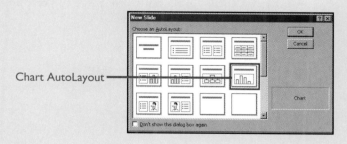

Figure 7.3
You can use a Chart AutoLayout as the basis for your new slide.

continues ▶

To Create a Data Chart   (continued)

4 Choose OK.

A new slide is inserted into your presentation with placeholders for a title and a chart (see Figure 7.4).

Figure 7.4
Want to create a chart? Use the Chart AutoLayout.

Title placeholder

Chart placeholder

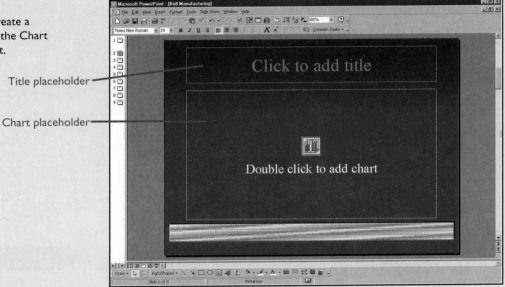

5 Click in the title placeholder, and then type Revenues 1998 vs. 1999.

This is the title for the chart. Now, you're ready to create the chart itself. To start Microsoft Graph so that you can develop your chart, double-click the chart placeholder.

6 Double-click the chart placeholder.

Microsoft Graph starts and a datasheet displays with sample data. Because Microsoft Graph is the active program, the Microsoft Graph Standard and Formatting toolbars are available so that you can use charting commands (see Figure 7.5).

The sample data is just a guide and is easily replaced with your own data. To enter your data, click the cell and type your entry. When you finish, press ⏎Enter or an arrow key. Try entering some data now.

7 Click the cell containing the word East.

A darkened border around the cell, called the *cell pointer*, indicates that this is the active cell—ready for an entry.

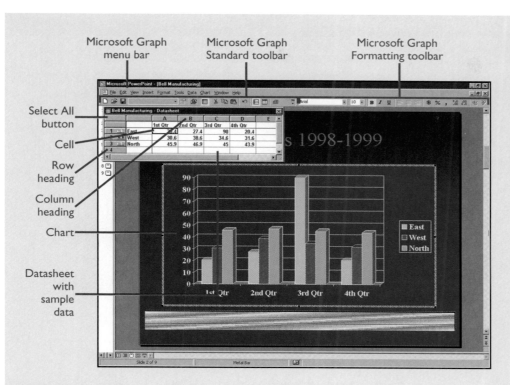

Microsoft Graph
menu bar

Microsoft Graph
Standard toolbar

Microsoft Graph
Formatting toolbar

Select All
button

Cell

Row
heading

Column
heading

Chart

Datasheet
with
sample
data

Figure 7.5
A sample chart and
datasheet display
whenever you activate
Microsoft Graph.

8 **Type 1998 and press ⬇.**
This enters 1998 in the cell and moves the cell pointer down one cell. (You can
also press ⏎Enter to move the cell pointer down one cell.)

9 **Click in the row 3 heading (North).**
The entire row is selected.

10 **Press Del.**
The sample data from the entire row 3 is deleted.

11 **Enter the data shown in Figure 7.6 into your datasheet.**

Close button

Figure 7.6
You can easily replace
sample data with your
own.

12 **When you finish entering the data, click the Close button in the
datasheet's upper-right corner.**
The datasheet closes and you can better see the column chart that is created.
This is the *default* chart type, which means that PowerPoint automatically uses
this type of chart unless you indicate otherwise. Additionally, the chart is embedded into the slide as an object. Black selection handles encompass the chart, indicating that it's still activated—Microsoft Graph is still active in memory (see
Figure 7.7).

continues ▶

To Create a Data Chart   (continued))

Figure 7.7
PowerPoint inserts the
graph on your slide as
an object.

Microsoft Graph
menu bar

Microsoft Graph toolbars

Embedded chart

Black selection handles

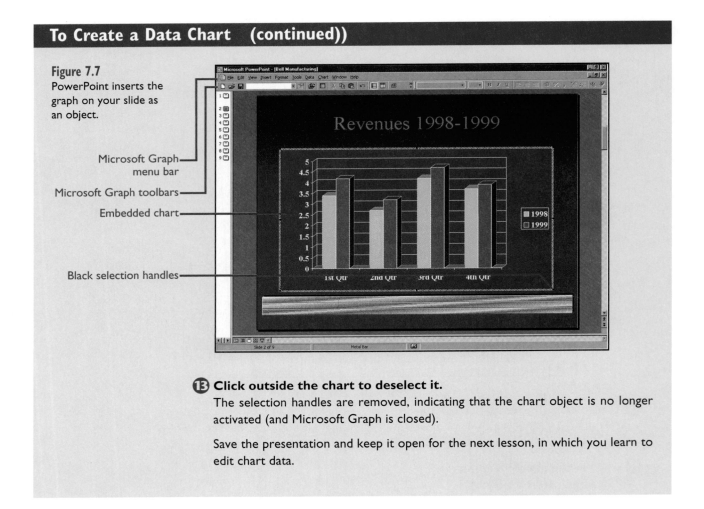

13 **Click outside the chart to deselect it.**
The selection handles are removed, indicating that the chart object is no longer
activated (and Microsoft Graph is closed).

Save the presentation and keep it open for the next lesson, in which you learn to
edit chart data.

 Exam Note: **Entering Information in a Datasheet**
It's handy to know some efficient ways to work with information that you enter
and edit in your datasheet. For example, you can click a column heading to select
an entire column for deletion—just as you selected an entire row for deletion in
the preceding lesson. In a similar way, you can click the Select All button (at the intersection of the row numbers and column headings) to quickly select the entire
datasheet, and then press Del to delete all the sample data at once.

Choosing a Chart AutoLayout as you create a new slide is an easy way to make a
chart. If you want to place a chart on a slide without a Chart AutoLayout, however,
you can choose Insert, Chart, or click the Insert Chart button on the Standard
toolbar.

 ## Lesson 3: Editing Chart Data

After you create a chart, you may want to edit its data. For example, you may want to update sales or production figures as they become available. In this lesson, you learn how to activate Microsoft Graph for an existing chart, as well as ways to edit your data.

Before you make changes to a chart, you must first activate it. There's a difference between
selecting a chart object and ***activating*** it.

Clicking a chart object one time selects it and places white selection handles around its border. (You use these handles in the next lesson to move and resize the chart.) In contrast, double-clicking the chart activates it and opens Microsoft Graph in memory so that you can again use Microsoft Graph's commands and features. You'll know when the chart is activated because you see black selection handles and a rope-like border.

Try activating your chart and editing its data now.

To Edit Chart Data

❶ In the Bell Manufacturing presentation, double-click the chart object you created on Slide 2.

The chart is activated, as shown by the rope-like border and black selection handles (see Figure 7.8).

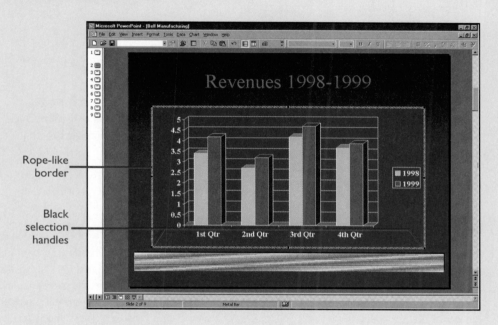

Rope-like border

Black selection handles

Figure 7.8
An activated chart displays a rope-like border and black selection handles.

✖ If You Have Problems...

It's sometimes tricky to activate rather than select the chart. If your chart doesn't look like the one in Figure 7.8, double-click on the chart again. Make sure to click in fairly rapid succession and to hold the mouse steady between clicks. If you really have trouble activating the chart by double-clicking, you can instead single-click the chart and press ⏎Enter.

❷ Click the View Datasheet button on the Standard toolbar.

The datasheet displays, which enables you to revise the data that it contains.

❸ Click the Select All button in the upper-left corner of the datasheet.

The entire datasheet is highlighted to show that it's selected (see Figure 7.9).

continues ▶

To Edit Chart Data (continued)

Figure 7.9
You can select the entire datasheet, and then delete its contents.

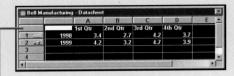

Click here to select the entire datasheet

④ **Press** ⌈Del⌋.
The datasheet contents are deleted. Now, you can enter new data.

⑤ **Enter the information shown in Figure 7.10 into your datasheet.**

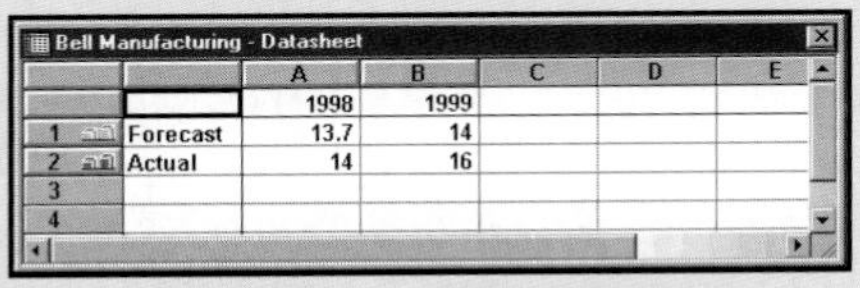

Figure 7.10
You can easily revise your chart by editing its data.

⑥ **When you finish entering the data, click the View Datasheet button.**
The datasheet closes, but the chart remains active. Keep your Bell Manufacturing presentation open for the next lesson, in which you learn to change the chart type, and move and resize your chart.

 Expert ## Lesson 4: Resizing, Moving, and Changing Chart Types

Congratulations! You've created a chart and revised its data. Now you're ready to move and resize your chart object on the slide, and to change the chart type. The easiest way to do this is to click the drop-down list arrow next to the Chart Type button. Keep in mind that the underlying data remains the same—the chart types just display the data differently. Because you don't affect the data when you change the chart type, you can experiment freely to see which chart type best conveys your data. (Plus, clicking the Undo button can get you out of any jams.)

Try resizing and moving your chart, as well as changing the chart type now.

To Resize, Move, and Change Chart Types

① **In the open Bell Manufacturing presentation, make sure that the chart on Slide 2 is active.**
Black selection handles indicate that the chart is still active. (If your chart isn't displayed in this manner, double-click the chart object to activate it.)

Now, hide the display of Microsoft Graph's Formatting toolbar. When you do this, you automatically uncover the Standard toolbar's buttons that you need to use.

2 **Choose <u>V</u>iew, <u>T</u>oolbars, Formatting.**

The Formatting toolbar's display is turned off so that only the Standard toolbar is visible. This toolbar includes the buttons that you use throughout the lesson. One of the most popular buttons is the Chart Type button, which includes a drop-down palette of chart types.

3 **On the Microsoft Graph Standard toolbar, click the Chart Type drop-down list arrow.**

The types of charts available on your system display on a palette, as shown in Figure 7.11. Notice that some of the charts are just variations of other types. For example, the palette shows both 2-D and 3-D bar and column charts.

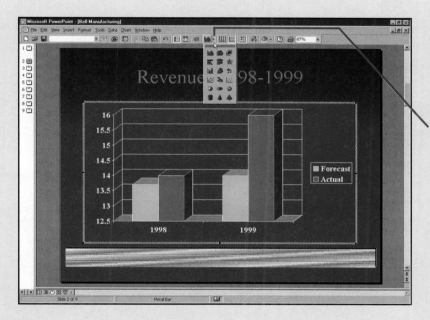

Figure 7.11
You can easily change the chart type.

Click this drop-down list arrow to display the chart types

4 **Rest the mouse pointer momentarily on any chart type on the palette.**

A ScreenTip displays and indicates the type of chart (see Figure 7.12). This is a handy feature that you can use to identify chart types.

5 **Move the mouse pointer to the 3-D Bar Chart button on the palette, and then click to select it.**

The chart displays as a bar chart (see Figure 7.13). For practice, spend a few minutes changing to other chart types. When you finish experimenting, choose the 3-D Bar Chart before continuing with the lesson.

continues ▶

To Resize, Move, and Change Chart Types   (continued)

Figure 7.12
A ScreenTip displays when you rest your mouse pointer on a button in the palette.

ScreenTip

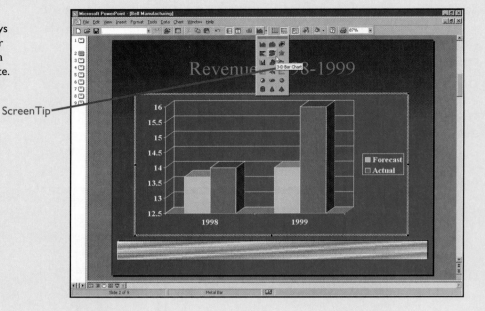

Figure 7.13
You can quickly change to a 3-D bar chart.

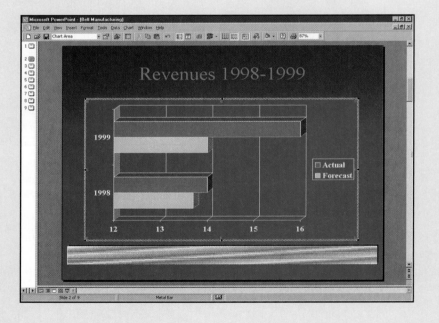

Besides changing chart type, you can make other modifications to your chart. For example, you may want to resize or move the chart on your slide. Luckily, PowerPoint makes this task easy.

6 **Click outside the chart to embed it as an object on your slide.**
The selection handles disappear because the chart is not activated. Now, select the chart so that you can move it.

7 **Click the chart object one time.**
White selection handles surround the chart object. They indicate that the chart is selected as an object, but that the Microsoft Graph program is not activated.

Now, resize the chart object.

8 **Move the mouse pointer to the white selection handle on the upper-right corner of the chart so that the pointer displays as a resizing arrow (see Figure 7.14).**

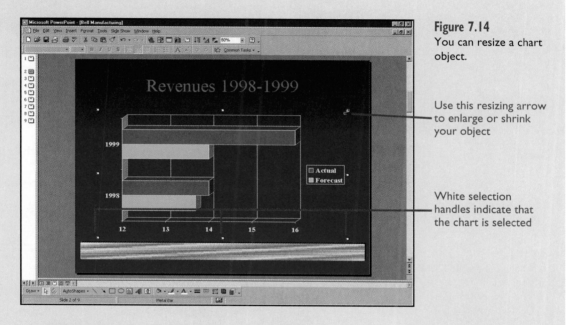

Figure 7.14
You can resize a chart object.

Use this resizing arrow to enlarge or shrink your object

White selection handles indicate that the chart is selected

9 **Drag toward the middle of the chart until the chart is approximately half the original size and release the mouse button.**
The object is resized on the slide. Now, move the object to the middle of the available space.

10 **Move the mouse pointer to the middle of the chart object until a four-sided arrow displays (see Figure 7.15).**

continues ▶

To Resize, Move, and Change Chart Types   (continued)

Figure 7.15
You can move a se-
lected chart object.

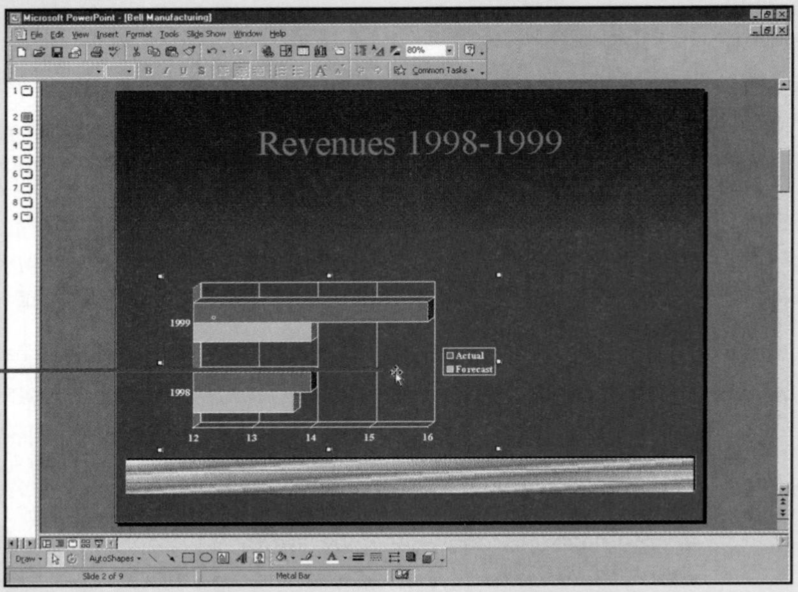

Make sure that the four-
headed arrow pointer is
displayed before dragging
the object

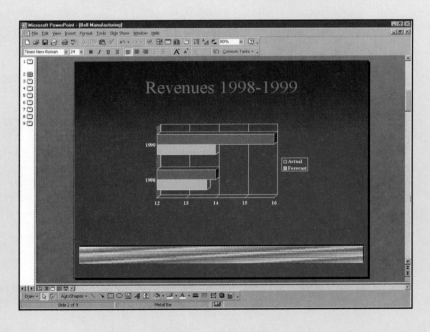

11 **Drag the chart object so that it displays in the middle of the slide and release the mouse button.**

12 **Click outside the chart object to deselect it.**
The slide should now look similar to the one shown in Figure 7.16.

Figure 7.16
You can resize and
move charts for a bet-
ter appearance.

13 **Save your changes and close the Bell Manufacturing presentation.**
Leave PowerPoint running for the next lesson, in which you format charts.

***Exam Note:*   Using Buttons to Modify Your Chart**
You can use a number of other buttons on Microsoft Graph's Standard toolbar to help display your data. For example, you can quickly switch the way your data appears by clicking the By Row or By Column buttons. You can also add or remove a legend by clicking the Legend button. To find out more about working with charts, activate a chart, and then choose <u>H</u>elp, Microsoft Graph <u>H</u>elp from the Microsoft Graph menu bar.

Lesson 5: Choosing a Chart Subtype and Formatting a Chart

So far in this project, you learned how to create charts and make some revisions. PowerPoint provides a number of tools you can use to make your charts more readable and understandable—and in this lesson, you learn how to wield them. For example, you learn how to choose a chart subtype and how to change a chart's text and color. You work with a safety campaign presentation, which includes a column chart. Try using some formatting options on this chart now.

To Choose a Chart Subtype

❶ **Open PP-0702 and save it as Safety.**

❷ **Double-click the existing chart on Slide 4, Total sick days per facility, and close the datasheet.**
Microsoft Graph is activated, as shown by the black handles around the chart. The chart is currently a column chart. For this presentation, however, you want to view the information in a stacked column chart. To change the chart's format to a different subtype, you use the Chart Type dialog box.

❸ **Choose <u>C</u>hart, Chart <u>T</u>ype.**
The Chart Type dialog box displays, as shown in Figure 7.17. You can use this dialog box to select a variation, or subtype, of the main chart type.

❌ ***If You Have Problems...***
If you don't see the <u>C</u>hart command on the menu bar, you probably accidentally selected (rather than activated) the chart. Just double-click the chart object to activate it.

Choose a subtype here ——

Choose a main chart type on this list ——

Choose the stacked column with a 3-D visual effect here ——

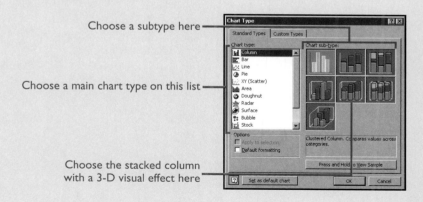

Figure 7.17
You can select and preview chart types in this dialog box.

continues ▶

To Choose a Chart Subtype   (continued)

4 **Click on the** `Stacked column with a 3-D visual effect` **subtype—the middle chart in the second row.**
A description of the selected subtype appears below the chart subtypes. You can also preview how your data looks when displayed by the subtype by using the special preview button that PowerPoint provides.

5 **Move the mouse pointer to the Press and Hold to <u>V</u>iew Sample button. Click and hold down the mouse button for a few seconds before releasing it.**
PowerPoint displays your data with the selected chart's format. You can select and preview other chart types (and subtypes). When you finish, choose the `Stacked column with a 3-D visual effect` subtype before proceeding.

6 **Click OK in the Chart Type dialog box.**
The selected chart type is applied to your chart. Keep your chart activated for the next tutorial, in which you explore some other methods of formatting your chart.

By now, you're familiar with creating a chart, editing data, and changing chart types. Next, you focus on working with individual elements in a chart, such as the data series, graph walls, legend, and so on. You can format or delete any of these elements, but first you must select the object. The easiest way to select a chart object is to use the Chart Objects drop-down list on the Standard toolbar. Try selecting, formatting, and deleting chart objects now.

To Format a Chart

| Chart Area ▼ |

1 **In the activated chart, click the drop-down list arrow to the right of the Chart Objects box.**
A list of the items in your chart displays. You can select an item by clicking it on the list.

2 **On the list, choose** `Series "Danville"`**.**
The data series that represents the Danville factory is selected. In fact, if you look carefully, you can see selected handles displayed around the series to help you identify your selection. A *data series* is a collection of values that pertain to a single subject. Now, format the data series.

3 **Choose F<u>o</u>rmat, Se<u>l</u>ected Data Series from the menu bar.**
The Format Data Series dialog box displays, as shown in Figure 7.18. Notice that PowerPoint includes several formatting categories—such as Patterns and Shape—each on a separate, tabbed page.

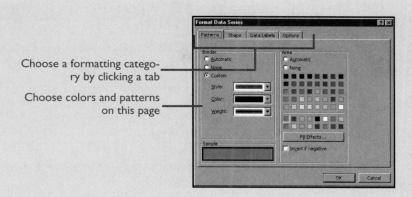

Figure 7.18
You can change many formatting features by using the Format Data Series dialog box.

Choose a formatting category by clicking a tab

Choose colors and patterns on this page

4 **In the Area section of the Patterns page, click the red color box.**
The Sample box displays the result of your choice. Now, change the pattern associated with the data series.

5 **In the Format Data Series dialog box, click the Fill Effects button.**
The Fill Effects dialog box displays (see Figure 7.19). You can choose a gradient, pattern, or texture for the data series.

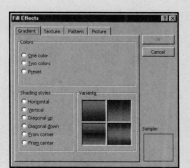

Figure 7.19
You can choose a variety of fills for your data.

6 **Click the Texture tab to display its page, and then click several fill textures.**
Each texture you choose is shown in the Sample box. Now, view the available patterns.

7 **Click the Pattern tab and choose the second pattern from the left on the fifth row (the red background with white dots).**
Your selected pattern is shown in the Sample box.

8 **Click OK in the Fill Effects dialog box and in the Format Data Series dialog box to accept your changes.**
The color and pattern you chose is applied to the data series. You can format any chart object in a similar way: Use the Chart Objects drop-down list to select an object, and then choose the S*e*lected (*name of object*) command from the F*o*rmat menu.

You can also double-click a chart object to open an associated Format dialog box. Use this method to change the legend's appearance now.

continues ▶

To Format a Chart   (continued)

⑨ Double-click the legend to display the Format Legend dialog box.
You use this dialog box to modify the colors, font, and placement for the legend.

⊗   If You Have Problems...
Make sure that you double-click the legend background, and not one of the legend entries (such as **Danville**).

---

⑩ In the Area section of the Patterns page, choose dark gray for your legend color, and then click OK.
The legend's background is formatted with the new color.

You can also delete a chart object by selecting it and pressing ⒹⒺⓁ. Delete a data series now.

⑪ Click the drop-down list arrow to the right of the Chart Objects box and choose Series "Samville".
The series is selected so that you can delete it.

⑫ Press ⒹⒺⓁ.
The selected series is removed from the chart. Notice that the legend entry for **Samville** is deleted simultaneously (see Figure 7.20).

Figure 7.20
You can select and then delete a chart object.

The Samville data series is deleted from the chart...

...and the legend entry is deleted at the same time

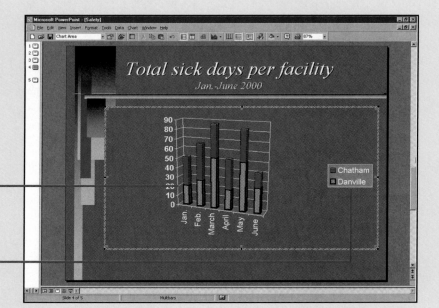

Before you close Microsoft Graph, turn the display for the Formatting toolbar back on.

⑬ Choose View, Toolbars, Formatting.
The Microsoft Graph Formatting toolbar is visible again. Now embed the chart on your slide.

⑭ Click outside the chart to embed it on the slide, and then save and close the Safety presentation.
Leave PowerPoint open for the next lesson, in which you learn how to animate a chart.

Lesson 6: Adding Animation to a Chart

You can animate almost any object on a PowerPoint slide, and a chart is no exception. **Animating** refers to displaying objects in sequence to produce the illusion of movement or to control the flow of information. For charts you can display data by element or by the entire data series. Try animating a chart now.

To Add Animation to a Chart

1 **Open** PP-0703 **and save it as** Record Sales.

2 **Click the chart to select it.**
White selection handles appear around the borders of the chart object, indicating that it is selected.

3 **Choose Slide Show, Custom Animation.**
The Custom Animation dialog box opens (see Figure 7.21). Notice that the Chart Effects page of this dialog box is automatically displayed.

> ❌ **If You Have Problems...**
> If the Chart Effects page doesn't appear in front, most likely you didn't select the chart before choosing Slide Show, Custom Animation. In the Custom Animation dialog box, click the Chart Effects tab, and then check the Chart box.

Preview area ⟶
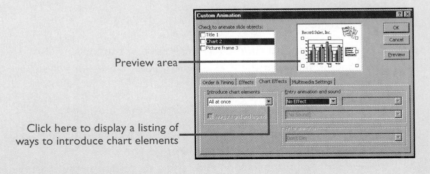
Click here to display a listing of ways to introduce chart elements

Figure 7.21
Use the Custom Animation dialog box to animate your chart.

4 **Click the Introduce chart elements drop-down list arrow.**
A listing of ways to animate your chart elements displays (see Figure 7.22).

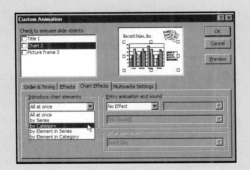

Figure 7.22
Choose an animation for your chart on this list.

5 **Choose by Category on the list.**
So that you can see how your animation effect looks, you can click the Preview button in the Custom Animation dialog box.

continues ▶

To Add Animation to a Chart   (continued)

6 Click the Preview button.

The miniature chart in the Preview area shows the animation effect. Just for fun, try another animation effect.

7 Click the Introduce chart elements drop-down list arrow, and then choose by Element in Category. (If you want, preview this effect as well.)

Now try changing the way that each chart element should appear. You can add a variety of animation effects to add interest to your presentation.

8 Click the Entry animation and sound drop-down list arrow.

A listing of effects you can use to introduce your chart elements displays (see Figure 7.23).

Figure 7.23
Choose the effect you want to use to introduce your chart elements here.

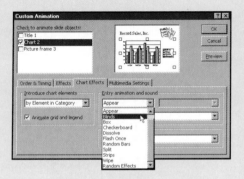

9 Choose Blinds, and then click the Preview button.

The effect is shown in the Preview area. Now try viewing the effect in an electronic slide show.

10 Click OK to close the Custom Animation dialog box.

11 Click the Slide Show button, and then left-click your mouse as many times as necessary to advance through the show.

PowerPoint uses the animation effects you set to display the chart elements.

12 Save your changes to the Record Sales presentation, and then close it.

Leave PowerPoint running for the next exercise, in which you learn how to create an organization chart.

Expert   Lesson 7: Building an Organization Chart

Organization charts are handy because they show the structure and relationship between people or functions within an organization. PowerPoint creates this type of chart by using a peripheral program, Microsoft Organization Chart. You can start this program and create the chart in two ways. First, choose the Organization Chart AutoLayout in the New Slide dialog box. On the slide, double-click the chart placeholder to start Microsoft Organization Chart. Alternatively, you can choose Insert, Object to display the Insert Object dialog box, and then choose MS Organization Chart from the Object type list. If you use the second method, the chart program automatically starts for you. In either case, Microsoft Organization Chart displays its own menu bar at the top of its window. Additionally, you can use the box tools displayed on the program's icon bar.

In this lesson, you create an organization chart, and then enter information in it. In Lesson 8, you change the organization chart structure and format the chart. Try creating an organization chart now.

To Build an Organization Chart

1 **Create a new presentation by clicking the New button on the Standard toolbar.**

The New Slide dialog box displays with available AutoLayouts. The Organization Chart AutoLayout is on the second row, second from the right.

2 **Double-click the Organization Chart AutoLayout.**

A new slide is created with a placeholder for the organization chart in the lower portion of the slide (see Figure 7.24).

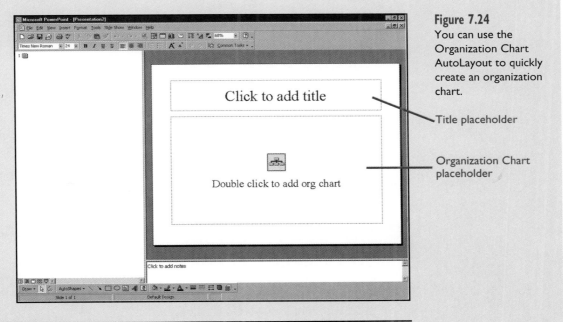

Figure 7.24
You can use the Organization Chart AutoLayout to quickly create an organization chart.

Title placeholder

Organization Chart placeholder

If You Have Problems...
If Microsoft Organization Chart has never run on your computer, PowerPoint displays a message box, telling you that the program isn't installed on your system. This is because PowerPoint 2000 has an *install upon demand* feature. Some features (such as Microsoft Organization Chart) are only installed if and when you need them. Luckily, this doesn't really present a problem. Just make sure that the Office 2000 program CD is inserted in the CD-ROM drive and choose Yes in the message box to install the Microsoft Organization Chart peripheral program. If you need additional assistance, ask your instructor.

3 **Click in the title placeholder, type Team Structure, and then double-click the Organization Chart placeholder to activate Microsoft Organization Chart.**

continues ▶

To Build an Organization Chart   (continued)

The chart program starts and the Microsoft Organization Chart window displays, as shown in Figure 7.25. When you create an organization chart, you actually use a peripheral program that comes with PowerPoint—Microsoft Organization Chart—as an embedded object on a slide. When Microsoft Organization Chart activates, it also displays box tools (on a special bar called the *icon bar*) and its own menu bar so that you can use its commands.

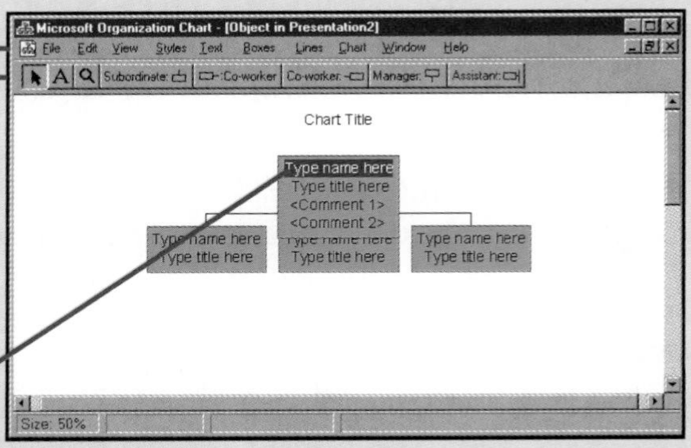

Figure 7.25
Microsoft Organization Chart displays in its own window.

Microsoft Organization Chart menu bar

Microsoft Organization Chart icon bar

Enter your information here

When you first open a new chart, the chart template displays with four boxes. The field names, such as name or title, act as placeholders for information that you type. You can enter information as you do in a word processor: by typing and revising text. Just click the box, type data, and then press Tab⇆ or ↵Enter to move to subsequent fields. Click outside the box when you finish. Try entering information by using these techniques now.

4 Type Lonnie Stegall, press ↵Enter, and then type President.
This enters the name and title into the top-level box.

5 Click in the lower-level boxes and enter the information shown in Figure 7.26; then click outside the boxes.

Figure 7.26
Enter the information shown to create an organization chart.

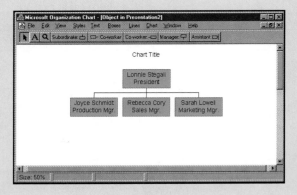

Notice that clicking outside a selected box (either in the background or another box) deselects it.

Now, you're ready to format the text you entered in the boxes. You can click a box to select all the text that it contains, or drag over just the characters you want. Choose Text, Font, or Text, Color to change the selected text's appearance. Try formatting the text now.

6 **Click in the top box, drag over Lonnie Stegall to select it, and then choose Text, Font from the Microsoft Organization Chart menu.**
The Font dialog box displays. You can use this dialog box to choose font or point size.

7 **Choose Impact, 16-point font, and then click OK. (If this font isn't available on your system, choose another font.)**
The selected font is formatted with the new font and point size. You can also select a box, and then change formatting for all the text included in the box. Try this now.

8 **Click the lower-left box, Joyce Schmidt, and choose Text, Color.**
The Color dialog box displays. The color you select is applied to all the text in the selected box.

9 **Click the red color, choose OK, and click outside the box to deselect it.**
The text in the selected box is formatted in red. Leave your presentation open for the next lesson, in which you modify your organization chart.

 Exam Note: **Selecting and Formatting Multiple Boxes**
You can select multiple boxes and apply formatting commands (such as changing text color) to the boxes simultaneously. To select more than one box, press and hold down ◆Shift while clicking the boxes you want.

Additionally, you can make formatting changes other than text and box color. For example, you can change how the boxes appear by choosing the Shadow or Border Style commands from the Boxes menu. You can modify text alignment by choosing Left, Right, or Center from the Text menu. To find out more about working with organization charts, open Microsoft Organization Chart, and then choose Help, Index.

Lesson 8: Modifying an Organization Chart

When you initially create an organization chart, PowerPoint automatically sets up the chart with a Manager box and three Subordinate boxes. However, this four-box organization chart is just a starting point. Unless your organization fits perfectly into this default setup, you'll need to make changes to the chart—such as adding, deleting, and generally restructuring the chart. Luckily, you can add Subordinates, Coworkers, Managers, and Assistants, as needed, by using the box tools on the icon bar.

To add new boxes, click the appropriate box tool, and then click the ***parent box***. The parent box is the existing box to which you want to attach the new one. For example, you can add an assistant to a manager by clicking the Assistant box tool and clicking the Manager box.

Table 7.2 summarizes the tools available on Microsoft Organization Chart's icon bar. You can use this table as a quick reference when working with organization charts.

Table 7.2 Microsoft organization chart icon bar tools

Icon Bar Tool	Function
[arrow]	Selects boxes or objects
[A]	Adds a text object to the organization chart
[magnifier]	Zooms the chart to larger or reduced views
Subordinate:	Adds a box directly below the selected (parent) box
:Co-worker	Adds a box to the left and at the same level as the selected (parent) box
Co-worker:	Adds a box to the right and at the same level as the selected (parent) box
Manager:	Adds a box directly above the selected (parent) box
Assistant:	Adds a box below and to the left of the selected (parent) box

You can also revise your chart by moving, formatting, and deleting boxes. Try modifying your organization chart by using these features now.

To Modify an Organization Chart

Assistant:

❶ **In the open organization chart window, click the Assistant box tool, and then click the Manager box (Lonnie Stegall, President).**
An Assistant-level box is added (see Figure 7.27). You enter information in this box as you did in Lesson 6.

Figure 7.27
You can easily add boxes to change your chart's structure.

Assistant box

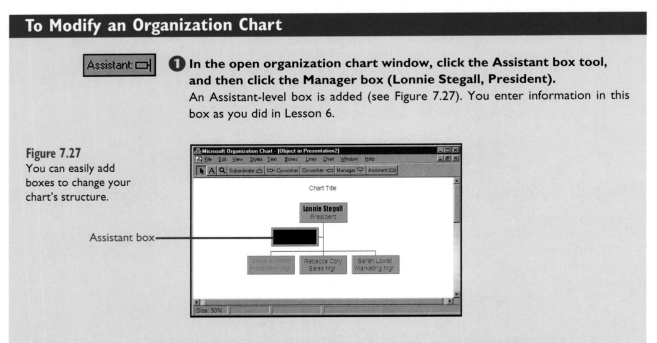

❷ **Type Betty Parks in the Assistant box, and then click outside of it.**
You can also select boxes and then format them by choosing Color or Shadow from the Boxes menu. When you finish, you can click in the background area to see the effects of your changes.

Before you apply formatting to your boxes, however, you must first select them. One quick way to select every box in your chart is to choose Edit, Select All. Alternatively, you can press Ctrl+A.

③ Choose Edit, Select All.

Your entire organization chart is selected (see Figure 7.28). The boxes are high-lighted and the lines show light gray dashes to indicate that they are also select-ed. After the boxes have been selected, you can format them to highlight information or for greater overall impact.

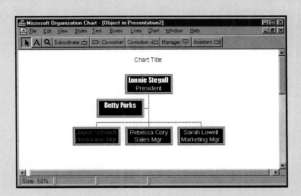

Figure 7.28
You can quickly select an entire organization chart and format it.

④ Choose Boxes, Color on Microsoft Organization Chart's menu bar.

The Color dialog box displays. You can choose a color from this dialog box, and then click OK to apply the color to the selected boxes.

⑤ Click the blue color box (the fourth from the left in the first row) and click OK.

The boxes display in blue, but are still selected. Now, try adding a shadow effect to the boxes.

⑥ With all boxes still selected, choose Boxes, Shadow to display a sub-menu (see Figure 7.29).

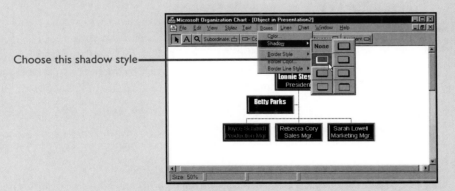

Choose this shadow style

Figure 7.29
You can enhance your chart by adding box shadows.

⑦ Click the shadow style indicated in Figure 7.29, and then click outside the boxes.

The selected shadow is applied to the boxes.

You can also move a box by dragging it to another location. Select the box you want to move, and then drag its border until it is on top of the box to which you want it attached. You can't just drop it next to the box because the program

continues ▶

To Modify an Organization Chart   (continued)

doesn't understand where you want the box placed. Keeping this in mind, move the Assistant box from its current location and attach it to Joyce Schmidt's box now.

8 **Select the Assistant box (Betty Parks), and then point to the border of the box until a white selection arrow appears.**
It's important to display this selection arrow before dragging the box. If the I-beam displays instead, you might accidentally place the box in editing mode (and expand it) when you start to drag it.

9 **Drag the Assistant box on top of (but slightly below) the Joyce Schmidt box until you see the special assistant pointer (see Figure 7.30). Release the mouse button.**

Figure 7.30
Modify your organization chart by dragging and dropping boxes to other locations.

Drag the Assistant box until you see this pointer

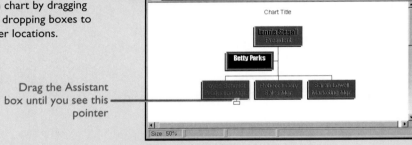

The Assistant box attaches to Joyce Schmidt's box.

You can also modify a chart's structure by deleting unwanted boxes. To remove a box, you select it, and then press Del.

10 **Select the Betty Parks box, if necessary, and then press Del.**
The box is removed from your chart. As usual, if you want to reverse the action, you can choose Edit, Undo. For now, you can leave the chart in its present state and close Microsoft Organization Chart to return to the presentation.

11 **In the Microsoft Organization Chart window, choose File, Exit and Return to Presentation.**
A confirmation box prompts you to update the organization chart in the presentation with the changes you made.

12 **Choose Yes to update the chart object, and then click outside the organization chart.**
Congratulations! You just added an organization chart to the presentation. If you later want to revise the chart, just double-click the organization chart object to launch the Microsoft Organization Chart program again.

13 **Save the presentation as My Organization, and then close it.**
If you finished your work session, exit PowerPoint and shut down Windows before turning off your computer. Otherwise, complete the exercises at the end of this project.

Summary

In this project, you learned the basics of creating charts in your PowerPoint presentations. First, you learned how to select which chart is most appropriate for the data you want to display. You used two peripheral programs—Microsoft Graph and Microsoft Organization Chart—to create and modify these charts. After you initially developed the charts, you explored ways of formatting and revising the charts.

To expand on your knowledge, spend a few minutes exploring Help on these topics. Additionally, complete some of the Skill Drill, Challenge, and Discovery Zone exercises.

Checking Concepts and Terms

True/False

For each of the following, check *T* or *F* to indicate whether the statement is true or false.

__T __F **1.** PowerPoint uses a peripheral program to create data charts. [L1]

__T __F **2.** Before you can change chart data, you must first activate the chart. [L3]

__T __F **3.** You can create an organization chart by using Word, a peripheral program. [L7]

__T __F **4.** You can enter or edit a data chart's information by using a datasheet. [L2–3]

__T __F **5.** A chart subtype is a variation of a main chart type. [L1, 5]

Multiple Choice

Circle the letter of the correct answer for each of the following questions.

1. The peripheral program that PowerPoint uses to create or revise data charts is called _____. [L2]
   a. Microsoft Datasheet
   b. Microsoft Organization Chart
   c. Microsoft Graph
   d. Microsoft PowerGraph

2. After a data chart has been created, you can _____. [L3–5]
   a. change the color of the data series
   b. change the chart type
   c. change the data
   d. all of the above

3. To activate Microsoft Graph and edit an existing data chart, _____. [L3]
   a. double-click the placeholder object that contains the chart
   b. click the Graphing Programs button on the Standard toolbar
   c. choose File, Graph from the menu bar
   d. all of the above

4. A pie chart is best used for showing _____. [L1]
   a. the relationship of parts to the whole
   b. data changes over time
   c. trends in data at equal intervals
   d. the magnitude of change over time

5. Which of the following is true regarding an organization chart? [L7–8]
   a. It is used to show changes over time.
   b. It is used to show stock prices in an organization.
   c. It shows comparisons of individual items.
   d. none of the above

Skill Drill

Skill Drill exercises reinforce project skills. Each skill reinforced is the same, or nearly the same, as a skill presented in the project. Detailed instructions are provided in a step-by-step format.

1. Using Help in the Microsoft Organization Chart Program

As assistant to the president of a large company, you're in charge of developing organization charts for each division. You're pleased that you can use the Microsoft Organization Chart from within PowerPoint, but need to know more about how to use the program more effectively. To do so, you use Help. [L7–8]

1. In PowerPoint, click the New button on the Standard toolbar to quickly create a new presentation.

2. In the New Slide dialog box that automatically displays, click the Organization Chart AutoLayout (the third AutoLayout on the second row), and then choose OK. Double-click the placeholder for the Organization Chart to open Microsoft Organization Chart.

3. On the Microsoft Organization Chart menu bar, choose Help, Index.

4. In the Microsoft Organization Chart Help window, click the first topic represented by a green hyperlink (Creating and updating charts). Click the second subtopic listed (Basic chart operations). Click the **Creating a new chart subtopic**.

5. Read through the information listed in the Help window, and then click the Back button twice (below the menu bar) to redisplay the main Microsoft Organization Chart Help window.

6. Choose the next subtopic (Opening and closing charts). Read through the information listed, and then click the Back button.

7. Continue to use the hyperlinks and the Back button to explore ways to create organization charts.

8. Click the close button in the upper-right corner of the Microsoft Organization Chart Help window. Also close Microsoft Organization Chart and your presentation without saving your work. Leave PowerPoint running if you plan to complete additional exercises.

2. Creating and Modifying a Line Chart

You need to show your boss that the cost of living is constantly rising, while your wages (adjusted for inflation, of course) are falling. Create a line chart to emphasize your point. [L2–5]

1. In PowerPoint, click the New button to create a new blank presentation.

2. In the New Slide dialog box, choose the Chart AutoLayout, and then click OK.

3. Click in the title placeholder; enter **I need a raise!** as the title for your slide.

4. Double-click the chart placeholder to activate Microsoft Graph. Enter the following information in the datasheet:

	Jan	Feb	March
Income	2000	1980	1967
Cost of Living	2000	2100	2150

5. Close the datasheet to display the chart as a column chart.

6. Choose Chart, Chart Type to display the Chart Type dialog box. Click Line in the Chart type list. Choose the **Line with markers** subtype (the first subtype on the second row). Click OK.

7. After looking over your data chart, you decide that you need to spiff it up with some formatting. Click the Chart Objects drop-down list arrow and choose **Series "Income"** from the list.

8. Choose Format, Selected Data Series from the menu bar. In the Line section, click the Weight drop-down list arrow and choose the thickest line available.

9. In the Format Data Series dialog box, click the Data Labels tab. Choose Show value, and then click OK.

10. Double-click the line that represents **Series "Cost of Living"** to display the Format Data Series dialog box. On the Data Labels page, choose Show value.

11. Click the Patterns page of the Format Data Series dialog box. Click the <u>W</u>eight drop-down list arrow and choose the thickest line. Choose OK to close the Format Data Series dialog box.

12. Click outside the chart to embed it as an object on your slide, and then print a copy of your slide.

13. Save the presentation as **Living Expenses**, and then close it. Leave PowerPoint running if you plan to complete additional exercises.

3. Creating and Modifying an Organization Chart

As secretary for the University Biking Club, you want to show how the club is structured. You decide to use an organization chart to do so. [L7–8]

1. In PowerPoint, click the New button to create a new blank presentation. In the New Slide dialog box, click the Organization Chart AutoLayout (the third AutoLayout on the second row). Click OK.

2. Click in the title placeholder and type **University Biking Club**.

3. Double-click the organization chart placeholder to activate Microsoft Organization Chart.

4. Enter the following data in the top-level box:

   Lucinda Samual, President

5. Enter the following data in the three lower-level boxes:

   Heather Parks, Vice President

   Grace Stegall, Treasurer

   David Reams, Secretary

6. Add an Assistant box to the President's box. To do this, click the Assistant box tool, and then click the President's box.

7. Enter **Sarah Jones, Assistant** in the Assistant box, and then click outside of it.

8. Press Ctrl+A to select all boxes and lines. Choose <u>B</u>oxes, <u>C</u>olor to display the Color dialog box. Click the gray color (the seventh color on the first row), and then choose OK.

9. Add a shadow effect. With your boxes still selected, choose <u>B</u>oxes, Shado<u>w</u>. From the Shado<u>w</u> sub-menu, choose the first shadow effect on the third row.

10. Change the text color by choosing <u>T</u>ext, <u>C</u>olor. In the Color dialog box, choose red (the last color on the first row), and then choose OK. Click outside the boxes to better view your changes.

11. Choose <u>F</u>ile, E<u>x</u>it and Return to Presentation. Choose <u>Y</u>es in the message box.

12. Save your presentation as **Club Organization**, and then close it. Leave PowerPoint running if you plan to complete additional exercises.

Challenge

Challenge exercises expand on, or are somewhat related to, skills presented in the lessons. Each exercise provides a brief narrative introduction, followed by instructions in a numbered-step format that are not as detailed as those in the Skill Drill section.

1. Creating, Formatting, and Animating a Data Chart

You need to create a presentation that includes sales data for your company. Because PowerPoint excels at creating good-looking charts, you decide to use it to develop the presentation. [L2–3, 5, 6]

1. Create a new blank presentation. For your first slide, create a slide based on the Chart AutoLayout.

2. Create a column chart with the title **Five Year Summary**, using the following data:

	1996	1997	1998	1999	2000
Sales	104	135	125	140	150
Expenses	65	89	67	60	88

3. Change the chart type to at least five other chart types. When you finish, change the chart to a 2-D horizontal bar chart.

4. Change the color for the Expenses data series to red. Change the color for the Sales data series to blue.

5. Add animation to the chart to display the information by Element in Category. Use Dissolve as the entry animation. View your animation in a slide show.

6. Save the presentation as **Sales Summary**. Print one copy of your presentation (as a slide); and then close it. Leave PowerPoint running if you plan to complete additional exercises.

2. Setting Up an Organization Chart

You are the communications director for a volunteer organization. To quickly get important information about upcoming meetings and events to those in your group, you create a phone tree using PowerPoint's organization chart feature. [L7–8]

1. Create a new blank presentation. For your first slide, create a slide based on the Organization Chart AutoLayout.

2. Enter **Phone Tree** in the title placeholder of the slide.

3. Add data to your organization chart so that it matches that shown in Figure 7.31.

4. Change the box color to white. Format the text in all boxes using Comic Sans, 12-point, blue font. Make the font bold.

5. Add a shadow effect of your choice to all the boxes.

6. Save the presentation as **Phone Tree**.

7. Print a copy of the organization chart, and then close the presentation. Leave PowerPoint running if you plan to complete additional exercises.

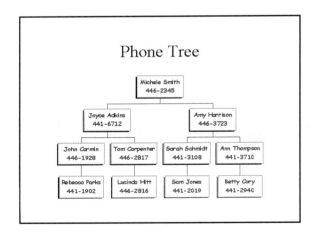

Figure 7.31
Use this figure as your guide.

3. Changing Chart Types and Formatting a Chart

You previously created a stacked column chart that shows expenses as a percentage of income. To spiff up the chart, you decide to change colors and patterns. [L4–5]

1. Open **PP-0704** and save it as **Income**. Activate Microsoft Graph.

2. Using the Chart Type drop-down list, change the chart to each of the following types:
   - Area Chart
   - 3-D Area Chart
   - 3-D Surface Chart

- Bar Chart

- 3-D Bar Chart

- Radar Chart

- Column Chart

- 3-D Column Chart

- Line Chart

- 3-D Line Chart

- (XY) Scatter Chart

- 3-D Cylinder Chart

- 3-D Cone Chart

- 3-D Pyramid Chart

3. Change the chart to a 3-D bar chart. Display the Chart Type dialog box. Choose the Stacked bar with a 3-D visual effect type, and then click OK.

4. Format the Income data series in blue. Choose a Gradient fill effect (*Hint:* Click the Fill Effects button in the Format Data Series dialog box.) Choose a Vertical Shading style.

5. Format the Expenses data series in red. Also apply a Gradient fill effect with the same Vertical Shading style you used for the Income data series.

6. Save, print, and close your Income presentation. Leave PowerPoint running if you plan to complete additional exercises.

Discovery Zone

Discovery Zone exercises require advanced knowledge of topics presented in *MOUS Essentials* lessons, application of skills from multiple lessons, or self-directed learning of new skills.

1. Finding Out More about Microsoft Graph

You're a newly hired employee in the Information System Department. Charts are extremely popular at your organization. So that you can do a better job of helping those in your company, you decide to research how to use Microsoft Graph more effectively. [L2–6]

Using the Help system in Microsoft Graph, find out the following:

- How can you format data series by using various fill effects?

- What options are available to format a legend?

- What options are available to format a chart's background?

- What options are available to format data walls and gridlines?

- How can you change a column chart to other shapes (such as pyramids)?

- How can you change one data series to a cone shape and another data series (on the same chart) to a cylinder shape?

- What is the purpose of a radar chart?

- How can you use a doughnut chart?

- What similarities are there between doughnut charts and pie charts? What differences are there between them?

- What are some methods you can use to animate the chart?

Outline the information you find in a logical, easy-to-follow sequence. (If you're familiar with Word, consider entering this information in a Word document.)

Practice by using each of the features that you researched on a chart, and present the information to at least one other user.

2. Finding Out More about Microsoft Organization Chart

Several people in your business use organization charts. You decide to research how to use the Microsoft Organization Chart program more effectively. [L7–8]

Using the Help system in Microsoft Organization Chart, find out the following:

- Which options are available to format lines on your chart?
- Which options are available to format boxes on your chart?
- How can you change background color for your chart?
- How do you align text?
- What are different ways of selecting boxes?
- How can you use a different layout (or style) for your chart?
- How can you adjust the view to better see your chart?
- What drawing tools are available in Microsoft Organization Chart? How are they used?
- How can you change the default setup for a new organization chart so that only one box is initially displayed?

Outline the information you find in a logical, easy-to-follow sequence. (If you're familiar with Word, consider entering this information in a Word document.)

Practice by using each of the features that you researched on a chart, and present the information to at least one other user.

PinPoint Assessment

You have completed this project and its associated lessons, and have had an opportunity to assess your skills through the end-of-project questions and exercises. Now use the PinPoint software Evaluation Mode to further assess your comprehension of the specific exam activities you have just learned. You can also use the PinPoint Trainer Mode and the Show Me tutorials to practice these exam activities.

Automating Electronic Slide Shows

Key terms introduced in this project include

- action items
- annotate
- annotation pen
- build
- multimedia
- slide transitions

Objectives	Required Activity for MOUS	Exam Level
➤ Adding Slide Transitions	Add slide transitions	Core
	Hide slides	Expert
➤ Adding Text Animation	Animate text and objects	Core
➤ Animating Objects	Animate text and objects	Core
	Apply animation effects	Expert
➤ Timing the Slide Show Presentation	Set automatic slide timings	Expert
➤ Using the Annotation Pen	Use the pen during a presentation	Core
➤ Using the Meeting Minder	Generate meeting notes	Expert
	Electronically incorporate meeting feedback	Expert

Why Would I Do This?

When you're giving a presentation, you want to make the strongest possible impression. Although your content should be center stage, PowerPoint includes a number of techniques you can use to emphasize the content *and* command your audience's attention at the same time. In this project, you learn a variety of ways to automate your presentation. Each of the techniques can help focus your audience's attention on your ideas.

One way to keep people's attention is to change the way PowerPoint displays the next slide—the program's slide transitions. Another way to create anticipation (and control the flow of information) is to animate the text so that your bullet points display one at a time. You can also animate objects to control the flow of information and redirect the audience's attention.

Finally, to help you keep track of ideas that pop up during a presentation, you can use the Meeting Minder. You use this feature to develop meeting minutes or ***action items*** onscreen. When you enter information in the Meeting Minder dialog box, for example, PowerPoint automatically creates a set of action items as a new presentation slide. As a finishing touch for your presentation, you can even print this slide and hand it out to participants as they leave.

To make your presentations more compelling, attention getting, and professional, take a look at these techniques now.

Lesson 1: Adding Slide Transitions

In Project 2, "Creating Presentations," you learned how to move through a presentation in Slide Show view. By now, you've probably run some other slide shows as well. As you ran the slide shows, you probably noticed that each new slide instantly replaced the previous one.

However, you'll be glad to know that you can change the way that one slide moves to the next by using a ***slide transition***. A slide transition is a visual effect that changes how one slide replaces another. Using PowerPoint's built-in slide transitions help you make more of an impact during an onscreen presentation. For example, you can set up a slide to fade, wipe, or dissolve into another. Table 8.1 describes some popular transition effects.

Table 8.1 Popular transitional effects

Transition Effect	Description
Blinds	Opens the screen in wide, even strips horizontally or vertically
Box In or Out	Redraws the screen from the center outward or from the outside to the center, using a box shape
Checkerboard	Changes the screen with a checkerboard pattern, either across or down
Cover	Redraws the screen as the new slide covers up the previous one
Fade Through Black	Fades away the old slide, shows black momentarily, and then fades in the new slide
Split	Redraws the screen by splitting it in different directions
Uncover	Opens the screen like a curtain, in a variety of directions
Wipe	Sweeps the screen in a choice of directions

The easiest way to add a transition is to use the Slide Transition Effects drop-down list, which is available on the Slide Sorter toolbar. Try adding some transition effects now.

To Add Slide Transitions

1 **Start PowerPoint, if necessary. Open** PP-0801 **and save it as** Quality Children's Clothing.

2 **Click the Slide Sorter View button to display the presentation in Slide Sorter view.**

Notice that the Slide Sorter toolbar automatically displays whenever Slide Sorter view is used (see Figure 8.1). You can use the Slide Sorter toolbar to add or change transition effects.

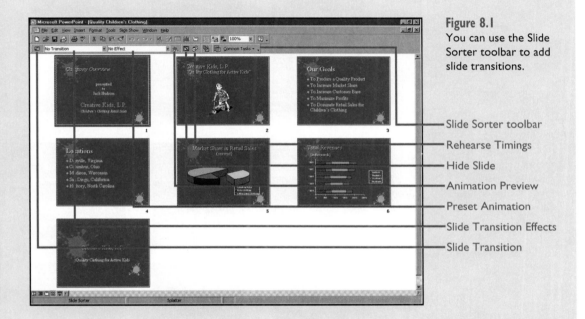

Figure 8.1
You can use the Slide Sorter toolbar to add slide transitions.

Slide Sorter toolbar
Rehearse Timings
Hide Slide
Animation Preview
Preset Animation
Slide Transition Effects
Slide Transition

3 **With Slide 1 selected, click the Slide Transition Effects drop-down arrow.**

A list of transition effects displays, as shown in Figure 8.2. You can choose an effect, and then preview it in Slide Sorter view.

4 **Choose Blinds Horizontal from the list.**

The transition effect is added for the selected slide and a slide transition icon is shown below the slide (see Figure 8.3). You can click this icon to preview the effect, which is handy because you don't have to run a slide show just to see how the transitions will look. Try using this feature now.

continues ▶

To Add Slide Transitions   (continued)

Figure 8.2
PowerPoint provides a number of transition effects.

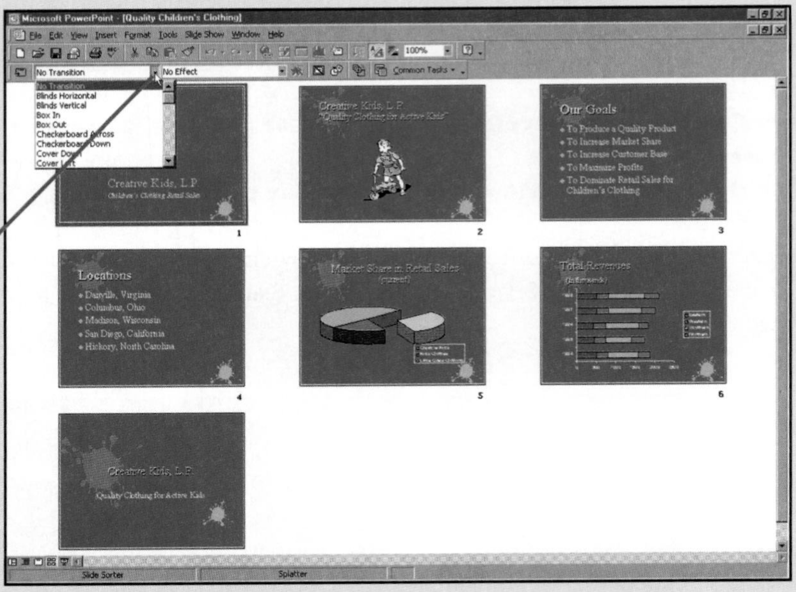

Click here to display a list of transition effects

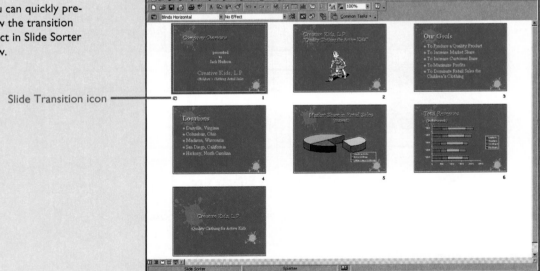

Figure 8.3
You can quickly preview the transition effect in Slide Sorter view.

Slide Transition icon

⑤ Click the Slide Transition icon for Slide 1.
Slide 1 displays a preview of the transition effect.

By now, you're probably convinced that it's helpful to judiciously add transitions to your slides. You'd like a more efficient method to do so than to add one transition at a time, however. Fortunately, you can select several slides and add the same transition to them simultaneously. Using this technique, try changing the transition effect for multiple slides at once.

6 **Click Slide 3, press ⬆Shift, and click Slides 4 and 5.**

A thick black line displays around each slide, indicating that they are selected.

7 **Click the Slide Transition Effects drop-down list arrow, and then choose Checkerboard Across.**

The transition effect is applied to the selected slides. Remember that you can tell whether a slide has a transition effect added because a slide icon displays beneath the slide.

Now, see how your transitions look by running the presentation as a slide show.

8 **Select Slide 1, and then choose View, Slide Show.**

9 **Click the left mouse button several times to advance completely through the slide show.**

The transitions you specified are used as you move through the slides. When you finish the slide show, the presentation again displays in Slide Sorter view.

After viewing your transitions, you might decide that you want to remove one of them. (After all, too many transitions might become distracting to your audience!) You're in luck—it's easy to remove a slide transition. Just select the slide, and then choose No Transition from the Slide Transition Effects drop-down arrow list. Try this now.

10 **Select Slide 3, click the Slide Transition Effects drop-down arrow list, and choose No Transition.**

The transition is removed from the selected slide and the Slide Transition icon no longer displays. (If you want, rerun the slide show to view this change before continuing with the tutorial.)

Save the presentation, but keep it open for the next exercise, in which you add animations to your bulleted text.

Exam Note: **Hiding Slides**

You can hide, or suppress the display of a slide during a slide show. For example, you might want to develop a slide with documentation or statistics you can use "just in case" a question arises on the topic during your presentation—but you normally don't expect to use it. To hide the slide, first display the presentation in Slide Sorter view. Select the slide and then click the Hide Slide button. During the slide show press Ⓗ to display the hidden slide.

Inside Stuff: **Adding Sounds to Transitions**

If you have a sound card and speaker, you can spice up your presentation even more by adding sound during the transition. Choose Slide Show, Slide Transition to display the Slide Transition dialog box. In the Sound section, click the drop-down list arrow and choose a sound. Choose Apply to associate the sound with the selected slide or Apply to All to add it to all slides. When you run the slide show, the sound will play during the transition.

Lesson 2: Adding Text Animation

An effective way to grab an audience's attention is to animate your text during a slide show so you can help them focus on important points, control the flow of information, or just add interest to your presentation. For example, you can have your bullet points display one by one (a process that's generally referred to as *building* or animating) to prevent your audience from losing focus by reading ahead on a slide. Text animation is a feature that operates independently from the slide transitions feature that you learned about in Lesson 1. In other words, you can add a slide transition to a slide, text animation, or both.

Try adding animation to bulleted text on a slide now.

To Add Text Animation

① **Make sure that the Quality Children's Clothing presentation is open in Slide Sorter view, and then select Slide 3, if necessary.**
Because Slide 3 has bullet points, you can set up the slide so that PowerPoint builds them separately.

② **From the Slide Sorter toolbar, click the Preset Animation drop-down arrow.**
A list of available methods for building your bulleted list displays (see Figure 8.4). When you select one of these methods, PowerPoint automatically builds the text one point at a time.

Figure 8.4
You can build bullet points in a number of ways.

Click this arrow to display a list of text animation effects

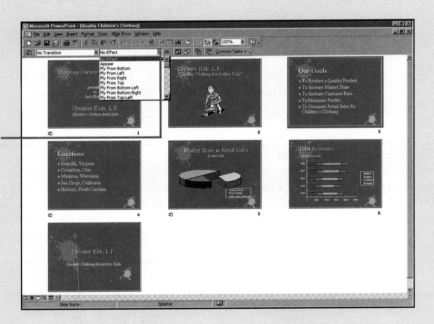

③ **Select Fly From Bottom-Left.**
PowerPoint shows the way the animation looks on the slide, which helps you decide whether you want to use the animation or not. Additionally, a special Text Animation icon displays at the bottom of the slide, as shown in Figure 8.5, indicating that Slide 3 is a build slide. (If the animation occurred too quickly, you can replay it by clicking the Text Animation icon.)

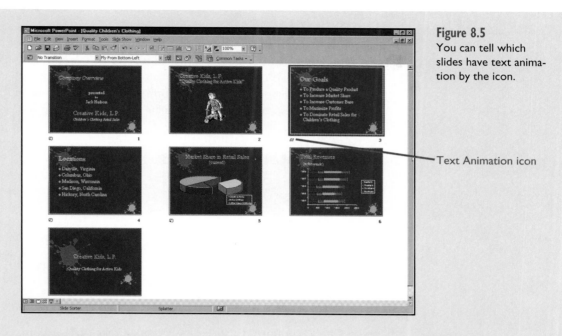

Figure 8.5
You can tell which slides have text animation by the icon.

Text Animation icon

4 **Click the Slide Show button.**
The slide show begins, starting with the selected slide (Slide 3).

5 **Click the left mouse button several times.**
PowerPoint builds the slide, one bullet point at a time, whenever you click the mouse button (or press Enter). After all of the slide text displays, clicking the mouse button advances the presentation to the next slide.

6 **Press Esc to end the slide show and redisplay the presentation in Slide Sorter view.**
Save the presentation and keep it open for the next lesson, in which you learn to customize your animation effects.

Lesson 3: Animating Objects

In the preceding lesson you learned how to animate, or build text on a slide, and in Project 7, "Working with Charts," you added animation to chart elements. From these experiences, you've probably already realized that you can animate almost any object—including clip art images, placeholders, and drawn objects—on a slide. In this lesson you'll expand your previous knowledge and learn to animate other objects on a slide.

To Animate Objects

1 **Display Slide 2 of the Quality Children's Clothing presentation in Normal view.**
You should display a slide in Normal or Slide view to add custom animation. (Also make sure there are no objects, such as placeholders, selected before continuing with the next step.)

continues ▶

To Animate Objects (continued))

2 **Choose Slide Show, Custom Animation, then click the Order & Timing tab.**

The Order & Timing page of the Custom Animation dialog box displays (see Figure 8.6). You use this page to determine which objects you want to animate, and in what order.

Figure 8.6
Determine which objects to animate on this page.

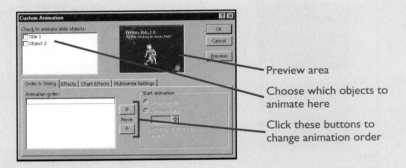

Preview area

Choose which objects to animate here

Click these buttons to change animation order

3 **In the Check to animate slide objects area, click the box for Title 1.**

The title is placed on the Animation order list. Additionally, the title placeholder in the Preview area is selected so you can confirm which object you picked (Figure 8.7).

Figure 8.7
Checking an object automatically places it on the Animation order list.

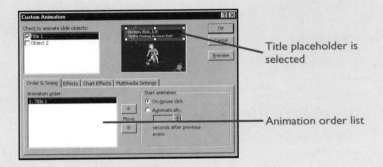

Title placeholder is selected

Animation order list

4 **Check the box for Object 2 (the clip art).**

The Object is added to the Animation order list. Now preview your animation.

5 **Click the Preview button.**

The title placeholder displays first, followed by the clip art object. By default, both objects used the Fly From Left effect. Try using and previewing other effects.

6 **Click the Effects tab.**

The Effects page of the Custom Animation dialog box displays (see Figure 8.8). You use this page to choose the specific type of animation effect you want to use for your objects.

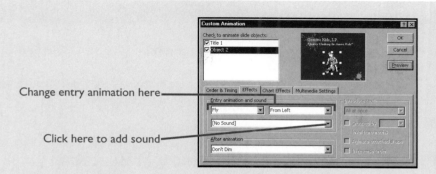

Figure 8.8
Change the animation effect for each object on this page.

Change entry animation here

Click here to add sound

7 **Click the Title 1 object on the list, then click the leftmost arrow in the Entry animation and sound area.**

A list of animation effects you can use to introduce your objects displays.

8 **Choose Zoom.**

The entry animation effect is set for Zoom. Now try changing the effect for the clip art object.

9 **Select Object 2 on the list, then click the rightmost arrow in the Entry animation and sound area. Choose From Right.**

Now add sound to the object.

10 **With Object 2 still selected, click the sound arrow in the Entry animation and sound area.**

A list of sound effects you can add to your animation displays (see Figure 8.9). Assuming you have the correct equipment, the sound will play when the object initially displays.

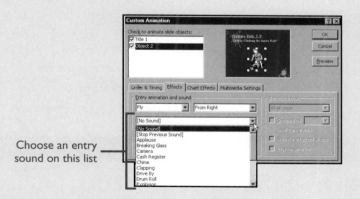

Figure 8.9
You can make sound play when your object displays.

Choose an entry sound on this list

11 **Scroll through the sound list, and then choose Whoosh.**

Now try previewing the animation.

12 **Click the Preview button.**

The effects you added are displayed. Next try viewing the animation in a full-screen electronic slide show.

13 **Choose OK to close the Animation Effects dialog box, and then click the Slide Show button.**

14 **Advance through your slide show by clicking the left mouse button until you've viewed all the animations on Slide 2.**

continues ▶

To Animate Objects   (continued)

15 Press Esc to end the slide show, and then save your Quality Children's Clothing presentation.
Leave the presentation open for the next exercise, in which you time the slide show.

Lesson 4: Timing the Slide Show Presentation

Because no one has an unlimited amount of time to give to a presentation, timing the slide show for the greatest impact is important. That's why PowerPoint includes a feature that you can use to find out how long you're spending on each slide, as well as to track the presentation's overall length.

You can set up your slide show to display a new slide automatically after a certain number of seconds or change slides only when the left mouse button is clicked. If you plan to use the slide show as a self-running presentation (such as at a trade show), you may opt for the former method. If you are presenting the show to a live audience, you'll definitely want control by using manual advance. Keep in mind that you don't want to spend so long on a slide that your audience loses attention, however. The general rule when using manual advancement is to allow a maximum of two–three minutes per slide.

Even if you use manual advance, you can rehearse your presentation by using the slide timings. This is a good way of measuring the overall length of the presentation. Here's how: Click the Rehearse Timings button to start your presentation as a slide show. Talk through your presentation as if you're presenting it to a live audience. When you finish, you'll have a good idea of the overall length of the presentation, as well as the time spent on each individual slide.

In contrast, automatic advancement is great if you have an onscreen show that you want to run continually (at a trade show exhibit, for example). When using automatic advancement, you need to spend only as much time on a slide as the average person needs to read it. If the slide stays onscreen too long, people lose interest.

Keeping these benefits in mind, try rehearsing your timings now.

To Time the Slide Show Presentation

 1 Display the Quality Children's Clothing presentation in Slide Sorter view, and then select Slide 1.

 2 On the Slide Sorter toolbar, click the Rehearse Timings button.
The slide show begins—but with a difference. A Rehearsal dialog box displays and keeps track of how many seconds you show each slide. This dialog box also records the overall length of the presentation (see Figure 8.10).

3 **After five seconds, click the left mouse button to advance to Slide 2.**

4 **In slides 2–6, set timings of your choice (pause from 3–10 seconds per slide or bullet point before clicking the mouse button to proceed).**
When you finish going through the entire show, PowerPoint displays a message box so you can decide whether you want to keep the timings as part of your presentation (see Figure 8.11).

Figure 8.11
PowerPoint confirms
that you want to save
the new timings.

5 **Choose Yes.**
The slides display in Slide Sorter view, including the number of seconds after which each slide will advance (see Figure 8.12).

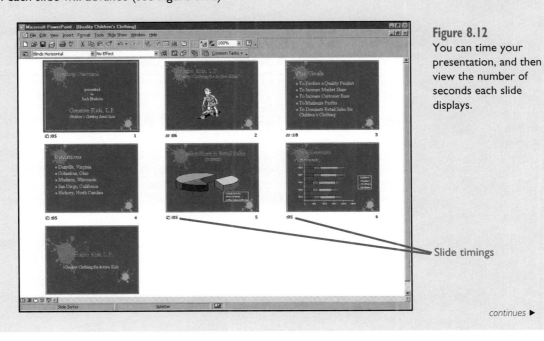

Figure 8.12
You can time your
presentation, and then
view the number of
seconds each slide
displays.

Slide timings

continues ▶

To Time the Slide Show Presentation   (continued)

Now, view your electronic slide show with the new timings.

 Select Slide 1, and then click the Slide Show button to start the slide show.
The show advances through the slides using the timings you specified.

7 When the slide show finishes and the black screen displays, click to exit the slide show.
The presentation displays in Slide Sorter view.

 If You Have Problems...
By default, PowerPoint 2000 ends each slide show with a black slide so that the audience redirects their attention to you. It's possible that this option may have been turned off for your system, however. If you like the effect, here's how to turn it back on: Choose <u>T</u>ools, <u>O</u>ptions, and then click the View tab. Check the <u>E</u>nd with a black slide box before clicking OK to close the Options dialog box.

---

8 Save the Quality Children's Clothing presentation, and then close it.
Keep PowerPoint open for the next lesson, in which you learn efficient methods of moving among slide show slides.

Exam Note: **Setting Up Self-Running Presentations**
If you want to use your slide show as a self-running presentation (such as at a trade show), set your slide timings just as you learned in this lesson. Then choose Sli<u>d</u>e Show, <u>S</u>et Up Show to display the Set Up Show dialog box. Choose **Loop continuously until 'Esc'**. Click OK when you finish.

For even more control over a self-running presentation, you can choose **Browsed at a kiosk (full screen)** in the Set Up Show dialog box. This runs the slide show full-screen continuously and restarts the show after five minutes of inactivity. The audience can advance slides manually, but can't make changes to the presentation.

Finally, you can add *multimedia* effects, such as music, sound, and videos to your presentation. To find out how to enhance your presentation with these effects, look at the Multimedia topic on Help's <u>C</u>ontents page.

 # Lesson 5: Using the Annotation Pen

Have you ever wished that you could write or draw on a slide during a slide show? Perhaps you want to draw attention to specific information or recapture your audience's attention. Luckily, PowerPoint provides an ***annotation pen***, which is an electronic pen that you use with the mouse to ***annotate*** the slide. Annotating is writing or drawing directly on the slide, and is an effective method of emphasizing information.

The comments you write are not permanent—when you display another slide, they're automatically erased. Alternatively, you can erase the notations but continue to display the slide.

For even more impact, you can change annotation pen colors. You might use white for most of the points that you're trying to make, for example, and then switch to orange for added emphasis. Try using the pen in a presentation now.

To Use the Annotation Pen

1 Open **PP-0802** and save it as `Recruiting TechHeads`.

2 Display Slide 3, and then click the Slide Show button.

The slide show begins. To use the pen, you must activate it. You do this by choosing P<u>e</u>n from the slide show shortcut menu.

3 Right-click to display the shortcut menu, then choose P<u>o</u>inter Options, P<u>e</u>n.
The pointer changes to an electronic annotation pen. You can use this pen to draw by holding down the left mouse button and dragging.

4 Drag to draw an arrow emphasizing the salary progression from Systems Support to Systems Analyst (refer to Figure 8.13).

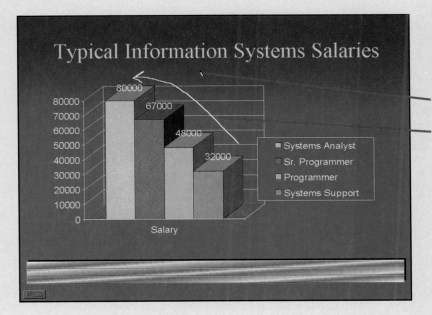

Figure 8.13
You can use the annotation pen to emphasize your points.

Use the annotation pen...

...to create this freehand drawing

The annotation is automatically erased whenever you move to another slide. If you want to continue to display the current slide (but erase the drawing), press E. Try this now.

5 Press E.
The drawing is erased. Notice that your pen is still active so that you can write other comments. Or you can activate the arrow, which automatically turns off the pen. The easiest way to turn off the pen is to press Esc.

6 Press Esc.
The arrow mouse pointer displays and the electronic pen is turned off.

Now, try an alternative method of turning on the pen—by pressing Ctrl+P. This method is not only quicker, but also more popular because the audience doesn't see the shortcut menu. Try activating the pen by using this technique.

7 Press Ctrl+P.
The electronic pen is activated. Now, try changing the pen color.

continues ▶

To Use the Annotation Pen   (continued)

8 **Right-click to display the shortcut menu, and then choose Pointer Options, Pen Color.**
A submenu displays with a list of available pen colors (see Figure 8.14).

Figure 8.14
You can choose from a variety of pen colors.

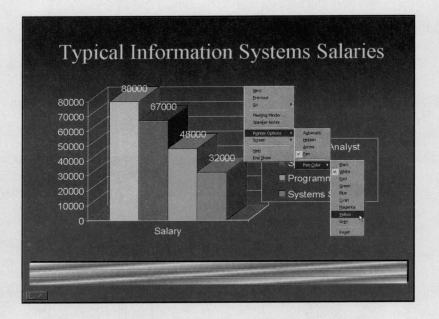

9 **Choose Yellow, and then draw freehand on your slide to see the new pen color.**
The drawing displays, using the color you indicated.

Earlier in this lesson, you saw how to use the keyboard shortcut Ctrl+P to display the pen. Now, try using a keyboard shortcut to switch back to the arrow.

10 **Press Ctrl+A.**
The pen icon changes to an arrow mouse pointer.

11 **Save and close your Recruiting Technical Personnel presentation.**
Leave PowerPoint running for the next lesson, in which you use the Meeting Minder.

 If You Have Problems...
When the annotation pen is active, clicking the left mouse button won't advance the slide show to the next screen, but just produces a dot on-screen. Press Esc (or Ctrl+A) to change the annotation pen back to an arrow, and then click.

Lesson 6: Using the Meeting Minder

The Meeting Minder is a PowerPoint feature that helps you take electronic notes during a presentation. You can use this tool to take minutes or record action items. Action items are any items that you want to assign to people during a meeting. You can display these items on a new slide at the end of your slide show or even print them.

The Meeting Minder is especially useful during an informal presentation, such as a staff meeting or brainstorming session. Try using this feature now.

To Use the Meeting Minder

1 **Open PP-0803 and save it as Recruiting Plan.**

2 **Display Slide 4, and then click the Slide Show button.**
This starts the presentation, beginning with the current slide.

3 **Right-click the mouse to display the shortcut menu, and then choose Meeting Minder.**
The Meeting Minder dialog box displays with two tabs: Meeting Minutes and Action Items (see Figure 8.15). You can click the tab you want, and then enter information.

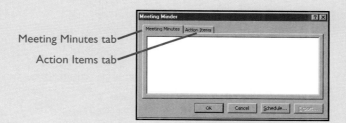

Meeting Minutes tab
Action Items tab

Figure 8.15
You can use the Meeting Minder to document your meeting and create action items.

4 **Click the Action Items tab to display the Action Items page (see Figure 8.16).**

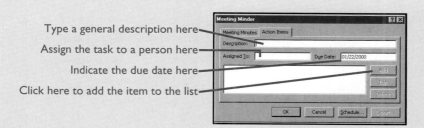

Type a general description here
Assign the task to a person here
Indicate the due date here
Click here to add the item to the list

Figure 8.16
You can enter action items by using the Meeting Minder.

5 **In the Description text box, type Attend job fairs at top colleges and universities to recruit employees, and then press Tab.**
The text you typed is entered in the text box and the insertion point moves to the Assigned To text box.

6 **Type L. Schmidt, and then press Tab.**
The insertion point moves to the Due Date text box. By default, this text box displays the current system date.

continues ▶

To Use the Meeting Minder   (continued)

7 **Enter 6/12/2000 to replace the current system date.**

After you create the basic information for an action item, you add it to the list.

8 **Click Add to place the item on the list.**

The action item displays on the list and the text boxes clear so that you can enter other tasks.

9 **Enter the following items in the Action Items page of the Meeting Minder dialog box:**

Description	Assigned To	Due Date
Coordinate advertising in national computer magazines	S. Black	2/7/2000
Network with other businesses	J. Reams	3/24/2000

10 **Choose OK to close the Meeting Minder dialog box.**

PowerPoint automatically creates a slide with the action items you entered and places it at the end of the presentation.

11 **Press Esc to end the slide show, and then press Ctrl+End.**

The slide show ends and the last slide—your action items—displays, as shown in Figure 8.17. You can display the slide, or print it to hand to your participants as they leave.

Figure 8.17
You can create an Action Items slide.

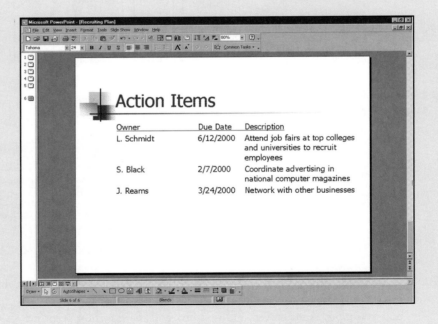

12 **With the Action Items slide displayed in Normal view, choose File, Print.**

The Print dialog box displays.

13 **Make sure that Current slide is chosen in the Print range section, and then choose OK.**

The Action Items slide prints.

14 **Save the presentation, and then close it.**

Leave PowerPoint running if you plan to complete the Skill Drill, Challenge, and Discovery Zone exercises at the end of this project. Otherwise, make sure to exit PowerPoint and shut down Windows properly before turning off your computer.

Exam Note: **Exporting Your Meeting Minutes to Word or Outlook**

You can export your meeting minutes (or action items) to Word or Outlook. To send the information to Word, click the Export button in the Meeting Minder dialog box. In the Meeting Minder Export dialog box, check the box to Send meeting minutes and action items to Microsoft Word, and then choose Export Now.

To add the information from the Meeting Minder to your Outlook calendar, click Schedule in the Meeting Minder dialog box.

Summary

In this project you learned some methods for spicing up your presentation when you run it as an onscreen slide show. You learned how to add transitions and animations to your slides to control the flow of information and keep your audience's attention. You also learned how to rehearse and time a slide show, so you can check its overall length, and as a preliminary step when you want your presentation to advance automatically. Finally, you practiced using the annotation pen and creating action items with the Meeting Minder feature.

To expand on your knowledge, spend a few minutes exploring Help on these topics. Additionally, complete some of the Skill Drill, Challenge, and Discovery Zone exercises.

Checking Concepts and Terms

True/False

For each of the following, circle *T* or *F* to indicate whether the statement is true or false.

__T __F **1.** You can use the Meeting Minder to create action items. [L6]

__T __F **2.** After you assign slide timings, they display in Slide Sorter view. [L3]

__T __F **3.** The only way to erase an annotation pen drawing is to advance to the next slide. [L4]

__T __F **4.** You can't add both a slide transition and a text animation to the same slide. [L1–2]

__T __F **5.** Annotation refers to the way bullet points display on a slide. [L5]

Multiple Choice

Circle the letter of the correct answer for each of the following questions.

1. You can use _____ to record action
items. [L5–6]

   a. Minute Taker

   b. Meeting Minder

   c. Notes Pages view

   d. annotation pen

2. The annotation pen is used to _____.
[L5–6]

   a. highlight information during an onscreen presentation

   b. create a list of action items

   c. take meeting minutes

   d. draw objects in Slide Sorter view

3. When you use the Action Items feature,
_____. [L6]

   a. PowerPoint automatically prints your presentation as an outline

   b. your speaker notes are updated

   c. an Action Items slide is automatically created

   d. action, or animation, is added to all bullet points

4. Blinds, Checkerboard Across, and Box In are all examples of _____. [L1, 5–6]

   a. annotations

   b. action items

   c. meeting minutes

   d. slide transitions

5. You might want to add text or object animation to
your bullet points _____. [L2–3]

   a. to control the flow of information

   b. to keep your audience from reading ahead

   c. to increase interest

   d. all of the above

Skill Drill

Skill Drill exercises reinforce project skills. Each skill reinforced is the same, or nearly the same, as a skill presented in the project. Detailed instructions are provided in a step-by-step format.

1. Using Help to Find Out About Slide Shows

You conduct a lot of meetings for a volunteer organization. To help you run the meetings more effectively, you use PowerPoint's slide show feature. To learn more about slide shows, you use Help. [L1, 4]

1. Start PowerPoint, if necessary, and make sure the Office Assistant is turned off. Choose <u>H</u>elp, Microsoft PowerPoint <u>H</u>elp. If necessary, click the Show button to split the window into two panes.

2. On the <u>C</u>ontents page, double-click the Running and Controlling a Slide Show icon. Click each of the following topics (write down what you learn about running a slide show before advancing to the next topic):

   ■ **Different ways to run a presentation**

   ■ **Start a slide show**

   ■ **Write or draw (annotate) on slides during a slide show**

   ■ **Hide the slide show pointer during a slide show**

   ■ **Set up a slide show to run in a continuous loop**

   ■ **Slide show controls**

3. Close the Help window.

4. Practice what you learned about running slide shows, using your notes as a guide.

5. Share what you learn with at least one other user. Leave PowerPoint running if you plan to complete additional exercises.

2. Adding Transitions and Animations

You're scheduled to conduct a new employee orientation session, but you're concerned that your audience will be bored with the information. To make the meeting more interesting, you decide to add slide transitions and text animations. [L1–2]

1. Open **PP-0804** and save it as **Spiffed-Up Orientation Session**. Display the presentation in Slide Sorter view and select Slide 1.

2. Click the Slide Transition Effects drop-down list arrow, and then choose Box In as the transition.

3. Select Slide 2, click the Slide Transition Effects drop-down list arrow, and choose Box Out.

4. Select Slides 3–4, click the Slide Transition Effects drop-down list, and choose Checkerboard Across.

5. Select Slide 5, click the Preset Animation drop-down list, and choose Crawl From Left.

6. Select Slide 6, click the Preset Animation drop-down list, and choose Spiral.

7. Select Slide 1, and then click the Slide Show button to run your presentation as a slide show. When you're finished, make sure the presentation displays in Slide Sorter view.

8. To get an idea of the overall presentation length, you record it by using the slide show timings.

9. Select Slide 1, and then click the Rehearse Timings button to set slide timings. Make each slide display for 5–10 seconds (with the exception of Slide 5, which takes longer to display because the text animation is slow).

10. In the Microsoft PowerPoint message box, choose Yes to accept the slide timings, and then view them in Slide Sorter view.

11. Click the Slide Show button to automatically run the slide show with the slide timings you set.

12. In Slide Sorter view, click the Rehearse Timings button again and set new timings. Choose Yes to accept the slide timings.

13. Run the slide show again, and then save and close the presentation. Leave PowerPoint running if you plan to complete the next exercise.

3. Using the Annotation Pen and Using Animations

You're trying to convince your parents that you need more money for college expenses. To do so, you give a presentation to them on college expenses, using the annotation pen to emphasize your main points. [L1–2, 5]

1. Open **PP-0805** and save it as **College is Expensive**. Display the first presentation slide, and then click the Slide Show button.

2. When Slide 1 displays in the slide show, press Ctrl+P to display the annotation pen. Use the pen to underline the word **successful** on the slide.

3. Press Esc (or Ctrl+A) to switch the pen to an arrow. Display Slide 3 in your slide show.

4. Right-click on the slide to display the slide show shortcut menu. Choose Pointer Options, Pen Color, Red.

5. Draw a line from the 1st year column to the 3rd year column to illustrate the increasing costs of college. Circle the words **Costs are rising!**. Press Esc (or Ctrl+A) to switch the pen back to a pointer.

6. Press ↵Enter to display the last presentation slide. Reactivate the pen, then use it to circle the word **ME**. Press E to erase the annotation on the slide. Press Esc to end the slide show.

7. Now add some animations and transitions. Click the Slide Sorter View button. In Slide Sorter view, click Slide 1 to select it. Click the Slide Transition Effects drop-down list arrow, and then choose Fade Through Black.

8. Click Slide 2 to select it. On the Slide Transition Effects drop-down list, choose Dissolve. With Slide 2 still selected, click the Preset Animation drop-down list arrow, and choose Zoom In From Screen Center.

9. Select Slide 3, and then choose Slide Show, Slide Transition from the menu bar. In the Effect section of the Slide Transition dialog box, click the drop-down list arrow. Choose Box In for the slide transition.

10. In the Slide Transition dialog box, click the Sound drop-down list arrow, and choose Cash Register from the list. Click the Apply button to add the sound and transition effects to Slide 3.

11. Click Slide 4 to select it, click the Slide Transition Effects drop-down list arrow, and choose Blinds Vertical.

12. Click Slide 1, and then press F5 to run your presentation as a slide show. Press ⏎Enter as many times as is necessary to completely advance through the slide show.

13. Save your College is Expensive presentation, and then close it. Leave PowerPoint running if you plan to complete additional exercises.

Challenge

Challenge exercises expand on, or are somewhat related to, skills presented in the lessons. Each exercise provides a brief narrative introduction, followed by instructions in a numbered-step format that are not as detailed as those in the Skill Drill section.

1. Animating Objects

You are giving a short talk to the local Chamber of Commerce organization about your company. The meeting is during lunch and you're concerned that people may get sleepy after eating a big meal. To keep their attention focused on your presentation, you add some animation effects to your slides. [L3]

1. Open **PP-0806** and save it as **Talk to the Chamber of Commerce**. Display Slide 2 in Normal view, and then choose Slide Show, Custom Animation.

2. Add check marks to both boxes in the **Check to animate slide objects** area. (This adds animation to the title and clip art object.) Click the Preview button to see the effect, and then click OK.

3. Display Slide 6, Total Revenues, in Normal view. Choose Slide Show, Custom Animation. Check the boxes for both the title and chart in the Check to animate slide objects area. Click the Preview button to see your effect.

4. Click the Chart Effects tab in the Custom Animation dialog box. Click the Introduce chart elements drop-down list arrow, and then choose by Series. Click the Preview button.

5. Change the way that the chart elements are introduced. Click the Introduce chart elements drop-down list arrow, and then choose by Category. Click Preview, and then choose OK.

6. Run your presentation as a slide show, starting from Slide 1.

7. Save your Talk to the Chamber of Commerce presentation, then close it. Leave PowerPoint running if you plan to complete additional exercises.

2. Adding Slide Transitions and Using Timings

For your college speech class, you're giving a talk on how to do presentations. To help hold the class's attention, you add slide transitions to your PowerPoint presentation. [L1, 4]

1. Open **PP-0807** and save it as **Presentation Guidelines**.

2. Display the presentation in Slide Sorter view. Use the Slide Sorter toolbar to add a transition of your choosing to each slide in the presentation. (*Hint:* Try combining opposite effects, such as using Box In for one slide, and Box Out for the next one. Another example of a possible combination is Cover Down/Uncover Up.)

3. Click the Slide Transition icon for each slide to preview the transition effect.

4. Add text animations to each slide that has a bulleted list. (Choose a different animation for each slide.)

6. Set slide timings by clicking the Rehearse Timings button, and then discuss the slide's contents—just as you would for a live audience.

7. View the timings that you set in Slide Sorter view. Run the presentation as a slide show.

8. Set up the slide show to play continuously (loop). (*Hint:* Use PowerPoint's Help to find out how to do this, or refer to information presented in Lesson 4 of this project.)

9. Run the slide show. When you finish viewing the show, press [Esc] to end it.

10. Save the Presentation Guidelines presentation. Leave the presentation running if you plan to complete the next exercise.

3. Using the Annotation Pen

To focus your audience's attention, you decide to use the annotation pen during your speech class presentation. To prepare for the presentation, you practice using the pen. [L5]

1. Select Slide 1 of the Presentation Guidelines presentation, open from the previous exercise, and then run the presentation as a slide show.

2. Advance to Slide 4. Use the annotation pen to draw an arrow to each of the sub-points listed on the slide. Erase the drawing, and then change the pen color to blue.

3. Practice using the keyboard shortcuts and the shortcut menu to switch between the arrow and the pen.

4. On a blank area of the slide, practice drawing the following items:

- Arrow
- Square
- Circle
- Your name (in cursive)
- Your company or school name (in cursive)

5. Save your Presentation Guidelines presentation, and then close it. Leave PowerPoint running if you plan to complete additional exercises.

Discovery Zone

Discovery Zone exercises require advanced knowledge of topics presented in *MOUS Essentials* lessons, application of skills from multiple lessons, or self-directed learning of new skills.

1. Learning about Multimedia

You want to incorporate multimedia effects, such as music, sound, and video, in your presentation. Using the Help system, find out about the following topics:

- How to add music background to a slide
- The difference between adding a clip from the Gallery and adding a clip from a file
- Adding a sound to a slide transition
- Adding a sound when a slide object or chart element is introduced
- Inserting a video in your presentation
- Resizing and moving a video

Write down what you learn. (If you're familiar with Word, you can instead develop a table.) Then develop a PowerPoint presentation that incorporates multimedia effects. Use the knowledge you gain from the book to develop the best possible presentation. Finally, give your presentation to your class. [L1]

2. Creating Presentations

Create each of the following types of presentations:

- A presentation you can use in a business setting
- A presentation you can use to promote a club, team, or organization
- A presentation you can use in a college class

Include the following elements in each presentation:

- A chart
- A bulleted list

After you initially develop the content (and objects, such as clip art and charts) for the presentations, automate the presentations by using the following PowerPoint features:

- Slide transitions
- Text animation
- Multimedia clips (sound, music, or video)
- Chart animation
- Slide timings
- Action items

Give your presentations to your class. Use the feedback that your classmates offer to revise and improve the presentations. Then, present the slide shows a second time.

Save all your presentations. When you finish working, close the presentations and exit PowerPoint.

PinPoint Assessment

You have completed this project and its associated lessons, and have had an opportunity to assess your skills through the end-of-project questions and exercises. Now use the PinPoint software Evaluation Mode to further assess your comprehension of the specific exam activities you have just learned. You can also use the PinPoint Trainer Mode and the Show Me tutorials to practice these exam activities.

Refining Your Presentation

Key terms introduced in this project include

- case
- fonts
- Presentation Assistant

- sentence case
- style
- summary slide

- TrueType fonts
- visual clarity

Objectives	Required Activity for MOUS	Exam Level
➤ Laying Out and Designing Professional-Looking Presentations		
➤ Replacing Fonts Automatically	Change and replace text fonts (individual slide and entire presentation)	Core
➤ Finding and Replacing Text	Find and replace text	Core
➤ Setting Style and Spelling Options	Check spelling	Core
➤ Using the Presentation Assistant to Check Styles and Spelling	Check spelling	Core
	Use Office Assistant	Core
➤ Creating a Summary Slide	Automatically create a summary slide	Expert
	Create a specific type of slide	Expert

Why Would I Do This?

How can you keep an audience in the palm of your hand during a talk? By being prepared, giving a targeted, compelling message—and using PowerPoint 2000. At this point in your career you're probably turning into a "PowerPoint power user," and have a good grasp of the program's basic commands. As you develop presentations, however, avoid the temptation to overload your slides with features just because they're available and you know how to use them. Lesson 1 of this project guides you through some design principles so that your presentations are top-notch.

Additionally, there's a big difference between an average presentation and an outstanding one. Luckily, PowerPoint provides a number of subtle but effective things you can do to refine a presentation and make it more professional looking. For example, you can globally replace all the *fonts*, or typefaces, in your presentation with ones that are more readable. You can also use PowerPoint's Presentation Assistant to ensure that your punctuation, case, and style are consistent throughout the presentation. Finally, you can quickly create an agenda for your audience by creating a summary slide.

Now, try using some PowerPoint 2000 features to help you improve and refine your presentations.

Lesson 1: Laying Out and Designing Professional-Looking Presentations

You can develop more powerful and persuasive presentations by implementing a few design principles. Because PowerPoint 2000 has so many impressive features, it's easy to overuse them and confuse your audience. The overall presentation layout needs to be carefully crafted to ensure a focused message, as well as balance and uniformity. As you refine your presentations, use the following principles as a guide:

- **Simplify your presentation.** Keep your message and slide show as concise as possible. Don't inadvertently include too many slides, slide elements, graphics, or extraneous text. Non-relevant information tends to distract the audience from your main message.
- **Use text effectively.** Avoid using too many fonts or colors on a slide. Additionally, use a mix of upper- and lowercase letters, and include proportionately more serif than sans serif fonts. Finally, use a font size of at least 24 points in the text placeholder and 36 points in title placeholders.
- **Keep the presentation balanced and uniform.** Rely on PowerPoint's templates, slide backgrounds, color schemes, and the Slide Master to keep a presentation balanced and uniform in appearance.

You can use Table 9.1 as a reference when designing presentations.

Table 9.1   Design guidelines

Design Guideline	How to Implement
Simplify	Plan three to five text slides per major concept in a presentation.
	Use just one main concept per slide.
	Use the minimum number of elements on a slide that will effectively convey your message.
	Limit each slide to six or fewer bulleted points that support the main idea.
	Use five or fewer data series per chart.
	Avoid too many objects (such as clip art or AutoShapes) on a slide.
Emphasize your main point	Use clip art and drawn objects to emphasize the most important point.
	Explode a pie slice or change a data series chart color to emphasize the most important data.
Make text readable	Limit the number of fonts.
	Use sentence case (upper- and lowercase lettering), not all capital letters.
	Make body text at least 24 points for onscreen display.
	Make title text a minimum of 36 points.
	Use more serif fonts than sans serif fonts.
	Use short, to the point phrases rather than complete sentences.
Keep slides uniform	Use the same slide background, color scheme, and template for all slides (except to emphasize a particular point).
	Use the same fonts, sizes, and attributes throughout the presentation.
	Limit slide transition effects.
Use color effectively	Keep the color contrasts high.
	Test the color combination on your final delivery system.
	Avoid juxtaposing red and green, especially in chart series; approximately four percent of men are red/green color-blind.
Limit animation	Include only animation features that enhance or emphasize your ideas. Don't include animation just because the feature is available.

Inside Stuff: **Font Usage**

The fine, ornamental cross-strokes that serif fonts use help "lead" the reader's eye to the next word. That's why the text of most books (including this one) uses serif fonts. In contrast, sans serif fonts are generally used for title and display purposes. How does all of this translate into how you use PowerPoint? Use sans serif fonts for titles; use serif fonts for body text.

For the following exercise, imagine that you're working in the Information Systems Department of a business. It's your job to plan and implement an upgrade to PowerPoint 2000. A coworker (with very little knowledge of PowerPoint) developed a presentation about the upgrade process. He broke multiple design rules—and now it's your job to "clean up" the presentation. Try using layout and design principles to fix the problems.

To Lay Out and Design Professional-Looking Presentations

❶ Start PowerPoint, and then open PP-0901 and save it as Design Principles.

This presentation slide contains a number of design flaws that you can quickly fix (see Figure 9.1). For example, you can eliminate extraneous objects to reduce clutter and focus the slide's message.

Figure 9.1

You can eliminate extra objects to reduce clutter and make a slide more attractive.

Adjacent green and red colors

Text too small

All caps used

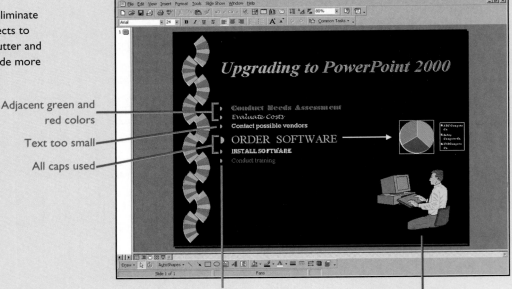

Different fonts used for each bullet

Extraneous objects

❷ Click the arrow object on the slide to place selection handles around it and press Del.

The arrow is removed. Now, you can remove the chart, which has no direct relation to the slide's main message.

③ Click the chart to select it, and then press ⌨Del.

The chart is deleted from the slide. Notice that the slide already appears less cluttered.

You can also improve this slide by enlarging the text and using a single font for the slide's body text. To do this, you first select the bulleted points by dragging the mouse pointer over them, and then choose a font from the Formatting toolbar.

④ Drag to select all bulleted points, click the Font drop-down list arrow on the Formatting toolbar, and choose Times New Roman.

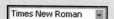

Times New Roman is a readable font that you can use to replace the mix of fonts originally used.

Because text should be a minimum of 24 points for onscreen display, you should enlarge it.

⑤ With the bulleted points still selected, click the Font Size drop-down list arrow and select 24.

The font size increases so that the text is easier to read. To make the slide even more cohesive, you should also limit the number of colors that you use—and preferably use those that coordinate with the presentation's template. The easiest way to change text color is to use the Font Color button on the Drawing toolbar.

✖ If You Have Problems...

By default, the Drawing toolbar displays at the bottom of the PowerPoint screen. If you don't see this toolbar, however, choose <u>V</u>iew, <u>T</u>oolbars to display a submenu of available toolbars. Choose Drawing from the submenu.

---

⑥ With the bulleted points still selected, click the Font Color button drop-down list arrow on the Drawing toolbar.

A palette of available colors displays (see Figure 9.2). The top row of colors contains those that are related to the current template and color scheme. Unless you are particularly artistic (or adventurous), you should choose from these colors. Also, notice that as you rest the mouse pointer over a color box, a ScreenTip displays. This ScreenTip indicates for which slide element the color is typically used.

continues ▶

To Lay Out and Design Professional-Looking Presentations   (continued)

Figure 9.2
Use the Font Color
button to quickly
change text color.

ScreenTip

Color scheme colors

Custom colors

Click this arrow to display
the color palette

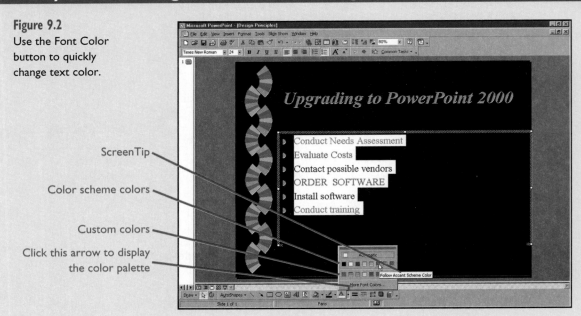

7 **On the top row of colors, rest the mouse pointer over the beige color (the second from the left) until the following ScreenTip displays: Follow Text and Lines Scheme Color. Click the color box.**

The beige color is applied to the selected bulleted points. (Don't worry if you can't see the color change—text always appears as a different color when it's selected.) Now, try converting the bullets to a numbered list.

8 **With the bulleted points still selected, click the Numbering button on the Formatting toolbar.**

The bullets are replaced by sequential numbering. Using numbers is appropriate when the order for the items on a list is important, as in this particular example.

Finally, to make the text more readable, you need to change the text in the placeholder to sentence case. *Case* is just the mix of upper- and lowercase letters used. *Sentence case* is text in which only the first letter of a phrase displays in uppercase. To quickly change case, you can use PowerPoint's Change Case feature.

9 **With the text still selected, choose F̲ormat, Change Cas̲e.**

The Change Case dialog box displays (see Figure 9.3). Notice that each command actually shows an example of the type of case. For example, the command associated with the uppercase option button displays as U̲PPERCASE. You can use this dialog box to view and apply a case to selected text.

Figure 9.3
You can quickly
change case by using
this dialog box.

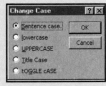

⑩ Click the Sentence case option button (if not already selected) and choose OK. Click outside the text placeholder to better see your changes.

The selected text displays, using sentence case. Your finished slide shows marked improvement by reducing clutter and extraneous fonts (see Figure 9.4).

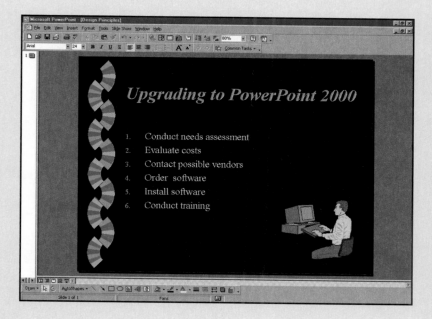

Figure 9.4
You can improve a slide's appearance by implementing simple design principles.

⑪ Save the presentation, and then close it.

Keep PowerPoint running for the next lesson, in which you learn how to replace fonts globally throughout a presentation.

 Inside Stuff: Making Your Presentation More Professional Looking
One way to make your presentation look more professional is to end the presentation with a black slide. This automatically refocuses your audience's attention on you. Luckily, PowerPoint's default option is to end a presentation in this manner. If you want to turn this option off, however, here's how: Choose Tools, Options; then click the View tab. Clear the End with black slide check box; then click OK. (On the other hand, if you want to enable the feature, check the box before closing the Options dialog box.)

Lesson 2: Replacing Fonts Automatically

One way to fine-tune your presentation is to replace a font with a more attractive one. For example, imagine that you're about to give an important presentation, when you discover that your font doesn't display well in the meeting room. Replacing the fonts throughout your presentation manually would be laborious and time-consuming. Fortunately, PowerPoint includes an automation feature to help you to quickly replace one font with another throughout your entire presentation. And, because the feature is so easy to use, you can experiment with replacing fonts until you find one that fits your needs.

For this exercise imagine that you're slated to give a talk to your speech class on presentation guidelines. You're not satisfied with the appearance of the fonts, however. You decide to replace fonts globally to fix your presentation.

To Replace Fonts Automatically

1 **Open PP-0902 and save it as Replacing Fonts.**

2 **Display Slide 2, Introduction; then choose F**o**rmat, R**eplace Fonts.

The Replace Font dialog box displays (see Figure 9.5). You can use this dialog box to quickly replace an existing font with another one.

Figure 9.5
You can automatically replace one font with another throughout an entire presentation.

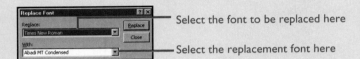

Select the font to be replaced here

Select the replacement font here

3 **Click the Replace drop-down list arrow to display a list of the fonts currently used in your presentation; then select Arial.**

This is the font used for title text in this presentation. Next, you designate the replacement font.

4 **Click the W**ith drop-down list arrow.

All the fonts available on your computer display (see Figure 9.6). The fonts listed depend, in part, on the printer you use as well as which fonts have been loaded on your system. Because of this, you should expect some variation from one system to the next. Choosing *TrueType fonts* (designated by the TT next to a font's name) helps you maintain consistency, however, if you show your presentation on different computers than the one on which it was created. A TrueType font is a scalable font that prints the same as it displays onscreen.

Figure 9.6
Most systems have a variety of fonts from which you can choose.

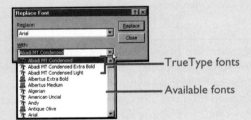

TrueType fonts

Available fonts

5 **Scroll down the list of available fonts and choose Comic Sans MS. (If Comic Sans MS isn't available on your system, choose a similar TrueType font or ask your instructor for assistance.)**

Even though you have designated the original and replacement fonts, you must click the R_eplace button to actually replace the fonts. Furthermore, the Replace Font dialog box remains open so you can make additional changes. To best see the effect of your change, however, you should move this dialog box.

6 **Drag the title bar for the Replace Font dialog box to view the slide's title and body text; then click the R**eplace button.

The Comic Sans MS font replaces the Arial font that was originally used in the title placeholder. Notice that the Replace Font dialog box is still open, so you can replace other fonts.

Now try replacing the font used for body text (Times New Roman) with another one.

7 Choose Times New Roman from the Replace drop-down list and Garamond from the With drop-down list; then choose Replace. (If you don't have Garamond on your system, choose another TrueType font.)

The new font replaces Times New Roman and the result displays on Slide 2. To see the changes on all the slides, however, you have to first close the Replace Font dialog box.

8 Click the Close button in the Replace Font dialog box, and then scroll through your presentation.

Notice that the fonts were replaced on all slides. Using this method, you can maintain consistency as well as see how different fonts will look in your presentation.

9 Save your presentation, and then close it.

Keep PowerPoint running for the next lesson, in which you learn how to find and replace text.

***Inside Stuff:* Checking Out Fonts**

To check which fonts a particular presentation uses, open the presentation and then choose File, Properties to display the Properties dialog box. Click the Contents tab to see a list of the fonts used.

Lesson 3: Finding and Replacing Text

In this lesson you focus on finding (and replacing) the actual text content rather than the font. Why would you do this? Well, using the Find command can help you quickly locate specific text in a long presentation. The Replace command is handy, too: For example, imagine that your company is bought out by another organization (or that you get a new boss). Relying on PowerPoint to quickly update your presentations with the new information can be a real time-saver. Try using the find and replace features now.

To Find and Replace Text

1 Open PP-0903 and save it as Safety First.

It's often handy to be able to quickly find information in a presentation, especially if the presentation includes a number of slides. Try using the Find feature to locate information now.

2 Display Slide 1 of the presentation in Normal view, and then choose Edit, Find.

The Find dialog box displays so that you can enter the text you want to locate (see Figure 9.7). If you see text in the Find what text box, don't worry—it's just left over from the last time someone used Find.

continues ▶

To Find and Replace Text (continued)

Figure 9.7
Use PowerPoint's Find feature to quickly locate text.

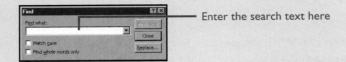

Enter the search text here

3 Enter OSHA in the Find what text box.
This is the text that you want to locate.

4 Click Find Next.
PowerPoint finds and highlights the first occurrence of "OSHA" in your presentation (see Figure 9.8). (If necessary, you may need to move the Find dialog box by dragging its title bar to better see the highlighted text.)

Figure 9.8
PowerPoint quickly locates the first occurrence of the search text.

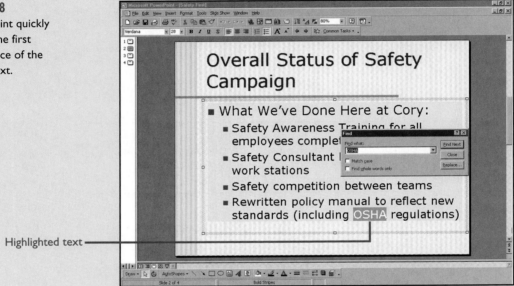

Highlighted text

5 Click Find Next again.
The next occurrence of the search text is highlighted. You can continue this process until you locate the text you want. (When PowerPoint systematically highlights all the occurrences of the text for your review, it displays a message that it's finished searching the document. If necessary, choose OK to close this message box.)

For now, however, you'll close the Find dialog box so that you can learn how to replace text globally throughout the presentation.

6 Close the Find dialog box, and then display the first presentation slide.
Now you're ready to search and replace text. By default PowerPoint searches from the beginning of the presentation to the end, so displaying the first slide ensures that text throughout the entire presentation will be replaced.

7 Choose Edit, Replace.
The Replace dialog box displays (see Figure 9.9). This dialog box includes text boxes for you to enter the text you want to find (Cory) as well as the replacement text (Reams).

Enter the text you want to find here ———

Enter the replacement text here ———

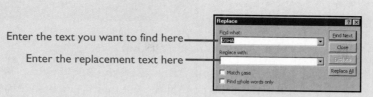

Figure 9.9
Use the Replace dialog
box to quickly replace
text throughout a pre-
sentation.

8 **Enter Cory in the Fi_n_d what text box and enter Reams in the Re_p_lace with text box.**
This indicates that you want to replace the name "Cory" with "Reams"—the new owner of the manufacturing plant.

9 **Click Replace A_ll_.**
PowerPoint replaces every occurrence of the word "Cory" with "Reams" and displays a message indicating the number of replacements (see Figure 9.10). (If the Office Assistant is not turned off the message may display in the Assistant's balloon rather than a message box.)

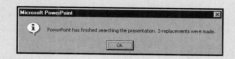

Figure 9.10
You can replace all oc-
currences of a word in
a flash.

10 **Click OK to close the message box, and then close the Replace dialog box.**

11 **Save the Safety First presentation, and then close it.**
Leave PowerPoint running for the next exercise, in which you learn how to set spelling and style options.

Lesson 4: Setting Style and Spelling Options

PowerPoint 2000 can automatically check your presentations for consistency, punctuation, vi-sual clarity, and style. **Style** refers to the way elements, such as text and graphics, are handled in a presentation. **Visual clarity**, the way in which text is used, includes appropriate font usage and the legibility of your slide text.

You can also use PowerPoint's automatic spell checking, which flags spelling errors and typos—any words that don't appear in the Office 2000 dictionary.

To give you flexibility in working with the program, you can change the way that spell check-ing and style checking work by setting options. And, of course, if you don't want PowerPoint to check style or spelling, you can turn off the features instead.

Imagine that you have "inherited" a presentation from a coworker that you're scheduled to give at an upcoming meeting. To make sure that the presentation is flawless, you set the style options. You also make sure that both style checking and the spell checker are turned on. (In Lesson 5, you will actually check the presentation for errors and inconsistencies.)

To Set Style and Spelling Options

1 **Open PP-0904 and save it as Guidelines.**

2 **Choose Tools, Options; then click the Spelling and Style tab.**
The Spelling and Style page of the Options dialog box displays (see Figure 9.11). You can change the options related to both spelling and style checking on this page. For now, you simply make sure that the features are turned on and the default settings are in place.

Figure 9.11
You can set the way spelling and style checking work in this dialog box.

Make sure that this box is not checked

Check this box to turn on style checking

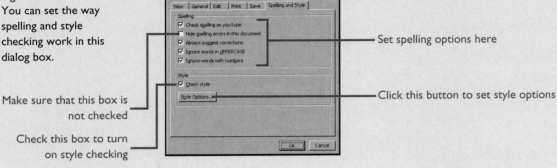

Set spelling options here

Click this button to set style options

3 **Make sure that all the boxes are checked in the Spelling area of the dialog box except Hide spelling errors in this document (refer to Figure 9.11).**
Choosing the first box, **Check spelling as you type**, is a good choice if you want to immediately see which words you might have misspelled or mistyped. When this feature is activated, PowerPoint flags possible misspellings with a red wavy underline.

4 **Check the box for Check style, if necessary.**
Checking this box turns on style checking in your presentations. (Conversely, if you don't want to check styles, you can easily turn off the feature by clearing the box.) Now, take a look at the options associated with style checking.

5 **Click the Style Options button.**
The Style Options dialog box displays (see Figure 9.12). This dialog box includes two tabbed pages—Case and End Punctuation, and Visual Clarity—so that you can make decisions regarding which items PowerPoint should examine.

Figure 9.12
You can set a variety of options related to checking style in this dialog box.

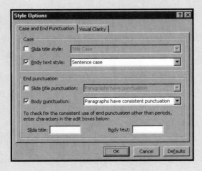

6 **Read over the options on the Case and End Punctuation page, and then click the Visual Clarity tab.**

The Visual Clarity page displays (see Figure 9.13). You use this page to make changes regarding the number of fonts allowed and the overall legibility.

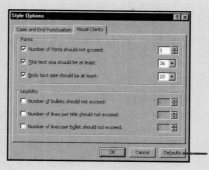

Figure 9.13
You can set font and legibility options by using the Visual Clarity page.

Click this button to restore default settings

7 **Read over the options on the Visual Clarity page; then click the Defaults button.**

PowerPoint restores the default settings associated with style checking. For example, by default, the maximum number of fonts is 3, and title text size should be at least 36 points. When you set the style-checking options, you help ensure that the presentation uses consistent case and punctuation.

8 **Click OK in both the Style Options and Options dialog boxes.**

The final step before you can check your presentation's style and spelling is to turn on the Office Assistant.

9 **Choose Help, Show the Office Assistant.**

The Office Assistant appears. Remember that style checking doesn't work if you don't activate the Assistant.

10 **Save your Guidelines presentation.**

Keep the presentation open for the next exercise, in which you check spelling and styles.

Lesson 5: Using the Presentation Assistant to Check Styles and Spelling

Using the Office Assistant, PowerPoint 2000's **Presentation Assistant** checks your presentation for problems with style. The Presentation Assistant offers help and tips on how to improve your presentation—including stylistic improvements. How does it work? Whenever the Presentation Assistant has a suggestion, a light bulb displays. Click the light bulb to show the associated "tip."

PowerPoint uses another method to help you quickly locate words that are misspelled: a red wavy line appears beneath them. You can right-click the misspelled word and choose a replacement word from the shortcut menu that displays.

To refine and improve the Guidelines presentation, try using these features now.

To Use the Presentation Assistant to Check Styles and Spelling

❶ Display Slide 1 in the Guidelines presentation from the preceding lesson.

When the automatic spelling checker is turned on, words that PowerPoint doesn't recognize are displayed with wavy red underlines—such as the word Presenttion on this slide.

❷ Right-click the misspelled word, Presenttion.

The spelling shortcut menu displays, showing suggested replacement words from which you can choose (see Figure 9.14). You can choose a replacement word from the list. Alternatively, you can choose Ignore All if you want to skip over all incidences of the word in the presentation, or choose Add if you want to place the word in the dictionary permanently. (You typically add a word to the dictionary that you might frequently use, such as your company name, personal names, or technical terms related to your job.)

Figure 9.14
Right-click a misspelled word to view the spelling shortcut menu.

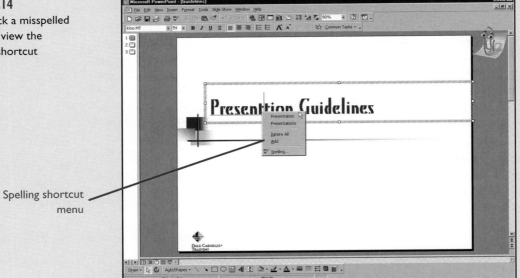

Spelling shortcut menu

❸ Select the word Presentation from the shortcut menu.

PowerPoint corrects the spelling by replacing the word. Now, try to use PowerPoint 2000's Presentation Assistant to help you refine your presentation.

❹ Press PgDn to display Slide 2.

Slide 2 of your presentation displays, complete with a light bulb "tip" (see Figure 9.15). This light bulb indicates that the Assistant has a way to improve your presentation (such as a stylistic correction).

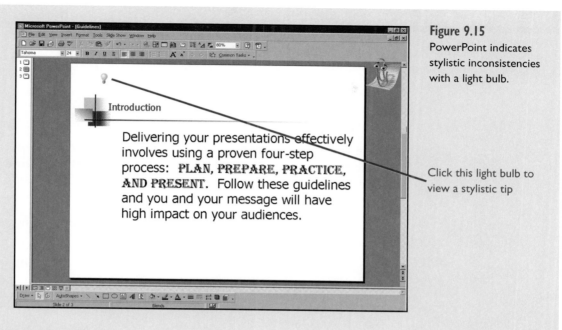

Figure 9.15
PowerPoint indicates stylistic inconsistencies with a light bulb.

Click this light bulb to view a stylistic tip

⑤ Click the light bulb.

A message balloon displays to indicate the main problem with this slide (the text is too small). You have a choice of whether or not to take the Assistant's advice—clicking the first option button fixes the stylistic problem. Alternatively, you can choose to ignore the style rule for this presentation or all presentations (see Figure 9.16).

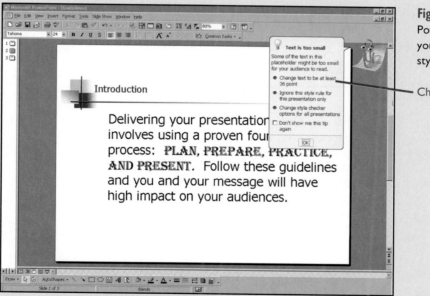

Figure 9.16
PowerPoint enables you to fix or ignore stylistic problems.

Choose this option

⑥ Click the first option button in the message balloon (Change text to be at least 36 point).

The title text is automatically reformatted in 36 points. Now, try to fix problems on other slides.

continues ▶

To Use the Presentation Assistant to Check Styles and Spelling   (continued)

7 Press PgDn to display Slide 3 and click the light bulb.

The Presentation Assistant indicates that there is a problem with capitalization. (Sentence case should be used for body text.)

8 Click the first option button in the message balloon to fix the capitalization problem.

The text in the lower placeholder displays in sentence case. However, a light bulb still appears on the slide, indicating that PowerPoint discovered another stylistic problem.

9 Click the light bulb.

PowerPoint indicates that the punctuation on the slide is not consistent with the style checker settings.

10 Click the second option button (Remove end punctuation).

PowerPoint removes the end punctuation for the slide.

Now, turn off the Office Assistant's display because you're finished checking styles in your presentation.

11 Right-click on the Office Assistant; then choose Options from the shortcut menu to display the Options dialog box (see Figure 9.17).

Figure 9.17
You can turn off the Office Assistant in this dialog box.

Clear this box to turn off the Office Assistant

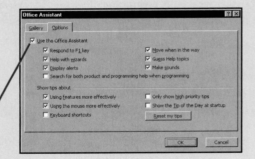

12 Click the Options tab, if necessary; then clear the Use the Office Assistant box. Choose OK.

The Office Assistant no longer displays.

13 Save the Guidelines presentation; then close it.

Keep PowerPoint running for the next lesson, in which you learn how to create a summary slide.

 ## Lesson 6: Creating a Summary Slide

One of the great things about PowerPoint 2000 is its capacity to help you create presentations more efficiently. Imagine, for example, that you have a presentation that includes a number of topics, yet you need to create a single slide that summarizes your presentation's main points. Luckily, PowerPoint includes an easy-to-use feature for this situation: creating a summary (sometimes called an agenda) slide.

A **summary slide** converts the titles of selected slides into bulleted points on a single slide. You usually place this slide immediately after the title slide so your audience can see what your presentation will cover. In fact, you can even print out the agenda slide as a handout.

For this exercise, imagine that you're developing a presentation for new employees at your company. You use PowerPoint's summary slide feature to quickly produce and print an agenda slide.

To Create a Summary Slide

① Open PP-0905 and save it as Summary Slide.

You can create a summary slide by using either Outline or Slide Sorter view.

② Choose View, Slide Sorter.

The presentation displays in Slide Sorter view. Now, you're ready to select the slides you want to include on the summary slide. You can select multiple slides by pressing ⬆Shift while clicking the slides.

③ In Slide Sorter view, click Slide 2, press ⬆Shift, and then click Slide 6.

Pressing ⬆Shift allows you to select multiple adjacent slides. (You can use Ctrl to select nonadjacent slides.) The selected slides appear with a darkened border (see Figure 9.18). Now, you can create a summary slide.

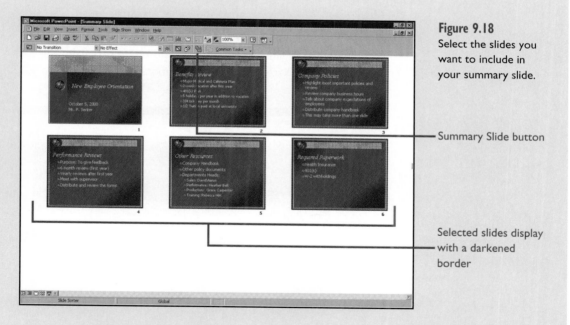

Figure 9.18
Select the slides you want to include in your summary slide.

—Summary Slide button

Selected slides display with a darkened border

④ Click the Summary Slide button on the Slide Sorter toolbar.

PowerPoint creates a summary slide and places it immediately before the first selected slide (see Figure 9.19).

continues ▶

To Create a Summary Slide   (continued)

Figure 9.19
PowerPoint creates a
summary slide and
places it before the
first selected slide.

Summary slide

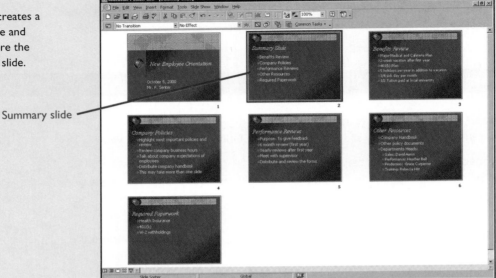

To better view your summary slide, switch to Slide view.

5 **Double-click the icon for Slide 2.**
Slide 2 displays in Slide view. Notice that the title text from the selected slides is
converted into bulleted points on the summary slide (see Figure 9.20).

Figure 9.20
A summary slide in-
cludes title text from
the selected slides.

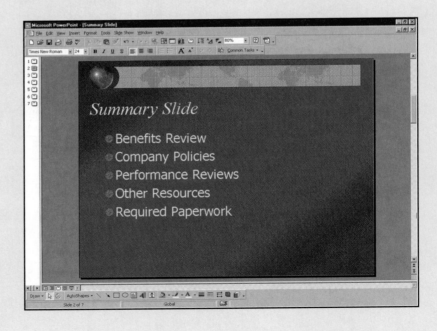

The default text in the title placeholder (Summary Slide) can easily be replaced
by more descriptive text. Try replacing the text in this placeholder now.

6 **Select the text in the title placeholder, and then type** Agenda.
Your new text replaces the default text.

Now, print the summary slide so that you can hand it out to your audience participants.

7 With Slide 2, Summary Slide, displayed in Slide view, choose File, Print.

The Print dialog box displays (see Figure 9.21). You can use this dialog box to specify which elements in your presentation (such as notes pages or slides) you want to print. Additionally, you can print the entire presentation or just the current slide.

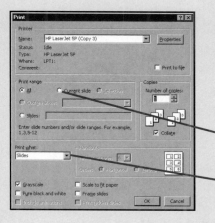

Figure 9.21
You can print the current slide or the entire presentation.

Click here to print only the current slide

Click here to specify which slide elements you want to print

8 Make sure that the Print what box is set for Slides.

9 Click the Current slide option button; then choose OK.

The summary slide prints, providing you with a useful handout for your audience.

10 Save the Summary Slide presentation; then close it.

If you're finished with your work session, exit PowerPoint and shut down Windows before turning off your computer. Otherwise, complete the Skill Drill, Challenge, and Discovery Zone exercises at the end of this project.

Summary

In this project, you learned several ways to refine your presentation. You applied design principles to make sure that your presentation was visually appealing. You efficiently replaced one font in a presentation with another. You ensured consistency in style, case, and punctuation by taking the Presentation Assistant's suggestions; and you made sure that the presentation's spelling was flawless. Finally, you learned how to create and print a summary slide. Together, these features can help you improve any presentation and make it more professional looking.

To expand on your knowledge, spend a few minutes exploring Help on these topics. Additionally, complete some of the Skill Drill, Challenge, and Discovery Zone exercises, as follows.

Checking Concepts and Terms

True/False

For each of the following, check *T* or *F* to indicate whether the statement is true or false.

__T __F   **1.** Font is a term used to refer to a particular combination of upper- and lowercase letters. [L1–2]

__T __F   **2.** You must have the Office Assistant turned on to view stylistic tips. [L5]

__T __F   **3.** Body text should be at least 24 points to be readable for most audiences. [L1]

__T __F   **4.** You can automatically replace one font with another throughout your entire presentation. [L2]

__T __F   **5.** To make a presentation interesting, you should include as many fonts as possible. [L1]

Multiple Choice

Circle the letter of the correct answer for each of the following.

1. Which of the following is a design principle you should use when refining a presentation? [L1]

   a. Use as many font colors as possible to add interest.

   b. Use a maximum of six bulleted points per slide.

   c. Use as many fonts on a slide as possible.

   d. all of the above

2. Which of the following can the Presentation Assistant examine? [L5]

   a. the number of fonts used on a slide

   b. the case used for titles

   c. the end punctuation used for text in a placeholder

   d. all of the above

3. Which of the following is true regarding a summary slide? [L6]

   a. It creates bulleted points from the titles of several slides.

   b. It is sometimes called an agenda slide.

   c. It can be printed.

   d. all of the above

4. What is the name for fonts that are scalable? [L1–2]

   a. ScaleFace

   b. TrueType

   c. Definable

   d. ScaleType

5. How can you find a list of replacement words for a misspelled word? [L4–5]

   a. Right-click the word.

   b. Double-click the word.

   c. Click the Word List button on the Standard toolbar.

   d. Choose Tools, Find Word.

Skill Drill

Skill Drill exercises reinforce project skills. Each skill reinforced is the same, or nearly the same, as a skill presented in the project. Detailed instructions are provided in a step-by-step format.

I. Replacing Fonts Automatically

You're trying to start up a small business that specializes in computer training and support. You created a business plan that you need to present to the Small Business Management Department in order to secure a loan. To make sure that you get the loan, you want to make the presentation as visually cohesive as possible. Because the fonts in your presentation are not easily readable, you decide to replace them. [L2]

1. Open **PP-0906** and save it as **Computer Consulting Business Plan**.

2. Display Slide 2, Mission Statement, and then choose Format, Replace Fonts.

3. Use the Replace and With drop-down list arrows to replace the Comic Sans MS font with Times New Roman. Click Replace.

4. Use the Replace and With drop-down list arrows to replace the Impact font with Arial. Click Replace.

5. Close the Replace Font dialog box. Scroll through your presentation to see that the fonts are replaced on all slides.

6. Display Slide 1, Software Solutions. Open the Replace Font dialog box. Replace Arial Black with Arial, and close the Replace Font dialog box.

7. If your teacher specifies, print a copy of your presentation. Save the Computer Consulting Business Plan presentation; then close it. Leave PowerPoint running if you plan to complete additional exercises.

2. Setting Style and Spelling Options

As a member of the Information Technology team at your company, you're helping to roll out a computer upgrade. Your boss will give a talk on the upgrade to your company's management team by using a presentation that one of your coworkers designed. [L3–4]

The presentation includes multiple problems with consistency, style, and spelling, however. Because you are familiar with PowerPoint, your boss has asked you to "clean up" the presentation. You decide to use PowerPoint's Presentation Assistant to quickly identify and fix the problems. Before you check the presentation, however, you set style and spelling options.

1. Open **PP-0907** and save it as **Upgrade Process**.

2. Choose Tools, Options; then click the Spelling and Style tab.

3. Make sure that all the boxes in the Spelling section are checked (except for Hide spelling errors in this document).

4. Make sure that the Check style box is checked; then click the Style Options button.

5. In the Style Options dialog box, click the Defaults button to restore the default settings. If you want, examine the default settings that PowerPoint uses.

6. Click OK in both the Style Options and Options dialog boxes.

7. If necessary, turn on the Office Assistant by choosing Help, Show the Office Assistant. Now you're ready to correct the stylistic and consistency problems in the Upgrade Process presentation by using the Presentation Assistant to guide you.

8. Click the Next Slide button on the vertical scroll bar to display Slide 2.

9. Click the light bulb that displays on Slide 2. In the Presentation Assistant balloon, click the second option button (Remove end punctuation).

10. Right-click each of the misspelled words on Slide 2. Replace the misspelled words with the correct spellings (training, assessment).

11. Press PgDn to display Slide 3, Background. Click the light bulb to display a tip on capitalization. Choose the first option button (Change the text to title case).

12. Click the next light bulb that displays on Slide 3 (on capitalization in the body text placeholder). Choose the first option button (Change the text to sentence case).

13. Scroll through your presentation to view your changes.

14. Turn off the Office Assistant. Right-click the Assistant; then choose Options. On the Options page of the Office Assistant dialog box, clear the box for Use the Office Assistant. Click OK.

15. Save your Upgrade Process presentation; then close it. Keep PowerPoint running if you plan to complete additional exercises.

3. Creating a Summary Slide

You work for a metal manufacturing plant, and you're creating a short presentation about your company to give to the local Chamber of Commerce. You create a summary slide to have an agenda to pass out to the audience. [L6]

1. Open **PP-0908** and save it as **Star Metal Business Summary**.

2. Click the Slide Sorter View button to display the presentation in Slide Sorter view.

3. Click Slide 3 to select it. Press (◆Shift) and click Slide 7.

4. On the Slide Sorter toolbar, click the Summary Slide button.

5. Double-click Slide 3 (Summary Slide) to display it in Slide view.

6. Replace the text in the title placeholder (Summary Slide) with Agenda.

7. Choose File, Print to display the Print dialog box. Click the Current slide option button; then choose OK.

8. Save the Star Metal Business Summary presentation; then close it. Keep PowerPoint running if you plan to complete additional exercises.

Challenge

Challenge exercises expand on or are somewhat related to skills presented in the lessons. Each exercise provides a brief narrative introduction, followed by instructions in a numbered-step format that are not as detailed as those in the Skill Drill section.

1. Improving a Presentation's Style and Spelling

You just started working for a travel agency. As part of your job, you give presentations to various groups on the types of tours that your agency can schedule. You developed a rough presentation using PowerPoint, but you need to check it for consistency in style and for spelling errors. [L4–5]

1. Open **PP-0909** and save it as **Affordable Travel Tours**. Display Slide 1, Affordable Travel Tours in Slide view.

2. Reset the style options to PowerPoint's default settings. Also, make sure that automatic spelling is turned on. Finally, display the Office Assistant.

3. Click outside of the Office Assistant's balloon to close it. Then, click the light bulb on Slide 1 to display a tip about capitalization. Choose the second option button in the balloon. (Ignore this style rule for this presentation only.)

4. Display Slide 2; then click the light bulb to display a tip (Too much text). Choose the first option button (Split this slide into two slides).

5. Redisplay Slide 2 and right-click on the first misspelled word in your presentation (Caribean). Replace the word with the correct spelling on the shortcut menu (Caribbean). Repeat the process to correct spelling errors throughout your presentation.

6. Scroll through your presentation to see your changes. If you wish, view your presentation as a slide show.

7. Turn off (not just hide) the Office Assistant.

8. Save your Affordable Travel Tours presentation; then close it. Leave PowerPoint running if you plan to complete additional exercises.

2. Replacing Fonts Throughout a Presentation

You developed a presentation for your company, which sells financial products. After eye-balling your presentation, however, you decide that the fonts don't look very appealing. To quickly replace the fonts, you use PowerPoint's capability to replace fonts globally throughout a presentation. [L2]

1. Open **PP-0910** and save it as **Financial Products**.

2. Replace the following fonts throughout your presentation:
   - Replace the Times New Roman font with Comic Sans MS.
   - Replace Antique Olive with Arial.
   - Replace Arial Black with Bookman Old Style.

3. Scroll through your presentation to see the changes. Move the text placeholder on Slide 3 slightly upward to better view the text.

4. Save the presentation. If requested by your instructor, print a copy of the presentation before closing it. Leave PowerPoint running if you plan to complete the additional exercises.

3. Creating a Summary Slide

As the safety manager for Cory Glass Company, you're spearheading a safety campaign. At this month's staff meeting, you're scheduled to report on safety issues. You decide to create and print an agenda slide so that you can hand it out to people at the meeting. [L6]

1. Open **PP-0911** and save it as **Safety Campaign Progress**.

2. Display the presentation in Slide Sorter view. Create a summary slide based on Slides 2–6.

3. Display your new agenda slide in Normal view. Replace the title text with **Agenda**.

4. Print a copy of the agenda slide. Save and close the presentation. Leave PowerPoint running if you plan to complete the additional exercises.

Discovery Zone

Discovery Zone exercises require advanced knowledge of topics presented in *MOUS Essentials* lessons, application of skills from multiple lessons, or self-directed learning of new skills. Each exercise is independent of the others, so you may complete the exercises in any order.

1. Using Design Principles

You're in charge of publicizing the company picnic. You assigned the task of making a flyer to your assistant, who unfortunately got carried away with using PowerPoint features. You decide to fix the problems with the flyer before printing it.

Open **PP-0912** and save it as **Company Picnic Flyer**. Using the design principles covered in this project, do the following:

- Eliminate the extraneous clutter on the slide. For example, delete all objects except the clip art image and the "Bring Your Family" object.
- Use a consistent (and appropriate) font and font size for the bulleted points. Make sure that the text displays in an appropriate case.
- Change the case in the title placeholder to title case. Change the font and make the font size at least 54 points.

- Change the font color to black.
- Move the clip art image to the most appropriate location.

Print a copy of your presentation. Save, and then close it. Leave PowerPoint running if you plan to complete the additional exercises. [L1]

2. Improving a Presentation's Design and Style

You work for J. Chapman, President of Appalachian Logging Company. He's well versed in the lumber business, but is not very good at putting presentations together. He's scheduled to give an overview of the organization to other business leaders at a meeting next Tuesday. To prevent him from being embarrassed, you stay late one evening to "clean up" the presentation.

Open **PP-0913** and save it as **Logging Company**. Use the principles you learned in this project to improve the presentation's style, visual clarity, and design. Correct any misspelled words or typos. If you wish, apply a different design template. Turn off the Office Assistant when you finish checking the presentation's style.

Print a copy of the presentation. Save the presentation, and then close it. [L1, 5–6]

PinPoint Assessment

You have completed this project and its associated lessons, and have had an opportunity to assess your skills through the end-of-project questions and exercises. Now use the PinPoint software Evaluation Mode to further assess your comprehension of the specific exam activities you have just learned. You can also use the PinPoint Trainer Mode and the Show Me tutorials to practice these exam activities.

Using Advanced Multimedia and Graphics

Key terms introduced in this project include

- animated GIF
- Clip Gallery
- Clip Gallery Live
- electronic clips

- keywords
- motion clip
- pop-up menu

- recoloring
- voice narration
- watermark

Objectives	Required Activity for MOUS	Exam Level
➤ Locating Clips by Category, Keyword, or Style	Add a picture from the ClipArt Gallery	Core
➤ Previewing and Inserting Pictures	Add a picture from the ClipArt Gallery	Core
	Scale and size an object including ClipArt	Core
➤ Modifying a Clip Using the Picture Toolbar	Customize clip art and other objects (resize, scale, etc.)	Expert
➤ Inserting and Playing Sound Clips	Add sound	Expert
➤ Inserting and Playing Motion Clips	Add video	Expert
➤ Adding Animated GIFs	Add animated GIFs	Expert

Why Would I Do This?

A quick and easy way to make a powerful impression is to embellish your presentation with **electronic clips**—including pictures, sounds, and movies. Clips refer to electronic graphic or multimedia files that you can purchase and use in your presentations. When well chosen, these clips can emphasize information or drive home ideas. PowerPoint groups the clips by pictures (including clip art created by artists and scanned photographs), sounds, motion (sometimes called movies), and GIFs. When you insert sounds, movies, and GIFs, you tap into PowerPoint's multimedia capabilities to make a strong impact. Multimedia is just a term that refers to the computer's capability to integrate various ways of communicating with others. These multimedia features are especially effective when you use them as part of an interactive slide presentation (such as at a trade show). They can also be used to spice up a live presentation as well.

So, where can you find clips? The first place to look is in Office's **Clip Gallery**, a peripheral program shared by all Office applications that you can use to find and insert clips into your presentation. Think of the Clip Gallery as a library where you can "check out" clips for your use.

If you need fresh clips, try locating picture, sound, or motion files on your computer's hard disk, CD-ROM, or network drives. For example, you might have scanned photographic images or clip art packages on your hard drive. Another rich source of clips is the World Wide Web. In fact, PowerPoint makes it easy to find and download the clips by helping you connect to Microsoft's **Clip Gallery Live**, a Microsoft Web site, which includes a wealth of free clips.

So, come along and learn how to dramatically improve your presentation's effectiveness. Remember that, because Office 2000 includes so many improvements to the Clip Gallery, you'll definitely benefit from spending a few minutes working through this project—even if you're an old pro at using clips in previous versions of PowerPoint.

Lesson I: Locating Clips by Category, Keyword, or Style

You can jazz up almost any presentation by inserting electronic pictures, commonly called clip art. PowerPoint includes a wide variety of pictures, or images, as part of the program. If you want more choices, however, you can purchase additional clip art packages or even download clips from the World Wide Web.

Before you can insert a clip, you have to find it—not always an easy task given the multitude of clips available. Fortunately, the "new and improved" Clip Gallery 5.0 in Office 2000 includes ways to search for clips by categories or keywords. For example, the Clip Gallery includes topical categories, such as *Academic* and *Business*, that you can use to locate clips.

Additionally, every clip has several **keywords** associated with it that help describe the clip. You can use these keywords to sift through the clips and display only the ones you want. For example, a picture of a person leading a meeting might have a keyword such as *leadership*, *communication*, or *goals* associated with it.

Finally, you can find a clip with the same artistic style (or color and shape) as the selected clip. Locating clips with this method can help you to create a consistent "look" for your presentation.

Throughout this project, imagine that you're the regional sales manager of SR Homes, a home-building company. You're conducting a motivational session to kick off a sales contest. Here's how the contest works: each salesperson has goals set up by his or her manager to sell a certain number of homes in the next two months. The division also has "group goals." If the salespeople reach the goals, they win a trip to the Caribbean. Your job is to encourage them to work toward common goals. To do so, you spice up a presentation by using clips.

To Locate Clips by Category, Keyword, or Style

1 **Open** PP-1001 **and save it as** Sales Contest. **Display Slide 1 in Slide view.**

2 **Click the Insert Clip Art button on the Drawing toolbar (or choose Insert, Picture, Clip Art from the menu).**

The Insert ClipArt dialog box displays (see Figure 10.1). This dialog box is analogous to the Clip Gallery, and includes three main groups of clips: Pictures, Sounds, and Motion Clips. Additionally, each page includes categories that you can use to locate clips by topic.

Click a tab to choose Pictures, Sounds, or Motion Clips ——

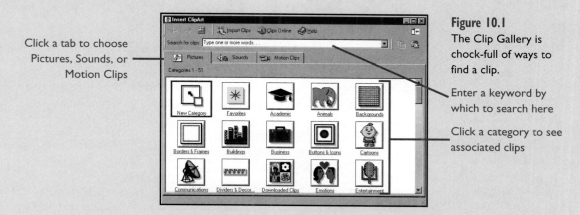

Figure 10.1
The Clip Gallery is chock-full of ways to find a clip.

Enter a keyword by which to search here

Click a category to see associated clips

Now try searching for a clip by category.

3 **Locate the Business category icon on the Pictures page, and then click it.**

The clips associated with this category display.

 If You Have Problems...
Don't worry if you don't have as many clips on your screen as those shown in the figures. It just means that your computer doesn't have as many clips loaded.

You can display a ***pop-up menu*** for a clip by left-clicking a clip. A pop-up menu is just one that displays whenever you click a clip. Try displaying this menu now.

4 **Point to the clip indicated in Figure 10.2 (working toward goals), and then click the left mouse button.**

The clip is selected (as shown by the blue border) and a pop-up menu for the clip displays (see Figure 10.2). You can find out each button's function on this menu by resting the mouse pointer over the button until a ScreenTip displays.

X ***If You Have Problems...***
Not sure if you're selecting the correct clip? Just rest your mouse pointer momentarily over any clip until the clip's name displays in a ScreenTip. Throughout this project, we'll refer to these names to help you choose the right clip.

---

continues ▶

To Locate Clips by Category, Keyword, or Style   (continued)

Figure 10.2
Use the pop-up menu to work with your clips.

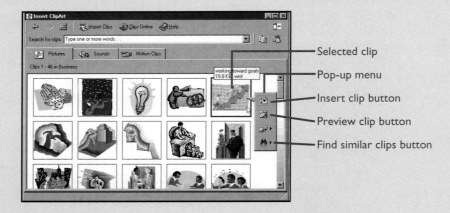

Selected clip
Pop-up menu
Insert clip button
Preview clip button
Find similar clips button

⑤ Move the mouse pointer to the Find similar clips button and click.
The `Find clips with similar` pane displays (see Figure 10.3). You can use this pane to search by keyword, artistic style, or color and shape.

Figure 10.3
PowerPoint hands you a variety of ways to locate clips.

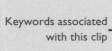

Keywords associated with this clip

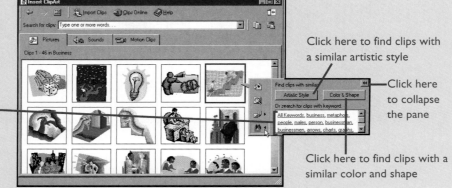

Click here to find clips with a similar artistic style

Click here to collapse the pane

Click here to find clips with a similar color and shape

⑥ Click the keyword for *arrows* in the `Find clips with similar` pane.
The clips that include this keyword display in the Clip Gallery (see Figure 10.4). (Remember, the clips shown on your computer may differ from those in the figure.) Now, try finding some clips with the same artistic style as a selected clip.

Figure 10.4
You can find clips that include the same keyword.

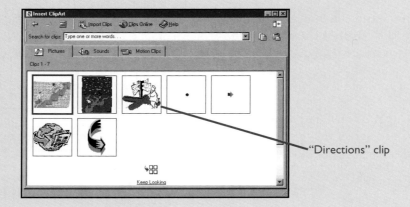

"Directions" clip

7 **Click the "directions" clip to display the pop-up menu, and then click the Artistic Style button. (If you don't have this clip installed on your computer, choose another one.)**

Several clips that use a similar artistic style display (see Figure 10.5). As you can tell, it's easy to quickly conduct so many searches that you lose track of your starting location! Luckily, the Clip Gallery includes some navigational methods that you can use. For example, you can click the Back, Forward, and All Categories buttons.

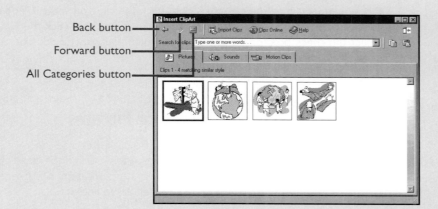

Back button
Forward button
All Categories button

Figure 10.5
The Clip Gallery quickly displays clips with a similar artistic style.

8 **Click the Back button.**

The preceding search in the Clip Gallery displays. In a similar fashion, you can click the Forward button to scroll forward through the Clip Gallery, or click the All Categories buttons to return to the original display of categories.

9 **Click the All Categories button (refer to Figure 10.5).**

All the categories on the Pictures page of the Clip Gallery display. Now, try another method of searching by keyword: using the Search for clips text box.

10 **Type reaching goals in the Search for clips text box, and then press ⏎Enter).**

Clips related to the keywords that you typed display (see Figure 10.6). Keep the Insert ClipArt dialog box open in this state for the next exercise, in which you preview and insert clips.

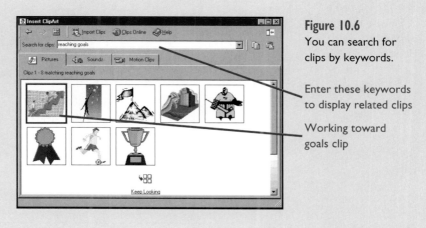

Figure 10.6
You can search for clips by keywords.

Enter these keywords to display related clips

Working toward goals clip

Inside Stuff: **Organizing Your Clip Art**

You don't have to live with the default keywords that Microsoft assigned to a clip. Instead, you can add your own keywords. Here's how: Right-click the clip to display a shortcut menu, and then click Clip P<u>r</u>operties. Click the Keywords tab and choose <u>N</u>ew Keyword. Enter the word in the New Keyword dialog box, and then close all dialog boxes.

You can also create your own category and then add clips to it. For example, you might want to add a category for research and development, sales, accounting, or other topics you regularly use in your job. To do this, click the New Category icon in the Clip Gallery. Enter a new category name in the text box, and then click OK. To add a clip to the category, right-click the clip you want to add, and then choose Clip P<u>r</u>operties. In the Clip Properties dialog box, click the Categories tab. Select the check box for the category to which you want to add the clip, and then close all dialog boxes.

 ## Lesson 2: Previewing and Inserting Pictures

As you saw in the preceding lesson, it's easy to locate a clip when you use keywords or stylistic similarities. Now, let's expand on your knowledge. After you find the clip, you can enlarge and preview it to see whether you really want it in your presentation. If you're sure you want the clip, you can insert it in your presentation and then resize and move it.

Because including clip art is a quick and easy way to spice up a presentation, try previewing and inserting a clip now.

To Preview and Insert Pictures

❶ **Make sure the Sales Contest presentation is open in Normal view, and that your Insert ClipArt dialog box matches that shown in Figure 10.6.**

❷ **Click the first clip on the top row (working toward goals), and then click the Preview clip button.**
The clip is magnified and displays in its own window, so you can determine whether you want the clip in your presentation (see Figure 10.7).

Figure 10.7
You can view an enlarged clip before inserting it in your presentation.

Preview window

Close button

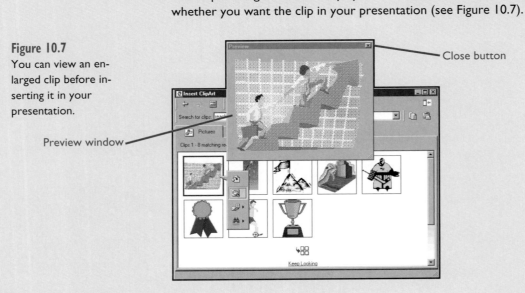

❸ Click the Preview window's Close button.

The Preview window closes. Now insert the clip into your presentation.

❹ Click the first clip on the top row again (working toward goals), and then click the Insert clip button on the pop-up menu.

The clip is inserted in your presentation. The Insert ClipArt dialog box remains open in case you want to add other clips to your presentation. For now, however, you can close the dialog box.

❺ Click the Insert ClipArt dialog box's Close button to close the Clip Gallery.

The clip displays on your slide. Additionally, the clip is automatically selected (as shown by the white selection handles) so that you can resize or move the clip—just like any other object.

❻ Move the mouse pointer over the handle on the lower-right corner of the clip, and then drag down and to the right, approximately two additional inches.

The image is resized. Now try centering it in the middle of the available space.

❼ Move the mouse pointer to the middle of the selected clip object, and then drag the clip so that it's centered in the middle of the available space, and then release the mouse button.

That's all there is to inserting, resizing, and moving your clip.

 Exam Note: Scaling an Object

It's pretty easy to resize a clip art object by dragging a handle. If you'd like more control over the exact size of the object, however, right-click it and then choose Format Picture. In the Format Picture dialog box, click the Size tab. Enter the percentage (compared to the original size) in the Height and Width boxes, and then click OK.

 Exam Note: Inserting Clips

Now you're familiar with how to insert a clip by using the Insert Clip Art button. But there's another method you can use if a slide already includes a clip art placeholder: Double-click the placeholder to display the Clip Gallery, and then insert the clip as usual (see Figure 10.8). Try your hand at using this method now.

---

continues ▶

To Preview and Insert Pictures   (continued)

Figure 10.8
You can double-click a clip art placeholder to access the Clip Gallery.

Clip art placeholder

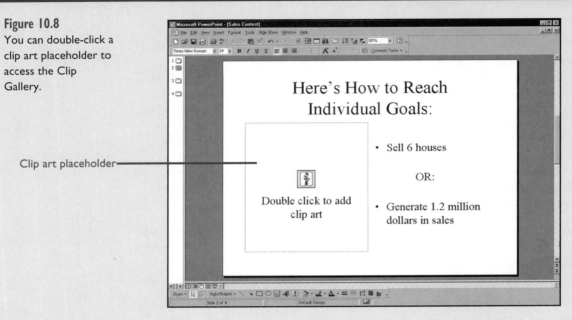

8 **Display Slide 2 in Slide view, and then double-click the clip art placeholder (refer to Figure 10.8).**
The Clip Gallery displays so you can view and select an image.

9 **Type money in the Search for clips text box, and then press ⏎Enter.**
Clips related to the word "money" display (see Figure 10.9).

Figure 10.9
You can quickly locate clips related to money.

Keyword

Choose this clip

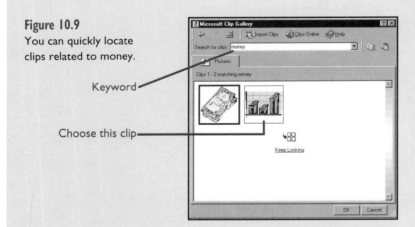

10 **Click the finance clip to display the pop-up menu, and then click the Insert clip button (refer to Figure 10.9 to help you identify the clip).**
The Insert ClipArt dialog box closes and the clip displays on your slide (see Figure 10.10). Notice that the clip automatically conforms to the size and location of the clip placeholder. Additionally, the Picture toolbar displays whenever the object is selected.

If You Have Problems...
Don't worry if the Picture toolbar doesn't display on your computer—someone has just turned it off. You'll turn on this toolbar in the next lesson if it's not already displayed.

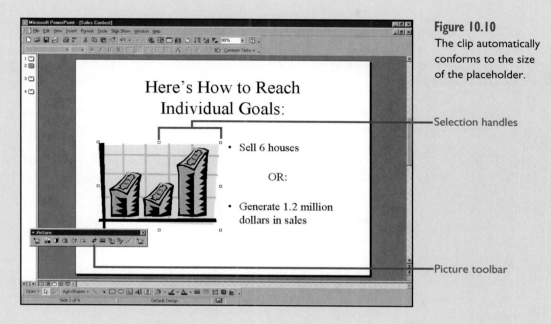

Figure 10.10
The clip automatically conforms to the size of the placeholder.

Selection handles

Picture toolbar

 Save the Sales Contest presentation.
Keep the presentation open for the next lesson, in which you use the Picture toolbar to modify a clip.

 Exam Note: Removing or Replacing a Clip
If you want to remove a clip from your presentation, just click to select it, and then press Del. Likewise, if you want to replace a clip image, delete the clip and insert your replacement.

Exam Note: Inserting an Object from a File
Keep in mind that you're not limited to inserting clips from the Clip Gallery. You can instead choose Insert, Object to display the Insert Object dialog box. Click the Create from file option button, and then enter the name of the file in the text box before clicking OK.

Lesson 3: Modifying a Clip Using the Picture Toolbar

PowerPoint 2000 has dramatically changed the way you can modify clips through the use of the Picture toolbar. By using buttons on this toolbar, you can change the clip's contrast and brightness, display the clip in black and white, crop and recolor the picture. To get more familiar with the toolbar's buttons, take a minute or two to scan Figure 10.11.

Figure 10.11
You can modify a picture by using this toolbar.

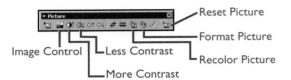

Image Control · Less Contrast · More Contrast · Reset Picture · Format Picture · Recolor Picture

Because of the wide variety of options available on the Picture toolbar, you can use it effectively to modify your clips. Try working with this handy toolbar now.

To Modify a Clip Using the Picture Toolbar

1 **Make sure that Slide 2 of the Sales Contest presentation is open in Slide view, and that the clip art image you inserted in the previous lesson is selected.**
By default, the Picture toolbar displays whenever you select a picture. If it doesn't, however, you can just turn on its display. (Skip Step 2 if the Picture toolbar already displays when you select a clip.)

2 **Choose View, Toolbars, Picture.**
The Picture toolbar displays. (Remember that you can find out about a button's function by resting your mouse pointer over the button until a ScreenTip displays. If you want, use the ScreenTips to identify each toolbar button before proceeding with the tutorial.)

Now, try using some of the buttons on the toolbar.

3 **Click the Image Control button, and then choose Grayscale.**
The clip displays in shades of black, white, and gray rather than in color. Now, try changing the clip back to color.

4 **Click the Image Control button, and then choose Automatic.**
The clip displays using the original colors.

5 **Click the More Contrast button 15 times.**
Each time you click the button, the clip is modified to show more contrast between colors.

6 **Click the Less Contrast button approximately 25 times.**
The clip displays with less contrast between colors. Now, use the Reset Picture button to quickly restore the original settings.

7 **Click the Reset Picture button.**
The clip displays using the original colors. Now, try changing the colors in the clip, a process called *recoloring*. Why would you want to recolor a clip? (To make the image display more attractively with the template's colors, to show your corporate colors, or to emphasize information.) For example, you might recolor a clip red in a safety presentation to convey the idea of a warning.

8 **Click the Recolor Picture button.**
The Recolor Picture dialog box displays (see Figure 10.12). It's easy to change colors for individual elements in the clip using this dialog box: just click the New drop-down list arrow for the color you want to change, and then choose a replacement color. A preview of your clip displays in the preview area of the dialog box, sporting the new color.

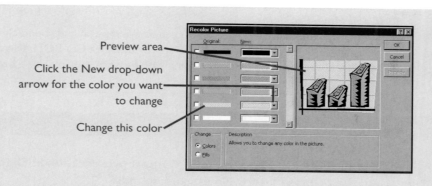

Preview area

Click the New drop-down
arrow for the color you want
to change

Change this color

Figure 10.12
You can recolor a clip
to better match your
slide.

9 **Click the beige color box's New drop-down list arrow (the fifth from the top of the list), and then choose the light gray color box (the eighth color on the top row).**
The new color replaces the original, and the results display in the preview area.

10 **Click OK to accept the color change.**
The new color displays in the clip.

11 **Resize and move the clip so that you can see your text, and then save the Sales Contest presentation.**
Leave the presentation open for the next exercise, in which you learn how to insert and play sound clips.

 Exam Note: **Creating a Watermark**
You can create a ***watermark***, which is a faint image of a picture that displays beneath other text or images on your slide. To do this, select the clip that you want to use for a watermark and display the Picture toolbar. Click the Image Control button on the toolbar, and then choose Watermark.

Lesson 4: Inserting and Playing Sound Clips

You can use sound in a variety of ways to "make or break" a presentation. You can use sound, for example, to indicate a slide transition or to set a mood. You add sound to a slide by inserting a sound file or clip. Once inserted, you can run an electronic slide show to actually play the sound clips.

PowerPoint includes different ways to add sound to your presentation. The method you choose depends on the sound file you want to use and the effect you want.

- You can add sound as part of a slide transition so that the sound plays when one slide replaces another during an electronic slide show.

- You can add audio sound clips from the Clip Gallery or a file. The sound clip is inserted as an object on the slide. You play the sound by clicking the object during an electronic slide show presentation, or set the sound object to play automatically.

- You can play a prerecorded CD as background music to set the mood—perhaps as your audience gathers for your presentation.

Because adding a sound clip or two can lend an air of professionalism and excitement to your presentation, try inserting and playing these types of clips now.

If You Have Problems...
To fully use the multimedia features, such as the motion and sound clips, you must have the proper equipment on your system—usually a CD-ROM drive, sound board, and speakers. Before proceeding with Lessons 4–6, make sure you have the necessary equipment.

To Insert and Play Sound Clips

1 **Display Slide 1 in the open Sales Contest presentation in Slide view, and then choose Insert, Movies and Sounds.**

The Movies and Sounds submenu displays (see Figure 10.13). Notice that you can insert sounds from the Clip Gallery, insert from a file, or even play a CD.

Figure 10.13
You can insert sounds in a variety of ways.

2 **Choose Sound from File.**

The Insert Sound dialog box displays (see Figure 10.14). To make sure you could find a sound file, we included one in the same location as this book's student data files.

Figure 10.14
You can insert a sound file.

3 If necessary, use the Look in drop-down list to locate the folder that contains the student data files for this book to find the Beetvn9 file.

Before you insert the sound clip in your presentation, you can listen to it to make sure it's to your liking.

4 Right-click the Beetvn9 file, and then choose Play from the shortcut menu.

The sound clip—the opening to Beethoven's Ninth Symphony—plays in a media player window. (If you don't want to wait until the entire sound clip plays just click the media player window's Close button.) Now you're ready to insert it in your presentation.

 If You Have Problems...

To play sounds (or motion clips) you must have a media player on your computer. Media players are typically installed with your operating system, browser, or other software. If a sound clip doesn't play, most likely a media player file has been accidentally deleted.

Also, if you see the media player window, but can't hear the sound, check your system to make sure the speakers and sound card are set up properly. You can also check Windows' volume control to make sure that the sound isn't muted.

---

5 Double-click the Beetvn9 file.

A PowerPoint message box displays, asking whether you want the sound clip to play automatically in the slide show (see Figure 10.15). If you choose Yes, the clip plays when the slide displays. On the other hand, choosing No gives you more control over when the sound plays because you must then click the clip to start it.

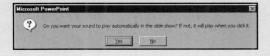

Figure 10.15
Decide whether you want the sound clip to play automatically.

6 Choose Yes.

The sound file is inserted on your slide as an object. Don't be surprised that you can't hear the sound clip—it only plays during a slide show. Now add a setting that ensures that your music will play continually until you move to the next slide during a slide show.

7 Right-click the sound object on your slide, and then choose Edit Sound Object from the shortcut menu.

The Sound Options dialog box displays (see Figure 10.16). You can check the `Loop until stopped` box to indicate that you want the music to play as long as the first slide displays.

Figure 10.16
Keep the music playing—check the Loop until stopped box!

continues ▶

To Insert and Play Sound Clips   (continued)

8 **Check the Loop until stopped box, and then click OK.**
Now move the sound object to an unobtrusive part of your slide so that it's less distracting.

9 **Drag the sound object to the lower-right corner of the slide.**

10 **Save the Sales Contest presentation.**
Keep the presentation open for the next lesson, in which you insert a video clip in it.

Inside Stuff: **Adding a Sound to a Slide Transition**
You can also add a sound to a slide transition. A slide transition, as you recall, is just the way that one slide replaces another. To set up sound so that it plays during the transition, display the slide in Normal or Slide view, and then choose Slide Show, Slide Transition. In the Slide Transition dialog box, click the Sound drop-down list arrow and choose a sound. (If the Sound Effects feature is not already installed, PowerPoint displays a message box, asking whether you want to install it. Make sure the CD is in the CD-ROM drive and choose Yes.) Choose Apply to add the sound to the current slide. The next time you run your slide show, the sound plays as you change slides—which should immediately grab everyone's attention.

Finally, using PowerPoint 2000 you can add **voice narration**—kind of a customized sound track—to your presentation that automatically plays whenever the presentation is given. To begin recording, choose Slide Show, Record Narration.

 Lesson 5: Inserting and Playing Motion Clips

You've already seen how inserting picture and sound clips can spiff up a presentation. PowerPoint can also play **motion clips** (also called *video* or *movie clips*) during an electronic slide show. You can insert videos from the Clip Gallery, a file on your hard disk, or even from the Web. Once inserted, you can play the video as part of your slide show. Videos are an impressive way of catching an audience's attention, emphasizing information or explaining procedures. Video and movie files typically have an extension of *.avi.

Try inserting a motion clip in your Sales Contest presentation now.

To Insert and Play Motion Clips

1 **In the open Sales Contest presentation, display Slide 4 in Slide view.**

2 **Choose Insert, Movies and Sounds, Movie from File.**
The Insert Movie dialog box displays (Figure 10.17).

Figure 10.17
You can insert a video file into your presentation.

Now, try previewing and inserting a movie, or video file.

③ Locate the folder where your student data files are normally located, and then right-click the Winner file.
The shortcut menu displays.

④ Choose Play from the shortcut menu.
A Media Player window displays and the motion clip automatically plays so that you can preview the effect (see Figure 10.18).

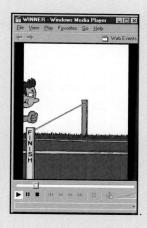

Figure 10.18
You can preview a motion clip before inserting it

⑤ Click the Media Player window's Close button.
The Media Player window closes. Now, you're ready to insert the clip in your presentation.

⑥ Double-click the Winner file.
PowerPoint asks whether you want the video file to automatically play when the slide displays in a running slide show.

⑦ Choose No.
The clip is inserted in your presentation, and displays on your slide, with white selection handles around its borders. You can resize and move this object, just as you can any other object.

⑧ Rest the mouse pointer over the lower-right corner's selection handle, and then drag down and to the right approximately two inches before releasing the mouse.

continues ▶

To Insert and Play Motion Clips (continued)

9 **Move the mouse pointer to the middle of the motion clip object, and then drag it so that it's centered beneath the title ("Be a Winner").**
Now, you're ready to see how the motion clip looks in a running slide show.

10 **With Slide 4 displayed, click the Slide Show button.**
The slide show displays, starting with Slide 4. To play the video, you need to click the video object.

11 **Rest your mouse pointer over the video object until a hand icon displays, and then click.**
The video plays. (You can click the object a second time if you want to see the video again.)

12 **Press** Esc **to end the slide show.**

13 **Save the Sales Contest presentation.**
Leave the presentation open for the next lesson, in which you add an animated GIF.

 Exam Note: **Inserting Objects from the Clip Gallery**
Instead of inserting sound and video clips from a file, you can insert these types of clips from the Clip Gallery. To do this, click the Insert Clip Art button, then click the Sounds or Motion Clips tabs. Click the clip you want, and then choose Insert clip from the pop-up menu.

Although the sound motion clips are not automatically installed during the default PowerPoint installation, there's a wealth of clips available on the Office CD #2. If you need help accessing these clips, see your instructor for help.

 ## Lesson 6: Adding Animated GIFs

What's an **animated GIF**? Simply a file that includes a series of Graphics Interchange Format (GIF) images. These images are played in rapid sequence to give the illusion of movement. (If you've cruised around the Web very much, you've probably seen this type of animation on various Web pages.) GIF files usually have an extension of .gif.

After you've discovered how easy it is to jazz up a presentation by using GIFs, you'll probably want to include them whenever appropriate. Try adding an animated GIF clip to your Sales Contest presentation now.

To Add Animated GIFs

1 **Display Slide 3 of the Sales Contest presentation in Slide view.**

2 **Choose Insert, Picture, From File.**
The Insert Picture dialog box displays (see Figure 10.19). This is the dialog box you use to locate the GIF files.

Figure 10.19
Use PowerPoint 2000 to insert GIF files.

③ Locate the folder where your student data files are normally located, and then double-click the House file.

The GIF file is inserted into your presentation as an object (see Figure 10.20). And, just like other objects, you can resize and move the file.

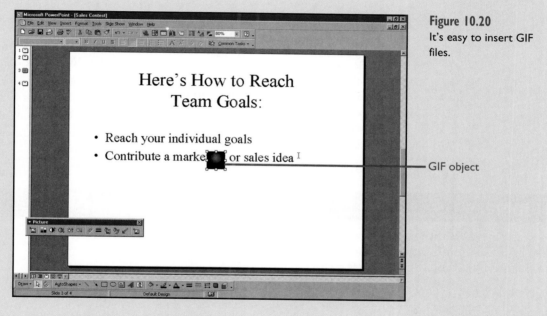

Figure 10.20
It's easy to insert GIF files.

GIF object

④ Resize and move the GIF object so that it displays in the center of the available space.

Now try viewing your entire presentation, complete with the clips you've inserted.

⑤ Display Slide 1, and then click the Slide Show button.

The first slide of the presentation displays. Notice that the sound clip automatically plays.

⑥ Click the left mouse button.

The second slide of your presentation displays—even though the sound clip might not have been finished playing. Remember that the clip continues to play only until you advance to the next slide.

⑦ Click the left mouse button.

Slide 3 displays—and the GIF file automatically plays.

continues ▶

To Add Animated GIFs (continued)

8 **Press ⏎Enter.**
Slide 4 displays.

9 **Move your mouse pointer over the video object until a hand icon displays, and then click.**
The video plays. (You can click the object again if you want to see the movie a second time.)

10 **Press Esc.**
The slide show again displays in Slide view.

11 **Save the Sales Contest presentation, and then close it.**
If you've finished with your work session, exit PowerPoint and shut down Windows before turning off your computer. Otherwise, complete the Skill Drill, Challenge, and Discovery Zone exercises at the end of this project.

Inside Stuff: **Using the Clip Gallery Live**
Tired of the same old clips? If you're hungry for more choices just turn to Microsoft's Clip Gallery Live site on the World Wide Web. The Clip Gallery Live includes thousands of clips—including clip art, sound files, movies and GIF animations—that you can download to use in your presentation. (Of course, you need a connection to the Web to tap into this resource.) To access the Clip Gallery Live, choose Clips Online in the Insert ClipArt dialog box.

Summary

Congratulations! You significantly improved a presentation's appearance and effectiveness by inserting picture, sound, video and GIF files on your slides. You're sure to develop a winning presentation by judiciously including a few clips.

To expand on your knowledge, spend a few minutes exploring Help on these topics. Additionally, complete some of the Skill Drill, Challenge, and Discovery Zone exercises.

Checking Concepts and Terms

True/False

For each of the following, check *T* or *F* to indicate whether the statement is true or false.

__T __F **1.** Picture, video, and sound files are collectively referred to as clips. [L1]

__T __F **2.** You can use the Picture Art Gallery to view and insert clips. [L2]

__T __F **3.** You find clips by keyword or category. [L1]

__T __F **4.** You cannot preview a video clip before inserting it in your presentation because the process uses too much memory. [L5]

__T __F **5.** You can add sound only for slide transitions. [L4]

Multiple Choice

Circle the letter of the correct answer for each of the following.

1. To use PowerPoint's multimedia capabilities effectively, your computer system should include which of the following? [L4–6]

a. a sound card

b. speakers

c. a CD-ROM drive

d. all of the above

2. Which of the following can you include in a presentation? [L3–6]

a. clip art images

b. GIF files

c. sound files

d. all of the above

3. What is the name of the Web site that includes clips you can download? [L6]

a. Art Gallery Online

b. Clippit Live

c. Clip Gallery Live

d. Picture Gallery

4. What is a GIF? [L6]

a. A type of file that displays images in sequence to give the illusion of movement

b. A Web site where you can download clips

c. A self-running presentation

d. A way of adding sound clips to your presentation

5. What can you do with a clip art image after you insert it on a slide? [L3]

a. recolor it

b. move it

c. resize it

d. all of the above

Skill Drill

Skill Drill exercises reinforce project skills. Each skill reinforced is the same, or nearly the same, as a skill presented in the project. Detailed instructions are provided in a step-by-step format.

1. Finding and Inserting Pictures

You work for the Information Technology Department at a hospital and are upgrading all the computers on-site. The hospital administrator asked you to conduct a brief presentation on the process for the doctors, so that they have an idea of how you plan to proceed with the project. To spiff up your presentation, you add some clip art. [L1–2]

1. Open **PP-1002** and save it as **Status of Computer Upgrade**.

2. Display Slide 1 of the presentation in Normal view, and then choose Insert, Picture, Clip Art.

3. In the Search for clips text box, type **computers**, and then press ↵Enter.

4. Drag a computer clip of your choice from the Insert ClipArt dialog box into the slide. Move and resize the clip so that it displays below the slide's title.

5. Display Slide 2 of the presentation in Normal view, and then double-click the clip art placeholder to open the Clip Gallery.

6. Click the icon for the Science & Technology category. Click a computer clip to display the pop-up menu, and then click the Find similar clips button. On the Find similar clips pane, click the keyword for technology.

7. Click a clip that you think you want to insert in your presentation. Then, click the Artistic Style button to find clips that use the same style.

8. Click the Back button to redisplay the preceding screen. Click a clip, and then choose the Insert clip button to add the clip to Slide 2.

9. Save the Status of Computer Upgrade presentation. Keep it open for the next exercise.

2. Adding a Sound Clip to a Presentation

So that you can get your audience keyed-in to your presentation, you decide to add a sound clip to the opening slide. You also set options so that the sound clip plays continually when the slide displays during a slide show. [L4]

1. Display Slide 1 in the Status of Computer Upgrade presentation, and then click the Insert Clip Art button. Click the Sounds tab.

2. Click the Entertainment category to display related sound clips. Click a sound clip, and then choose Play clip from the pop-up menu. Repeat the process with at least five other sound clips. Close the Insert ClipArt dialog box without inserting a clip.

3. Choose Insert, Movies and Sounds, Sound from File.

4. Listen to the Lazym sound file, and then double-click the file to insert it in your presentation.

5. When the PowerPoint message box displays, choose Yes to specify that your sound clip should play automatically.

6. Drag the sound clip to the lower-right corner of the slide.

7. Right-click the clip and choose Edit Sound Object. In the Sound Options dialog box, check the **Loop until stopped** box. Choose OK to close the dialog box.

8. Click the Slide Show button to run your slide show. Advance completely through the slide show, and then press Esc to end the show.

9. Save the Status of Computer Upgrade presentation. Keep it open and PowerPoint running for the next exercise.

3. Finding and Inserting a Motion Clip from the Web

To add a finishing touch to your presentation, you decide to use a motion clip (rather than a picture clip) on Slide 1. After searching the Clip Gallery, however, you can't find a suitable clip. To find more choices, you decide to look on the World Wide Web. [L7]

1. Display Slide 1 of the Status of Computer Upgrade presentation in Normal view, and then click the clip object. Press Del to remove the clip object.

2. Connect to the Web to find more clips. Click the Insert Clip Art button to display the Insert ClipArt dialog box. Then, click Clips Online.

3. In the Connect to Web for More Clip Art, Photos, Sounds dialog box, click OK. Complete whatever steps are necessary on your system to connect to the Web.

4. When the End-User License Agreement page of the Clip Gallery Live displays, click the Accept button.

5. On the opening page of the Clip Gallery Live, enter **technology** (or **celebration**) in the Search Clips by Keyword text box. Press ↵Enter.

6. Click the Motion tab to display motion clips that include the keyword technology.

7. Click a clip of your choice to display it in the Preview area. Then, click the Preview area (or the red down-pointing arrow) to download the clip.

8. When the Insert ClipArt dialog box displays, click the downloaded motion clip and choose Insert clip. Close the Insert ClipArt dialog box and the Clip Gallery Live. (Also, close the connection to the Web, if prompted.)

9. Move and resize the motion clip on Slide 1 so that it displays below the title.

10. Run the presentation as a slide show to see the effects you added.

11. Save the Status of Computer Upgrade presentation, and then close it. Keep PowerPoint running if you plan to complete additional exercises.

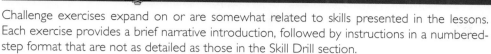

Challenge

Challenge exercises expand on or are somewhat related to skills presented in the lessons. Each exercise provides a brief narrative introduction, followed by instructions in a numbered-step format that are not as detailed as those in the Skill Drill section.

1. Inserting and Recoloring Pictures

You work for a scientific research facility and were asked to represent the company at a trade show. To spiff up an existing presentation, you decide to add some clips to it. [L2–3]

1. Open **PP-1003** and save it as **ABC Research**.

2. Display Slide 1 in Normal view, and then display the Pictures page of the Clip Gallery. Locate all clips related to science or technology.

3. Use the **Find similar clips** button to locate clips that include the following keywords: **chemical**, **mixing**, **research**, and **measuring instruments**.

4. Preview several clips. When you find a suitable clip that you like, insert it in your presentation.

5. Using the Picture toolbar, modify the picture as follows:

   - Display the clip in <u>G</u>rayscale, <u>B</u>lack & White, and as a <u>W</u>atermark. Then, choose <u>A</u>utomatic on the Image Control button.

   - Click the More Contrast button several times to see the effect. Click the Less Contrast button several times.

   - Click the More Brightness button repeatedly until you see a change. Click the Less Brightness button as many times as necessary, until you see a change.

   - Click the Recolor Picture button. Change several colors on the image.

   - Click the Reset Picture button. Resize and move the picture, as necessary, to display in the center of the available space.

6. Save your changes. Keep the ABC Research presentation open for the next exercise.

2. Adding Motion and Sound Clips

Make sure that the ABC Research presentation you developed in the preceding exercise is open. Display Slide 2 in Normal view, and then make the following changes to the slide: .[L4, 6]

1. Insert a motion clip from the Clip Gallery Live or a file. (*Hint:* Search for clips by the keywords you used in the previous exercise. Also preview several motion clips in the Clip Gallery Live before choosing one for your presentation.) Resize and move the clip, as necessary, to display in the middle of the available space.

2. Add a sound clip of your choice (either from Office's Clip Gallery or from the Clip Gallery Live) to Slide 1 and Slide 2. Set the sounds to play automatically and move the sound objects to the lower-right corner of each slide.

3. Edit the sound objects so that they play as long as the associated slide displays.

4. If you want, add voice narration to the first slide. Develop your own "script" that describes your company, and then record it as part of the slide. (If necessary, use Help to find out how to add voice narration to a slide.)

5. Run your presentation as a slide show to see the effects. Save the presentation, and then close it.

3. Working with Clips

As a manager for your company, you're working on a presentation to give to your staff. The purpose of the presentation is to motivate people to set goals. To help inspire them, you decide to insert both motion and sound clips in your presentation. [L4–5]

1. Open **PP-1004** and save it as **Setting Goals**. Make the following changes to Slide 1:

    - Insert a sound clip from the Clip Gallery, the Clip Gallery Live, or a file. Set the clip to play automatically and continuously as the slide displays. Move the sound object to the lower-right corner of the slide.

    - Use the Picture toolbar to modify the picture clip on Slide 1. Experiment with the different effects (including creating a Watermark). When you finish, click the Reset Picture button.

2. Make the following changes to Slide 2:

    - Locate all the picture clips in Office's Clip Gallery that have the following keywords: **goals**, **success**, **accomplishment**, **challenges**, **victories**, and **problem**. Then find clips in the Clip Gallery Live with the same keywords.

    - Display the Clip Properties for several of the clips you find in the Clip Gallery. (*Hint:* Use the shortcut menu.)

    - Choose an appropriate clip and insert it on Slide 2. Resize, format, and move the clip, as necessary.

    - Add a sound clip to the slide. Edit the object so that it plays continually when the slide displays in a slide show. Move the sound object to the lower-right corner of the slide.

3. Make the following changes to Slide 3:

    - Search the Clip Gallery Live by the following categories: Business, Office, People, and People at Work.

    - Preview several motion clips in the Clip Gallery Live.

    - Insert an appropriate motion or GIF clip from the Clip Gallery Live (or a file). Move and resize the clip, as necessary.

    - Add a sound clip. Set the clip to play automatically and continuously. Move the clip object to the lower-right corner of the slide.

4. View your presentation as a slide show. Save the presentation, and then close it. Keep PowerPoint running if you plan to complete additional exercises.

Discovery Zone

Discovery Zone exercises require advanced knowledge of topics presented in *MOUS Essentials* lessons, application of skills from multiple lessons, or self-directed learning of new skills. Each exercise is independent of the others, so you may complete the exercises in any order.

1. Troubleshooting Clip Gallery Problems

You provide support for 50 Office users at an accounting firm. Recently, your company upgraded to Office 2000, but never provided training for you so that you could effectively help the end users. As a result, you're on your own in finding out about different Office features. One particularly troublesome feature is the Clip Gallery. Users are having problems...they can't find motion and sound clips, they're getting messages that the main catalog (Artgal50.mmc) is corrupted, and so on. To help them out, you spend some time researching these types of problems.

In a new blank presentation, click the Insert Clip Art button to display the Insert ClipArt dialog box. Click Help to display the Microsoft Clip Gallery 5.0 Help dialog box.

Find out why your users are experiencing the following problems:

- They can't find buttons or functions in the Clip Gallery that were present in the previous version that they used.
- They can't locate motion or sound clips.
- They imported clips from the Clip Gallery Live, yet they can't find the clips.
- They can't find a catalog (or clips) that were previously available.
- The Artgal50.mmc file is corrupt.
- They can't find the media player.

Close the Clip Gallery's help. Create a multiple-slide presentation (complete with clips) that outlines the information that you find. Share the presentation with at least one other user or with your class. If your instructor wants, save the presentation. Otherwise, close it without saving it. Keep PowerPoint running if you plan to complete the additional exercises. [L1–6]

2. Inserting and Playing Clips

You work for a travel agency and are slated to give a presentation to a community group during a luncheon meeting. In preparation for the talk, you create a presentation that includes picture, motion, and sound clips. To find some of the clips, you use the Clip Gallery Live.

Open **PP-1005** and save it as **Travel Agency**. Modify the presentation, referring to Help or the information in this project if you can't remember how to complete a step.

Make the following changes to Slide 2 (Go to Japan):

- Search for picture clips in the Clip Gallery and the Clip Gallery Live by the keywords **travel**, **trip**, **Japan**, **world**, and **tour**.
- Preview several clips and view their keywords.
- Insert, resize, move, and recolor a clip that is appropriate for this slide's content.

Make the following changes to Slide 3 (or China):

- Search for picture clips in the Clip Gallery and the Clip Gallery Live by the keywords **travel**, **trip**, **China**, **world**, and **tour**.
- Preview several clips and view their keywords.
- Find clips with a similar artistic style to the one you inserted on Slide 2. (You can choose either a scanned photograph or a clip art image.)
- Insert, resize, move, and recolor a picture clip appropriate for this slide's content. (It doesn't have to match the artistic style of Slide 2).

Make the following changes to Slide 4 (Travel the World!):

- Search for motion clips in the Clip Gallery and the Clip Gallery Live by the keywords **travel**, **trip**, **world**, and **tour**.
- Preview several clips and view their keywords.
- Insert, resize, move, and recolor a motion clip appropriate for this slide's content.

Add a sound clip to the first slide. Set the clip to play automatically when the slide displays, and to loop continually.

Copy the same sound clip to each slide. (*Hint:* You can use copy and paste to quickly duplicate the sound clip and its properties.) Move the clip to a corner of the slide.

Run your presentation as a slide show and share the presentation with at least one other user (or your instructor). Make any revisions necessary to improve the show, based on feedback from other users. Save the Travel Agency presentation, and then close it. Exit PowerPoint.

PinPoint Assessment

You have completed this project and its associated lessons, and have had an opportunity to assess your skills through the end-of-project questions and exercises. Now use the PinPoint software Evaluation Mode to further assess your comprehension of the specific exam activities you have just learned. You can also use the PinPoint Trainer Mode and the Show Me tutorials to practice these exam activities.

Using Drawn Objects

Key terms introduced in this project include

- adjustment handle
- array
- AutoShapes
- drawn objects

- fill effects
- Format Painter
- freehand shapes

- rotate handles
- semitransparent fill
- sweep

Objectives	Required Activity for MOUS	Exam Level
➤ Drawing Freehand Objects	Add and group shapes using WordArt or the Drawing toolbar	Core
	Create a text box for entering text	Core
	Use the Wrap Text in TextBox feature	Core
➤ Using AutoShapes	Place text inside a shape using a text box	Core
	Use the Wrap Text in AutoShape feature	Expert
➤ Manipulating and Grouping Objects	Add and group shapes using WordArt or the Drawing toolbar	Core
	Size and scale an object, including ClipArt	Expert
	Rotate and fill an object	Expert
	Customize clip art and other objects (resize, scale, etc.)	Expert
➤ Formatting Objects with Fill Effects	Apply formatting	Core
	Rotate and fill an object	Core
➤ Formatting Objects with 3-D Effects	Apply formatting	Core
➤ Formatting Objects with a Shadow Effect	Apply formatting	Core
➤ Using WordArt	Add and group shapes using WordArt or the Drawing toolbar	Core
	Customize clip art and other objects (resize, scale, etc.)	Core

Why Would I Do This?

As you saw in Project 10, "Using Advanced Multimedia and Graphics," PowerPoint's clip art images are handy for jazzing up a presentation. These clips won't fit all your needs for illustrating your presentation, however. Luckily, PowerPoint includes a wealth of tools on the Drawing toolbar that you can use to quickly produce your own **drawn objects** such as arrows, rectangles, circles, and other shapes. These objects are useful for emphasizing key information on a slide or to capture an audience's attention. You might want to have an arrow point to the highest sales for the year, for example, or to just draw interest to information. Figure 11.1 shows how drawn objects can enhance a slide.

Figure 11.1

You can use a variety of drawn objects on a slide.

In addition to adding interest or emphasizing information, you can also use PowerPoint's drawing tools to create rather complicated drawings that are not available as predrawn clip art. For example, you may want to design a company, department, or personal logo and can't find clip art to fit the bill. If you're ambitious (and creative), you can use the drawing tools that PowerPoint provides to design your own logo.

After you draw an object, you can move, resize, scale, format, and otherwise modify it. To give you even more choices, PowerPoint 2000 also includes tools that you can use to apply 3-D and shadow effects to objects. Finally, you can use WordArt to create text objects and then manipulate them.

In this project you'll learn a variety of advanced drawing techniques. Because drawn objects can add so much pizzazz to a presentation, try working with them now.

 Inside Stuff: Freehand or AutoShape?

In PowerPoint, you can draw either freehand or AutoShape objects. **Freehand shapes**, such as lines, rectangles, and ovals, are those that you draw from scratch using the mouse. In general, you must have good control of the mouse, a creative mind, drawing skills, and time to create complicated freehand shapes. In contrast, you can quickly reproduce professionally designed objects, such as stars, banners, bubble callouts, and so on, by using **AutoShapes**. These are predesigned shapes included with PowerPoint.

Lesson 1: Drawing Freehand Objects

You can draw freehand objects by using the tools on PowerPoint's Drawing toolbar (see Figure 11.2). By default, this toolbar displays at the bottom of the PowerPoint screen when your presentation is shown in Normal or Slide view.

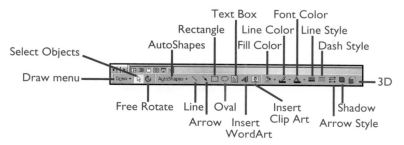

Figure 11.2
The Drawing toolbar gives you quick access to a multitude of tools.

Luckily, it's easy to draw a freehand shape: Just click the tool you want, and then drag to draw the shape on your slide.

To have more control over the way your freehand shapes are created, however, you can use the following methods:

- Press **⬆Shift** while dragging to produce a straight line or arrow, and to create a perfect circle or square.

- Press **Ctrl** as you drag to make the point where you begin the center of your object.

- Press **Ctrl** and **⬆Shift** to create a symmetrical object (such as a perfect circle or square) from the point where you began.

Additionally, you can double-click a tool to keep it active to draw more than one object. When you finish drawing objects with it, click the tool again to turn it off.

Try using these techniques to draw some freehand objects now.

To Draw Freehand Objects

❶ Start a new presentation and display a blank slide.
You'll have the most room to work with objects on a slide if you display the presentation in Slide view.

❷ Click the Slide View button in the lower-left corner of the application window.
The presentation displays in Slide view to give you more "screen real estate" with which to work. Another way to make working with objects easier is to use PowerPoint's horizontal and vertical rulers.

You turn the rulers on or off by choosing <u>V</u>iew, <u>R</u>uler. When turned on, the rulers appear at the top and left sides of the slide window. The **0** marks on the horizontal and vertical rulers represent the center of the slide. When you draw an object, the movement reflects on the rulers to show your exact location on the slide. This helps you accurately place drawn objects.

❸ If the rulers don't display on your screen, choose <u>V</u>iew, <u>R</u>uler.
The rulers display (see Figure 11.3).

To Draw Freehand Objects (continued)

> **X** **If You Have Problems...**
> Because the <u>R</u>uler command is a toggle, don't complete Step 3 if the rulers already display. Another snag is that the Drawing toolbar's display may be turned off. If this is the case, choose <u>V</u>iew, <u>T</u>oolbars; then choose Drawing from the submenu.

Figure 11.3
Rulers help you draw objects more precisely on your slide.

Horizontal ruler

Vertical ruler

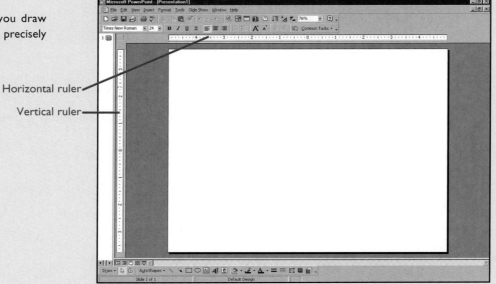

4 **Click the Rectangle tool on the Drawing toolbar, and then move the mouse pointer into the slide area.**
The mouse pointer changes to a crosshair so that you can accurately place the drawn object. The mouse pointer's appearance changes, depending on the type of tool you choose.

5 **On the slide, position the crosshair where the two 0-inch marks intersect; then click and drag downward until the rectangle's lower-right corner is at the place where the 3-inches horizontal mark and the 2-inches vertical ruler mark intersect. Release the mouse button.**
A rectangle is added to your presentation (see Figure 11.4). The color and line colors used for the object are whatever was used most recently for the Fill Color and Line Color tools. Additionally, white selection handles appear around the object to indicate that it is selected. You can easily deselect the object—just click on the slide (outside of the object) or draw another object. (You learn more about how to select and modify drawn objects in Lesson 3.)

You can use other drawing tools in the same manner: click the tool, and then drag to draw the object on the slide. And remember: You can press ⬆Shift) while dragging to create a symmetrical object.

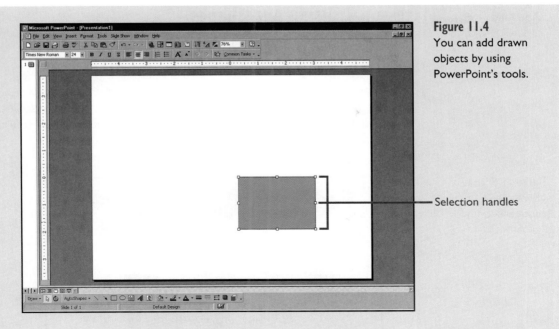

Figure 11.4
You can add drawn
objects by using
PowerPoint's tools.

Selection handles

6 **Click the Oval tool; then press** ◆Shift **as you drag to draw a 1-inch circle in the lower-left corner of the slide.**
A perfect circle is added to your slide. Now, try drawing an oval that originates from the center.

7 **Click the Oval tool; then press** Ctrl **and draw a 1-inch oval in the upper-right corner of the slide.**
The oval is drawn from the point where you first clicked the mouse.

8 **Save the presentation as** Freehand Drawing, **and then close it.**
Keep PowerPoint running for the next lesson, in which you use PowerPoint's AutoShapes.

 Exam Note: **Using Text Boxes**

Drawing a text box is similar to drawing a rectangle, except that the box includes an area in which you can enter and edit text. In a sense, a text box is like a "mini-document." To draw a text box, click the Text Box tool. Click at the beginning location on the slide, and then drag the mouse until the text box is the size you want. Alternatively, choose the Text Box tool, and then click once on the slide where you want the text to appear.

After you have created a text box, you can enter and edit text as you would in a word processor. When you're finished, click outside the box to deselect it. If you later decide to make text revisions, click inside the box to place the insertion point in it before entering your replacement text.

To change how the text wraps within the box, you can resize the box. Alternatively, right-click the box's border and choose Format Text Box. Click the Text Box tab. To make the text wrap horizontally in the text box, check the box for Word wrap text in AutoShape. To adjust the Text Box's size so that the text fits within it, check the box for Resize AutoShape to fit text.

Finally, to delete a text box, click within it to select it. Then, click the border and press Del.

Lesson 2: Using AutoShapes

If you're not very artistic, or just don't have a great deal of time, you'll appreciate PowerPoint's AutoShapes. By using AutoShapes, you can easily insert professionally designed objects, such as circles, rectangles, and arrows, in your presentation to spice it up or empha-size certain information (see Figure 11.5). Once inserted, you can move, color, resize, or even add text to an AutoShape. After you discover how easy it is to place AutoShapes into your presentation, you'll probably find that it's quicker and more efficient to use them instead of drawing the same type of objects from scratch.

Figure 11.5
Give a slide a snappy appearance with AutoShapes.

To give you plenty of variety, PowerPoint includes eight categories of AutoShapes:

- Lines—Six line tools to draw straight and curved lines freehand.
- Connectors—Nine connector tools that you can use to draw lines between other ob-jects. Once connected, they stay connected, even if you move the objects. They are useful for flow charts, organizational charts, and so on.
- Basic Shapes—Thirty-two commonly used shapes.
- Block Arrows—Twenty-eight block (thick) arrows.
- Flowchart—Twenty-eight shapes to help you build elements to create a flow chart or document processes.
- Stars and Banners—Sixteen stars and banners that you can use to announce news, em-phasize information, and otherwise add an element of excitement.
- Callouts—Twenty ways to draw text annotations.
- Action Buttons—Twelve button shapes that you can use as buttons on a slide. After you draw the button, you can associate the action with a sound or movie file, or link it to the World Wide Web.

The basic process of creating an AutoShape is the same, no matter which type of shape you choose. First, click the AutoShapes tool to display the AutoShapes menu. Choose a menu category, and then click a shape from the submenu. Drag in the drawing area of the screen to create a shape.

To create a symmetrical shape, press (◆Shift) while drawing, just like you did earlier when you used the basic drawing tools. Likewise, you can press (Ctrl) to draw the shape from the center outward. Because you can create such a variety of drawings using AutoShapes, try using them now.

For this exercise, imagine that you own Star Training Company, a small computer consulting and training organization. To get your new trainer/consultants up to speed, you periodically conduct a training seminar that outlines how you want your trainers to work with businesses. To emphasize the information in an easy-to-remember way, you use AutoShapes in your presentation, including connector lines, a banner, and a callout.

To Use AutoShapes

① **Open PP-1101 and save it as** `Computer Training Procedures`.

② **Display Slide 2 in Slide view, and then click the A̲utoShapes tool on the Drawing toolbar and move your mouse pointer to S̲tars and Banners.**
The S̲tars and Banners submenu displays (see Figure 11.6). You can rest your pointer over any of the AutoShapes on this submenu and a ScreenTip pops up to indicate the AutoShape's name. When you find the AutoShape you want, you can click to select it.

> AutoShapes ▾

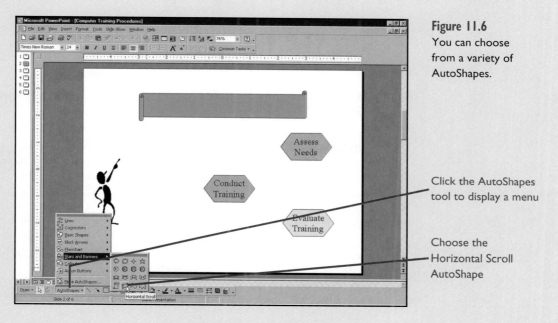

Figure 11.6
You can choose from a variety of AutoShapes.

Click the AutoShapes tool to display a menu

Choose the Horizontal Scroll AutoShape

③ **Rest the mouse pointer over the Horizontal Scroll AutoShape to display its ScreenTip, and then click the shape.**
The AutoShape's tool activates. Now, you can draw the shape by dragging to indicate the size and location you want.

④ **Move the crosshair pointer to the intersection of the 3-inch horizontal and vertical marks in the upper-left corner of the slide; then click and drag down and to the right to the 3-inch mark on the horizontal ruler and 2-inch mark on the vertical ruler. Release the mouse button.**
The banner is drawn with the dimensions you indicated (see Figure 11.7). Notice that the object has white selection handles that you can use to move or resize the object. The object, like many AutoShapes, also has an **_adjustment handle_**. An adjustment handle is a diamond-shaped handle you can use to change the appearance (not the size) of an AutoShape. For example, you can change the size of the point of an arrow. Some AutoShapes even contain more than one adjustment handle so that you can change several of the shape's elements. In this case, you use the adjustment handle to make the scroll's curve tighter or looser.

continues ▶

To Use AutoShapes (continued)

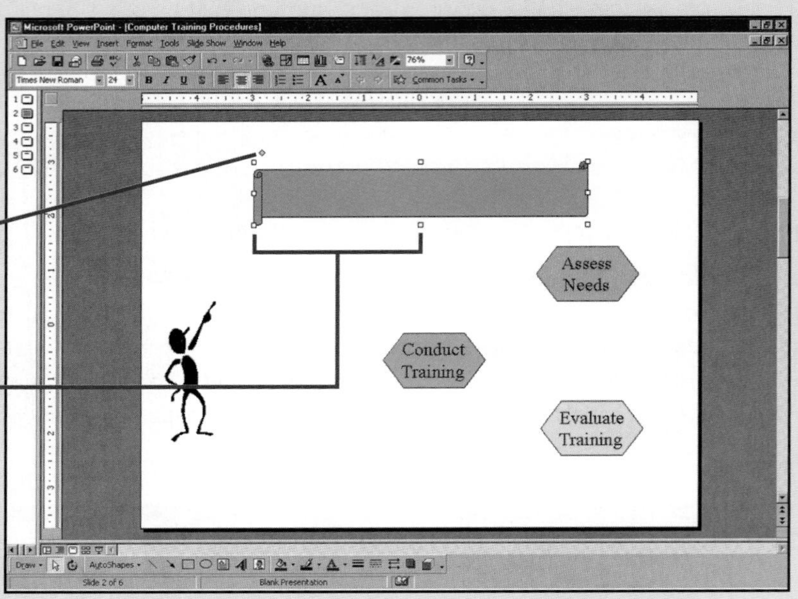

Figure 11.7
Many AutoShapes include an adjustment handle.

Use the adjustment handle to change the object's shape

Use the selection handles to move or resize the object

5 **Drag the adjustment handle to the right to increase the curve on the scroll; then release the mouse button.**

The AutoShape's appearance changes. If you want, experiment by dragging the adjustment handle to the left and right until you are satisfied with the scroll's appearance. (Although PowerPoint enables you to change the AutoShape's appearance, you can only drag a certain amount to the right or to the left for this particular shape. When you're finished, proceed with the next step.)

You can also add text to an AutoShape—just click in the shape and start typing. The text you add becomes part of the shape. If you subsequently change the shape's size or location, the text moves with it. Try adding some text to your AutoShape now.

6 **Make sure that the scroll is still selected, and then type** `Computer Training Procedures.`

The text is added to the AutoShape. (You can select text, and then format it like any other text in PowerPoint. For now, however, leave the text as it is and add another AutoShape to the slide.)

Exam Note: **Wrapping Text in an AutoShape**

You'll sometimes find that the text doesn't display as you want within the AutoShape. Here's the workaround: Select the shape, and then choose Format, AutoShape. In the Format AutoShape dialog box, click the Text Box tab. To make the text wrap horizontally in the AutoShape, check the box for Word wrap text in AutoShape. To adjust the AutoShape's size so that the text fits within it, check the box for Resize AutoShape to fit text.

---

7 **Click the AutoShapes tool; then choose Callouts, Rounded Rectangular Callout.**

8 **Starting at 0 inch on the vertical ruler and 3 inches on the left side of the horizontal ruler, drag up and to the right to draw a callout approximately 1-1/2" high by 2-1/2" wide. Release the mouse button.**

A callout bubble is added to your slide (see Figure 11.8). You can add text to the callout as you did to the scroll.

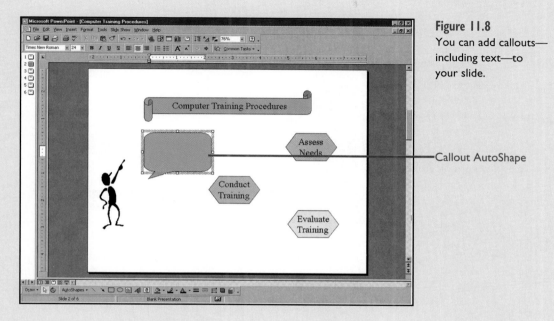

Figure 11.8
You can add callouts—including text—to your slide.

Callout AutoShape

9 **With the callout still selected, type Be sure to follow the steps.**

The text wraps to fit within the callout. Now, try adding some connector lines between the three shapes on the right side of the slide. You can do this by using PowerPoint's connector lines to connect the objects. The connector lines are handy because they keep objects connected—even if you later move or resize them.

10 **Click the AutoShape tool; then choose Connectors, Straight Arrow Connector and draw a line from the Assess Needs object to the Conduct Training object. Release the mouse button.**

When you move the special connector pointer over an object, square blue handles display at the corners of the object. These handles indicate locations where the objects can be connected to another. When you drag the line to the second object, it also displays connector handles (see Figure 11.9). Finally, when you release the mouse button, red connector handles display. Now try adding another connector line.

continues ▶

To Use AutoShapes   (continued)

Figure 11.9
Connector lines are useful for keeping objects together

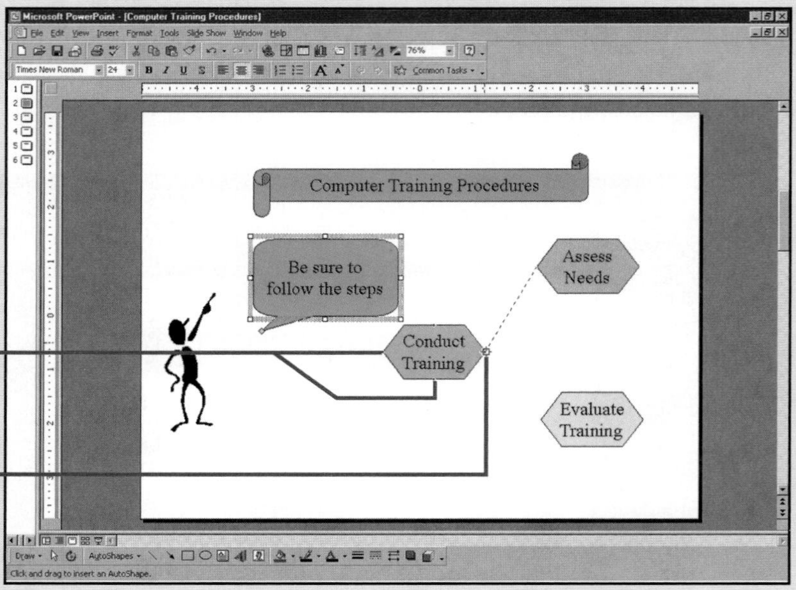

Connector handles indicate where an object can be connected to another

Special connector pointer

⑪ Click the AutoShape tool; then choose Connectors, Elbow Arrow Connector and draw a line from the Conduct Training object to the Evaluate Training object. Release the mouse button.
The objects connect. Now, try moving the Evaluate Training object.

⑫ Click the Evaluate Training object to select it, and then display the four-headed arrow over the object's border and move the object to the bottom of the slide.
When you rearrange objects, the connectors remain attached. Remember, if you accidentally move an object to the wrong location, you can click PowerPoint's Undo button to reverse your action.

⑬ Save the Computer Training Procedures presentation.
Keep the presentation open for the next lesson, in which you learn to manipulate objects by flipping, rotating, and aligning them.

✏ Exam Note: **Creating Default-Size AutoShapes**
You don't have to click and drag in the slide to create an AutoShape. To quickly create an AutoShape using PowerPoint's default size, choose the AutoShape from the AutoShapes palette; then click in the slide.

      # Lesson 3: Manipulating and Grouping Objects

If you're a typical PowerPoint user, you probably revise objects in various ways after you draw them. For example, you might draw several objects and then change your mind about how they are laid out. Luckily, you can flip, align, rotate, and otherwise manipulate objects to give you maximum flexibility in designing (or redesigning) your slide.

Use Table 11.1 as a reference when you want to manipulate your drawings:

Table 11.1   Methods of selecting objects

To	Do This
Select a drawn object	Click the object.
Select multiple objects	Press (◆Shift) as you click the objects.
Deselect objects	Click outside the objects.
Resize an object	Select the object, rest the mouse pointer on a selection handle until a two-sided arrow displays, and drag to resize.
Move an object	Select the object, move the mouse pointer over the object until a four-sided arrow displays, and drag to the new location.
Duplicate an object	Select the object and choose Edit, Duplicate.
Delete an object	Select the object and press (Del).
Rotate an object	Select the object and click the Free Rotate button to place green rotate handles around the object. Move the mouse pointer over a handle and drag to spin the object.
Flip an object	Select the object and choose Draw, Rotate or Flip, Flip Horizontal (or Flip Vertical).
Align objects	Select the objects and choose Draw, Align or Distribute.
Change the stacking order of objects	Select the object and choose Draw, Order.
Group objects	Select the objects to group and choose Draw, Group.
Ungroup an object	Select the object and choose Draw, Ungroup.

Most of the commands that manipulate objects are found on the Draw menu (Figure 11.10).

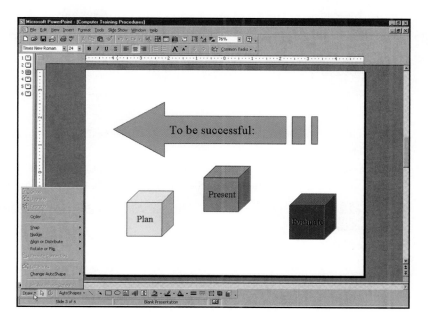

Figure 11.10
You can execute many commands by using the Drawing toolbar's Draw menu.

To make your Computer Training Procedures presentation more polished and professional looking, try manipulating and grouping objects in it now.

To Manipulate and Group Objects

1 **Display Slide 3 in the Computer Training Procedures presentation, and then click the arrow object (`To be successful`).**
Before you can manipulate an object, you must first select it. As usual, white selection handles appear around any selected object.

2 **Click the D̲raw tool on the Drawing toolbar, and then choose Rotate or Flip, Flip H̲orizontal.**
The object flips 180 degrees horizontally. Now try lining up multiple objects.

3 **Click outside the arrow to deselect it; then press ⬆Shift as you click the Plan, Present, and Evaluate cube objects.**
Each object appears with white selection handles around the border (see Figure 11.11). Because you selected all the objects, any command you use will apply to all selected objects.

Figure 11.11
You can select multiple objects.

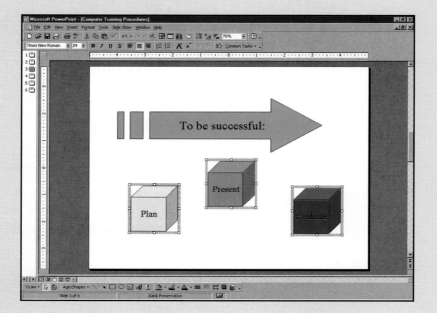

4 **Click the D̲raw tool, and then choose A̲lign or Distribute, Align B̲ottom.**
The bottoms of the selected objects line up on an imaginary line. Now, try using a command that spaces them evenly between the left and right objects.

5 **Click the D̲raw tool, and then choose A̲lign or Distribute, Distribute Horizontally.**
The objects rearrange so that an even amount of space is between each of them (see Figure 11.12).

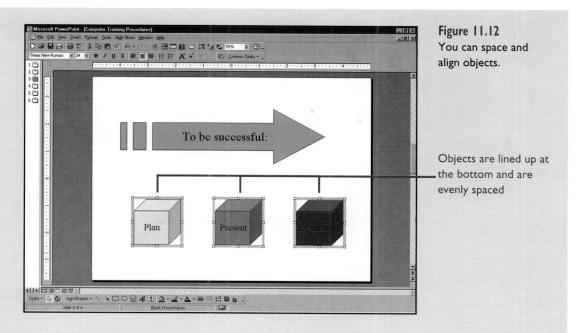

Figure 11.12
You can space and align objects.

Objects are lined up at the bottom and are evenly spaced

You can also manually rotate objects to the angle you want. Try this now.

6 **Display Slide 4 in the open presentation, and then click to select the curved green arrow.**

7 **Click the Free Rotate button on the Drawing toolbar.**
Green *rotate handles* appear around the object (see Figure 3.14). You can place the mouse pointer over any rotate handle, and then drag to rotate the object.

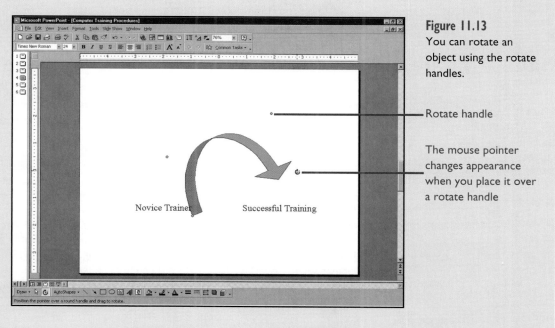

Figure 11.13
You can rotate an object using the rotate handles.

Rotate handle

The mouse pointer changes appearance when you place it over a rotate handle

8 **Move the mouse pointer over the lower-right rotate handle.**
The mouse pointer changes appearance (refer to Figure 11.13).

continues ▶

To Manipulate and Group Objects   (continued)

9 Drag downward to spin the object until the object's outline looks like that shown in Figure 11.14, and then release the mouse button.

Figure 11.14
You can rotate the arrow for a better appearance.

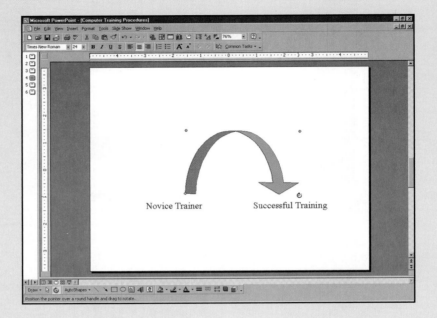

 If You Have Problems...
Be careful not to click outside the green rotate handle, or else you'll turn off the Free Rotate command. If this happens, make sure that the object is selected, and then click the Free Rotate button again.

---

10 Click the Free Rotate button to turn it off. (Alternatively, you can press Esc.)

11 Save the Computer Training Procedures presentation.
Keep the presentation open for the next lesson, in which you create interesting visuals by using various fill effects.

Exam Note: **Creating Arrays and Sweeps**
Two special effects that have gained recent popularity are arrays and sweeps. An *array* is an arrangement in which duplicates of an object are evenly distributed on a slide (horizontally or vertically). A *sweep* is an arrangement in which duplicates of an object slightly overlap. To create either effect, select the object and choose Edit, Duplicate. To find out more about these visual effects, refer to PowerPoint's Help.

Exam Note: **Sizing, Scaling, and Grouping Objects**

If you don't like the size of a drawn object (such as an AutoShape), you can just re-size it with the mouse. For more precise control over the size of an object, select it, and then choose F**o**rmat, Aut**o**Shape. In the Format AutoShape dialog box, click the Size tab. Enter the percentage relative to the original shape in the **H**eight and **W**idth text boxes, and then click OK.

You can also group objects so that you can apply a command or formatting to all the objects at once. Press (**◆Shift**) while clicking the objects you want to group, and then choose D**r**aw, **G**roup. To work with the objects individually again, select the grouped object and then choose D**r**aw, **U**ngroup.

Lesson 4: Formatting Objects with Fill Effects

You probably already discovered that PowerPoint automatically formats ovals, rectangles, and other objects with the template's default color for fills. Luckily, PowerPoint hands you a vast assortment of ways to format your objects. You can format the object with solid colors, or choose from PowerPoint's rich array of effects—such as shading styles, textures, or semi-transparent fills.

In this lesson, you use PowerPoint's ***fill effects*** to format objects in your presentation and to create a logo for your company.

To Format Objects with Fill Effects

❶ Make sure that Slide 4 in the Computer Training Procedures presenta-tion displays; then click the green curved arrow to select it.

You can confirm that an object is selected by the presence of white selection handles around the object's border.

❷ Click the Fill Color button's drop-down list arrow; then choose Fill **Effects from the palette.**

The Fill Effects dialog box displays (see Figure 11.15). You can use effects in this dialog box to format a selected object with a gradient, texture, or pattern. In this exercise, you learn how to add a gradient fill to your object. Just keep in mind that the same principles apply when you want to add a textured or patterned fill.

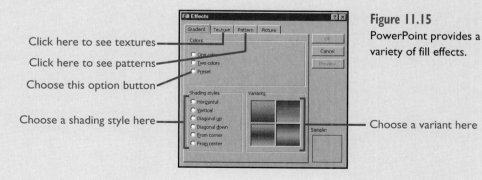

Click here to see textures
Click here to see patterns
Choose this option button
Choose a shading style here
Choose a variant here

Figure 11.15
PowerPoint provides a variety of fill effects.

On the Gradient page, you can use a single color (which is automatically com-bined with black shading), or click the **T**wo colors option button. You can also click the P**r**eset option button and P**r**eset colors drop-down list arrow; then choose a professionally designed gradient fill from the list.

continues ▶

To Format Objects with Fill Effects   (continued)

3 Click the Preset option button; then click the Preset colors drop-down list arrow and choose Rainbow from the list.

The preset color combination you chose (Rainbow) displays in the Sample box in the lower-right corner of the dialog box (see Figure 11.16). Now, select a shading style. To do this, click the effect you want in the Shading styles section; then click a Variants block.

Figure 11.16
You can choose from a wide variety of gradient fill effects.

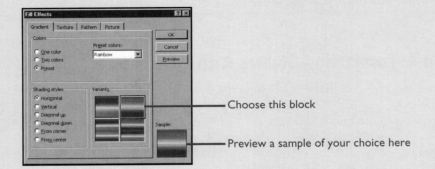

Choose this block

Preview a sample of your choice here

4 Make sure that the Horizontal Shading style is selected, and then click the upper-right block in the Variants section (refer to Figure 11.16). Click OK.

The effect you chose is applied to the arrow object. Now, try copying the effect to another object—instead of re-creating the effect from scratch. You can copy formatting from one object to another by using the *Format Painter*. The Format Painter is a feature that you can quickly use to copy text or object formatting from one area of text (or an object) to another. Because this is an efficient method of applying the same formatting to multiple objects, try using it in your presentation now.

5 With your object still selected, click the Format Painter button on the Standard toolbar.

The Format Painter activates. Now, you move to another slide and apply the formatting from the arrow to another object.

6 Press PgUp to display Slide 3; then click the arrow.

The formatting—including the fill effect—is copied to the object (see Figure 11.17).

Now, try using PowerPoint's semitransparent fills. A *semitransparent fill* is one in which the object is not completely filled with color. Using this fill, you can create various visual effects. In this exercise, you use a semitransparent fill to create a logo for your company.

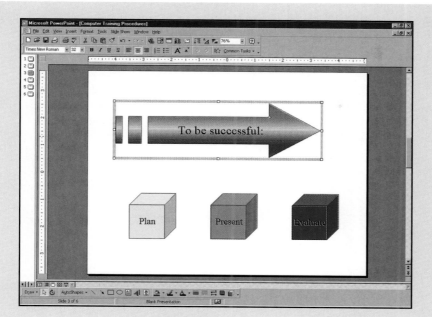

Figure 11.17
You can copy formatting from one object to another.

7 **Press** Ctrl+Home **to display the first slide in your presentation, move the circle over the star until it completely covers the star, and release the mouse button.**

You can layer objects in PowerPoint. Now, format the circle with a semitransparent fill to create an interesting visual effect.

8 **Double-click the circle.**

The Format AutoShape dialog box displays (see Figure 11.18) (You can also display this dialog box by right-clicking the object and choosing Format AutoShape, or choosing F**o**rmat, Aut**o**Shape from the menu bar.)

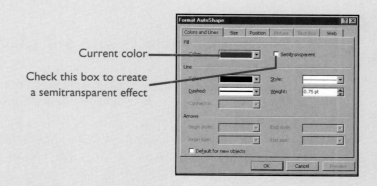

Figure 11.18
You can create special fill effects in PowerPoint.

Notice that the color in the Fill section of the dialog box is solid. However, you can quickly create a visual effect by checking the Semi**t**ransparent box.

9 **Check the Semi**t**ransparent box; then click OK.**

The effect is applied to the circle (see Figure 11.19).

continues ▶

To Format Objects with Fill Effects   (continued)

Figure 11.19
An object with a semi-transparent fill enables you to see objects layered beneath it.

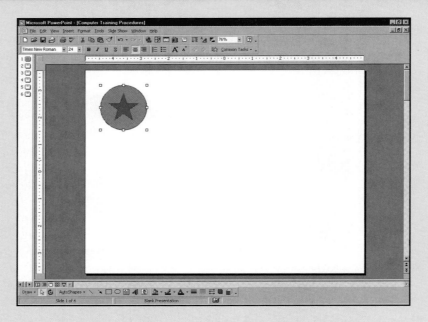

 Save your Computer Training Procedures presentation.
Keep the presentation open for the next lesson, in which you create 3-D effects.

 Inside Stuff: **Moving Objects**
Have you ever had trouble controlling the mouse well enough to move an object in small increments? If so, don't despair. Instead, click to select the object, press Ctrl, and use the keyboard's arrow keys to move the object in one-pixel increments.

Lesson 5: Formatting Objects with 3-D Effects

One of the slick things about PowerPoint is its capability to add a 3-D effect to lines, AutoShapes, and freeform objects. With 3-D settings, you can change the depth of the object and its color, rotation, angle, direction of lighting, and surface texture.

To add or change a 3-D effect for an object, select the object, and then click the 3-D tool on the Drawing toolbar. Choose an effect from the palette. You can also change the 3-D settings for an object or remove the 3-D effect altogether.

To enhance your presentation, try adding some 3-D effects now.

To Format Objects with 3-D Effects

1 **In the open Computer Training Procedures presentation, display Slide 5, and then choose E̲dit, Select Al̲l (or press Ctrl+A) to select all the objects.**
You must select the objects before you can modify them. In this case, you selected all objects to apply a 3-D effect to them simultaneously. (Remember that you can tell when objects are selected because white selection handles appear around their borders.)

2 **On the Drawing toolbar, click the 3-D tool.**

The 3-D palette displays (see Figure 11.20). You can display the name of a 3-D effect by momentarily resting your mouse pointer over it until a ScreenTip displays. When you find a 3-D effect you like, click the effect to apply it to selected objects.

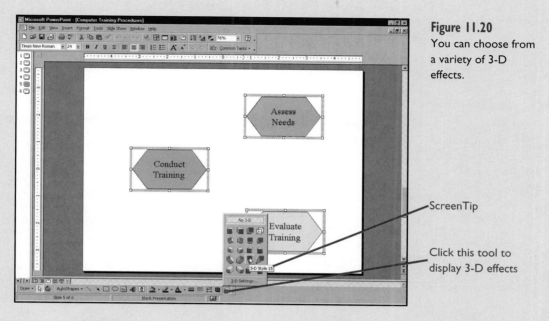

Figure 11.20
You can choose from a variety of 3-D effects.

ScreenTip

Click this tool to display 3-D effects

3 **Move your mouse pointer over the 3-D effects until a ScreenTip displays for 3-D Style 15, and then click.**

The effect is applied to the selected objects (see Figure 11.21). (If you want, experiment by choosing other 3-D effects. Make sure that you choose 3-D Style 15 before proceeding with the next step.)

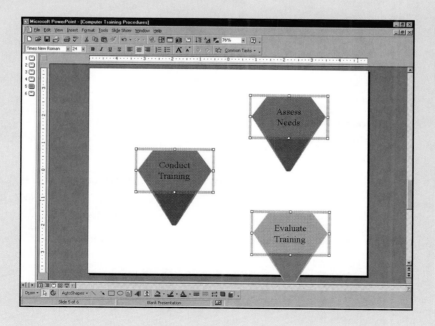

Figure 11.21
The 3-D effect applies to all selected objects.

continues ▶

To Format Objects with 3-D Effects   (continued)

You can further modify the 3-D effect by changing its depth, perspective, surface appearance, and so on. You make these revisions by using the 3-D Settings toolbar. Try making some modifications to the effect now.

4 **With the objects still selected, click the 3-D tool, and click the <u>3-D</u> Settings button on the 3-D palette.**
The 3-D Settings toolbar displays (see Figure 11.22). You can use this toolbar to refine your 3-D effect. Like all other PowerPoint toolbars, you can also find out any button's function by resting the mouse pointer over the button until a ScreenTip appears.

Figure 11.22
PowerPoint provides a wealth of settings to apply to your 3-D objects.

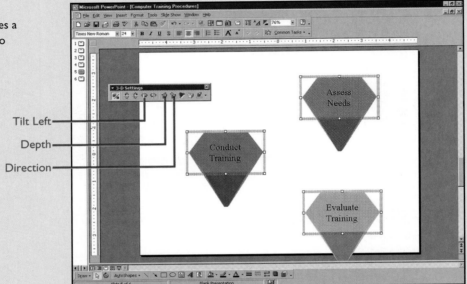

Tilt Left

Depth

Direction

 5 **Click the Tilt Left button three times.**
The 3-D effect changes. Now, try changing the depth for the objects.

 6 **Click the Depth tool.**
The Depth palette displays so that you can choose a depth (in points) for your effect.

7 **Choose <u>1</u>44 pt.**
The new depth applies to the selected objects. You can also change the direction of the 3-D effect.

 8 **Click the Direction tool and choose the third icon on the last row.**
The 3-D effect changes to the direction you choose. (If you want, experiment with other 3-D effects before proceeding to the next step.)

9 **On the 3-D Settings toolbar, click the Close button, and then click outside the objects.**
The toolbar closes, and the effects you added are clearly seen onscreen (see Figure 11.23).

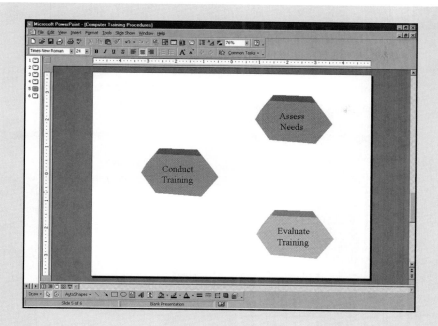

Figure 11.23
You can use 3-D effects to spice up your presentation.

⑩ Save the Computer Training Procedures presentation.
Keep the presentation open for the next lesson, in which you further improve your presentation by adding shadow effects.

 Exam Note: **Removing 3-D Effects**
If you want to remove a 3-D effect, first select the object. Click the 3-D tool and choose No 3-D from the palette.

Lesson 6: Formatting Objects with a Shadow Effect

PowerPoint also provides another great way to enhance objects: shadow effects. These effects give depth to an object and can make it appear more realistic. You can add a shadow to any object you create, including AutoShapes.

To add a shadow effect, select the object, and then click the Shadow tool on the Drawing toolbar. Next, choose a Shadow style or effect, from the palette that displays.

You can also use tools on the Shadow Settings toolbar to change the direction and angle of the shadow. Try working with shadow effects now to jazz up your presentation.

To Format an Object with a Shadow Effect

① Display Slide 6 in the open Computer Training Procedures presentation, and then click the star object to select it.
As usual, you have to adhere to the "select before you effect" rule. In other words, you must first select an object before you modify it.

continues ▶

To Format an Object with a Shadow Effect (continued)

② Click the Shadow tool on the Drawing toolbar.

A palette of shadow effects displays (see Figure 11.24). You can rest the mouse pointer over any palette icon to see a ScreenTip that identifies it. After you've located the shadow effect you want, you can click to select it.

Figure 11.24
You can choose from a variety of shadow effects.

ScreenTip

Click the Shadow tool to see these effects

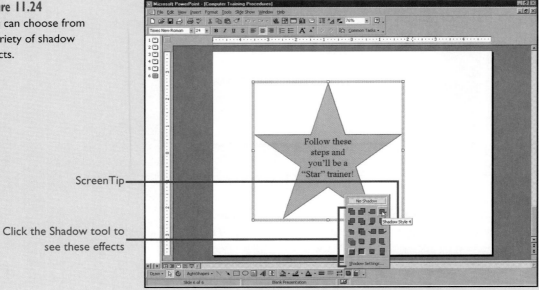

③ Move your mouse pointer over the shadow effects until a ScreenTip displays for Shadow Style 4, and then click.

The shadow effect is added to your object (see Figure 11.25). You can further modify the effect by using the Shadow Settings toolbar.

Figure 11.25
You can quickly add a shadow to your objects.

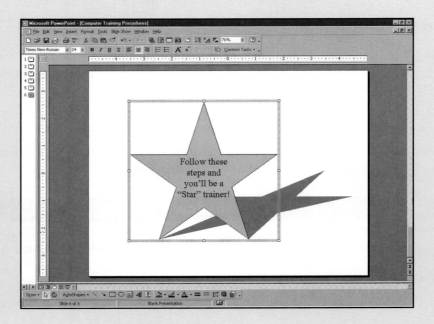

4 **Click the Shadow tool again; then click the <u>S</u>hadow Settings button on the palette.**

The Shadow Settings toolbar displays (see Figure 11.26). You can use these tools to move the shadow or change the shadow's color.

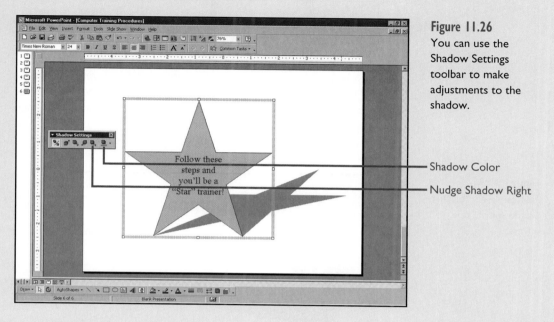

Figure 11.26
You can use the
Shadow Settings
toolbar to make
adjustments to the
shadow.

Shadow Color

Nudge Shadow Right

5 **Click the Nudge Shadow Right tool five times.**

The shadow moves slightly to the right (one point) every time you click the mouse. (If you want to change the shadow effect in larger increments, press ⭡Shift) while clicking the tool to move it six points at a time.) Now, try changing the shadow's color.

6 **Click the Shadow Color drop-down list arrow.**

The Color palette displays. The first row of colors contains those that coordinate with the presentation's color scheme. The second row shows custom colors—those that are used in the presentation, but are not part of the color scheme. You can choose any of the colors shown or click <u>M</u>ore Shadow Colors for additional choices.

7 **Click the light gray color box (the last color in the first row).**

The shadow's color changes.

8 **Click the Close button on the Shadow Settings toolbar; then click outside the star object to deselect it.**

The effects you added display.

9 **Save the Computer Training Procedures presentation.**

Keep the presentation open for the next lesson, in which you work with WordArt.

Inside Stuff: **Working with Shadow and 3-D Effects**
You may find yourself growing fond of both 3-D and shadow effects. Just like a woman with two beaus, however, you'll eventually have to make a choice. Why? Because you can't add both effects to the same object. In fact, if you try to add a second effect, the first one is removed automatically.

 ## Lesson 7: Using WordArt

By now, you used PowerPoint's drawing tools to make several changes to your Computer Training Procedures presentation. PowerPoint still has another trick up its sleeve, however: WordArt. Using WordArt, you can stretch, emboss, and otherwise change the way text appears. This is because text you enter in WordArt is not really text at all—it's an object. Figure 11.27 shows examples of some of WordArt's special effects.

Figure 11.27
You can use WordArt to add special text effects.

Once you work with WordArt, you'll probably turn to it whenever you want to spiff up a text object. Try adding some finishing touches to your presentation now by adding a WordArt object.

To Use WordArt

 ❶ **Display Slide 1 in the open Computer Training Procedures presentation, and then click the Insert WordArt tool on the Drawing toolbar.**
The WordArt Gallery displays, showing the available styles you can use for your text (see Figure 11.28).

Figure 11.28
You can choose a text style from the Gallery.

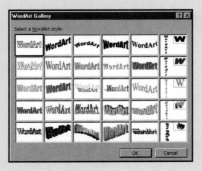

2 **Click the fifth style from the left on the bottom row, and then choose OK.**

The Edit WordArt Text dialog box displays so that you can enter text (Figure 11.29).

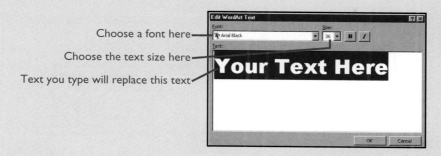

Choose a font here⎯

Choose the text size here⎯

Text you type will replace this text⎯

Figure 11.29
You enter your text in this dialog box.

3 **Type `Star Training Company`, and then click OK.**

WordArt creates an object on your slide with the text and style you chose (see Figure 11.30). Notice that the object has both selection handles (to move and/or resize it) and an adjustment handle (to change the shape). Additionally, WordArt automatically displays the WordArt toolbar that you can use to make further modifications to the object.

⊠ ***If You Have Problems...***
If the WordArt toolbar doesn't display on your screen, right-click the Standard toolbar. Choose WordArt from the shortcut menu that displays.

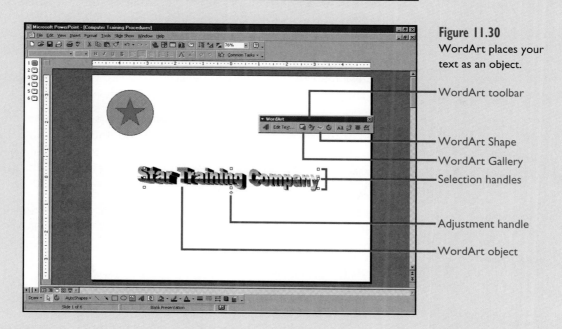

Figure 11.30
WordArt places your text as an object.

⎯WordArt toolbar

⎯WordArt Shape

⎯WordArt Gallery

⎯Selection handles

⎯Adjustment handle

⎯WordArt object

4 **Click the WordArt Gallery tool on the WordArt toolbar.**

The WordArt Gallery again displays, so you can choose another style.

5 **Double-click the fourth style from the left on the third row.**

The text displays with the new style. Now, try modifying the object by using the WordArt Shape tool.

continues ▶

To Use WordArt   (continued)

6 Click the WordArt Shape tool on the WordArt toolbar.
A palette of shapes that you can apply to a WordArt object displays (see Figure 11.31). You can click a shape to quickly modify a WordArt style.

Figure 11.31
You can apply a number of shapes to your style.

7 Display the ScreenTip for the Wave 2 shape, and then click.
The WordArt object displays with the new shape. (If you want, experiment with other shapes from the palette. Before you continue with the next step, make sure that you choose Wave 2.)

Because the WordArt object has selection handles, you can resize (or move) it like any other object. Try increasing the object's size now.

8 Move the mouse pointer over the upper-right selection handle, and then drag upward and to the right until you double the object's size.
The object enlarges so you can see it better. Because you're done working with the object for now, you can deselect it.

9 Click outside the WordArt object.
The object is deselected. Notice that both the object's handles and the WordArt toolbar disappear when the object is deselected. (If you later decide to modify the object, you can click it again to display the handles and the toolbar.)

10 Choose View, Ruler.
It's a good idea to turn off the rulers' displays when you're not using them, because it gives you a bit more screen space to work with other objects.

11 Save the Computer Training Procedures presentation, and then close it.
If you finish your work session, exit PowerPoint and shut down Windows before turning off your computer. Otherwise, complete the Skill Drill, Challenge, and Discovery Zone exercises at the end of this project.

Summary

In this project, you learned how to wield PowerPoint's drawing tools. Not only did you learn how to draw freehand and insert AutoShapes, but you learned how to modify them in various ways, as well. You also developed some stunning visuals, including gradient and semi-transparent fills, and 3-D and shadow effects. Furthermore, you saw how quick and easy it was to create impressive visual effects by using WordArt. Combined, these drawing features constitute a wealth of tools you can pull from PowerPoint's toolbox whenever you want to jazz up a presentation.

To expand on your knowledge, spend a few minutes exploring Help on these topics. Additionally, complete some of the Skill Drill, Challenge, and Discovery Zone exercises.

Checking Concepts and Terms ✓

True/False

For each of the following, check *T* or *F* to indicate whether the statement is true or false.

__T __F **1.** AutoShapes are created by using the AutoDraw program. [L2]

__T __F **2.** You can add a shadow effect to an object to create a feeling of depth. [L6]

__T __F **3.** You must first select objects before you group them. [L3]

__T __F **4.** You can add text to AutoShapes. [L2]

__T __F **5.** WordArt is a program you use to write text. [L7]

Multiple Choice

Circle the letter of the correct answer for each of the following.

1. Which of the following are AutoShapes? [L2]

  a. connector lines between objects

  b. stars and banners

  c. callouts

  d. all of the above

2. Which type of handle(s) do you use to change the shape of an AutoShape? [L2–3]

  a. white square handle(s)

  b. red square handles(s)

  c. yellow diamond handle(s)

  d. green round handle(s)

3. Which of the following is true regarding 3-D effects? [L5]

  a. You must remove one effect before applying another.

  b. You make modifications to them by using the 3-D Settings toolbar.

  c. They are the same as shadow effects.

  d. all of the above

4. Which of the following can you use to draw a perfectly symmetrical circle? [L1]

  a. Double-click the Oval tool; then draw.

  b. Select the Oval tool; then press ◆Shift while drawing.

  c. Select the Oval tool; then press Ctrl while drawing.

  d. Select the Circle tool; then press Ctrl while drawing.

5. Which of the following are modifications you can make to an object? [L3]

  a. flip it

  b. rotate it

  c. group it with other objects

  d. all of the above

Skill Drill

Skill Drill exercises reinforce project skills. Each skill reinforced is the same, or nearly the same, as a skill presented in the project. Detailed instructions are provided in a step-by-step format.

1. Using AutoShapes

You are in charge of the company picnic. To create an attention-getting flyer for the event, you decide to add some AutoShapes to the flyer. After you add the AutoShapes, you spiff them up by changing the fill color. [L2]

1. Open **PP-1102** and save it as **Company Picnic**. Display the presentation in Slide view.

2. Click the AutoShapes tool, and then choose Stars and Banners. Display the ScreenTips for the various AutoShapes on the Stars and Banners submenu, and then click Up Ribbon.

3. Draw a banner across the top third of the slide, and then enter the text **Company Picnic!**

4. Select the text in the AutoShape, and then click the Font Size drop-down list arrow and choose 36 points. (Resize the banner, if necessary, to accommodate the new text size.)

5. With the AutoShape still selected, click the Fill Color drop-down list arrow. Choose one of the light gray colors, and then click outside the AutoShape to deselect it.

6. Add the Rectangular Callout to the clip art ("Screen Bean") figure. Use the adjustment handle to reshape the callout if necessary. Enter the following text: **Be sure to come!**

7. With the callout AutoShape still selected, click the Fill Color drop-down list arrow and choose No Fill. Click outside the AutoShape.

8. Print one copy of the presentation.

9. Save the Company Picnic presentation, and then close it. Leave PowerPoint running if you plan to complete additional exercises.

2. Using Connectors and 3-D Effects

Because everyone at your company considers you a "tech head," they've put you in charge of upgrading other computer users to PowerPoint 2000. To outline the upgrade process, you decide to add connector lines to the shapes on a PowerPoint slide. Then, to increase interest, you add 3-D effects to the objects. [L5]

1. Open **PP-1103** and save it as **Upgrade Process**. Display the presentation in Slide view.

2. Click the AutoShapes tool, and then choose Connectors.

3. Display ScreenTips for the connectors on the submenu, and then choose Straight Arrow Connector. Connect the right side of the Evaluate Needs object to the left side of the Order Software object.

4. Connect the bottom of the Order Software object to the top of the Provide Training object by using the same connector type.

5. Move the Provide Training object approximately 2 inches to the right. (Notice that the connector line resizes automatically to keep the two objects connected.)

6. Select the three objects by pressing (Shift) as you click each object.

7. Click the 3-D tool, and then choose the 3-D Style 3 to apply to the objects.

8. With the objects still selected, click the Fill Color button's drop-down list arrow and choose Fill Effects. On the Gradient page of the Fill Effects dialog box, click the From center Shading style. Click the left variant block, and then click OK.

9. Click outside the objects to better view your changes.

10. Print a copy of your Upgrade Process presentation. Save the presentation, and then close it. Leave PowerPoint running if you plan to complete additional exercises.

3. Working with WordArt, Fill Effects, and 3-D Effects

To earn some spending money while in college, you work at a toy store. The boss, who is impressed with your computer skills, asked you to develop a flyer to promote the newest line of model rockets. You use WordArt, fill effects, and 3-D effects to create the flyer in a flash. [L4–5,7]

1. Open **PP-1104** and save it as **Model Rocket Promotion**. Display the presentation in Slide view.

2. Click the Insert WordArt button on the Drawing toolbar. Choose the third style from the left on the fourth row, and then click OK.

3. Enter **Rocket Flyers** in the Edit WordArt Text dialog box. Change the Font to Impact, and then click OK.

4. Move and resize the WordArt object so that it fills the upper one-third of the slide. Then, click the WordArt Shape button on the WordArt toolbar and choose Triangle Up.

5. With the WordArt object still selected, click the 3-D button and choose the 3-D Style 3.

6. Display the Fill Effects dialog box. Click the Preset option button and click the Preset colors drop-down list arrow. Choose Daybreak, the Horizontal Shading style, and the upper-left variant block. Click OK.

7. Add another WordArt object. Choose the first style on the second row, and enter **for an out-of-this-world experience!** in the Edit WordArt Text dialog box. Click OK.

8. Move the object so that it displays in the center of the available space at the bottom of the slide. Resize it, if necessary.

9. Add solid blue fill color to the second WordArt object you created.

10. Save your Model Rocket Promotion presentation. Print a copy, and then close the presentation. Leave PowerPoint running if you plan to complete additional exercises.

Challenge

Challenge exercises expand on or are somewhat related to skills presented in the lessons. Each exercise provides a brief narrative introduction, followed by instructions in a numbered-step format that are not as detailed as those in the Skill Drill section.

1. Using a Text Box

As Production Manager for a manufacturing operation, you're concerned with minimizing the scrap produced as a byproduct of the manufacturing process. You developed a presentation that charts waste, but are concerned that the chart's information won't be clear to others. To help explain the chart's data, you decide to include and format a text box on the slide. [L1]

1. Using PowerPoint's Help and the information included in this project, brush up on how to create and format text boxes.

2. Open **PP-1105** and save it as **Scrap**. Display the presentation in Slide view.

3. Click the Text Box tool, and then click in the lower-left corner of the slide.

4. Type **Scrap amounts have been reduced with increased management** in the text box. If necessary, size or scale the text box.

5. Format the text in the box as blue. Change the font size to 20-point text.

6. Use the Line Style tool to add a 6-point, triple line style border to the text box.

7. Deselect the text box to view your changes.

8. Save the presentation, and then close it. Leave PowerPoint running if you plan to complete additional exercises.

2. Using AutoShapes

You work for Star Training Company, and you need to develop a promotional flyer to help recruit good-quality trainers for your organization. To do so, you use PowerPoint's AutoShapes. [L2]

1. Open **PP-1106** and save it as **Recruiting Trainers**. Display the presentation in Slide view.

2. Using Figure 11.32 as a guide, create the publicity flyer. Keep the following in mind as you develop the presentation:

   - Use the Duplicate command to copy the star object.
   - Use the Format Painter to copy formatting from one object to another.
   - Format text within AutoShapes.

Figure 11.32
Use your drawing skills to develop this slide.

3. Save your presentation; then print and close it. Leave PowerPoint running if you plan to complete additional exercises.

3. Using WordArt and a Text Box

You're in charge of this year's county fair. To create publicity materials, you decide to use PowerPoint, including WordArt. [L1–7]

1. Create a new, blank presentation and display it in Slide view.

2. Using Figure 11.33 as a guide, create the publicity flyer. Keep the following in mind as you develop the presentation:

   - Download a clip similar to the one shown from the Web.
   - Use a text box (and bullets within the text box) to create the text below the clip art image.
   - Format the lower WordArt object (**Be sure to come!**) using a gradient fill effect.
   - Use the first WordArt style on the third row for the upper WordArt object (Gallia County Fair).

Figure 11.33
Use this slide as an
example when you
design your own slide.

3. Save your presentation as **County Fair**; then print and close it.

4. Leave PowerPoint running if you plan to complete the additional exercises.

Discovery Zone

Discovery Zone exercises require advanced knowledge of topics presented in *MOUS Essentials* lessons, application of skills from multiple lessons, or self-directed learning of new skills. Each exercise is independent of the others, so you may complete the exercises in any order.

1. Using Freehand Drawings and Fill Effects

Many families have a coat-of-arms—a holdover from their European roots. A modern-day version of this idea is a personal logo.

Think about what you would include in a personal logo—items or ideas that symbolize what's important to you. Then use PowerPoint's drawing tools, AutoShapes, and fill effects (including semitransparent fills) to create a logo. If appropriate, also use 3-D or shadow effects. Include a text box on the slide that explains the symbolism of your personal logo. If your instructor indicates that you should do so, save and print the presentation.

Next, obtain a local phone directory. Look through the yellow pages to see what types of logos the organizations use. Select three different industries (such as real estate, banking, manufacturing, and so on). Use PowerPoint's drawing tools, AutoShapes, fill effects, 3-D, and shadow effects to create a logo for each industry. Save and print the presentations, and then close them.

Leave PowerPoint running if you plan to complete the final exercise. [L1, 4]

2. Using WordArt and 3-D Effects

You're starting up an Internet service provider (ISP) in a rural area. To drum up business, you create a publicity flyer.

Create a new, blank presentation and save it as **GoldNet**. Using Figure 11.34 as a guide, create the publicity flyer. Use AutoShapes, WordArt, fill effects, and 3-D effects to create the look of the flyer.

Figure 11.34
Use your drawing skills to make this slide.

Save and print the presentation, and then close it. If you're finished with your work session, exit PowerPoint and shut down Windows before turning off your computer. [L5, 7]

PinPoint Assessment

You have completed this project and its associated lessons, and have had an opportunity to assess your skills through the end-of-project questions and exercises. Now use the PinPoint software Evaluation Mode to further assess your comprehension of the specific exam activities you have just learned. You can also use the PinPoint Trainer Mode and the Show Me tutorials to practice these exam activities.

Sharing Information with Other Programs

Key terms introduced in this project include

- destination file
- destination program
- docked
- embedding
- floating toolbar
- integration

- linking
- move bars
- Object Linking and Embedding (OLE)
- Office Clipboard
- source file

- source program
- stylistic problems
- table
- title case
- Windows Clipboard
- worksheet

Objectives	Required Activity for MOUS	Exam Level
➤ Importing Text from Word	Import text from Word	Core
➤ Using the Presentation Assistant to Fix Stylistic Problems	Use Office Assistant	Core
➤ Drawing and Formatting a Table Within PowerPoint	Create tables within PowerPoint	Core
	Change and replace text fonts	Core
	Modify PowerPoint tables	Expert
➤ Using the Slide Finder to Combine Presentations	Create a new presentation from existing slides	Core
	Add a presentation within a presentation	Expert
➤ Linking an Excel Chart to a PowerPoint Presentation	Insert an Excel chart	Expert
➤ Embedding a Word Table Within a Presentation	Add a table (from Word)	Expert
➤ Formatting an Embedded Word Table	Modify PowerPoint tables	Expert
	Apply diagonal borders to a table	Expert
➤ Using the Office Clipboard	Use the Office Clipboard	Core
➤ Exporting an Outline to Word	Export an outline to Word	Expert

Why Would I Do This?

Working with the entire Office 2000 suite has several advantages over using individual programs—the similar menus and toolbars, the Office Assistant, Web integration, and so on. Perhaps no reason is more dramatic and powerful, however, than the capability of programs to easily share information with each other, and to produce top-notch documents by integrating features.

What's **integration**? It's just combining two or more software functions or program features to produce a result that you couldn't have otherwise. You can link an Excel chart to a PowerPoint presentation, for example, to combine features from both programs.

Depending on your needs, you can use a variety of methods to help programs "talk" with each other. If you want to just insert information that exists in another program, and you don't need to have PowerPoint automatically update the information, a simple copy-and-paste operation probably fits the bill. For example, you can copy data from Word or Excel into PowerPoint, using the **Windows Clipboard** as a facilitator. The Windows Clipboard is an area in memory that acts as sort of a "halfway house" for your data. Whenever you cut (or copy) information, it's placed in the Clipboard. You can then move to a different location—either in the same application or a different one—and then use the Paste command to insert the data at the new location.

To make copying and pasting operations easier, Office 2000 includes its own version of the Clipboard: the **Office Clipboard**. You can use the Office Clipboard to insert data from multiple sources all at once. You can "collect" data from several Excel and Word files, for example, and then paste it simultaneously into a PowerPoint presentation.

In contrast to copying and pasting, **Object Linking and Embedding**, commonly known as **OLE**, is a capability of Windows programs to constantly share updated information with each other because they maintain an active connection. The program in which the data is originally created (or modified) is called the **source program**; the program that accepts the data is called the **destination program**. If you embed a Word table in a PowerPoint presentation, for example, Word is the source program and PowerPoint is the destination program.

What's the difference between using the Clipboard and using OLE? When you copy and paste via the Clipboard, the transfer of information is a one-shot deal. In contrast, **linking** creates an electronic pipeline between programs that lets them actively share information. **Embedding** refers to inserting one program within another as an object.

Here's how you can use linking to keep a presentation up-to-date: Imagine that you have an Excel chart with production data and that you include this information in a monthly staff presentation. Rather than copy and paste the information every time you need to update your presentation, you can just link the chart to your presentation. Then, when the information in the worksheet changes, the linked information in your presentation changes as well.

This project focuses on how to make you more efficient by using the integration features inherent in the Office 2000 suite. Try your hand at a few of them—and you'll be amazed at the increase in efficiency!

Lesson 1: Importing Text from Word

If you've worked with Office 2000 for a while, chances are that you've prepared an outline in Word and then wanted to use the same information as the basis for a PowerPoint presentation. Of course, you could re-create the information in PowerPoint, but it's much easier to open the Word document as a PowerPoint presentation. Luckily, in PowerPoint 2000 you can do this! Try using this helpful technique now.

To Import Text from Word

1 **Start PowerPoint, if necessary, and then click the Open button on the Standard toolbar.**

The Open dialog box displays, as shown in Figure 12.1. Although you're already familiar with using this dialog box to open existing PowerPoint presentations, you've probably never opened a Word document in PowerPoint before. Fortunately, the steps for doing so are similar to those you use for opening a presentation: just locate the file, and then click <u>O</u>pen.

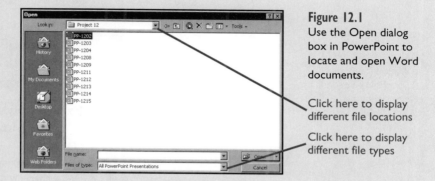

Figure 12.1
Use the Open dialog box in PowerPoint to locate and open Word documents.

Click here to display different file locations

Click here to display different file types

2 **Click the Look <u>i</u>n drop down list arrow and choose the drive and folder where your student data files are located.**

3 **Click the Files of <u>t</u>ype drop down list arrow and choose All Files from the list.**

All the files located on the selected drive and folder—whether created in PowerPoint or not—display (see Figure 12.2). Notice, too, that the icon next to PP-1201 indicates that the file was created in Word.

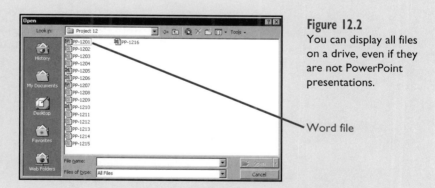

Figure 12.2
You can display all files on a drive, even if they are not PowerPoint presentations.

Word file

Now that you've located the Word file that you want to use as the basis for the PowerPoint presentation, you can open it.

4 **Click PP-1201, and then choose <u>O</u>pen.**

The Word outline opens as a new PowerPoint presentation in Normal view (see Figure 12.3). The text from the outline extends beyond the lower (text) place-holder—not a very good design for a slide. For right now, however, don't worry about this. You learn how to use the Presentation Assistant to split the slide into multiple slides in the next lesson.

continues ▶

To Import Text from Word   (continued)

X ***If You Have Problems...***
The feature responsible for inserting a Word outline in your presentation is installed "on first use." If PowerPoint displays an error message telling you that the feature isn't installed, insert your Office 2000 CD in the CD-ROM drive and choose <u>Y</u>es to install the feature.

Notice that the presentation automatically uses a blank template. To spiff up your presentation, try applying a different design template.

Figure 12.3
You can open a Word outline within PowerPoint—even if a bit of cleanup is necessary.

Text extends beyond placeholder

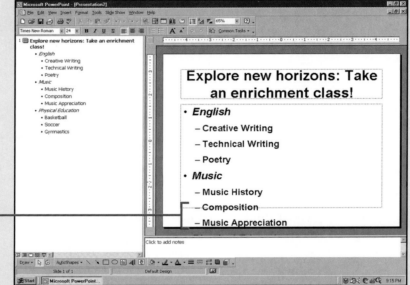

⑤ **Right-click on the slide (but not within a placeholder), and then choose Apply Design Template from the shortcut menu.**
The Apply Design Template dialog box displays.

⑥ **Choose the Strategic template, and then click Apply.**
The template is applied to your presentation. Now save your newly created presentation. Remember, it's always a good idea to save (or resave) your presentations every few minutes.

⑦ **Save your new presentation as Enrichment Classes.**
Keep the presentation open and PowerPoint running for the next lesson, in which you learn how to better arrange the outline information by splitting it into multiple slides.

 Exam Note: Inserting Word Text
Here's an alternative method you can use to insert a Word outline in a PowerPoint presentation: Display your PowerPoint presentation in Slide Sorter view, and then place the insertion point where you want to insert the information from Word. Choose <u>I</u>nsert, Slides from Out<u>l</u>ine. Double-click the file you want in the Insert Outline dialog box.

Lesson 2: Using the Presentation Assistant to Fix Stylistic Problems

In the preceding lesson, you opened a Word outline as a PowerPoint presentation. You were probably impressed by PowerPoint's capability to seamlessly open the file, but at the same time may have been a bit distressed by its inability to logically arrange the information onto multiple slides.

Fortunately, you can use PowerPoint's Presentation Assistant to quickly fix problems such as these. The Presentation Assistant integrates several features from previous PowerPoint versions (such as the Style Checker and AutoClipArt). In a sense, the Presentation Assistant is an offshoot of the Office Assistant—designed to help you correct ***stylistic problems*** such as incorrect capitalization, too much text on a slide, and so on. To use the Presentation Assistant, you must first activate the Office Assistant. When activated, the Presentation Assistant flags potential problems by displaying a light bulb. You can click the light bulb to display a list of possible corrections for the problem and choose an option from the list.

In this lesson, you learn how to activate the Presentation Assistant and how to use it to split a single slide into multiple slides. Try working with this handy feature now.

To Use the Presentation Assistant to Fix Stylistic Problems

1 **Make sure that the Enrichment Classes presentation you created in the preceding lesson is open in Normal view, and then choose Help, Show the Office Assistant.**

 If you have problems...
In Project 1 of this book, you learned how to turn off the display of the Office Assistant. If the Assistant has been turned back on since you worked on that project, however, you can skip over Steps 1 and 2 and proceed directly to Step 3.

The Office Assistant appears onscreen. Remember that the Office Assistant must display before the Presentation Assistant can show you suggestions for improving your presentation.

2 **Click outside the Office Assistant's message bubble (if necessary) to clear the bubble.**
A light bulb displays near the title placeholder (see Figure 12.4). Whenever the light bulb appears, it's a sure sign that the Presentation Assistant has a tip or idea about how to improve your presentation.

continues ▶

To Use the Presentation Assistant to Fix Stylistic Problems   (continued)

Figure 12.4
PowerPoint's
Presentation Assistant
helps you clean up
presentations.

Click this light bulb to see a
Presentation Assistant tip

Office Assistant

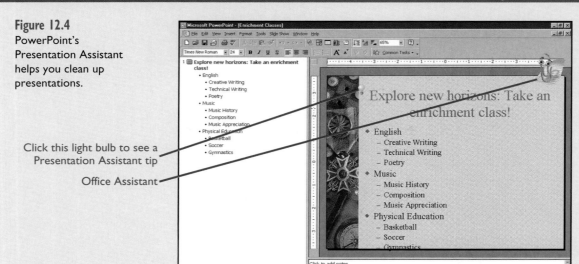

3 **Click the light bulb.**

The Presentation Assistant indicates that the capitalization for the title placeholder should be in **title case**. Title case is the combination of upper- and lowercase
letters used to capitalize the first letter of each word. You can choose to have
the Presentation Assistant automatically change the text in the placeholder to
title case or ignore its suggestion.

4 **Click Change the text to title case (the first option button.)**

The text in the title placeholder is formatted as title case. At the same time, a
light bulb appears next to the lower (text) placeholder, indicating that there is
another stylistic or formatting problem that needs to be fixed.

5 **Click the light bulb that appears next to the word English.**

Again, the Presentation Assistant indicates that the text in the lower placeholder
is not formatted according to the default setting of sentence case. Sentence case
is where only the first letter of a sentence or phrase is capitalized. In this in-
stance, you should ignore the suggestion.

6 **Click Ignore this style rule for this presentation only (the second option button).**

A light bulb appears near the bottom of the lower placeholder (next to `Physical
Education`).

7 **Click the light bulb.**

The Presentation Assistant indicates that there is too much text to fit in the
placeholder (see Figure 12.5). You'll find that this is a typical problem when
opening Word outlines in PowerPoint.

If you choose the `Split this slide into two slides` option, you'll end up with
one slide that contains two of the main topics (`English` and `Music`). In contrast, if
you choose `Make a new slide for each paragraph on this slide`, you'll create three slides, each with the same title, but having different topics for the bulleted points. Try splitting the single slide into multiple slides by using this technique.

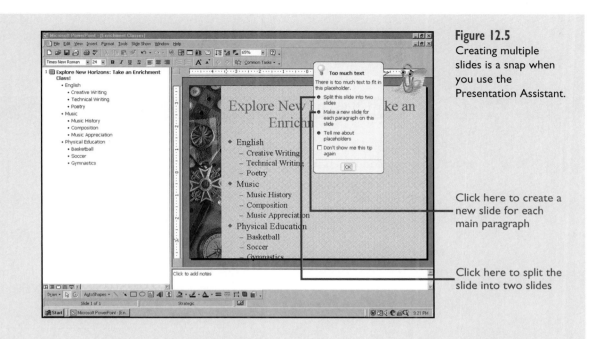

Figure 12.5
Creating multiple slides is a snap when you use the Presentation Assistant.

Click here to create a new slide for each main paragraph

Click here to split the slide into two slides

8 **Click** `Make a new slide for each paragraph on this slide.`
PowerPoint breaks the information included on the original slide into three individual slides. Each slide includes information for one of the main topics (such as English, Music, and Physical Education), but includes the same title.

9 **Press** PgUp **twice to scroll through the presentation and view your newly created slides.**
Now, turn off the Office Assistant's display because you're finished fixing stylistic problems in this presentation.

10 **Right-click on the Office Assistant, and then choose Options.**
The Options page of the Office Assistant dialog box displays.

11 **Clear the Use the Office Assistant check box, and then click OK.**
The Office Assistant no longer displays.

12 **Save the Enrichment Classes presentation.**
Keep the presentation open and PowerPoint running for the next lesson, in which you draw and format a table.

Lesson 3: Drawing and Formatting a Table Within PowerPoint

One great way to organize your data is by drawing a **table**. A table is simply a grid of columns and rows that you can use to display your data in an organized manner. If you've worked with spreadsheet programs (such as Excel), you'll instantly recognize the similarities between the way a **worksheet** and a table are set up.

You can create a table within PowerPoint or by using Word. If you need to create only a simple table that doesn't need much formatting, use PowerPoint. On the other hand, if you want to have full access to more powerful formatting tools for your table, use Word. For now, focus on creating a simple table—right from within PowerPoint. (In Lessons 6 and 7, you'll tap into Word's more powerful table features by embedding and formatting a Word table in a presentation.)

For this exercise, imagine that you need to create a table to display registration information for the English classes. You want to locate a table at the bottom of a slide that includes the relevant information for the classes. To do this, you create and format a table in PowerPoint. Try drawing and formatting a table now.

To Draw and Format a Table Within PowerPoint

❶ Display Slide 1 in the Enrichment Classes presentation, open from the preceding lesson.
This is where you draw the table.

❷ On the Standard toolbar, click the Tables and Borders button.
The Tables and Borders toolbar displays (see Figure 12.6). This handy toolbar, which is universally available in the Office 2000 programs, enables you to draw a table electronically. To draw the table, make sure that the Draw Table button is activated, and then drag to create a table on your slide. If you make a mistake, just click the Eraser button and drag over the line(s) you want to remove. It's that easy!

  If You Have Problems...
By default, the Tables and Borders toolbar displays as a *floating toolbar*, which means that it shows in its own window. Because of this, the toolbar on your screen may not display in the same location as the one in this book. If you'd like, just drag the toolbar's title bar to the location you want.

Alternatively, the toolbar may be *docked*, or attached, to one side of the application window. You can convert it into a floating toolbar by moving it into the screen. To do so, drag the double bars (called *move bars*) on the toolbar.

Figure 12.6
The Tables and Borders toolbar puts tools for creating tables at your fingertips.

Draw Table tool
Table menu
Eraser tool
Fill Color tool
Tables and Borders toolbar

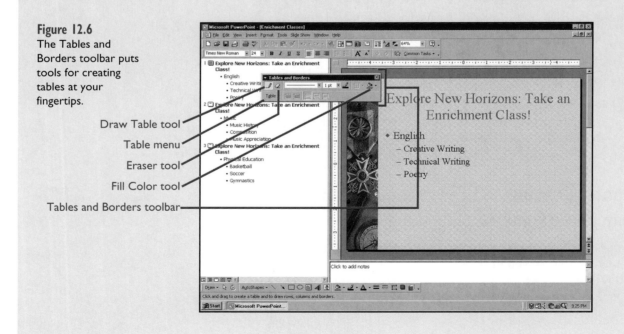

3 **If necessary, click the Draw Table tool, and then drag from immedi-ately below the word** Poetry **to the lower-right corner of the slide (see Figure 12.7). Release the mouse button.**

A rectangle is drawn in the lower half of the slide. Notice that the border in-cludes selection handles so that you can resize the table. Additionally, the Draw Table pencil pointer remains active so that you can add more lines to your table.

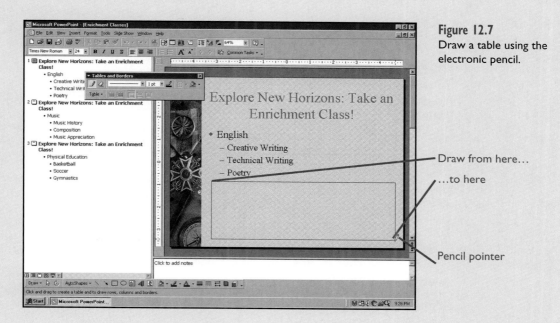

Figure 12.7
Draw a table using the electronic pencil.

Draw from here...

...to here

Pencil pointer

Now, you're ready to add more lines to your table.

4 **Drag to draw a horizontal line from the left center selection handle to the right center selection handle, and then release the mouse button.**

A horizontal line divides the rectangle evenly, so that two rows are displayed. Now, try adding two vertical lines so that you have three columns.

5 **Drag to draw two vertical lines to create three columns that are approximately equal in width.**

You created a table that includes three columns and two rows (see Figure 12.8).

 If You Have Problems...

If you can't seem to get the lines drawn exactly where you'd like, don't despair. Just click the Eraser tool, and then drag over the line you want to remove. Then, "go back to the drawing board" by clicking the Draw Table tool and trying again.

continues ▶

To Draw and Format a Table Within PowerPoint   (continued)

Figure 12.8
You can organize your data in columns and rows.

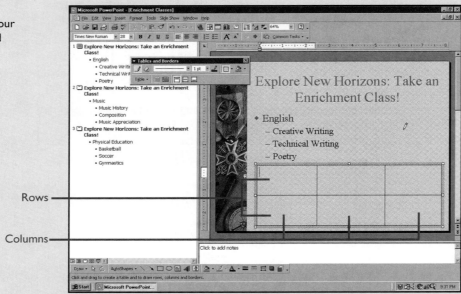

Rows ——

Columns ——

Next, you'll add shading to the top row to emphasize its information. First, select the row so that PowerPoint understands what part of the table you'd like to shade.

6 **Press Esc to turn off the Draw Table tool, and then click in any cell in the top row.**

7 **On the Tables and Borders toolbar, click the T̲able tool.**
The T̲able menu displays (see Figure 12.9). This menu gives you a slew of choices related to working with your tables.

Figure 12.9
PowerPoint offers a variety of methods to format and structure your table.

Click the Table tool to display this menu

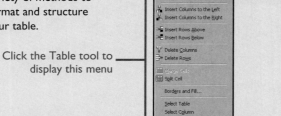

8 **Choose Selec̲t Row from the menu.**
The top row is selected and shown in reverse video. Now, add some shading to it.

9 **On the Tables and Borders toolbar, click the Fill Color drop-down list arrow, and then choose the light brown (the third color box from the left).**
The row is formatted in the chosen color. You can't see the color change until you deselect the table, however.

⑩ Click outside the table.
The table is deselected and you can more easily see the first row's shading. Now, turn off the display of the Tables and Borders toolbar.

⑪ Click the Tables and Borders toolbar's Close button, and then save and close the Enrichment Classes presentation.
Keep PowerPoint running for the next exercise in which you learn how to combine two existing presentations.

 Exam Note: **Entering Text in a Table**
After you've created and formatted a table, entering your information is a snap. Click in the *cell* (the intersection of a column and row) where you want the data and type. To move to the next cell in the table, press (Tab⇥).

Lesson 4: Using the Slide Finder to Combine Presentations

One quick way to include information from multiple existing presentations is to combine them. Luckily, PowerPoint includes a feature—the Slide Finder—that helps you do this almost effortlessly. You can combine all the slides from the presentations, or pick and choose the slides from each presentation that you want to use. So, come along as we show you how to seamlessly combine presentations.

For this and the next few lessons, imagine that you own a chain of stores that sells sports equipment. Because you're busy running the business, you don't have a lot of time to develop presentations—but when you need to, you like to "pull out the big guns" and create the presentation as efficiently as possible.

To Use the Slide Finder to Combine Presentations

❶ In PowerPoint, open PP-1202 and save it as `Sports Company`.
The two-slide presentation displays onscreen. You want to give a presentation to your store managers—and this presentation is a start. To create the complete presentation quickly and easily, you plan to add slides from other existing presentations.

First, you get ready to combine the slides by displaying the open presentation in Slide Sorter view. Even though you can combine presentations in any view (except Slide Show), it's probably easiest to see the results of your actions in Slide Sorter view.

❷ Click the Slide Sorter View button.
Your next step is to select the slide that's located immediately before the spot where you want to insert slides from another presentation, and then open the Slide Finder dialog box.

continues ▶

To Use the Slide Finder to Combine Presentations   (continued)

③ Click the last slide (Slide 2), and then choose Insert, Slides from Files.
The Slide Finder dialog box displays (see Figure 12.10). This dialog box gives you quick access to existing presentations on your system. You can use the Find Presentation page, for example, to locate any presentation on your system, or click the List of Favorites tab to display the files previously added to your Favorites folder. For now, we'll just use the Find Presentation page and the Browse button to locate presentations.

Figure 12.10
The Slide Finder helps you insert one presentation within another.

Click here to locate presentations

④ On the Find Presentation page, click the Browse button.
The Browse dialog box displays. The layout of this dialog box is similar to the Open dialog box, and you use it in much the same way.

⑤ Use the Look in drop-down list to choose the drive and folder where your student data files are located, select PP-1203, and choose Open.
The Slide Finder dialog box redisplays, complete with thumbnails, or miniatures of slides, in PP-1203 (see Figure 12.11). You can also display slides as slide miniatures or as a list. Either way, you can pick and choose which slides you want to insert in your open presentation, or click the Insert All button to quickly insert all slides.

Figure 12.11
The Slide Finder offers you ways to view and insert slides.

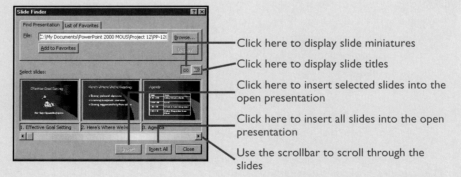

Click here to display slide miniatures

Click here to display slide titles

Click here to insert selected slides into the open presentation

Click here to insert all slides into the open presentation

Use the scrollbar to scroll through the slides

⑥ Click the button to display only the titles of your slides, and then click the fourth slide on the list (This Year's Goals). (Refer to Figure 12.11 to locate the slide title button, if necessary.)
A preview of the selected slide displays beside the list. Remember, if you want to see how a slide looks, you can click the slide title on the Select slides list.

⑦ Choose Insert, and then click Close.
The selected slide is added to the end of the Sports Company presentation. Now, try adding all the slides of another presentation to the open presentation.

⑧ Choose Insert, Slides from Files, and then click the Browse button.
The Browse dialog box displays, so you can locate a presentation to insert in the Sports Company presentation.

⑨ Double-click PP-1204.
The presentation opens in the Slide Finder dialog box.

⑩ Click Insert All, and then click Close.
All the slides from PP-1204 are added at the end of your Sports Company presentation (see Figure 12.12).

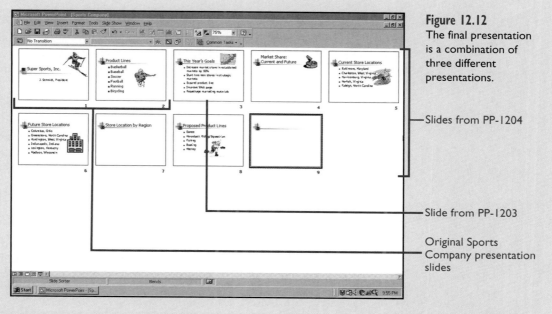

Figure 12.12
The final presentation is a combination of three different presentations.

—Slides from PP-1204

—Slide from PP-1203

Original Sports Company presentation slides

⑪ Save your Sports Company presentation.
Keep the presentation open for the next lesson, in which you link an Excel chart to your PowerPoint presentation.

Lesson 5: Linking an Excel Chart to a PowerPoint Presentation

If you've worked with PowerPoint for a while, you probably know that you can place a chart on a slide by double-clicking a chart placeholder, or clicking the Insert Chart button on the Standard toolbar. Either command activates Microsoft Graph, a peripheral program that you use to create charts within PowerPoint.

You can also link an existing Excel chart to a PowerPoint slide. This helps you take advantage of Excel's powerful formulas to create charts initially in Excel and then insert them in PowerPoint presentations. Another reason why you might want to link to an existing Excel chart is so the information in the presentation is always kept up-to-date.

Here's how it works: Linking enables you to actively share information from a **source file** in Excel (or another program) to a **destination file** in PowerPoint. A **source program** is the program used to create the object (such as a chart or table). In contrast, a **destination**

program is one that accepts the source file. When objects are linked, any changes made to the source file are automatically reflected in the destination file. For example, you can link sales, marketing, or production figures that exist in an Excel worksheet to a PowerPoint slide, so the changes in Excel are automatically reflected in the presentation.

Think about it this way: a linked object is a door between two rooms—an "Excel" room and a "PowerPoint" room. Creating the link opens the door between programs so that information can be freely shared from Excel to PowerPoint.

For this lesson, you'll link an Excel chart that shows your company's market share to the Sports Company presentation. If you haven't linked programs before, you'll be amazed at this powerful feature. Try linking an Excel chart to your presentation now.

 Exam Note: Linked and Embedded Objects
Embedded objects are those objects placed in the file of a destination program by another program. After an object has been embedded, it becomes part of the destination file. You can double-click an embedded object to reactivate the source program and make revisions to the object.

In contrast to embedded objects, linked objects are those created in a source file, and then placed in the destination file while maintaining a connection between the two. The object in the destination file is automatically updated whenever you make changes to the source file. For example, you can link an Excel chart to a Power-Point slide. Any changes you make on the Excel chart are reflected automatically on the PowerPoint slide.

 If You Have Problems...
To share information between programs, they must both be installed on your computer system. You'll be using Word and Excel throughout the remainder of the project, so make sure that these programs are installed before continuing.

To Link an Excel Chart to a PowerPoint Presentation

❶ In the open Sports Company presentation, double-click Slide 4, Market Share: Current and Future.
This is the slide where you want to place the linked chart. Double-clicking a slide in Slide Sorter view is a quick way to display the slide in Normal view.

❷ Click the Start button, and then choose Microsoft Excel from the Programs menu.
Excel 2000 loads into memory and a blank worksheet displays.

 If You Have Problems...
If Excel doesn't start, or you can't locate it on the Programs menu, it is most likely in a different folder on your system. Ask your instructor for help. Also, if the Office Assistant window displays in Excel, click its Close button.

❸ In Excel, open PP-1205 and save it as Market Share.
This worksheet file contains the chart that you want to link to a PowerPoint presentation. Because charts in Excel reflect underlying data, any time you change the data in the Excel worksheet, the chart also automatically changes.

Now select the chart object that you want to link.

④ Click the chart object on the Excel worksheet.

The chart object is selected, as indicated by the black selection handles (see Figure 12.13). In addition, Excel places colored borders around the data that was used to create the chart. Any changes to this data will be reflected on the chart.

⊠ If You Have Problems...

Make sure that the selection handles appear as shown in Figure 12.13—not just around a chart object such as the chart title.

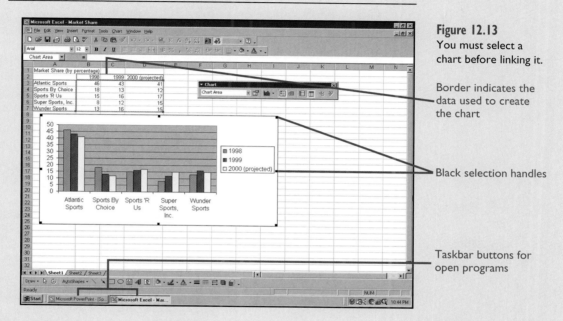

Figure 12.13
You must select a chart before linking it.

Border indicates the data used to create the chart

Black selection handles

Taskbar buttons for open programs

⑤ Click the Copy button on Excel's toolbar.

The chart is copied to the Clipboard. In addition, the selected chart has a moving border, sometimes called a "marching marquee."

Now you're ready to create the link. To do this, you must choose the Edit, Paste Special command in PowerPoint. This command enables you to create an active link between the Excel chart and the PowerPoint presentation. First, you need to switch to PowerPoint. You can quickly switch to another program by clicking the program's Taskbar button.

⊠ If You Have Problems...

Don't fall into the trap of just switching to PowerPoint and clicking the Paste button. If you do, you'll paste the Excel chart in the presentation, but won't create an active link. Be sure to choose Edit, Paste Special in PowerPoint.

⑥ Click the PowerPoint (Sports Company) button on the Taskbar, and then choose Edit, Paste Special.

The Paste Special dialog box displays (see Figure 12.14). You use this dialog box to create a link.

continues ▶

To Link an Excel Chart to a PowerPoint Presentation (continued)

Figure 12.14
You can create an active link between programs by using this dialog box.

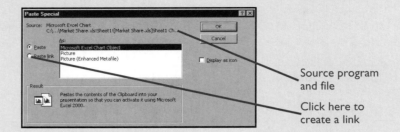

Source program and file

Click here to create a link

7 **Click the Paste link option button.**
This command creates a shortcut to the source file (in Excel), so the changes you make to the chart or worksheet data reflect in your presentation slide (the destination file).

8 **Make sure that Microsoft Excel Chart Object is selected in the As list box in the Paste Special dialog box, and then choose OK.**
The Excel chart is placed in the presentation as an object (see Figure 12.15). Because the chart is linked to the source file, changes you make to the source file will also be updated in PowerPoint.

Figure 12.15
Use the Paste Special command to create a link.

Linked object

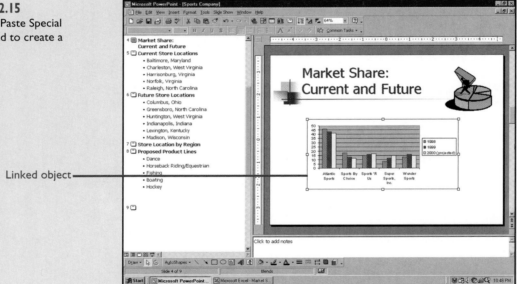

9 **Move and resize the chart object to display in the center of the available space.**

10 **Save the Sports Company presentation.**

11 **Switch to Excel, save the Market Share file, and then exit Excel.**
Keep your presentation open and PowerPoint running for the next lesson.

Exam Note: **Updating and Breaking Links**

After you link an Excel chart to a PowerPoint presentation, you can change information in Excel and then watch it automatically update the associated data in the presentation. Remember that data changes to the Excel worksheet reflect in the Excel chart, which is linked to the PowerPoint presentation. In addition to changes in data, you can also change the chart's structure or layout.

If your changes to the Excel chart aren't reflected in the PowerPoint presentation, your link may be set for manual (not automatic) updating. In PowerPoint, choose <u>E</u>dit, Lin<u>k</u>s to display the Links dialog box. Make sure that the Update option button is set to <u>A</u>utomatic, and then click <u>U</u>pdate Now. Close the Links dialog box.

Here's an even quicker way to update a linked object: Right-click the object (such as a chart), and then choose <u>U</u>pdate Link.

What happens when you want to break a link between the source and destination file? Just choose <u>E</u>dit, Lin<u>k</u>s to display the Links dialog box. Click the <u>B</u>reak Link button, and then close the dialog box.

 Exam Note: **Importing Excel Charts**

You can also import an entire chart file into a PowerPoint presentation. Double-click a chart placeholder on the slide in which you want to import the file to activate Microsoft Graph. Then, click the Import File button on the Standard toolbar to display the Import File dialog box. Specify the filename and location, and then choose <u>O</u>pen. In the Import Data Options dialog box that displays, choose whether to import the <u>E</u>ntire sheet or just a specific <u>R</u>ange. Finally, click OK to import the file.

Lesson 6: Embedding a Word Table Within a Presentation

Tables provide a good way of organizing information in PowerPoint. A table is just a grid with columns and rows for entering data, similar to a worksheet. The intersection of a column and row, called a cell, is the area in which you enter data. You can use cells to group related information together.

You can create a table directly in PowerPoint by using PowerPoint's <u>I</u>nsert, Ta<u>b</u>le command, or by using tools on the Tables and Borders toolbar. If you want to use Microsoft Word's more powerful formatting commands, however, you should instead embed a Word table within the slide.

When you create a table using Word, you **embed** it as an object on a slide. An embedded object is an object created by one program (in this case, Word) within another program (PowerPoint). Whenever you access the embedded object—by double-clicking it—you can use the original program's commands to revise or format it.

It is not necessary to have Word running in memory before you create a table. PowerPoint automatically accesses Word when you create or edit the table, but closes it when you finish working with it.

In the Sports Company presentation, you want to insert a table that shows store location by regions. To do so, you'll insert a Word table as an embedded object on a PowerPoint slide. Try working with a Word table now.

To Embed a Word Table Within a Presentation

1 **In the open Sports Company presentation, display Slide 7, Store Location by Region, in Normal view.**
This is where you want to insert your table.

2 **Choose Insert, Picture, Microsoft Word Table.**
The Insert Table dialog box displays (see Figure 12.16). By default, Word creates a table with two columns and two rows. However, you can create a table with more columns and rows by typing the number you want in the dialog box. For now, you'll create the default-sized table.

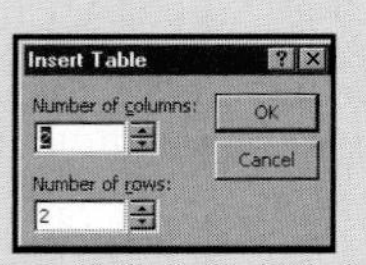

Figure 12.16
Indicate the number of columns and rows you want for your new table.

3 **Click OK in the Insert Table dialog box.**
A Word table with two columns and two rows is embedded on your slide (see Figure 12.17). Notice the dark rope-like border and the selection handles that surround the table, indicating that the source program, Word, is activated. Additionally, Word's toolbars, menu commands, and rulers display. That's because when you use an embedded object, you have access to the source program's features.

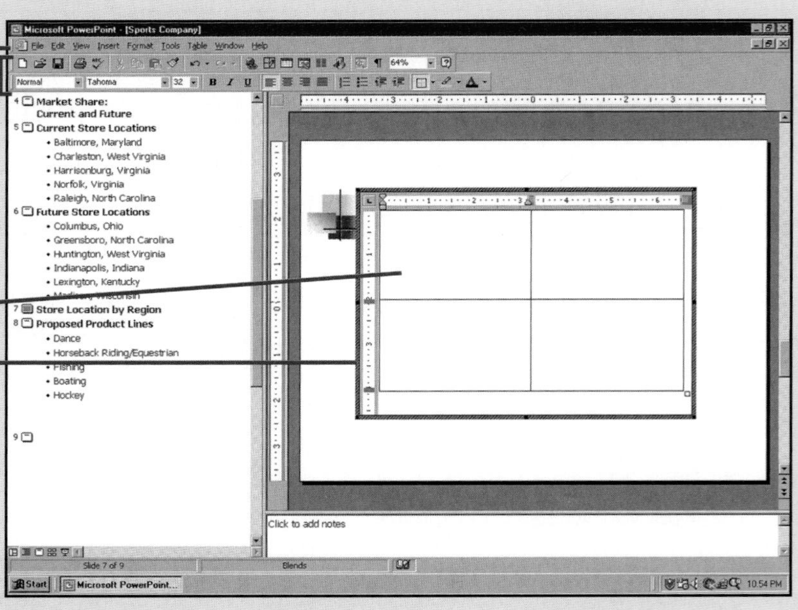

Figure 12.17
Embedding a Word table gives you access to Word commands.

Word's menu bar

Word's toolbars

Cell

Rope-like border indicates an activated object

✖ *If You Have Problems...*
Don't worry if your Word toolbars appear differently than those shown in the book. Most likely, another user has changed the toolbar arrangement (such as separating the Standard and Formatting toolbars).

Also, if you don't see lines separating the cells, choose Format, Borders and Shading. On the Borders page, click All before closing the dialog box.

4 **Type** Mid-Atlantic **in the first cell, press** (Tab⇥)**, and type** Baltimore, MD**.**
The text is entered in the cells. Happily, you're not limited to only one line of text per cell. Instead, you can press (⏎Enter) to create a new line within a cell—and the cell automatically expands to accommodate the new text. Try using this technique to enter more stores in the cell.

5 **Press** (⏎Enter) **to create another line, and then type** Charleston, WV**. Press** (⏎Enter)**.**

6 **Enter the following information in your table (press** (Tab⇥) **or** (⬆Shift) **+**(Tab⇥) **to move forward or backward between cells):**

Mid-Atlantic   Baltimore, MD

                            Charleston, WV

                            Greensboro, NC

                            Harrisonburg, VA

                            Huntington, WV

                            Lexington, KY

                            Norfolk, VA

                            Raleigh, NC

Midwest   Columbus, OH

                            Indianapolis, IN

                            Madison, WI

The information is entered into your table. Now, try moving and resizing your table. First, however, you must finish creating the table by clicking outside of it. When you do so, you embed the table as an object on the slide.

7 **Click outside the table object.**
The table is embedded as an object on your slide. Also, notice that you no longer have access to Word's commands. Instead, PowerPoint's toolbars and menu commands redisplay. Don't worry about how the table text looks, because you'll "clean up" the table's formatting (and size) in the next lesson.

8 **Save the Sports Company presentation.**
Leave the presentation open and PowerPoint running for the next exercise, in which you format the table.

Lesson 7: Formatting an Embedded Word Table

If you completed the preceding lesson, you successfully embedded a Word table in a presentation. One of the main advantages of embedding a Word table (instead of creating a native PowerPoint table) is to use Word's formatting commands. In this lesson, you spiff up the table by using Word's formatting features. Try working with formatting commands now.

To Format an Embedded Word Table

1 **In the Sports Company presentation, make sure that Slide 7, Store Location by Region, is open in Normal view.**
Now, try to activate the source program, Word, so that you can make changes to the table's formatting. Before you do, however, here's a brief primer on the difference between selecting and activating an embedded object.

continues ▶

To Format an Embedded Word Table   (continued)

You single-click an embedded object to select it so that you can resize, move, or delete it. In contrast, when you double-click the object, you reactivate it and place a rope-like border around it. When an object is activated, you have complete access to the commands of the source program that created it. In the next step, you double-click your table to activate Word.

2 **Double-click the table to activate it.**
The dark rope-like border appears around the table to indicate that it is activated. Remember that when a table is activated, you can use Word's features to format the table—such as using the AutoFormat command.

3 **Choose T_able, Table Auto_Format.**
The Table AutoFormat dialog box displays (see Figure 12.18). You can use this dialog box to view and quickly apply a preset format to your table.

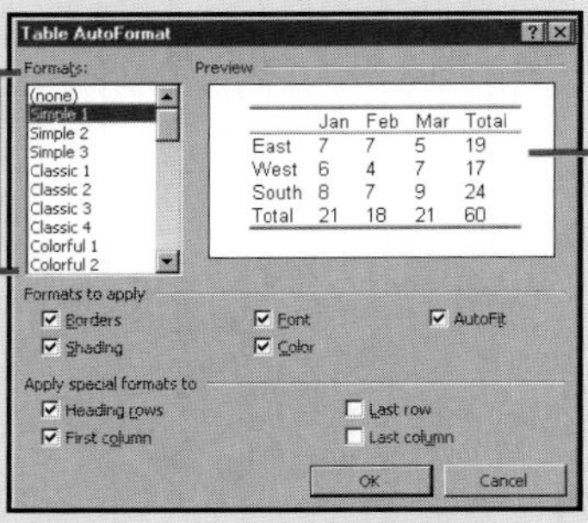

Figure 12.18
You can quickly apply a table format by using this dialog box.

Choose a format here

Preview the selected format here

4 **From the Forma_ts list, select Grid 1.**
A preview of the format displays in the Preview section, so you get an idea of the way the formatting looks. (If you want, preview several other formats. Just make sure that you select Grid 1 before proceeding with the next step.)

5 **Choose OK.**
The Table AutoFormat dialog box closes, and the format is applied to the table.

Now, try changing the font size for your table's text. Before you change the font size, you must select the text that you want to change. An easy way to do this is to use Word's T_able menu.

6 **Choose T_able, Sele_ct, _Table.**
The table is selected, and it appears with an inverse color scheme. Now choose a font size from the Font Size drop-down list on Word's Formatting toolbar.

7 **Click the Font Size drop-down arrow, and then choose 22.**
The new font size is applied to your text. To make your text more readable, you can also add bullets.

8 **Click in the right column, and then choose T_able, Sele_ct _Column.**
The right column is selected.

9 **Click the Bullets button on Word's Formatting toolbar.**
Bullets are added to each line in the right column.

10 **Click outside the table to embed it on your slide.**

Now, select the table so that you can move and resize it. You move and resize embedded objects by using the same procedures that you use to resize other objects.

11 **Single-click the table.**

White selection handles appear around the border of the table, so you can move or resize it.

12 **Resize and move the table so that it appears in the center of the available space, and then click outside the table to deselect it.**

The white selection handles are no longer displayed. The formatted table should appear similar to that shown in Figure 12.19.

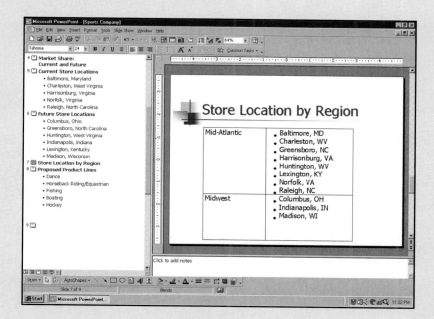

Figure 12.19
You can format a table to add visual appeal.

13 **Save the Sports Company presentation.**

Keep this presentation open and PowerPoint running for the next lesson, in which you collect and paste data from several sources all at once.

 Exam Note: **Applying Diagonal Borders to a Table**

If you want a bit more control over the borders used for your table, select the table and then choose Format, Table to display the Format Table dialog box. On the Borders page, click the buttons that represent the borders you want (outside, diagonal, and so on), and then click OK.

Lesson 8: Using the Office Clipboard

Chances are that you're an old hand at using the Windows Clipboard to copy and paste data. For example, you've probably selected data on one PowerPoint slide, clicked the Copy button, switched to another slide, and clicked Paste to insert the information. You may have even copied data from one program to another—such as copying Word or Excel data, and then pasting it in your presentation. If you've performed functions like these, you know that the process was facilitated by the Windows Clipboard, and that you were basically limited to transferring one piece of data at a time.

Office 2000 includes its own Clipboard—the **Office Clipboard**. The Office Clipboard can "collect" up to 12 pieces of data at a time, and then insert them all at once in your presentation. You can collect a logo from a PowerPoint presentation, a WordArt object in Word, and an Excel chart, for example, and then insert them simultaneously into your presentation. Of course, this makes "pooling" data from different sources quicker and more efficient.

In your Sports Company presentation, you want to quickly create a slide that combines objects from different programs. Try using the time-saving Office Clipboard to insert data from multiple sources into your presentation now.

To Use the Office Clipboard

❶ Start Excel, and open PP-1206.
This is the first program from which you want to pull information. To see the Office Clipboard in action, you can open it before you begin collecting data. Luckily, it's easy to open the Office Clipboard as a toolbar, and then watch it collect data.

❷ Choose View, Toolbars, Clipboard.
The Clipboard toolbar displays (see Figure 12.20). You can use this toolbar to copy information (even from multiple sources), and then paste it into other locations. Before you get started, however, you should clear the Clipboard of any items by clicking the Clear Clipboard button.

Figure 12.20
The Clipboard toolbar helps you collect and paste multiple items.

Clear Clipboard button
Copy button
Paste All button
Copied data appears here

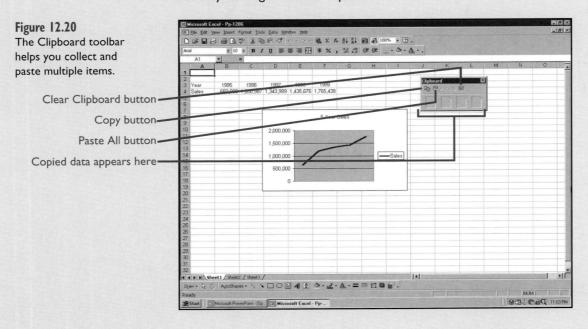

3 Click the Clear Clipboard button.
The items (if any) on the Clipboard are deleted. Now, try copying an Excel chart to the Office Clipboard.

4 Click the chart in the Excel worksheet, and then click the Copy button on the Clipboard toolbar (or on the Standard toolbar).
The chart is copied and appears on the Clipboard toolbar (see Figure 12.21). Now, try copying data from other programs to the Office Clipboard.

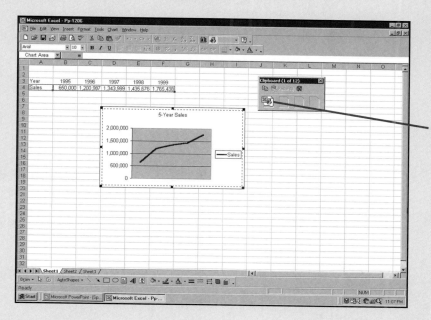

Figure 12.21
Data that you copy appears as an icon on the Clipboard toolbar.

— Copied chart data

5 Start Word, and open PP-1207.
This document includes a WordArt object that you want to use to spiff up a slide. Notice also that the Clipboard toolbar continues to display—even if you switch to another program. Now, try selecting and copying the WordArt object.

6 Click the WordArt object (Sales are up!), and then click the Copy button on the Clipboard toolbar.
The WordArt object is copied and appears on the Office Clipboard as a Word icon. Now, try opening a second presentation in PowerPoint so that you can copy data from it to the Sports Company presentation.

7 Click the Microsoft PowerPoint taskbar button to switch to PowerPoint, and then open PP-1208.
You can open multiple presentations in memory at one time. Each presentation or open program, such as Word, is represented by a taskbar button.

8 Select the clip art object on the slide, and then click the Copy button on the Clipboard toolbar.
The copied data displays as a PowerPoint icon on the Clipboard toolbar. Now try inserting the data that you collected to a new PowerPoint slide.

9 Close PP-1208, switch to the Sports Company presentation, and display the last presentation slide.
This blank slide is the location where you want to paste the data that you collected.

continues ▶

Use the Office Clipboard (continued)

⑩ Click the Paste All button on the Clipboard toolbar.
The data from all three sources is copied to the slide. Of course, you might need to do a bit of cleaning up and rearranging the objects, but collecting and pasting multiple items still saves you time.

 If You Have Problems...
Don't panic if you don't initially see all three of the pasted objects. Most likely, they are "stacked" on top of each other. Also, some of the objects (such as the Excel chart) may appear very small. Just select and resize the objects until they display the way you want them to.

⑪ Move and resize the objects on your new slide until they appear similar to the slide shown in Figure 12.22.

Figure 12.22
You can rearrange your data after you paste it on a slide.

WordArt object from Word

Clip from PowerPoint presentation

Chart from Excel

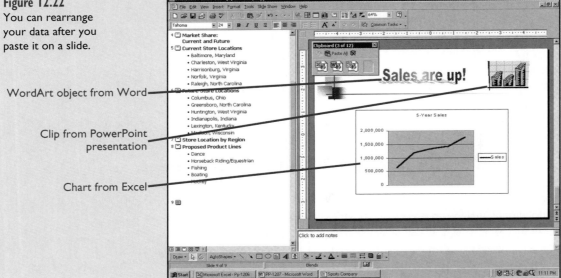

⑫ Close the Clipboard toolbar, and then exit Word and Excel without saving the open files.

⑬ Save the Sports Company presentation.
Keep the presentation open and PowerPoint running for the next lesson, in which you learn how to send a presentation to Word.

 Exam Note: Pasting Individual Items
You aren't limited to pasting all the items that happen to be in the Office Clipboard. Instead, click an individual item on the Clipboard toolbar to insert it in the open presentation. Remember that if you accidentally insert an object in the wrong location, just click Undo.

Lesson 9: Exporting an Outline to Word

If you've ever wanted to convert a PowerPoint presentation to a Word document, you'll be happy to know that PowerPoint includes a feature that allows an almost seamless transfer of information to Word. After the information has been exported to Word, you can modify and save the new Word document, just as you can with any other Word document.

Imagine, for example, that you want a copy of your presentation to hand out to your store managers. You can create an outline in Word, or a set of handouts that have slide miniatures and blank lines for taking notes. Try creating these Word documents from your presentation now.

To Export an Outline to Word

❶ Display Slide 1 in the Sports Company presentation, and then choose File, Send To, Microsoft Word.

The Write-Up dialog box displays (see Figure 12.23). You can use this dialog box to designate the page layout for the Word document that you're creating. You can export slide miniatures to the document, or only the text. Additionally, you can paste the information from PowerPoint into Word as a one-time occurrence, or create an active link (by choosing Paste link). For now, you create an outline in Word without linking the documents.

Choose the main page layout here ——

Choose linking options here ——

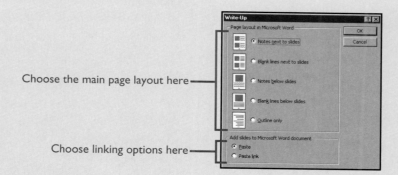

Figure 12.23
You can choose from a variety of page layouts.

❷ Click the option button for Outline only; then choose OK.

PowerPoint sends the presentation to Word and creates an outline in Word (see Figure 12.24). After the presentation is sent to Word, you can modify the Word document by editing or formatting it. Also notice that the Word document has a generic name assigned, such as PPT983, which displays in the title bar. This name is assigned based on the temporary file that Windows uses for the new Word file, and has no real significance. Also, don't be concerned if the name on other students' computers differs from yours.

continues ▶

To Export an Outline to Word   (continued)

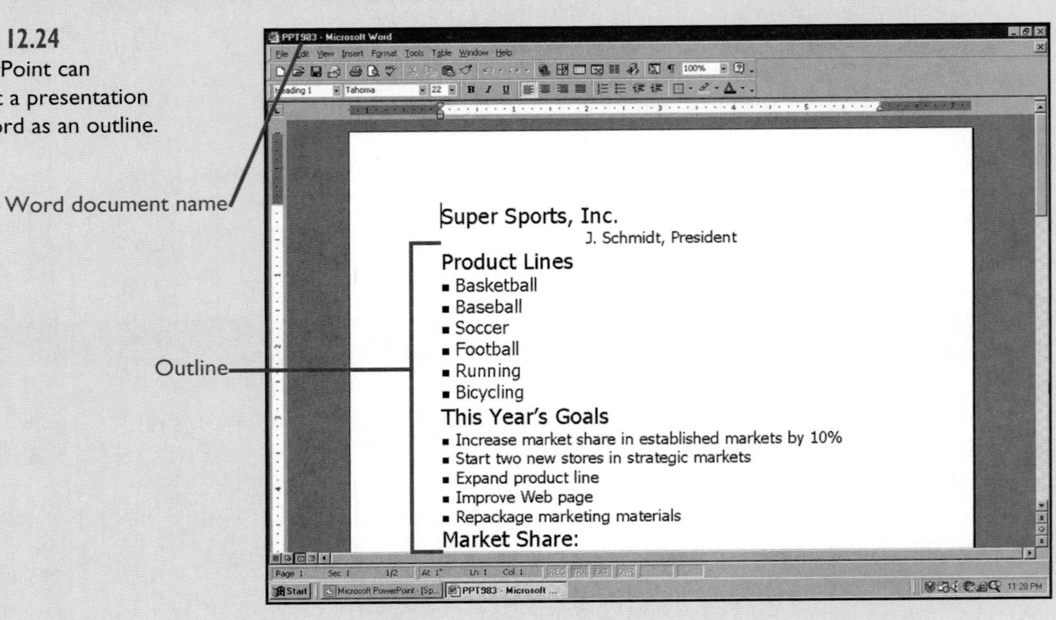

Figure 12.24
PowerPoint can
export a presentation
to Word as an outline.

Word document name

Outline

After you create an outline and view it, you can revise the outline text or formatting by using any of Word's commands. You can also save the file in Word by using the File, Save As command. For right now, however, you can close the file without saving it, so that you can try linking a PowerPoint presentation to Word.

3 Exit Word without saving the outline, and then display your Sports Company presentation.

4 Choose File, Send To, Microsoft Word.
The Write-Up dialog box displays.

5 Choose the Blank lines next to the slides option button.
You choose this page layout to create a Word document with slide miniatures and blank lines next to them.

Now, try linking the presentation to the Word document. When you do this, any changes made to the presentation are automatically reflected in the Word document.

6 Choose Paste link, and then click OK.
After a brief delay, a Word document is produced that includes each of your PowerPoint slides with blank lines next to them (see Figure 12.25). If you're familiar with Word's tables, you'll quickly realize that your presentation is laid out within a table.

Why is this type of page layout handy? Because you can print and hand it out to participants during a meeting, and they can use it to take notes.

Now, watch what happens when you change information in the PowerPoint presentation. Because it's linked to the Word document, the changes automatically reflect in Word.

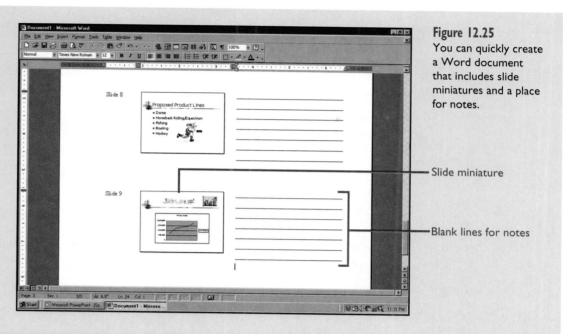

Figure 12.25
You can quickly create a Word document that includes slide miniatures and a place for notes.

Slide miniature

Blank lines for notes

How do you access the source data to change it? It's easy: just double-click a linked object to display the source document for the link, and then make your revisions. Try this method of updating information now.

7 **Press Ctrl+Home to display the first presentation slide in Word, and then double-click the first slide miniature.**
The Sports Company presentation—the source file that's linked to the Word document—displays.

8 **Change the word President to CEO on Slide 1.**
The information is changed in the source file. The destination file automatically refreshes, or updates, the link whenever you reopen the file. You can also choose to update the links whenever you like by choosing the Update Now button in the Links dialog box. Try this method of updating your new Word document now.

9 **Switch to Word, and then choose Edit, Links.**
The Links dialog box displays with a list of the links that exist between the documents (see Figure 12.26).

Selected slide

Click here to automatically update the link when the file opens

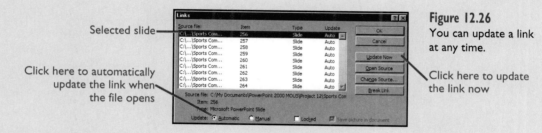

Figure 12.26
You can update a link at any time.

Click here to update the link now

10 **Make sure that the first slide is selected, and that the Update section is set to Automatic.**

continues ▶

To Export an Outline to Word   (continued)

⑪ Choose <u>U</u>pdate Now, and then click OK.

The information on Slide 1 changes to reflect the modified information from the source file.

Now, try saving and printing your new Word document. Remember that you save and print it by using the same commands that you use in PowerPoint. For example, you can choose <u>F</u>ile, <u>P</u>rint, and click OK to print the document.

⑫ Save the Word document as Super Sports, print it, and then close it. Exit Word.

⑬ Save your Sports Company presentation, and then close it.

If you're finished with your work session, exit PowerPoint and shut down Windows before turning off your computer. Otherwise, complete the Skill Drill, Challenge, and Discovery Zone exercises at the end of this project.

Summary

In this project, you learned several ways to share information between PowerPoint and the other Office 2000 programs. From linking Excel charts to embedding Word tables, you learned some powerful ways of integrating programs with PowerPoint. Furthermore, you learned how to combine slides from multiple PowerPoint presentations to quickly create a finished presentation. You also saw how you could use the Office Clipboard to quickly insert multiple objects in a presentation. Finally, you learned methods for sending (and linking) information from PowerPoint to Word. These integration features can help you powerfully and seamlessly create more dynamic and forceful presentations.

To expand on your knowledge, spend a few minutes exploring Help on these topics. Additionally, complete some of the Skill Drill, Challenge, and Discovery Zone exercises.

Checking Concepts and Terms

True/False

For each of the following, check *T* or *F* to indicate whether the statement is true or false.

__T __F   **1.** Linking and embedding are the same thing. [L5–6]

__T __F   **2.** Information that you cut or copy is sent to a temporary area in memory called the Exporter. [L8]

__T __F   **3.** You can combine multiple PowerPoint presentations by using the Slide Finder feature. [L4]

__T __F   **4.** A taskbar button displays for each program in memory. [L5–7]

__T __F   **5.** The Windows Clipboard and the Office Clipboard are the same thing. [L8]

Multiple Choice

Circle the letter of the correct answer for each of the following questions.

1. How can you share information between Office programs? [L1, L4–9]

a. Link an Excel chart to a PowerPoint presentation.

b. Embed a Word table within a PowerPoint presentation.

c. Export a PowerPoint presentation to Word as an outline.

d. any of the above

2. Which of the following is *not* an advantage of embedding a Word table within a PowerPoint presentation? [L6–7]

a. You maintain an active connection between Word and PowerPoint.

b. You can use Word's more sophisticated and powerful formatting commands.

c. You can double-click the embedded table to activate Word's features and toolbars.

d. The table is automatically kept in memory so that you can paste it in multiple presentations.

3. Which of the following is a way to share information between Word and PowerPoint? [L1, 6, 8]

a. Copy information to PowerPoint via the Office Clipboard.

b. Send a PowerPoint presentation to Word.

c. Embed a Word table within PowerPoint.

d. all of the above

4. How many items can you collect and store on the Office Clipboard? [L8]

a. 1

b. 6

c. 12

d. 100

5. What happens when you double-click an embedded Excel chart on a PowerPoint slide? [L5]

a. The Links dialog box displays, so you can decide whether to update the link.

b. The Insert Object dialog box displays, so you can insert an updated version of the chart.

c. The source file in Excel displays, so you can make modifications to it.

d. none of the above

Skill Drill

Skill Drill exercises reinforce project skills. Each skill reinforced is the same, or nearly the same, as a skill presented in the project. Detailed instructions are provided in a step-by-step format.

1. Sending a Presentation to Word

Your supervisor asked you to give a quick update on a safety campaign you're spearheading five minutes before a staff meeting. You have the information in a PowerPoint presentation, but would like to develop handouts to give staff members. Luckily, you remember that you can send a PowerPoint presentation to Word—including slide miniatures. [L9]

1. In PowerPoint, open **PP-1209**, and save it as **Staff Meeting**.

2. Choose File, Send To, Microsoft Word.

3. In the Write-Up dialog box, choose Blank lines next to slides. Also choose the Paste link option button. Click OK.

4. In Word, press Ctrl+Home to display the top of your document.

5. Save the Word document as **Staff Meeting Handouts**.

6. Close the Word document and exit Word.

7. In PowerPoint, save the Staff Meeting presentation. Keep the presentation open and PowerPoint running if you plan to complete the additional exercises.

2. Embedding and Formatting a Word Table

To make the data in your Staff Meeting presentation easier to follow, you decide to embed and format a Word table. [L6–7]

1. In PowerPoint, press Ctrl+End to display the last presentation slide.

2. Click the New Slide button to display the New Slide dialog box. Choose the Title Only AutoLayout, and then click OK.

3. Enter **Sick Days Per Facility** in the title placeholder.

4. Choose Insert, Picture, Microsoft Word Table to display the Insert Table dialog box.

5. Press Tab to select the text for the Number of rows box, and then type **3**. Click OK.

6. Enter the following information in the table:

Facility	Sick Days
Danville	45
Madison	38

7. Now move and format the table: Move the table down on the slide so that it is centered in the available space.

8. Make sure the embedded table is activated so that Word's toolbars and commands display. Choose Table, Table AutoFormat.

9. In the Table AutoFormat dialog box, preview several formats by clicking them on the Formats list. Choose Grid 8 on the Formats list; then click OK.

10. Click outside the table to better see your changes.

11. Save the Staff Meeting presentation. Keep it open and PowerPoint running if you plan to complete the additional exercises.

3. Linking an Excel Chart to the PowerPoint Presentation

You want to include visual, up-to-date information in the Staff Meeting presentation. To do so, you link an existing Excel chart to your PowerPoint presentation. You also use the Office Clipboard to collect and paste information from several sources. [L2, 8]

1. Start Excel, and open **PP-1210**. Click the chart object, and then choose Edit, Copy.

2. Switch to PowerPoint. Display the last presentation slide in the Staff Meeting presentation, and then click the New Slide button. In the New Slide dialog box, choose the Title Only AutoLayout, and then click OK.

3. Type **Sick Days: First Quarter** in the title placeholder.

4. Choose Edit, Paste Special. In the Paste Special dialog box, click the Paste link button. Make sure that Microsoft Excel Chart Object is selected in the As list box, and then click OK.

5. Resize and move the chart object on Slide 6 to fill the available space.

6. You want to create an ending slide for your presentation that hammers home some of your main points. Because you already have the information and pictures you need in other files, you decide to use the Office Clipboard to collect the data and paste it in your presentation. Display the last slide in the Staff Meeting presentation. Add a new blank slide to the end of the presentation.

7. Display the Office Clipboard by choosing View, Toolbars, Clipboard. Clear the Clipboard's contents by clicking the Clear Clipboard button.

8. Open **PP-1211**. Select the text in the placeholder, and then click the Copy button on the Clipboard toolbar. Close the **PP-1211** presentation.

9. Open **PP-1212**. Click the object in the upper-left corner of the slide (Cory Glass). Click the border of the object to select it, and then click the Copy button on the Clipboard toolbar.

10. Click the arrow (drawn object) in the lower half of the slide, and then click its border to select it. Click the Copy button. Close the **PP-1212** presentation.

11. Display the blank slide you created in Step 6. Click Paste All on the Clipboard toolbar.

12. Move the Cory Glass logo to the upper-right corner of the slide. Resize the object so that you can read the text on the slide. Move the arrow object beneath the text. Close the Clipboard toolbar.

13. Save the Staff Meeting presentation, and then close it. Leave PowerPoint running if you plan to complete the Challenge or Discovery Zone exercises.

Challenge

Challenge exercises expand on or are somewhat related to skills presented in the lessons. Each exercise provides a brief narrative introduction, followed by instructions in a numbered-step format that are not as detailed as those in the Skill Drill section.

1. Using the Slide Finder to Combine Presentations

You work for a travel agency, and frequently need to create new presentations to market your agency. To make creating these new presentations a breeze, you decide to combine slides from two existing presentations. [L4]

1. Open **PP-1213**, and save it as **Travel Trips**. Display the presentation in Slide Sorter view.

2. Choose Insert, Slides from Files.

3. Click the Browse button. Locate the folder where your student data files are stored, and then double-click **PP-1214**.

4. In the Slide Finder dialog box, click Insert All. Leave the Slide Finder dialog box open.

5. In the Slide Finder dialog box, click the Browse button.

6. Locate the folder where you store your data files, and then double-click **PP-1215**. Choose Insert All. Close the Slide Finder dialog box.

7. Save your Travel Trips presentation. Keep the presentation open and PowerPoint running for the next exercise.

2. Linking to an Excel Chart

To drive home the idea that your agency is less expensive than others, you decide to include a chart in your presentation. Because the information you want to use for the chart already exists in Excel, however, you plan to link the chart to your presentation instead of creating it from scratch. [L5]

1. In the Travel Trips presentation open from the preceding exercise, display Slide 5 (Here's the Deal:).

2. Insert a new slide following Slide 5, based on the Title Only AutoLayout. Type **Our Deals are Steals!** in the title placeholder.

3. Start Excel, if necessary, and open **PP-1216**. Click the chart object, and then click the Copy button.

4. Insert the chart on Slide 6 as a linked object. Move and resize the chart so that it fills the available space on the slide.

5. Double-click the chart object. In the Excel worksheet, click cell D2. Enter **2895** in the cell, and then press Enter.

6. Click the Close button for your Excel worksheet. Choose <u>Y</u>es in the message box that displays.

7. In PowerPoint, update the linked chart.

8. Save the Travel Trips presentation. Keep the presentation open and PowerPoint running if you plan to complete the additional exercises.

3. Sending a Presentation to Word

You want a copy of the presentation as a Word outline. To quickly create the outline, you send the presentation to Word. [L9]

1. Send the Travel Trips presentation to Word as an outline. Save the Word outline as **Spring and Summer Trips**. Close the document and Word.

2. Send the Travel Trips presentation to Word as slides with blank lines below. Make sure that you create the slide miniatures as linked objects.

3. Save the Word document as **Publicity Meeting Handouts**. Print a copy of your Word document, and then close it.

4. Exit Word.

5. Save and close the Travel Trips presentation. Keep PowerPoint running if you plan to complete the additional exercises.

Discovery Zone

Discovery Zone exercises require advanced knowledge of topics presented in *MOUS Essentials* lessons, application of skills from multiple lessons, or self-directed learning of new skills. Each exercise is independent of the others, so you may complete the exercises in any order.

1. Finding Out About Integration Features

You're scheduled to conduct a training seminar on PowerPoint for advanced users. One of the main topics is on linking and embedding objects in a PowerPoint presentation. Using Help, research the following subjects:

- How to set up an OLE object to open during a slide show
- How to convert an embedded object to a PowerPoint object
- How to insert an object from a program (such as Paint) that is *not* an Office 2000 program
- How to edit a linked object
- How to display a linked object as an icon
- How to insert a presentation as an embedded object in Word or Excel
- Ways to insert and edit an equation in PowerPoint
- How to create a table and enter text
- How to add or delete rows from a table
- How to select items in a table
- How to add, change, or remove fill from a table cell
- How to merge and split cells in a table
- How to insert an Excel chart in a presentation

- How to change text and data in a chart
- How to change colors, patterns, and fills for a chart
- How to import chart data from other programs

Develop a presentation based on the information you find. Your presentation should feature about 25–35 slides. Use clip art, and linked and embedded objects to help illustrate your presentation. Practice giving the presentation to another user or to your class. Save the presentation. Leave PowerPoint running if you plan to complete the final exercise. [L1–9]

2. Using Integration Features to Create a Presentation

Pick a topic that interests you, and then use the World Wide Web (and your library) to research information about the topic. Be sure to locate statistical and numeric data related to your topic.

Organize the information that you find, and then develop a presentation based on the data. Include an embedded Word table and a linked (or imported) Excel chart in your presentation. Format the chart and table by using commands you learned in this project.

Use the Office Clipboard to copy objects from several sources, and then paste them on a title (or ending) slide for your presentation.

Send the presentation to Word as an outline, and then save and close the newly created outline. Create handouts in Word, based on your PowerPoint presentation. Make sure to link the slide miniatures to the PowerPoint presentation. Save the Word document.

Give your presentation to at least one other user or to your class. Save the presentation, and then close it and exit PowerPoint. [L2–7]

PinPoint Assessment

You have completed this project and its associated lessons, and have had an opportunity to assess your skills through the end-of-project questions and exercises. Now use the PinPoint software Evaluation Mode to further assess your comprehension of the specific exam activities you have just learned. You can also use the PinPoint Trainer Mode and the Show Me tutorials to practice these exam activities.

Creating Interactive Slide Shows

Key terms introduced in this project include

- action buttons
- custom slide shows
- interactive slide shows
- intranet
- mouse over action

Objectives	Required Activity for MOUS	Exam Level
➤ Creating a Custom Slide Show	Add links to slides within the presentation	Expert
	Add a presentation within a presentation	Expert
➤ Running a Custom Slide Show	Add a presentation within a presentation	Expert
➤ Creating Hyperlinks	Insert hyperlink	Core
	Add links to slides within the presentation	Expert
➤ Using Hyperlinks	Insert hyperlink	Core
	Add links to slides within the presentation	Expert
➤ Creating Action Buttons	Add links to slides within the presentation	Expert
	Add an action button	Expert
➤ Editing and Removing a Hyperlink		
➤ Using Hyperlinks in a Slide Show		

Why Would I Do This?

PowerPoint includes a wide variety of ways you can create ***interactive slide shows***—those that perform an action in response to user input. Interactive slide shows are useful when you want to involve the users or require input from them. For example, you might want to create an interactive slide show for use at a trade show, on the Web, or on your company's ***intranet***, which is a network used within an organization. Interactive slide shows usually have ***action buttons*** that the user can click to quickly display supporting data or to jump to another location (such as a Web site).

One way to make a presentation interactive is to create ***custom slide shows***—presentations that have several variations based on which slides you choose. You might begin a presentation with the same set of slides, for example, but then branch to one set of slides for sales, another for marketing, and so on.

You can also insert ***hyperlinks*** in your presentation. A hyperlink is text or an object in your presentation that provides a pathway (or link) to another slide, presentation, graphic, file, intranet, or World Wide Web location. Hyperlinks enable you (or other users) to access additional information and display related slides or presentations. You can place your mouse pointer over a hyperlink to display a pointing hand icon, and then click to jump to the linked information. Even better, some hyperlinks require you to only move the mouse pointer over the linked object to jump to that link.

In this project, you learn how to create custom slide shows. You also learn how to create, edit, and remove hyperlinks in your document. When you finish setting up the hyperlinks, you run an interactive slide show that contains hyperlinks.

Imagine that you represent a training organization and are preparing a presentation to give to the local Chamber of Commerce. Because you're not sure what type of organizations (small or large) will be attending the meeting, you create an interactive presentation that addresses the needs of both. The presentation contains custom slide shows, hyperlinks, and action buttons so that you have maximum flexibility in giving the presentation.

Lesson 1: Creating a Custom Slide Show

You can use PowerPoint's custom slide show feature to create multiple subsets of the same presentation. Instead of developing several almost-identical presentations for different audiences, you can create a main presentation and then jump to custom shows when appropriate.

For example, you might want to give similar presentations to different groups within your company. You can use the same slides to begin the show, and then jump to the custom slide show that's appropriate for each group. For example, you might give one presentation for salaried employees, another for hourly workers, and so on.

You can jump to a custom slide show by choosing <u>G</u>o, <u>C</u>ustom Show from the slide show's shortcut menu. Alternatively, you can set up a hyperlink to the show (as you learn in Lessons 2 and 3). After you create the show, you can also edit it by adding or removing slides.

Because using this feature can be a time-saver and enables you to quickly customize a presentation, try creating a custom show now.

To Create a Custom Slide Show

① Open PP-1301 and save it as Promotional Information.

② Display the presentation in Normal view, and then choose Slide Show, Custom Shows.

The Custom Shows dialog box displays (see Figure 13.1). You use this dialog box to manage custom slide shows by adding, revising, or deleting shows.

Click here to create a new custom slide show

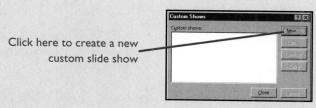

Figure 13.1
You can create a variety of presentations from the same set of slides.

③ Click the New button.

The Define Custom Show dialog box displays (see Figure 13.2). You use this dialog box to choose slides from your presentation that you want to include in a custom show.

Enter the custom show's name here

All the slides in your presentation appear here

Slides included in your custom show appear here

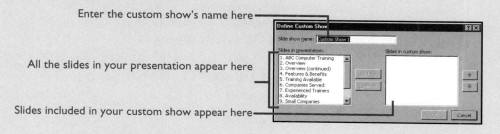

Figure 13.2
You can pick and choose presentation slides to add to a custom show.

Before you decide which slides you want in your custom show, you should assign a descriptive name (up to 31 characters in length) to your show. This is a good idea, so that you and others can quickly determine a custom show's purpose.

④ In the Slide show name text box, type Large Companies.

Now you're ready to choose slides from your presentation that you want to include in the custom show. PowerPoint provides a couple of ways to add slides to a custom show. You can click to select individual slides, and then click the Add button to insert them in the custom show. Alternatively, you can double-click each slide you want to add.

You can also select multiple adjacent slides by pressing ◆Shift while clicking the first and last slides you want. Alternatively, you can click and drag the mouse over them.

Try adding some slides to your custom show now.

⑤ In the Slides in presentation list box, scroll down, and then click and drag over Slides 10–11.

The slides are selected.

continues ▶

To Create a Custom Slide Show (continued)

6 **Click the Add button.**
The specified slides are added to the custom slide show, and display on the Slides in custom slide show list (see Figure 13.3).

Figure 13.3
You can quickly create a custom slide show.

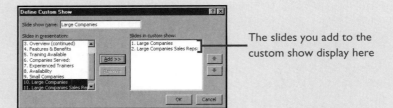

The slides you add to the custom show display here

7 **Click OK to close the Define Custom Show dialog box.**
The Custom Shows dialog box redisplays. Notice that the Large Companies slide show that you just created displays on the Custom shows list. Now, try creating a second custom slide show—this time for Small Companies.

8 **In the Customs Shows dialog box, click New, and then type Small Companies in the Slide show name text box.**
If you want to select nonadjacent slides to add to your presentation, press Ctrl while clicking them. After you select the slides you want, you can click the Add button.

9 **Press Ctrl, and then click Slide 9 and Slide 12 on the Slides in presentation list.**
The slides are selected.

10 **Click Add.**
The selected slides are added to your Small Companies custom show.

11 **Click OK to close the Define Custom Show dialog box.**
The Custom Shows dialog box redisplays. Notice that both custom shows you developed display on the Custom shows list (see Figure 13.4).

Figure 13.4
You can create multiple custom shows that are based on the same set of slides.

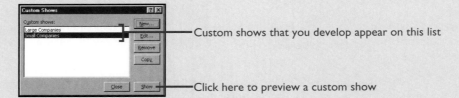

Custom shows that you develop appear on this list

Click here to preview a custom show

Keep the Custom Shows dialog box open for the next exercise, in which you learn two methods of running your custom shows.

 Exam Note: Modifying Custom Shows
If you work with custom shows very often, you'll probably find yourself modifying existing shows. Luckily, this is easy to do. Select the show you want to revise in the Custom Shows dialog box, and then choose Edit. To remove a slide, select it on the Slides in custom show list, and then click Remove. To change slide order, select a slide on the Slides in custom show list, and then click the Move Up and Move Down arrows. When you finish modifying the custom show, close the Define Custom Show and Custom Shows dialog boxes.

Lesson 2: Running a Custom Slide Show

After you define which slides you want in a custom show, you can run the show. You can run a custom slide show in two ways. First, you can click the Show button in the Custom Shows dialog box to get a preview of the show. Second, you can click the Slide Show button, and then use the Slide Show shortcut menu to select a custom show. Try running a custom show now.

To Run a Custom Slide Show

1 **Make sure that Small Companies is selected on the Custom shows list, and then click the Show button.**

 If You Have Problems...
If you accidentally close the Custom Shows dialog box, choose Slide Show, Custom Shows to reopen it.

The custom slide show begins, and the first slide displays full screen. You can advance through a custom slide show by clicking the left mouse button.

2 **Click the left mouse button twice to advance completely through the custom show. Click once more, if necessary, to clear the black screen.**
When all the slides are shown, the presentation displays in Normal view. Now, try using the second method of running a custom slide show—while you run your presentation as a slide show.

3 **Make sure that Slide 1 displays, and then click the Slide Show button.**
The slide show begins. You can view the entire slide show in sequence, or branch to a custom show whenever you want. First, advance to the slide location from which you want to branch.

4 **Click the left mouse button seven times.**
The slide titled Availability should display on your screen. Now, try branching to the Small Companies custom show from this slide.

5 **Right-click the mouse on the slide show, and then choose Go, Custom Show.**
The presentation's custom shows display on the Custom Show submenu (see Figure 13.5). When you select a custom show, the slide show branches to display the custom show's slides.

continues ▶

To Run a Custom Slide Show (continued)

Figure 13.5
You can use the short-cut menu to branch to a custom show.

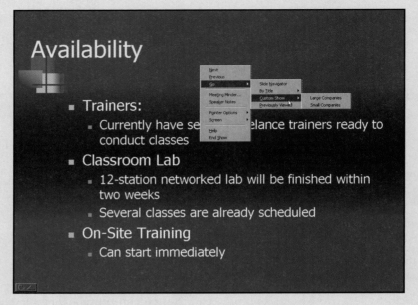

6 **Choose Small Companies from the submenu.**
The first slide for the Small Companies custom show displays.

7 **Click the left mouse button as many times as is necessary to completely advance through the slide show.**
PowerPoint advances through the remaining slides and then redisplays the presentation in Normal view. (In the next lessons, you learn how to set up a custom show so that you can display the remainder of the slide show instead.)

8 **Save the Promotional Information presentation.**
Keep the presentation open for the next lesson, in which you add hyperlinks.

 Exam Note: **Inserting One Presentation Within Another**
PowerPoint includes another way to dovetail presentations: inserting one presentation within another. Inserting a presentation within the main presentation enables you to quickly branch to supporting information.

To insert one presentation within another, display the main presentation, and then choose Insert, Object. In the Insert Object dialog box, click the Create from file option button, and then choose Browse. In the Browse dialog box, double-click the file you want to insert in the main presentation. (You can also check the Display as icon box.) Close the Insert Object dialog box.

Here's how to use the inserted presentation after you set it up. Run your main presentation as a slide show, and then click the object that represents the inserted presentation. When you finish using the inserted presentation, press Esc to redisplay the main presentation.

Lesson 3: Creating Hyperlinks

One great way to make your presentations interactive is to add hyperlinks to them. Hyperlinks are text, graphics, or other objects to which you assign a mouse action. For example, you can jump to slides, presentations, files, or even a Web site when you click a hyperlink. You can also make a sound (such as a recorded message) play when you move the mouse over a hyperlink. Hyperlinks are effective because you can add them to the presentations that you use at trade shows, on your company's intranet, or even on a Web home page. Hyperlinks become active when you run a slide show—not when you create them in Normal view.

One way to create a hyperlink is to use the Action Settings command on the Slide Show menu to display the Action Settings dialog box. Using this dialog box, you can attach different actions to the same object, depending on whether you click the object or just move the mouse pointer over it. You might assign a sound to play when you move the mouse over an object, for example, but require that users click the object to jump to another file or Web site.

Because hyperlinks give you the means to create a truly interactive slide show, try adding some to your presentation now.

 Inside Stuff: Saving Presentations

Before you add hyperlinks, it's a good idea to save a presentation. Because you just saved the Promotional Information presentation at the end of the preceding exercise, however, you don't need to save it again before creating a hyperlink.

To Create Hyperlinks

❶ In the Promotional Information presentation, display Slide 6, Companies Served, in Normal view.
You must display your presentation in Normal (or Slide) view to create a hyperlink. These views are the easiest to use because you can select the text (or object) before you convert it to a hyperlink.

❷ Select the text associated with the first bulleted point, Large Companies, and then choose Slide Show, Action Settings.
The Action Settings dialog box displays (see Figure 13.6). You use this dialog box to specify the object or file to which you want to create a link.

Click this tab to set mouse over actions ——
Click here to set a hyperlink ——
Click here to display link locations ——

Click here to choose a sound ——

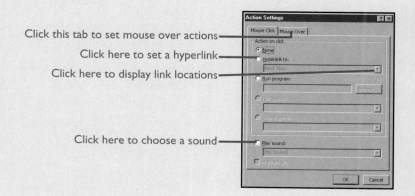

Figure 13.6
You set hyperlinks in this dialog box.

continues ▶

To Create Hyperlinks (continued)

③ Click the Hyperlink to option button, and then click its drop-down list arrow.

A list of possible hyperlink sites displays (see Figure 13.7). Notice that you can use the hyperlink to jump to other slides within the current presentation, other files, custom shows, or even URL sites (on the Web).

Figure 13.7
You can link to a variety of locations.

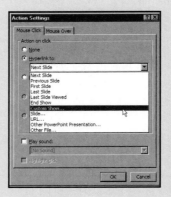

④ Click Custom Show.

The Link to Custom Show dialog box displays (see Figure 13.8). Notice that the custom shows you developed in the preceding lesson display on the Custom shows list.

Figure 13.8
You can link to custom shows that you previously created.

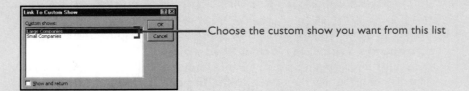

Choose the custom show you want from this list

⑤ Make sure that Large Companies is selected in the Link to Custom Show dialog box, and then click OK in both the Link to Custom Show and Action Settings dialog boxes.

A hyperlink is created for the text, Large Companies, on Slide 6. Notice that PowerPoint displays the hyperlink in a color that coordinates with the presentation's color scheme. (You can click outside the selected text to see the hyperlink's true color if you want.) Remember, however, that the link is only active in Slide Show view—not in Normal view.

Now, try setting a hyperlink to another presentation. Before you proceed with the next step, make sure that your instructor has copied PP-1302—the file to which you are creating a link—to the same folder as your other student files.

⑥ Display Slide 4, Features & Benefits, in Normal view, and then select the first two words associated with the first bulleted point (Cost Effective).

This is the text to which you want to add a hyperlink.

7 **Choose Slide Show, Action Settings.**
The Action Settings dialog box displays.

8 **Click the Hyperlink to option button, and then select Other File from the Hyperlink to drop-down list.**
The Hyperlink to Other File dialog box displays (see Figure 13.9). You can select a file from this dialog box to link to your presentation. You can also browse your hard disk or network drives (or even the Web) to locate the file you want.

 If You Have Problems...
It's likely that your instructor has copied your files to a different location than the one shown in Figure 13.9. If necessary, use the Look in drop-down list arrow to help locate PP-1302.

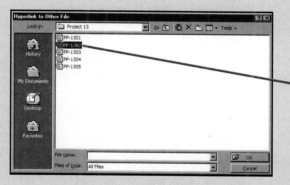

Figure 13.9
You can link to other files or presentations.

Link to this file

9 **Double-click PP-1302 to select it, and then click OK in the Action Settings dialog box.**
A hyperlink is added to the Cost Effective text.

10 **Save the Promotional Information presentation.**
Keep the presentation and PowerPoint open for the next lesson, in which you use the hyperlinks to run your slide show.

 Exam Note: Creating Links to the Web
You can also use the Insert Hyperlink dialog box to quickly create links to slides in your presentation, other files, or the World Wide Web. To do this, select the text to which you want to add the hyperlink, and then click the Insert Hyperlink button on the Standard toolbar. Click the type of link (such as Existing File or Web Page) that you want on the bar, and then choose the link location on the list. When you finish, click OK.

Lesson 4: Using Hyperlinks

Now that you set hyperlinks in your presentation, try using them while running a slide show. You do this by clicking the hyperlink in Slide Show view.

To Use Hyperlinks

1 **In your open presentation, make sure that Slide 4 still displays, and then click the Slide Show button.**
The slide show begins, starting with the current slide. Notice that the words to which you added a hyperlink (Cost Effective) display in a different color. Now, try using the hyperlink.

2 **Move the mouse pointer over the text Cost Effective.**
A pointing hand icon (and a ScreenTip that shows the link location) displays (see Figure 13.10). Whenever you see a pointing hand icon, it's a sure sign that you can click the object to jump to the linked location.

Figure 13.10
You can identify hyperlinks by the special hand pointer.

Pointing hand icon
ScreenTip indicates link location

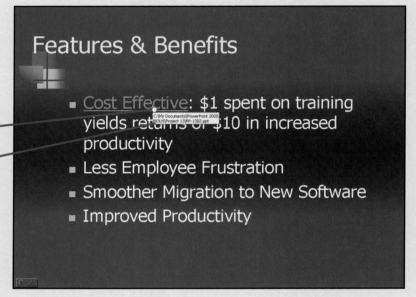

3 **Click the hyperlink.**
Because this hyperlink is linked to another presentation file, the linked presentation displays (see Figure 13.11). In this case, the linked file contains supporting information for data in the main presentation. When you've finished viewing the linked file, you can return to your original presentation by pressing Esc.

4 **Press Esc to close PP-1302 (the slide with the graph) and return to the Promotional Information presentation.**
Now, try using the hyperlink on Slide 6 to jump to a custom slide show. By using hyperlinks to jump to a custom slide show, you create a smoother transition than when you use the slide show's shortcut menu.

5 **Press ↵Enter twice to display Slide 6, Companies Served, and then click the hyperlinked text (Large Companies).**
The presentation jumps to the Large Companies custom slide show.

6 **Press Esc to end the slide show, and then save the presentation.**
Keep the presentation open for the next lesson, in which you create action buttons with hyperlinked text.

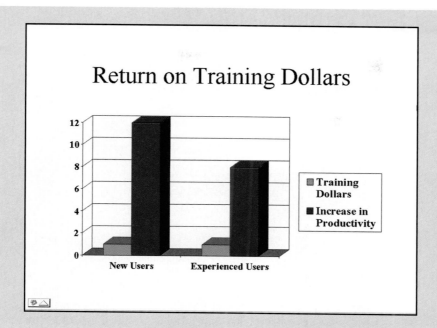

Figure 13.11
You can jump to
another presentation
to display supporting
data.

Lesson 5: Creating Action Buttons

In the preceding lesson, you learned how to hyperlink text to custom slide shows and an-other file. You can also create action buttons and then link them to files, locations, or Web sites. Action buttons work in much the same way as text hyperlinks, but because they are graphical, many people consider them to be easier to use.

You can add an action button from the AutoShapes menu on the Drawing toolbar, or by choosing Slide Show, Action Buttons from the menu. In either case, you can add text to your action buttons, and then use them to jump to other locations.

You can choose from a variety of action buttons. Furthermore, when you draw an action button, the Action Settings dialog box automatically displays so that you can view (and change) the default settings. Most of the buttons contain default settings and are already linked to a particular action. For example, the second button in the second row contains a hyperlink to the next slide. You can use the preset action buttons or choose the Custom button to designate your own hyperlink settings.

Try adding some action buttons to the Promotional Information presentation now.

To Create Action Buttons

❶ In the open Promotional Information presentation, display Slide 1 in Slide view, and then choose Slide Show, Action Buttons.
The Action Buttons submenu displays (see Figure 13.12). As usual, you can rest your mouse pointer over any button to display a ScreenTip that identifies the button.

continues ▶

To Create Action Buttons (continued)

Figure 13.12
Use ScreenTips to identify the type of action button you want.

2 **Click the Action Button: Forward or Next (the second button from the left on the second row) from the submenu.**

The mouse pointer changes to a crosshair so that you can accurately place the button. You can drag to draw the size of button that you want, but you can also just click the location for the button—PowerPoint automatically creates a button using the default size. When you click the mouse, PowerPoint not only creates the button, but also displays the Action Settings dialog box—complete with the appropriate settings for the type of button. Try creating the button now.

3 **Move the mouse pointer to the lower-right corner of the slide, and then click once.**

PowerPoint automatically creates an action button and displays the Action Settings dialog box. Notice that this dialog box already contains hyperlink settings to the next slide (see Figure 13.13).

Figure 13.13
When you create an action button, the hyperlink location is already set.

Preset hyperlink location

Action button

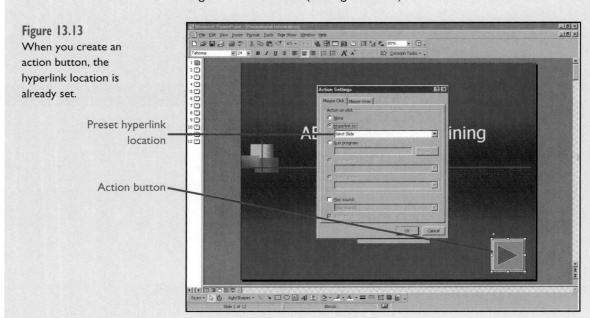

 If You Have Problems...

Make sure that you don't accidentally move and drag the mouse when you create your action button, or you will create a small, hard-to-see button.

Also, don't worry if the button isn't drawn exactly where you want it. You can always move and resize an action button, just as you can any other object.

Even though PowerPoint automatically assigns a hyperlink location, you can change it (or other settings) if you want. For now, however, you can accept the predetermined settings that PowerPoint assigned to the button.

4 **Click OK in the Action Settings dialog box.**
The Action Settings dialog box closes, and the button you added displays on your slide. Notice that the button has square selection handles, so you can move (or resize) the button—just like any other object.

5 **Move the button so that it appears approximately 1/4 inch from the edge of the lower-right corner of the slide.**
Now try adding a custom action button, for which you specify the link location.

6 **Display Slide 6, Companies Served, in Slide view and then choose Slide Show, Action Buttons.**

7 **Click Action Button: Custom (the first button on the top row), drag to draw a button 6 inches wide by 2 inches deep in the bottom-center of the slide, and release the mouse button.**
The action button is created and the Action Settings dialog box displays. Because the button is a Custom button, you must specify the link location rather than relying on PowerPoint's default settings.

8 **Click the Hyperlink to option button, click the drop-down arrow, and choose Custom Show.**
The Link to Custom Show dialog box displays (Figure 13.14). You can indicate which custom show you want to view in this dialog box. Additionally, you can check the box for Show and return so that the current slide (Slide 6) redisplays when the custom show is finished.

Check this box to redisplay the original presentation after the custom slide show is finished

Figure 13.14
Choose a custom show in this dialog box.

9 **Select Small Companies in the Link to Custom Show dialog box, check the Show and return box, and then choose OK.**

10 **Choose OK in the Actions Settings dialog box.**
The button you created displays on your slide. You can add text to the button so users understand what action it performs.

11 **Make sure that the action button is selected, and then type** `Click here for information on Small Businesses.` **Click outside the button.**
Text is added to the button (see Figure 13.15). After you add text, you can change the way the text looks by selecting and formatting it in a variety of ways. For now, however, you'll leave the text as it was when you entered it.

continues ▶

To Create Action Buttons (continued)

Figure 13.15
You can customize action buttons by adding text.

Action button

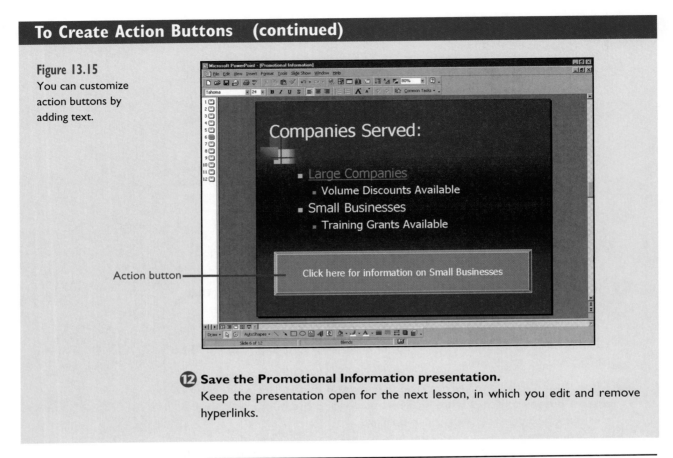

12 **Save the Promotional Information presentation.**
Keep the presentation open for the next lesson, in which you edit and remove hyperlinks.

 ***Inside Stuff:* Formatting Action Buttons**
Action buttons are technically AutoShapes. Because of this, you can change their colors, lines, and otherwise format them. To format them, double-click an action button in Slide view or Normal view to display the Format AutoShape dialog box. Choose the formatting settings that you want, and then click OK.

Lesson 6: Editing and Removing a Hyperlink

After you create hyperlinks, you might find that you need to edit the link location or make other changes. Luckily, you can modify any hyperlink you want. For example, you can add sound, a mouse over action, or change the object to which it is linked. A ***mouse over action*** is just a command that PowerPoint executes whenever you move your mouse pointer over a hyperlink.

To change a hyperlink's settings, you select it, and then choose Slide Show, Action Settings to display the Action Settings dialog box. You can then make the modifications you want by using commands and options with which you are now familiar.

You can also remove a hyperlink. To do this, select the hyperlinked text or object, and then choose the None option button in the Action Settings dialog box.

Try editing and removing a hyperlink now.

To Edit and Remove a Hyperlink

1 **Make sure that Slide I displays in the Promotional Information presentation, and then click the action button object.**
Because this object has a hyperlink associated with it, selecting the object selects the hyperlink as well.

2 **Choose Slide Show, Action Settings.**
The Action Settings dialog box displays and shows the settings for the selected hyperlink. You can revise the hyperlink (which is an action button in this case) by changing the settings.

3 **Click the Mouse Over tab.**
The Mouse Over page displays (see Figure 13.16). You can set options on this page so that an action occurs whenever the mouse pointer moves over the hyperlink. For example, you can change the settings so that a sound plays as soon as you move your mouse over the hyperlink.

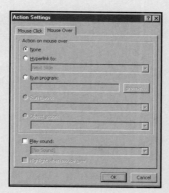

Figure 13.16
You can set actions to occur when the mouse pointer moves over a hyperlink.

4 **On the Mouse Over page, check the Play sound box.**
The Play sound command becomes active.

5 **Click the Play sound drop-down list arrow, and then choose Applause and click OK. (If this sound file isn't available on your system, choose another.)**
The action settings are modified. When you run a slide show, applause will sound whenever you move the mouse pointer over the hyperlink.

Now, try deleting a hyperlink that you added earlier in this project. First, select the text with which the hyperlink is associated.

6 **On Slide 6, select the Large Companies hyperlink text, and then choose Slide Show, Action Settings.**
The Action Settings dialog box displays with the settings for the selected hyperlink.

7 **On the Mouse Click page, choose the None option button before clicking OK.**
This removes the hyperlink from the text.

8 **Save the Promotional Information presentation.**
Keep the presentation open for the next lesson, in which you run the slide show and use the hyperlinks.

Inside Stuff: **Recording Custom Messages**

If you have the proper equipment, you can record and save a message as a sound file, and then associate it with a hyperlink. To do this, open the Action Settings dialog box for the hyperlink. Check the Play sound box, and then click the drop-down list arrow. Choose Other Sound from the list to display the Add Sound dialog box. Locate and then double-click the sound file you want to associate with your hyperlink. Play the sound in your presentation by clicking the associated hyperlink.

Lesson 7: Using Hyperlinks in a Slide Show

After you add hyperlinks to text and objects, you can use them in a slide show. When you run the slide show, you have the option of clicking the hyperlinks or not. For example, you may create a hyperlink to a file or Web site that supports your position. Depending on the audience, however, you can decide whether to use it.

Try using the hyperlinks that you created in your presentation now.

To Use Hyperlinks in a Slide Show

1 **In the open Promotional Information presentation, display Slide 1, and then click the Slide Show button.**

The slide show displays, starting on Slide 1. Notice that this slide contains an action button. You previously added both Mouse Click and Mouse Over actions to this button.

2 **Move the mouse pointer over the object.**

Assuming that you have the computer's speakers turned on, the applause sound clip plays. Now, try clicking the button to perform the associated action.

3 **Click the action button.**

The slide show advances to the next slide according to the settings you specified earlier in this project.

4 **Press ⏎Enter twice to advance to the Features and Benefits slide, and then click the Cost Effective hyperlink.**

This type of hyperlink, which links to another file, is handy when you need to quickly access supporting information during a talk.

5 **Right-click, and then choose Go, Previously Viewed from the shortcut menu that displays.**

The Features and Benefits slide redisplays.

6 **Press ⏎Enter twice.**

The Companies Served slide displays. You added an action button to this slide with a hyperlink to a custom show. Clicking on the button launches the slides in the custom show.

7 **Click the action button.**

The Small Companies custom show begins.

8 **Press ⏎Enter twice to advance through the custom show.**

The Companies Served slide reappears after you view the custom show because you used the Show and return option.

9 Press Esc twice to end the slide show.

10 Save the Promotional Information presentation, and then close it.
Keep PowerPoint open if you plan to complete the end-of-chapter exercises.

Summary

In this project, you learned critical skills that you can use to make your presentations interactive. You learned how to add hyperlinks to text and buttons so that you can make the presentations more user friendly, especially if you plan to use them on the Web or an intranet. You also learned how to create custom slide shows to quickly individualize presentations for any audience.

To expand on your knowledge, spend a few minutes exploring Help on these topics. Additionally, complete some of the Skill Drill, Challenge, and Discovery Zone exercises.

Checking Concepts and Terms ✓

True/False

For each of the following, check *T* or *F* to indicate whether the statement is true or false.

__T __F **1.** You can create hyperlinks only by using action buttons—you can't use text as a hyperlink. [L2–5]

__T __F **2.** You can create a hyperlink to a Web site. [L3]

__T __F **3.** A custom slide show must contain hyperlinked objects. [L1–2]

__T __F **4.** You cannot modify hyperlinks after you create them. [L4]

__T __F **5.** When you rest the mouse pointer over a hyperlink, a pointing hand icon appears. [L4–5]

Multiple Choice

Circle the letter of the correct answer for each of the following questions.

1. You can create a hyperlink to which of the following? [L2]

a. a custom show

b. another slide in the same presentation

c. another file

d. all of the above

2. Which of the following is true regarding a custom slide show? [L1]

a. You must create a hyperlink in order to launch it.

b. It cannot be revised.

c. You can display it by choosing <u>G</u>o, <u>C</u>ustom Show from the shortcut menu.

d. none of the above

3. Which of the following can you use to make your presentation interactive? [L1–5]

a. action buttons

b. hyperlinks

c. custom shows

d. all of the above

4. Which of the following is a good use of an interactive slide show? [L1]

a. an onscreen presentation at a trade show

b. printing a presentation to hand out to your audience

c. printing a presentation as overhead transparencies

d. all of the above

5. What is the name for the worldwide association of hundreds of computer networks used to distribute information? [L1]

 a. home page

 b. intranet

 c. World Wide Web

 d. hyperlink

Skill Drill

Skill Drill exercises reinforce project skills. Each skill reinforced is the same, or nearly the same, as a skill presented in the project. Detailed instructions are provided in a step-by-step format.

1. Creating and Using Hyperlinks

You are developing a presentation for your sales force that you plan to distribute over your company's intranet. To help your sales team quickly find the information they need, you develop a presentation that includes hyperlinks to your product line. You also test your hyperlinks by using them in a slide show. [L2, 5]

1. Open **PP-1303** and save it as **Product Information**. Display the presentation in Slide view.

2. Select the text (Workstations) in the Workstations object, and then choose Slide Show, Action Settings.

3. Click the Hyperlink to option button, and then click its drop-down list arrow and choose Slide.

4. In the Hyperlink To Slide dialog box, choose Slide 4, Workstations.

5. Click OK in both the Hyperlink To Slide and Action Settings dialog boxes.

6. Repeat Steps 2–5 for the Keyboards, Monitors, and Chairs objects. Create a hyperlink for each to the appropriate slide in the presentation.

7. Display the first slide of the Product Information presentation in Slide view.

8. Click the Slide Show button to start the slide show. Click the Workstations hyperlink to display the linked slide.

9. Right-click the mouse to display the Slide Show shortcut menu. Choose Go, Previously Viewed to quickly display the first presentation slide.

10. Repeat Steps 2–3 for each of the hyperlinks in your presentation (Monitors, Chairs, Keyboards).

11. Save your Product Information presentation and keep it open for the next exercise.

2. Creating Action Buttons

You want your sales team to be able to return to the first slide in your presentation (the home page) after they have jumped to another slide—without using the Slide Show shortcut menu. To enable them to do this, you create an action button on each of Slides 2–5. [L3]

1. In the open Product Information presentation, display Slide 2, Monitors, in Slide view.

2. Choose Slide Show, Action Buttons to display the submenu.

3. Choose the Action Button: Home (the second button on the first row), and then click in the lower-right corner of the slide.

4. Look over the settings in the Action Settings dialog box, and then click OK to accept them.

5. Repeat Steps 2–4 for each of Slides 3–5.

6. Save the presentation and keep it open for the next exercise.

3. Creating a Hyperlink to Another File

To help your sales team to quickly access ordering information, you create a link from the Product Information presentation to another file. And before you place your presentation on your company's intranet, you decide to test it out by running it as a slide show. [L2, 5]

1. In the open Product Information presentation, display Slide 1 in Slide view.

2. In the middle button select the text, **Ordering Information**.

3. Choose Sli_d_e Show, _A_ction Settings.

4. Choose the _H_yperlink to option button. Click the _H_yperlink to drop-down list arrow, and then choose Other File.

5. In the Hyperlink to Other File dialog box, choose **PP-1304** and click OK.

6. Click OK in the Action Settings dialog box.

7. Now test the links in your presentation. Display Slide 1 in the open Product Information presentation, and then click the Slide Show button.

8. Click the Ordering Information hyperlink to jump to the linked file. Press Esc to return to your Product Information presentation.

9. Click the Monitors hyperlink to jump to the Monitors slide. Click the action button to return to Slide 1.

10. Click each of the other hyperlinks on Slide 1. Use each slide's action button to return to the first slide.

11. Press Esc to end the slide show.

12. Save the Product Information presentation, and then close it. Leave PowerPoint running if you plan to complete the Challenge or Discovery Zone exercises.

Challenge

Challenge exercises expand on or are somewhat related to skills presented in the lessons. Each exercise provides a brief narrative introduction followed by instructions in a numbered-step format that are not as detailed as those in the Skill Drill section.

1. Creating Custom Shows

You work for a large travel agency and use PowerPoint to create presentations about available vacation packages. You promote trips to two distinct groups: those interested in luxury accommodations and budget travelers. To keep from creating two presentations, you create custom shows that branch from one main presentation. [L1]

1. Open **PP-1305** and save it as **Vacations**.

2. Create two new custom slide shows, as follows:

   - Create a custom show called Deluxe Tours. Include Slides 5–7 in this custom show.

   - Create a custom show called Bargain Tours. Include Slides 8–12 in this custom show.

3. Display each custom show from the Custom Shows dialog box. Also view the shows by using the Slide Show shortcut menu.

4. Save the Vacations presentation and keep it open. Leave PowerPoint running if you plan to complete additional exercises.

2. Creating Action Buttons

You plan to use your presentation at trade shows, and want to make it easy for prospective clients to use the presentation. To make the presentation more user friendly, you decide to add some action buttons. [L1, 3]

1. Display Slide 4, Travel the World, of your Vacations presentation in Normal or Slide view. Add two custom action buttons to the bottom of the slide.

2. Enter **Deluxe Tour Information** as the text for the first action button. Create a link to the Deluxe Tour custom slide show. Make sure that you indicate that you want to **show and return**.

3. Enter **Bargain Tours** as the text for the second action button. Create a link to the Bargain Tour custom slide show. Make sure that you indicate that you want to **show and return**.

4. Run your presentation as a slide show. Test all the hyperlinks and make any necessary adjustments.

5. Save the Vacations presentation and keep it open. Leave PowerPoint running if you plan to complete additional exercises.

3. Creating a Hyperlink to the Web

You decide to add some hyperlinks in your presentation to travel information on the World Wide Web. [L2]

1. In the open Vacations presentation, display Slide 13, More Tours, in Normal view.

2. Enter **Click here to see more tours** as text for the Arrow AutoShape. Select the text.

3. Use the Insert Hyperlink dialog box to link to a Web page. The Web page should include a wide variety of tours (**http://vacations.yahoo.com** or **http://travel.yahoo.com** are good places to start.)

4. Test all the links in your presentation. Make any revisions necessary so that working with the presentation is seamless.

5. Save the Vacations presentation, and then close it. Leave PowerPoint running if you plan to complete the additional exercises.

Discovery Zone

Discovery Zone exercises require advanced knowledge of topics presented in *MOUS Essentials* lessons, application of skills from multiple lessons, or self-directed learning of new skills.

I. Learning About the Insert Hyperlink Dialog Box

You want to link presentations to a wide variety of locations, including other files and the World Wide Web. You heard that the Insert Hyperlink dialog box provides ready access to a variety of link locations. You decide to use the What's This? button to find out more about the Insert Hyperlink dialog box.

Create a new blank presentation. Enter your name in the title placeholder of the first slide. Select the text, and then click the Insert Hyperlink button on the Standard toolbar.

Click the What's This? button in the upper-right corner of the dialog box, and then click in the Link to area. Read the information displayed in the ScreenTip, and then click to clear the ScreenTip.

Click the What's This? button, and then click the ScreenTip button in the Insert Hyperlink dialog box. Clear the tip when you finish reading it.

Click the Existing File or Web Page icon in the Link to section. Use the What's This? button to research each of the elements and text boxes that are displayed in the middle of the dialog box.

Click the Pl<u>a</u>ce in This Document icon in the Link to section. Use the What's This? button to display a ScreenTip for each element displayed in the dialog box.

Click the Create <u>N</u>ew Document icon in the Link to section. Notice the options associated with this selection. Use the What's This? button to find out more about the options.

Click the E-<u>m</u>ail Address icon in the Link to section. Notice the text boxes that are associated with this icon. Use the What's This? button to find out more about the options. Close the Insert Hyperlink dialog box.

Leave PowerPoint running if you plan to complete the last Discovery Zone exercise. [L2]

2. Creating Hyperlinks in a Presentation

Pick a topic that interests you, and then use the World Wide Web (and your library) to research information about the topic. Be sure to write down the addresses of the most interesting Web sites related to your topic.

Organize the information you find, and then develop a presentation based on the data. Include at least two custom slide shows as part of the presentation. Also develop several hyperlinks that connect to the custom slide shows, slides within the presentation, other files, and Web sites. Be sure to include action buttons that you can click to redisplay the original presentation.

Let at least one other user test your presentation's hyperlinks. Save the presentation, and then close it and exit PowerPoint. [L1–5]

PinPoint Assessment

You have completed this project and its associated lessons, and have had an opportunity to assess your skills through the end-of-project questions and exercises. Now use the PinPoint software Evaluation Mode to further assess your comprehension of the specific exam activities you have just learned. You can also use the PinPoint Trainer Mode and the Show Me tutorials to practice these exam activities.

Using PowerPoint's Web and Collaboration Features

Key terms introduced in this project include

- broadcast
- collaborate
- home page
- Hypertext Markup Language (HTML)

- install on first use feature
- Internet
- NetMeeting
- Pack and Go Wizard
- PowerPoint Viewer

- real-time
- upload
- Web browser
- Web Page Preview
- World Wide Web (WWW)

Objectives	Required Activity for MOUS	Exam Level
➤ Packing Up Your Presentation	Save presentation for use on another computer (Pack and Go)	Expert
➤ Formatting Your Presentation for the Web	Format presentations for the Web	Expert
➤ Using Web Page Preview	View a presentation on the Web	Expert
➤ Saving a Presentation as a Web Page	Publish a presentation to the Web	Core
	Save HTML to a specific target browser	Expert
➤ Sending a Presentation via Email	Send a presentation via email	Core
➤ Scheduling an Online Meeting	Subscribe to a presentation	Expert
	Use NetMeeting to schedule a broadcast	Expert
	Use NetShow to deliver a broadcast	Expert
	Electronically incorporate meeting feedback	Expert

Why Would I Do This?

One of the slickest things about PowerPoint 2000 is its tight, seamless integration with the Internet, especially the Internet's graphical, user-friendly side—the World Wide Web (WWW). PowerPoint has built-in Web support, for example, so that anyone who uses the Web can view your presentations. As a result, saving and publishing your presentation as a Web page enables you to share it with an extremely large audience—virtually everyone connected to the Internet. All they need to view your presentation is a Web browser, software you use to view Web pages. Popular examples of this type of software include Internet Explorer and Netscape.

You can also publish presentations to your company's intranet. This makes it easy to distribute sales or production information using an interactive presentation that others in your company can view—no matter where they're located.

Additionally, PowerPoint 2000 includes many features that help you to work interactively with others and to **collaborate**, or work together, on projects. Many of these features depend on being connected electronically through your company's intranet or the World Wide Web.

PowerPoint also includes other ways to communicate with others. For example, you can attach comments to a presentation—PowerPoint's version of the yellow sticky notes! Another way to share your presentation is to send it as an email attachment. This is especially useful when you want to quickly distribute the presentation to selected people for feedback or to share information.

You can also pack up, or compress, your presentation to a floppy or portable Zip disk, so that you can use it on any computer, even if the computer doesn't have PowerPoint installed on it. Finally, you can share presentations during a meeting, even if the participants are in different locations. How? By using the online collaboration features to set up an electronic meeting.

As you work through this project, you'll experience some of the powerful Web-based and collaborative features available in PowerPoint. You learn how to use PowerPoint's built-in Web and collaboration features to publish to the Web and to work effectively with others. So come along and learn the ropes for working in a Web-based and collaborative environment—using PowerPoint as a tool.

Inside Stuff: The Internet and World Wide Web

You almost can't go through a day without hearing about the **Internet**. Originally designed as a way for government and university facilities to share information, the Internet has grown to become a loose association of thousands of networks worldwide. The Internet is an electronic city of sorts—by using it, you can access libraries; scientific, medical, or business information; and so on.

The **World Wide Web** (abbreviated **WWW**, or just known as the Web) is the graphical, user-friendly way to explore the Internet. Using the Web is easy for most people because Web pages are chock-full of hyperlinks that you can click to quickly jump to related information.

You can't put a document with just any kind of file format on the Web, however. Documents used on the Web need to be saved by using **Hypertext Markup Language (HTML)** file format. HTML controls the display of graphics, formatting, and hyperlinks that are the hallmarks of the World Wide Web.

Others can view the HTML documents if they have a **Web browser**—software that helps you locate and view Web pages by clicking hyperlinks to move from one Web page to another. Because so many people can access the Web, businesses (and individuals) can greatly increase their marketing leverage by publishing to it.

Lesson 1: Packing Up Your Presentation

You can use the **Pack and Go Wizard** to package all presentation files (including linked files and fonts) on a disk, so that you can run the presentation on another computer. Additionally, you have the option of packing the **PowerPoint Viewer**, which is a program used to run slide shows on computers that don't have PowerPoint installed on them. A wizard is an interactive help utility that guides you through each step of a multi-step operation. Wizards help automate processes that would otherwise be tricky or complicated to accomplish.

For this lesson, imagine that you work for a sports equipment company, and you hope to open a store in a town several hours from your home office. To promote your company in the new location, you're scheduled to give an overview of your company's products and goals to the Chamber of Commerce. Because the Pack and Go Wizard makes it easy to take your presentation "on the road," you decide to use it to package your presentation on a floppy disk.

To Pack Up Your Presentation

1 **Open PP-**1401 **and save it as** New Store.

2 **Choose File, Pack and Go.**
The first page of the Pack and Go Wizard displays (see Figure 14.1). You can make choices on each page of the wizard, and then click Next to proceed to the following page.

Track your progress here——

Click here to exit the wizard——

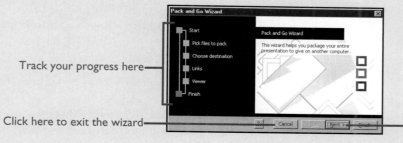

Figure 14.1
The Pack and Go Wizard helps you pack up your presentation.

Click here to display the next page

X *If You Have Problems...*
The Pack and Go Wizard is an *install on first use feature*. This means that you're prompted (through use of a message box) to install the feature the first time you try to use it. If necessary, make sure the Office 2000 CD is inserted in the CD-ROM drive, and then choose Yes in the message box. When the feature is installed, continue with the lesson.

---

3 **Click the Next button.**
The second page of the wizard displays. This page gives you the choice of packaging the open presentation or another one.

4 **Make sure that the Active presentation box is checked, and then click Next.**
The third page of the wizard displays (Choose destination), so you can specify where you want to store the packed presentation. In most cases you'll accept the default option—placing the presentation on floppy disks. You can also place the presentation on your hard drive, a Zip disk, or on another computer to which you are networked.

continues ▶

To Pack Up Your Presentation (continued)

5 **Make sure the A:\ drive option button is selected, and then click Next.**
The Links page of the wizard displays (see Figure 14.2). You can include any linked files so that they're available on the destination computer. You can also choose to embed the fonts, which ensures that the text displays properly on the destination computer (even if the font isn't installed on it). Although linked files and embedded fonts take up more room on your disk, it gives you peace of mind to know that everything you need to give your presentation is included.

Figure 14.2
You can choose to include linked files.

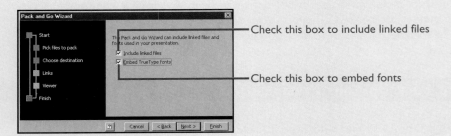

Check this box to include linked files

Check this box to embed fonts

6 **Check both boxes on the Links page, and then click Next.**
The Viewer page of the wizard displays. Including the PowerPoint Viewer takes up room on your disk, but it ensures that you can give your presentation from virtually any computer—whether or not it has PowerPoint installed. For this lesson, however, you use the default setting (Don't include the Viewer).

7 **Make sure that the Don't include the Viewer option button is selected, and then click Next.**
The final page of the Pack and Go Wizard displays.

8 **Make sure that you have a blank, formatted disk in the A: drive, and then click Finish.**
PowerPoint packages your presentation (including the linked files and embedded fonts) onto the floppy disk. How long should this process take? It depends on the size of your presentation (and the processing speed of your computer). Eventually, you see a PowerPoint message box, indicating that your presentation has been successfully packed (see Figure 14.3).

Figure 14.3
PowerPoint lets you know when Pack and Go is finished.

 If You Have Problems...
If there's not enough room on the floppy disk for a presentation, PowerPoint prompts you to insert another disk. Just pop the second disk into the your drive and press ⏎Enter).

9 **Click OK in the message box.**
Congratulations! You successfully packaged up your presentation for use at another time, place, or computer.

10 **Save the New Store presentation, and then close it.**
Leave PowerPoint running for the next lesson, in which you preview how a presentation will look as a Web page.

Exam Note: **Unpacking Your Presentation**

So you packed up your presentation… but how do you unpack it? On the computer you plan to use for your presentation, display the contents of the A: drive. Double-click the pngsetup.exe file icon. In the Pack and Go Setup dialog box, specify the drive and folder location where you want to unpack the files, and then click OK. When the presentation is successfully unpacked, a message box displays, asking whether you want to display the presentation as a slide show. Choose <u>Y</u>es, and your show is off and running.

Lesson 2: Formatting Your Presentation for the Web

You don't have to jump through hoops to create a presentation to use on the Web. You can instead rely on the AutoContent Wizard to help you create a Web-ready presentation, already formatted to publish to the Web. How? Just select Web Page as your output option on the appropriate AutoContent Wizard page, and you automatically add information that displays on each page of a Web presentation, such as a copyright notice, the last date updated, and your email address.

Because PowerPoint includes such strong Web support, try using the AutoContent Wizard to create a Web-ready presentation now.

 Exam Note: **Creating Web Pages**

When you are creating a presentation for the Web, keep a couple of things in mind. First, make sure you keep the text and graphics readable and interesting, but don't add so many graphics that your pages are sluggish to display. Many users will give up on your presentation rather than wait for poky pages to appear onscreen.

Also, keep in mind that some of PowerPoint's animation features (such as slide transitions, text builds, and so on) are not supported by some Web browsers. Unless you install the PowerPoint Animation Player (and can count on all viewers to do the same), your audience won't be able to see these enhancements.

Finally, make sure hyperlinks point to targets within your presentation (or on the network), or they won't work. Links to other presentation pages or Web sites generally work well, for example, but not those to your hard drive.

To Format a Presentation for the Web

❶ Choose <u>F</u>ile, <u>N</u>ew, and then double-click the AutoContent Wizard icon on the General page of the New dialog box.
The first AutoContent Wizard page displays.

❷ Click <u>N</u>ext.
The Presentation type page appears so that you can select a topic for your presentation.

❸ Click the <u>A</u>ll button.
All the presentation topics available through the AutoContent Wizard are listed (see Figure 14.4).

continues ▶

To Format a Presentation for the Web (continued)

Figure 14.4
You can create a variety of presentation types.

Click this button to display all presentation types

❹ **Choose Product/Services Overview as the presentation type, and then click <u>N</u>ext.**
The Presentation style page displays (see Figure 14.5). You use this screen to designate that you want to use the presentation on the Web.

Figure 14.5
PowerPoint makes creating a Web presentation a snap.

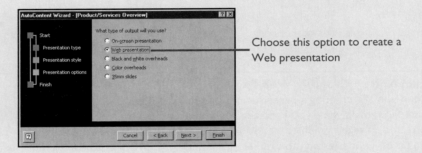

Choose this option to create a Web presentation

❺ **Choose the W<u>e</u>b presentation option button, and then click <u>N</u>ext.**
The Presentation options page displays.

❻ **Enter your email address in the F<u>o</u>oter text box and click <u>N</u>ext.**
PowerPoint displays the final AutoContent Wizard page.

❼ **Click <u>F</u>inish.**
The AutoContent Wizard creates your presentation. Now try adding an action button that links each page to the first presentation slide—your home page.

❽ **Display Slide 2 in Normal view, and then choose Sli<u>d</u>e Show, Act<u>i</u>on Buttons, Home.**
The crosshair pointer displays so that you can accurately place the button on your slide.

❾ **Click in the lower-right corner of the slide.**
An action button is created and the Action Settings dialog box displays. When you create this type of action button, PowerPoint automatically sets the <u>H</u>yperlink option to the first presentation slide.

❿ **Click OK in the Action Settings dialog box.**
The Action Settings dialog box clears. Now try copying this button to the other presentation slides.

⓫ **With the action button still selected, click Copy and then display Slide 3.**
The button (and its hyperlink settings) are copied to the Clipboard. From there you can copy it to multiple locations.

12 Click Paste.
The action button is copied to Slide 3.

13 Repeat Step 12 for Slides 4–7, and then save your presentation.
You should have action buttons at the lower-right corner of each slide.

14 Save your presentation as My New Company **and then close it.**
Leave PowerPoint running for the next lesson, in which you use Web Page Preview.

 Exam Note: **Web Options**
You can change the way PowerPoint creates and formats Web pages by using the Web Options dialog box. Choose <u>T</u>ools, <u>O</u>ptions, and then click the General tab. Click the <u>W</u>eb Options button to display the Web Options dialog box.

Lesson 3: Using Web Page Preview

You can publish presentations to your company's intranet or to the World Wide Web. Publishing a presentation refers to converting a copy of it to HTML format so that you can use it on the Web. Before you save the presentation using HTML, however, it's a good idea to see how it will actually look on the Web. To help you out, you can use PowerPoint 2000's **Web Page Preview**. This view helps you see how your presentation will display as a Web page by opening it in your Web browser. Try using this view now.

To Use Web Page Preview

1 Open PP-1402 **and save it as** Ergonomic Products.

2 Scroll through the presentation, one page at a time.
This presentation includes a number of hyperlinks to other locations. It's typical for Web-based documents to include hyperlinks to related information or Web sites. For example, Slides 2–6 include buttons that you can click to display the first slide. Regardless of whether you've already developed hyperlinks in your presentation, they are added when you use Web Page Preview in a frame at the left side of the window.

Now use Web Page Preview to see how your presentation will look on the Web.

3 Choose <u>F</u>ile, We<u>b</u> Page Preview.
The presentation displays in your browser, giving you a good idea of the way your presentation will look when you actually save it as a Web page (see Figure 14.6). Notice that the first page of your presentation is automatically used as the *home page*. (A home page, which is the opening page of a Web site, is usually devoted to the main topic for the site.) Additionally, a hyperlink for each slide appears on the left side of the window—making it easy to access a page by clicking its hyperlink.

continues ▶

To Use Web Page Preview   (continued)

Figure 14.6
Hyperlinks appear for each presentation slide.

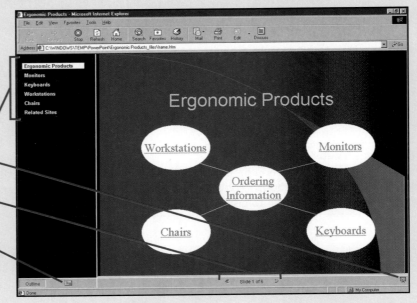

Hyperlinks for each presentation slide appear in this frame

Click here to view your presentation as a slide show

Click here to scroll through your slides

Click here to expand or collapse the outline in the frame

> ### ☒ If You Have Problems...
> Don't worry if your screen doesn't exactly match Figure 14.6, in which Internet Explorer is used as the browser. The way your screen appears depends on which Web browser you use.
>
> Additionally, you may need to maximize the browser window to better see the presentation.

Now try testing out the hyperlinks.

❹ Click the hyperlink on the left side of the browser window for Chairs.
The Chairs page of the presentation displays. Now try to redisplay the home page.

❺ Click the Home Page button in the lower-right corner of the Web page.
The first presentation slide (analogous to the home page) redisplays. Remember that you can use either the hyperlinks that you create within the presentation or the ones that automatically display in the browser window to move between locations.

When you're satisfied that a presentation will work well for Web use and it includes the hyperlinks you want, you can close the browser window.

❻ Click the Close button in the upper-right corner of the browser window.
The browser window closes and your presentation (in PowerPoint) redisplays.

❼ Save the Ergonomic Products presentation.
Keep the presentation and PowerPoint open for the next exercise, in which you save the presentation as a Web page.

Lesson 4: Saving a Presentation as a Web Page

Have you ever been in front of a large audience? How about an audience of several million people? By placing your PowerPoint presentations on the Web, you can do just that! However, publishing to the Web can seem daunting for many people. Luckily, PowerPoint 2000 makes it easy to convert an existing presentation to a series of HTML files that Web browsers can recognize.

In the preceding lesson, you saw what your presentation would look like on the Web. You also tested the presentation's hyperlinks to make sure that they would work as expected in the Web environment.

Now you're ready to publish your presentation to the Web by saving the presentation in HTML format—as a Web page.

To Save a Presentation as a Web Page

① **In the open Ergonomic Products presentation, choose File, Save as Web Page.**
The Save As dialog box displays, but with some differences from the "run-of-the-mill" Save As dialog box that you typically use to save presentations (see Figure 14.7). For example, HTML is automatically chosen for the file format.

Click here to change file storage location

Places Bar

Web Page (HTML) file format is automatically chosen

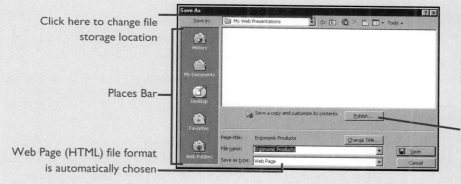

Figure 14.7
You can save a presentation in HTML format for use on the Web.

Click here to set publishing options

Now specify where you want to save the Web pages you're about to create. Because literally tens (or even hundreds) of HTML files can be created for any presentation, you should carefully select an appropriate location. If you're not sure where to place the HTML files, ask your instructor before proceeding with the next step.

② **Click the Save in drop-down list arrow and designate the location where you want to store your Web page files.**
Next, assign a name for the Web page file and folder you're about to create.

③ **In the File name box, enter Company.**
Now take a look at some of the additional settings that you can change when you save a presentation for Web use.

④ **In the Save As dialog box, click the Publish button.**
The Publish as Web Page dialog box displays (see Figure 14.8). This dialog box includes a variety of options related to saving your presentation in HTML format. You can publish the entire presentation, for example, or choose a selected range of slides.

continues ▶

To Save a Presentation as a Web Page   (continued)

Figure 14.8
Set up the way you want to publish your presentation in this dialog box.

Choose which slides to publish here

Choose the browser support here

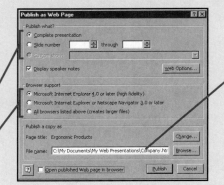

Designate where you want to save the presentation here

Now you're ready to create the HTML files.

⑤ In the Publish as Web Page dialog box, click Publish.
The presentation is saved as a group of HTML files. Because you're finished with the Ergonomic Products presentation, you can close it.

⑥ Close the Ergonomic Products presentation.
Now take a look at the HTML files that you created. A handy way to do this within PowerPoint is to use the Open dialog box.

⑦ Choose File, Open.
The Open dialog box displays (see Figure 14.9). (If necessary, select the location where your Web page files are stored in the Look in drop-down list.)

Notice that both a Company file and a Company_files folder are shown. Try displaying the properties associated with the Company file to confirm that PowerPoint saved it by using HTML file format.

Figure 14.9
Saving your presentation as a Web page automatically creates many supporting HTML files.

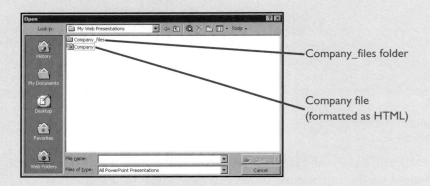

Company_files folder

Company file (formatted as HTML)

⑧ Right-click on the Company file, and then choose Properties from the shortcut menu.

⑨ If necessary, click the General tab.
The General page of the Properties dialog box is displayed (see Figure 14.10). Notice that this file uses the HTML format.

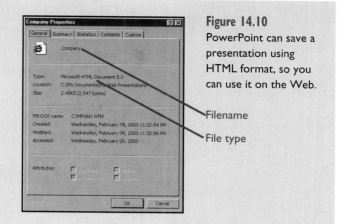

Figure 14.10
PowerPoint can save a presentation using HTML format, so you can use it on the Web.

Filename

File type

⑩ Click OK to close the Company Properties dialog box, and then double-click the Company_files folder.
A listing of files created for your Web pages displays. You can confirm that each of these files uses the HTML format by displaying the associated Properties dialog boxes.

⑪ Display the Properties dialog box for several of the files listed.
Each of the files shows HTML as the file type. After you *upload* (copy files) to your Web server, you're ready to appear—electronically speaking—before millions!

⑫ Close any Properties dialog boxes that may be open.

⑬ Close the Open dialog box.
Keep PowerPoint open for the next lesson, in which you learn now to send a presentation via email.

 Exam Note: **Using the Web Toolbar**
PowerPoint includes a wealth of built-in Web features, including a Web toolbar that you can use to browse presentations on your intranet or on the Internet—right from within PowerPoint. To display the Web toolbar, choose <u>V</u>iew, <u>T</u>oolbars, Web.

Lesson 5: Sending a Presentation via Email

Most likely, you know how to send email, which is using a network to send and receive messages. In a sense, email is just an electronic version of sending regular mail. In addition to sending messages, you can also send files (such as PowerPoint presentations) as attachments that a recipient can view.

PowerPoint 2000 takes this process a step further by providing a seamless way for you to attach a PowerPoint presentation to an email message. This makes it easy for you to share your presentations with others via email. Try sending your presentation as an attachment now.

 If You Have Problems...
Before you proceed with Lesson 5, make sure that your computer has an email program, such as Outlook, set up on it.

To Send a Presentation via Email

① **Open PP-1403 and save it as** Travel Bargains.

② **Choose File, Send To, Mail Recipient (as Attachment) on the menu bar.**
A new email message is created (see Figure 14.11). The presentation's title is automatically entered in the Subject text box, and the presentation appears as an icon within the message area.

Figure 14.11
It's easy to send an attached presentation via email.

Enter the recipient's email address here

The presentation's name is automatically entered as the subject

The attached presentation file appears here as an icon

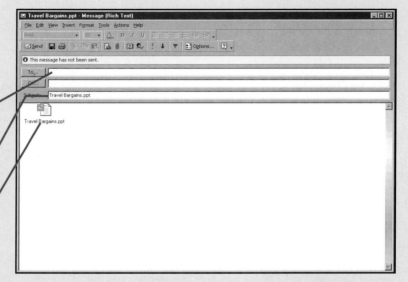

> **✗** **If You Have Problems...**
> Don't worry if your email message looks a little different from the one shown in Figure 14.9. The exact appearance of the message depends on which email messaging software you use and which options are set.

③ **Enter a person's email address in the To text box. (If you don't know an email address, enter your own or ask the instructor for help.)**
Now add a message so that the recipient knows why you're sending the presentation.

④ **Click in the message area (to the right of the presentation icon), and then press ↵Enter until the insertion point displays below the icon.**

⑤ **Type:** Hi! Here's the presentation I'm planning to use for the next Chamber of Commerce meeting. Please let me know what you think by Thursday.
The message is added. Now you're ready to send it.

⑥ **Click Send, and then complete whatever steps are necessary to connect to your email server.**
After the connection has been made, the message is sent and the message clears. (If you sent the email to yourself, you can open your Inbox and see the message. Open the presentation by double-clicking its icon on the Attach line.)

⑦ **If necessary, disconnect from your email server.**

8 **Save the Travel Bargains presentation.**
Keep the presentation and PowerPoint open for the next lesson, in which you learn how to set up an online meeting.

 Inside Stuff: **Using Comments**

Another way to use PowerPoint to communicate your ideas effectively with others is to create a presentation, and then attach comments to it. Comments are a handy way to write notes to yourself or others. For example, you might want to add a note that explains information on a slide or asks for feedback. Comments are even more powerful when you include them in a presentation that you plan to send to others by email. Others can then add additional comments before sending the presentation to others or back to you.

To add a comment, display the slide in Slide or Normal view, and then choose Insert, Comment. Enter your text in the yellow comment text box, and then click outside of it. You can also move, resize, or delete the box as you would any other object.

What happens when you want to include comments on a slide show, but don't want them to display during a slide show? Simple: Just hide them by choosing View, Comments. This command acts as a toggle to hide or display comments, as needed.

Lesson 6: Scheduling an Online Meeting

As part of the Office 2000 suite, PowerPoint 2000 includes a feature called Microsoft **NetMeeting**. You can use this feature to set up an online meeting and share information with others in **real-time** over the Internet or your company's intranet. Real-time is the actual time when events occur. When you communicate in real-time, you see the changes and make decisions immediately. Real-time differs from communicating via email because responses to email are usually delayed in time. Although you can use the NetMeeting feature in any Office 2000 program, it's ideally suited for use in conjunction with a PowerPoint presentation because you can clearly present your ideas with PowerPoint. Try setting up an online meeting now.

 Exam Note: **NetMeeting and NetShow Services**

It's easy to get confused about the difference between Office 2000's NetMeeting and NetShow Services features. Here's the difference: NetShow Services is used to **broadcast** one-way meetings that others can only view (but not give feedback to except via email). Broadcasting a presentation is like giving an onscreen presentation to an audience—except that the audience is scattered at remote locations rather than in a conference room.

In contrast, the NetMeeting feature enables active, electronic participation by those in the meeting. Meeting attendees can give immediate, electronic feedback through the whiteboard and chat windows. Because of this, it's typically used for teams collaborating on a project or document.

To Set Up an Online Meeting

❶ In the open Travel Bargains presentation, choose Tools, Online Collaboration.

The Online Collaboration submenu displays (Figure 14.12). Conducting an online meeting includes two main steps: scheduling the meeting (including inviting participants), and activating the meeting. First, you can schedule the meeting.

Figure 14.12
Use these menu options to schedule and activate an online meeting.

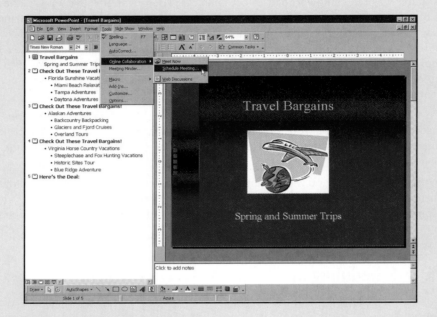

❷ Choose Schedule Meeting from the submenu.

☒ If You Have Problems...

Some of the features related to online collaboration are installed the first time you use them. If you don't see the Schedule Meeting menu option, most likely it's never been installed. See your instructor or Help for assistance.

Additionally, if this is the first time you've used the NetMeeting feature, you may be prompted to enter information about your email address and server before the Outlook window displays.

Outlook (the messaging and scheduling software program that is packaged with Office 2000) displays (see Figure 14.13). You can use this window to invite others to participate in your electronic meeting by entering their email addresses in the To section of the text box.

Enter email addresses
for meeting participants
here

Enter your meeting's
topic here

Indicate the meeting
time here

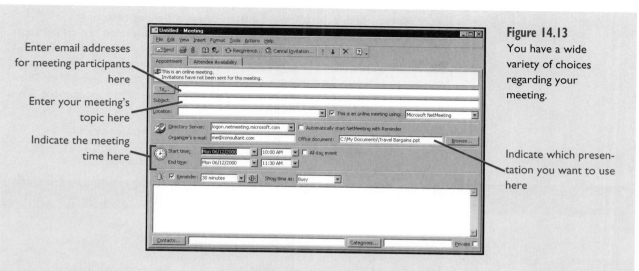

Figure 14.13
You have a wide
variety of choices
regarding your
meeting.

Indicate which presen-
tation you want to use
here

❸ Click in the To text box, and then enter the email address of another student. (If you don't know any email addresses, ask your instructor.)
This is the address of the person you want to invite to the meeting. You can enter as many addresses as you want. Now add a topic for the meeting.

❹ In the Subject text box, type `Publicity Materials`.
This information displays when your meeting recipients get their invitations via email.

❺ In the message text box area (at the bottom of the dialog box), type
`Let me know if you can make this meeting.`

❻ Make sure that Microsoft NetMeeting displays in the Location section of the dialog box.
Now take a look at the starting and ending times. By default, the meeting is scheduled for the next available 30-minute time block. You can change the meeting time, however, by clicking the Start time: and End time: drop-down list arrows, and choosing a different time. For now, however, leave the defaults in place and send the message.

❼ Click the Send button.
Outlook sends your message to the recipients. (You may, however, have to connect to the Internet or an intranet if you're not already online.)

After you receive replies from your recipients, you can choose Tools, Online Collaboration, Meet Now to start the meeting. While the meeting is being held, you can use buttons on the Online Meeting toolbar to display or hide the whiteboard or chat windows so that you can incorporate meeting feedback electronically. For now, however, close your presentation and PowerPoint.

❽ Save and close the Travel Bargains presentation.
If you've finished your work session, exit PowerPoint and shut down Windows before turning off your computer. Otherwise, complete the Skill Drill, Challenge, and Discovery Zone exercises at the end of this project.

Exam Note: Using NetShow to Broadcast a Presentation
You can broadcast a presentation over the Web, including video and sound clips. Broadcasting is especially handy when you have a large or widespread audience. And because the presentation is saved in HTML format, any person who has a browser can view it. You set up a broadcast presentation by choosing Slide Show, Online Broadcast, Set Up and Schedule. To run an online broadcast, choose Slide Show, Online Broadcast, Begin Broadcast.

For more information on setting up a broadcast presentation, see Help.

Summary

In this project, you learned several ways to use PowerPoint as a communication tool. You learned how to pack up your presentation to take it with you to other locations. You also learned how to interface PowerPoint with the Web or your company's intranet by previewing and saving the presentation as a Web page. As further collaboration tools, you added comments to a presentation and sent it by email. Finally, you used PowerPoint to set up an online meeting.

To expand on your knowledge, spend a few minutes exploring Help on these topics. Additionally, complete some of the Skill Drill, Challenge, and Discovery Zone exercises.

Checking Concepts and Terms

True/False

For each of the following, check *T* or *F* to indicate whether the statement is true or false.

__T __F **1.** The Web is a text-only way to explore the Internet. [L2–4]

__T __F **2.** A home page is the opening page for a Web site and is usually dedicated to a certain topic or company. [L2–3]

__T __F **3.** Saving a presentation for Web use typically creates many files. [L4]

__T __F **4.** You can send a PowerPoint presentation via email. [L5]

__T __F **5.** You schedule an online meeting by using PowerPoint's Schedule Meeting Wizard. [L7]

Multiple Choice

Circle the letter of the correct answer for each of the following questions.

1. HTML stands for which of the following? [L2–4]

a. HyperLink Text in Many Languages

b. HyperTransport Markup LANs

c. HyperText Markup Language

d. none of the above

2. Which of the following is true regarding a Web home page? [L2–4]

a. It usually contains a number of hyperlinks to other documents.

b. It makes your computer display in *home mode*.

c. It is the same as a Web browser.

d. It is software that you use to post information to a Web server.

3. How can you use PowerPoint to communicate with others? [L1–6]

a. Use NetMeeting

b. Attach a presentation to an email message

c. Publish your presentation as a Web page

d. all of the above

4. Which of the following can you use to format and prepare your presentation for use on the Web? [L2]

    a. AutoContent Wizard

    b. Wizard Preview

    c. Save As a NetShow Wizard

    d. none of the above

5. What is the difference between collaborating via email and via an online meeting? [L5–6]

    a. An online meeting happens in real-time; email does not.

    b. You cannot respond during an online meeting; you can reply to an email message.

    c. You can view a presentation during an online meeting; there is no way to attach a presentation to an email message.

    d. all of the above

Skill Drill

Skill Drill exercises reinforce project skills. Each skill reinforced is the same, or nearly the same, as a skill presented in the project. Detailed instructions are provided in a step-by-step format.

1. Using the Pack and Go Wizard

You're scheduled to give an orientation meeting for employees at one of your company's offices. To make it easy to take your presentation along, you decide to use Pack and Go.

After you pack up the presentation, imagine that you arrive at the office where you plan to give the talk. To set up for the seminar, you unpack the presentation and then run it as a slide show. [L1]

1. Open **PP-1404** and save it as **Orientation Session**. Choose File, Pack and Go. Click Next to proceed past the opening page of the wizard.

2. Make sure that Active presentation is selected on the second page of the wizard, and then click Next.

3. On the third page—Choose destination—make sure that A:\ drive is chosen, and then click Next.

4. Check both boxes on the Links page of the wizard, and then click Next.

5. On the Viewer page, choose Don't include the Viewer. Choose Next.

6. Read over the information on the final page of the wizard. Make sure that you have a blank disk in the A: drive, and then click Finish. Click OK in the message box.

7. Close the Orientation Session presentation, but keep PowerPoint running so that you can practice unpacking the presentation.

8. Click PowerPoint's Minimize button to shrink PowerPoint to a taskbar button. On the Windows desktop, double-click the My Computer icon. In the My Computer window, double-click the 3 1/2 Floppy (A:) icon.

9. Double-click the pngsetup icon. In the Pack and Go Setup dialog box, enter **C:\Session**. Click OK.

10. Another Pack and Go Setup message box prompts you to create the directory. Click OK.

11. Another message box displays, indicating that the presentation was installed in C:\Session. Click Yes in the message box to run the slide show.

12. Press (↵Enter) as many times as is necessary to advance completely through the slide show.

13. Close the 3 1/2 Floppy window on your desktop, and then click the Microsoft PowerPoint button on the taskbar to maximize the program window.

14. Now, practice opening the presentation from within PowerPoint. In PowerPoint, display the Open dialog box. Locate and open the Session folder on the C: drive.

15. Open the Orientation Session, run it as a slide show, and then close it. Leave PowerPoint running if you plan to complete the additional exercises.

2. Viewing a Presentation as a Web Page

You work for a company that produces children's clothing. You're the most computer-literate employee at your office, so your boss asked you to develop a Web site for the company. Because you don't know how to code in HTML, you decide to use a PowerPoint presentation as the basis of your Web site instead. To do so, you add action buttons to the presentation and then view it by using Web Page Preview. Finally, you save the presentation as a Web page. (If you need to brush up on how to create action buttons, see Project 13, "Creating Interactive Slide Shows.") [L3–4]

1. Open **PP-1405** and save it as **Clothing Company**. Display Slide 2 in Normal view.

2. Choose Slide Show, Action Buttons to display the Action Buttons submenu. Click the Home action button (the second button from the left on the top row). Click in the lower-left corner of the slide.

3. Click OK to confirm the default settings in the Action Settings dialog box.

4. Repeat Steps 2–3 for Slides 3–5. Move and resize the button on Slide 4 so that it doesn't cover any text. When you're finished, Slides 2–5 should each have an action button to display the first presentation slide.

5. Display the first presentation slide in Normal view, and then choose File, Web Page Preview. Maximize the browser window.

6. Click the Our Goals hyperlink on the left side of the window to display that page.

7. Click the Home button to redisplay the home page for your presentation.

8. Repeat Steps 6–7 for each of the hyperlinks and buttons in your presentation.

9. Close the browser window. Now you're ready to save the presentation as a Web page.

10. Display the presentation in Normal view, and then choose File, Save as Web Page. In the Save As dialog box, enter **Creative Kids** in the File name box. Indicate a file location, and then click Publish.

11. In the Publish as Web Page dialog box, click the Change button. Enter **Creative Kids** in the Set Page Title dialog box. Click OK to redisplay the Publish as Web Page dialog box.

12. In the Publish as Web Page dialog box, check the box for Open published Web page in browser. Click Publish.

13. Maximize the browser window. Click each hyperlink and action button to test it.

14. Close the browser window. Save the Clothing Company presentation, and then close it. Leave PowerPoint running if you plan to complete additional exercises.

3. Attaching a Presentation to a Mail Message

To quickly get a presentation in the hands of your coworkers, you email it as an attachment. [L6]

1. Open **PP-1406** and save it as **Computer Support Company**. Display the first slide of the presentation in Normal view.

2. Choose File, Send To, Mail Recipient (as Attachment) to display a mail message.

3. In the To text box, enter the email address of a friend or fellow student.

4. In the Cc text box, enter the name of another friend or student.

5. Enter the following text in the message area:
    Please let me know what you think of the presentation. I need your feedback by Tuesday. Thanks.

6. Click the Send button, and then complete whatever steps are necessary to connect to your mail server (via an intranet or the Internet).

7. Save the Computer Support Company presentation, and then close it. Leave PowerPoint running if you plan to complete the Challenge or Discovery Zone exercises.

Challenge

Challenge exercises expand on or are somewhat related to skills presented in the lessons. Each exercise provides a brief narrative introduction followed by instructions in a numbered-step format that are not as detailed as those in the Skill Drill section.

I. Finding Out About Online Collaboration

You're the sales manager for a cookie company. Most of your sales representatives are far-flung across your district, and bringing them to a central office for meetings has been hard to do. However, you've recently learned that PowerPoint has an online collaboration feature that enables you to conduct electronic meetings over the Internet. You decide to find out more. [L7]

1. Choose Help, Microsoft PowerPoint Help. Display the Answer Wizard page, and then enter **online meetings** as your search text.

2. Research each of the following topics. Make sure to take notes about what you find.
   - How to set up an online meeting
   - How to join an online meeting
   - How to work on the whiteboard
   - How to send typed messages in an online meeting
   - How to set up NetMeeting
   - The difference between online broadcasting and online meetings

3. Develop a slide show that explains how to host, run, and end an online meeting.

4. Display your presentation using Web Page Preview, and then save the presentation as a Web page.

5. Add comments to the presentation, asking for specific feedback from other PowerPoint users. Send them the presentation as an email attachment. When they reply, incorporate their feedback and resave the presentation.

6. Present the slide show to at least one other user, and then close it. Leave PowerPoint running if you plan to complete the additional exercises.

2. Previewing and Saving Your Presentation as a Web Page

As the head of Information Technology for your organization, you're in charge of upgrading all employees to Office 2000. So that you can keep everyone appraised of the project's progress, you develop a presentation and save it as HTML so that you can put it on your company's intranet. [L2–3]

1. Open **PP-1407** and save it as **Upgrading to Office 2000**.

2. Create action buttons on Slides 2–7 that you can click to display the first presentation slide. Position the buttons in the lower-right corner of each slide. Resize the buttons, if necessary, so they don't cover any slide text.

3. Preview the presentation in Web Page Preview. Test each of the hyperlinks and action buttons in the presentation. Close the browser window.

4. Save the presentation as a Web page, using the name **R & S Consultants** for the Page title and the filename.

5. Use Help to find out how to post the presentation on an intranet. If possible, actually complete the steps to post the presentation on your organization's intranet (or the Internet).

6. Save the presentation, and then close it. Leave PowerPoint running if you plan to complete additional exercises.

3. Packing and Unpacking a Presentation

You work for a large company that manufactures steel ball bearings. As a regional safety manager, you periodically give Safety Report presentations at the corporate office. To make it easy to take your presentation with you, you use the Pack and Go Wizard to compress it. When you arrive at headquarters, you unpack and run it. [L1]

1. Open **PP-1408** and save it as **Cory Manufacturing**.

2. Use the Pack and Go Wizard to pack up the presentation on a floppy (or Zip) disk. Choose the following options in the Pack and Go Wizard dialog box:

   - Include linked files
   - Embed TrueType fonts
   - Don't include the Viewer

3. Close the Cory Manufacturing presentation and PowerPoint.

4. Unpack the Cory Manufacturing presentation from the floppy (or Zip) disk to C:\Safety.

5. Run the slide show from the Pack and Go Setup dialog box.

6. Open PowerPoint. Locate the Cory Manufacturing presentation in the C:\Safety folder. Open the presentation and run it as a slide show from within PowerPoint.

7. Close the presentation. Leave PowerPoint running if you plan to complete additional exercises.

Discovery Zone

Discovery Zone exercises require advanced knowledge of topics presented in *MOUS Essentials* lessons, application of skills from multiple lessons, or self-directed learning of new skills.

I. Getting Help on the Web

You're regarded as the "PowerPoint guru" at your office. Because of this, others continually ask you questions about how to use PowerPoint more effectively. You decide to bolster your knowledge by accessing help resources on the Web.

Connect to the Web and display Microsoft's home page for Microsoft Office (http://microsoft.com/office/).

Use the hyperlinks on the site to find out the following:

- What new features are included in PowerPoint 2000?
- How much does PowerPoint cost to buy as a stand-alone application? How much does it cost if you purchase the program as part of the Office 2000 suite?
- What known bugs and problems exist in the software?
- Where can you find more clips?
- What are some "tips and tricks" that you can employ to use the software more effectively?

If you want, use your browser's search engine to find more Web sites with information about PowerPoint. (*Hint:* Type **PowerPoint 2000** in the search text box.)

Disconnect from the Web. Develop a presentation that includes the information you found. Include links in your presentation to the Web sites that you found most useful.

Send your presentation via email to another user to obtain his or her feedback. After you have incorporated the feedback, save the presentation as a Web page. If you know how and have access to a Web server, post the presentation. [L2–6]

2. Using Comments and Sending Presentations

As a manager for Star Metal Manufacturing Company, you plan to post a PowerPoint presentation in HTML format on your company's intranet. Before you do, however, you'd like to elicit feedback from other managers. To do so, you use the Insert, Comments command to add comments and send the presentation to them via email.

Open **PP-1409** and save it as **Star Metal Manufacturing**. Add the following comments to the presentation, resizing and moving them as necessary, so that they don't cover text on the slides.

- Slide 1: **What do you think of the template? It's one of the new ones packaged with PowerPoint 2000!**
- Slide 3: **Should I insert a picture on this slide to spiff it up?**
- Slide 5: **Is it OK to post this information on our intranet?**

Also do the following:

- Change the comment boxes' color to orange (to match the template).
- Display the presentation as a slide show—with and without comments displayed.
- Send the presentation as an email attachment to at least one other person.
- Preview the presentation in Web Page Preview, and then save the presentation as a Web page, using **Star Metal** for the page title. Use the name **Star Metal** for the Web page file and folder.

Close the presentation (and the Web browser). If you're finished with your work session, exit PowerPoint and Windows. [L5–6]

PinPoint Assessment

You have completed this project and its associated lessons, and have had an opportunity to assess your skills through the end-of-project questions and exercises. Now use the PinPoint software Evaluation Mode to further assess your comprehension of the specific exam activities you have just learned. You can also use the PinPoint Trainer Mode and the Show Me tutorials to practice these exam activities.

Customizing PowerPoint for Your Needs

Key terms introduced in this project include

- docked toolbars
- floating toolbars
- usage data

Objectives	Required Activity for MOUS	Exam Level
➤ Customizing Existing Toolbars	Customize the toolbar	Expert
➤ Creating a New, Custom Toolbar	Create a toolbar	Expert
➤ Restoring Original Settings	Customize the toolbar	Expert

Why Would I Do This?

Have you ever tried to wear "one-size-fits-all" clothing? If so, you probably quickly discovered that the garment didn't fit very well. Why? Because you're an individual, and certain types and styles of clothing fit you better than others. The same principle holds true for software such as PowerPoint. When you're forced to use the default toolbars—a "one-size-fits-all" type of setup—you're not as efficient as you might be. Luckily, you can tailor PowerPoint's settings to fit your individual working style.

For example, you can hide or display PowerPoint's toolbars and change the buttons they include. There are two ways to do this. First, PowerPoint 2000 includes a personalized toolbars and menus feature that continually tracks which commands and buttons you use most frequently, and then removes those that you don't use. You don't have to wait for PowerPoint to change the commands for you, however. Instead, you can cut short the process by using the Customize dialog box to add or remove buttons from toolbars, or to create a new toolbar from scratch. If you later decide that you don't like the changes, you can quickly restore the original settings. So come along and learn how to customize PowerPoint to your needs.

Inside Stuff: **Floating and Docked Toolbars**

You've probably already noticed that PowerPoint dictates which toolbars display—and when they display. That's because the program automatically shows the appropriate toolbars for the view you're using. But you're not limited to using the toolbars that PowerPoint hands you by default. Instead, you can expand your horizons and gain quick access to commands by displaying other toolbars. And, after they're displayed, you can move them to other locations on the screen. You can display them in their own window as *floating toolbars* or attach them to the side of the application window as *docked toolbars*. Either way, you'll have ready access to their buttons.

To display (or hide) a toolbar, choose it from the View, Toolbars submenu. To move a docked toolbar, drag the move handle (on the left side of the toolbar); to move a floating toolbar, drag its title bar.

 ## Lesson 1: Customizing Existing Toolbars

Have you ever wished that your favorite button was on a toolbar, but the default setup didn't include it? Wish no longer! You can customize any of PowerPoint's existing toolbars so that they better fit the commands you frequently use by adding or removing buttons from the toolbars. You do this by displaying the Customize dialog box, and then dragging buttons to or off of a displayed toolbar. Because customizing your toolbars can directly lead to increased productivity, try mastering the techniques for customizing an existing toolbar now.

To Customize Existing Toolbars

❶ Open PowerPoint and display a new, blank presentation in Normal view.

By default, the Standard, Formatting, and Drawing toolbars show when you use this view (see Figure 15.1).

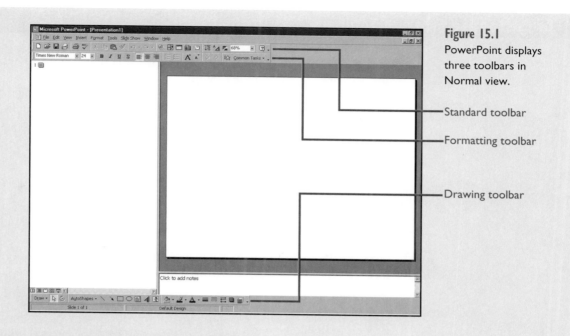

Figure 15.1
PowerPoint displays three toolbars in Normal view.

Standard toolbar

Formatting toolbar

Drawing toolbar

> ### ✗ If You Have Problems...
>
> Before continuing, make sure the toolbars on your screen match those shown in Figure 15.1. To turn the display of a toolbar on or off, right-click the menu bar to display a list of available toolbars. Left-click the toolbar you want to turn on or off.

❷ Choose Tools, Customize, and click the Toolbars tab.

A listing of the toolbars available on your system displays in the Customize dialog box (see Figure 15.2). Notice that checks indicate which toolbars are currently displayed in PowerPoint. You can turn on a toolbar by checking its box, and then modify it by adding or removing buttons.

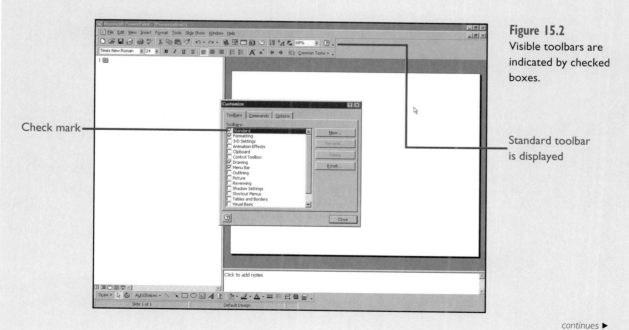

Figure 15.2
Visible toolbars are indicated by checked boxes.

Check mark

Standard toolbar is displayed

continues ▶

To Customize Existing Toolbars   (continued)

3 In the Customize dialog box, scroll down through the Toolb̲ars list, and then check the box for Web.
The Web toolbar displays as soon as you check the box. Now you're ready to customize this toolbar to better fit your needs. Imagine, for example, that you frequently print pages that you find on the Web. You can add a Print button to the toolbar so that you can quickly access the print command. How? By finding the Print button on the C̲ommands page and dragging it from the Customize dialog box to the toolbar. Try this now.

4 Click the C̲ommands tab.
The C̲ommands page of the Customize dialog box displays (see Figure 15.3). The Categories on the list indicate main menu commands or categories. Furthermore, the Comman̲ds list shows the buttons associated with a particular category. (If you want, you can click several of the categories to see how the associated commands change. When you finish, make sure to choose File on the Categories list.)

Figure 15.3
PowerPoint gives you a slew of command buttons that you can add to a toolbar.

Drag the button to the Web toolbar

Choose a main category here

Choose a command or button here

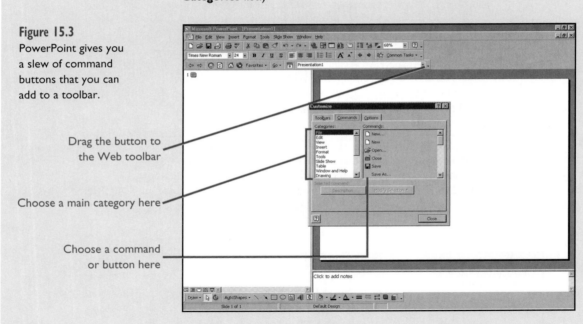

5 With File selected on the Categories list, scroll down the Comman̲ds list until you see the Print... button.

6 Drag the Print... button from the Customize dialog box to the right end of the Web toolbar until a black I-beam displays (see Figure 15.4). Release the mouse button.

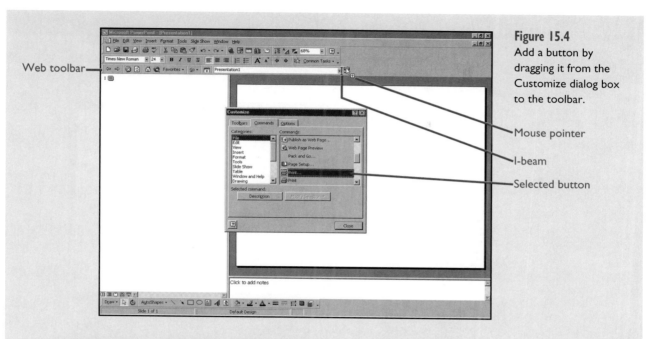

Figure 15.4
Add a button by dragging it from the Customize dialog box to the toolbar.

Web toolbar

Mouse pointer

I-beam

Selected button

The Print... button is added to the Web toolbar. Now try adding another button to the toolbar.

7 Drag the Page Setup button from the Customize dialog box to the right end of the Web toolbar, and then release the mouse button.
The button is added to the toolbar.

But you're probably wondering... what happens if you accidentally add a button to the wrong location, or you decide you don't want it on the toolbar at all? Simple. With the Customize dialog box still displayed, just drag the button off the toolbar. Try this technique now.

8 Drag the Page Setup button from the Web toolbar into the PowerPoint screen, and then release the mouse button.
The button is removed from the toolbar. Don't forget: The Customize dialog box must be open and the toolbar must be visible for you to add or remove buttons on the toolbar.

Now that you're finished using the Customize dialog box, you can close it.

9 Click the Close button in the Customize dialog box.
The dialog box closes, but the Web toolbar still displays. You turn off the display of this toolbar with a separate action.

10 Right-click the Web toolbar.
A listing of available toolbars displays (see Figure 15.5).

continues ▶

To Customize Existing Toolbars   (continued)

Figure 15.5
Right-click the menu
bar or a visible toolbar
to display this listing.

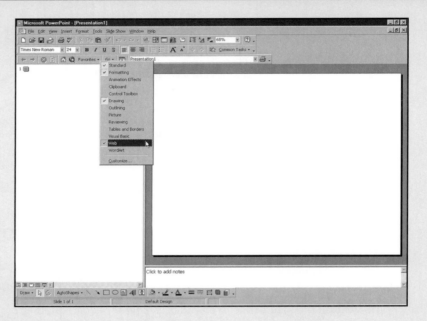

 Click Web on the listing.
Unchecking, or clearing, the toolbar on the list turns off its display. Now you're
well on your way to customizing toolbars effectively and easily.

Leave PowerPoint running for the next lesson, in which you create a new toolbar
from scratch.

Exam Note: Moving Toolbar Buttons

If you customize your toolbar buttons frequently, you probably occasionally drag a
button to the wrong location on the toolbar. To move it to where you'd like it, display the Customize dialog box (and the toolbar), and then drag the button left or
right on the toolbar. When the black I-beam displays at the correct location, release the mouse button.

 ## Lesson 2: Creating a New, Custom Toolbar

In the preceding lesson, you learned how to customize existing toolbars by adding or removing buttons. You can use similar techniques to create a new customized toolbar. This gives
you the flexibility because you include only the buttons that you plan to use most frequently.
Try creating a new toolbar now.

To Create a New Custom Toolbar

❶ Choose Tools, Customize, and then click the Toolbars tab.
The Customize dialog box displays. This handy dialog box isn't used just to modify existing toolbars—you can also use it to create completely new toolbars.

2 **Click the <u>N</u>ew button.**

The New Toolbar dialog box displays, so you can give a name to your toolbar (see Figure 15.6). Usually, you want to use a descriptive name to remember the toolbar's purpose.

Type a descriptive
name here ───────

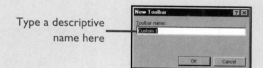

Figure 15.6
You can assign a name to your new toolbar.

3 **Type** Productivity **in the <u>T</u>oolbar name text box, and then click OK.**

Congratulations! You just created a new toolbar with the assigned name. Notice that the toolbar not only appears on the screen, but also on the list in the Customize dialog box (see Figure 15.7).

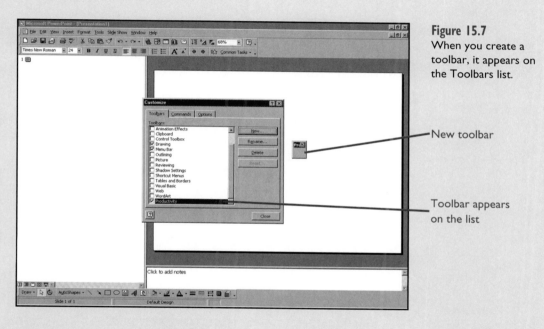

Figure 15.7
When you create a toolbar, it appears on the Toolbars list.

New toolbar

Toolbar appears on the list

Now try adding some buttons to the Productivity toolbar. You do this by using the same technique that you used to customize an existing toolbar: Drag a command or button from the Customize dialog box to the toolbar.

4 **Click the <u>C</u>ommands tab, and drag the New button from the Comman<u>d</u>s list to the Productivity toolbar until an I-beam displays. Release the mouse button.**

The New button is added to the toolbar (see Figure 15.8).

continues ▶

To Create a New Custom Toolbar   (continued)

Figure 15.8
Add a button by dragging it from the Customize dialog box into the toolbar.

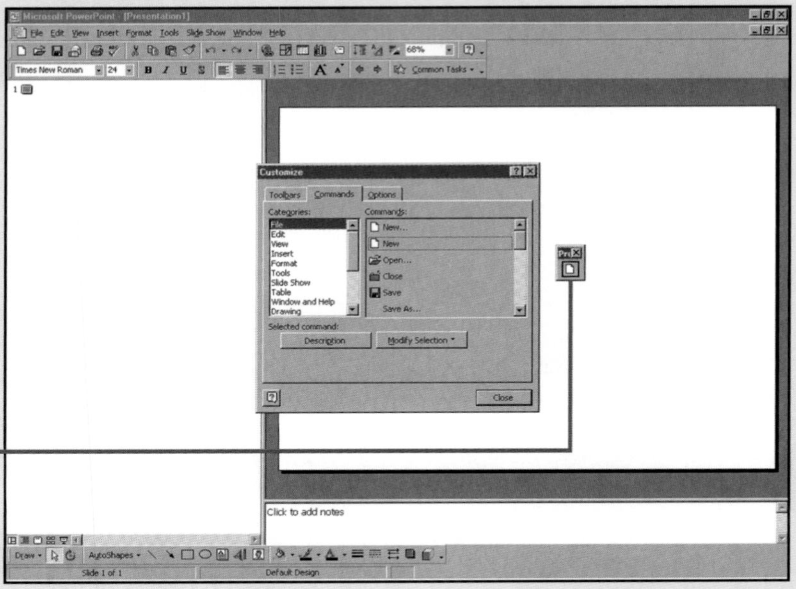

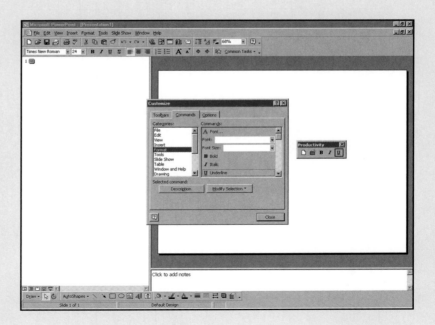

The New button is added to your custom toolbar

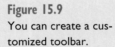

Now try adding another button.

⑤ Drag the Close command to the right of the New button in the Productivity toolbar, and then release the mouse button.

Two buttons appear on the toolbar. Remember that if the button isn't "dropped" in the exact location you want, you can move it by dragging the button left or right. To get more practice, add some additional buttons to your toolbar.

⑥ Click Format on the Categories list, and then drag the Bold, Italic, and Underline buttons to the Productivity toolbar.

When you finish, your toolbar should look similar to the one shown in Figure 15.9.

Figure 15.9
You can create a customized toolbar.

Now that you created the toolbar, try using it. First, you need to close the Customize dialog box.

7 **Close the Customize dialog box.**

8 **Choose Insert, New Slide, then double-click the Title Slide AutoLayout.**
You'll use this slide to try out the commands on the new toolbar.

9 **Click in the Title placeholder of your open presentation. (If necessary, move the Productivity toolbar out of the way by dragging its title bar.)**

10 **Click the Bold, Italic, and Underline buttons on the Productivity toolbar, and then type How to Customize PowerPoint.**
Now try deleting the toolbar.

11 **Display the Toolbars page of the Customize dialog box, and then click the Productivity toolbar. (You may need to scroll through the list to find the toolbar.)**

12 **Click Delete.**
A message box displays to confirm your action. (The Office Assistant displays your message if it is turned on instead.)

13 **Choose OK.**
The toolbar no longer appears on the list or on your screen.

14 **Close the Customize dialog box.**
Leave PowerPoint running for the next lesson, in which you restore PowerPoint's original settings for your toolbars.

Lesson 3: Restoring Original Settings

In Project 1, "Getting Started with PowerPoint," you learned that PowerPoint automatically personalizes your commands based on which ones you frequently use. In this project, you seize more control over the program by customizing toolbars yourself. In either case, however, you end up with commands that differ from the default, or original, settings.

Luckily, if you changed the buttons on a toolbar and are unhappy with the results you can restore the original configuration in a flash.

On the other hand, if PowerPoint automatically created new personalized menus based on your usage, you'll need to use the Options page in the Customize dialog box to reset your **usage data**. The usage data is just an internal list that PowerPoint employs to track the commands you use (or don't use). When you reset this list, your toolbars and menus appear as they did when the program was first installed. (Keep in mind that clearing the usage data does not change or delete customized toolbars.)

With these principles in mind, try changing toolbar and menu commands to their original settings now.

To Restore Original Settings

1 **Choose Tools, Customize, and then click the Commands tab.**
Before you get into the nitty-gritty of how to restore settings, change the buttons on the Formatting toolbar—you'll be able to better see the effect.

continues ▶

To Restore Original Settings   (continued)

2 **Using techniques you learned in Lesson 1, add the Increase Paragraph Spacing and Decrease Paragraph Spacing buttons to the Formatting toolbar, and then close the Customize dialog box. (*Note:* These buttons are part of the Formatting category.)**
The new buttons display on the toolbar (see Figure 15.10).

Figure 15.10
The buttons you added display on the Formatting toolbar.

Added buttons

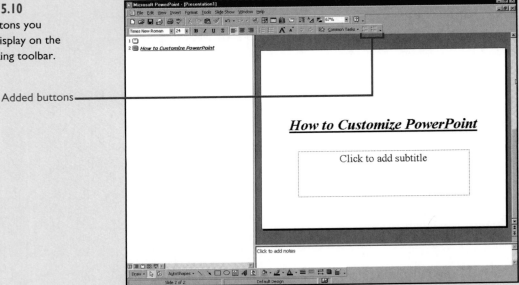

Now you're ready to restore the original settings to this toolbar. When you do, the buttons you added will be automatically removed.

3 **Right-click any toolbar, and then choose <u>C</u>ustomize.**
The Customize dialog box displays.

4 **Click the Tool<u>b</u>ars tab.**
You can select a command bar from the list, and then restore the original settings.

5 **Click Formatting—but not the check box next to Formatting—on the list, and then click <u>R</u>eset.**
A message box displays, asking whether you're sure you want to reset the changes that you made to the Formatting toolbar (see Figure 15.11).

Figure 15.11
Use this message box to confirm your action.

 If You Have Problems...
Make sure you don't accidentally clear the check box next to the Formatting toolbar in the Customize dialog box. Doing so turns off the display of this toolbar.

6 **Click OK, and then close the Customize dialog box.**
Notice that the original (default) buttons display on the Formatting toolbar (see Figure 15.12).

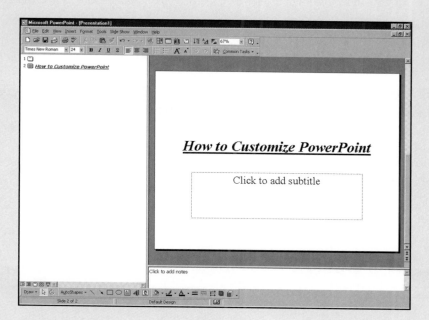

Figure 15.12
The default buttons on the Formatting toolbar display.

Now, restore the original settings to your system to clear the usage data list.

7 **Display the Customize dialog box, and then click the <u>O</u>ptions tab.**
The <u>O</u>ptions page of the Customize dialog box displays (see Figure 15.13). This page includes a number of ways to customize your system.

Check this box to display the Standard and Formatting toolbars on one row

Check this box to turn on personalized menus

Click here to reset your usage data

Click here to animate your menus

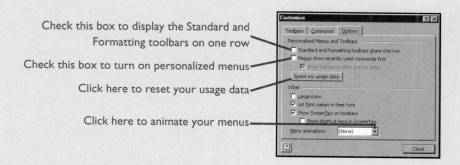

Figure 15.13
The Options page is chock-full of ways to customize or reset your settings.

8 **Click the <u>R</u>eset my usage data button.**
A message box displays, indicating that the listing of commands you used will be cleared, and the default commands will be restored to your menus and toolbars (see Figure 15.14).

Figure 15.14
You can quickly restore the default settings to menus and toolbars.

9 **Choose <u>Y</u>es, and then close the Customize dialog box.**
The original commands and settings for your toolbars and menus are restored.

continues ▶

To Restore Original Settings (continued)

⑩ Close the open PowerPoint presentation without saving it.
Keep PowerPoint running if you plan to complete the Skill Drill, Challenge or Discovery Zone exercises.

Summary

In this project, you learned how to take more control of PowerPoint by customizing it to fit your needs. You learned how to turn the display of toolbars on or off, and how to relocate them on your screen. To give you even more flexibility, you added and removed buttons to toolbars and created a new toolbar. Finally, you learned how to restore PowerPoint's original settings and reset usage data.

To expand on your knowledge, spend a few minutes exploring Help on these topics. Additionally, complete some of the Skill Drill, Challenge, and Discovery Zone exercises.

Checking Concepts and Terms ✓

True/False

For each of the following, check T or F to indicate whether the statement is true or false.

__T __F **1.** A toolbar must be visible for you to add buttons to it. [L1]

__T __F **2.** You can move a floating toolbar by dragging its title bar. [L1]

__T __F **3.** You can turn the display of toolbars on or off. [L1]

__T __F **4.** You can create new toolbars, but not revise PowerPoint's "built-in" ones. [L1–2]

__T __F **5.** The only way to restore default toolbar settings after you revised them is to reinstall PowerPoint. [L3]

Multiple Choice

Circle the letter of the correct answer for each of the following questions.

1. In which of the following ways can you change a toolbar? [L1–2]

  a. move it

  b. add buttons

  c. remove buttons

  d. all of the above

2. Which of the following conditions must be in effect for you to add or remove buttons from a toolbar? [L1–2]

  a. The Options dialog box must be open and the Toolbar shortcut menu must be displayed.

  b. The Customize dialog box must be open and the toolbar must be visible.

  c. The toolbar must be docked and the Toolbars dialog box must be open.

  d. The default toolbar must be displayed and the Options dialog box must be open.

3. How do you move a docked toolbar? [L1]

  a. by dragging its title bar

  b. by choosing Toolbar, Modify from the menu

  c. by dragging its move handle

  d. You can't move a docked toolbar.

4. To what does the term *default settings* refer? [L3]

  a. the original settings that were in place when you installed the software

b. the custom toolbars you develop

c. your individualized settings

d. none of the above

5. What happens when you reset usage data? [L3]

a. It erases the record of commands used.

b. It makes the selected toolbar a floating toolbar.

c. It reverses your last action.

d. none of the above

Skill Drill

Skill Drill exercises reinforce project skills. Each skill reinforced is the same, or nearly the same, as a skill presented in the project. Detailed instructions are provided in a step-by-step format.

1. Using Help to Find Out More About Toolbars

You've been working with PowerPoint for awhile, and would like to exert more control over the way that toolbars operate. Before you start modifying and moving the toolbars, however, you decide that it would be wise to spend a few minutes brushing up on how to work with them. [L1–3]

1. Start PowerPoint, if necessary; then choose Help, Microsoft PowerPoint Help. If necessary, click the Show button to split the window into two panes.

2. Click the Answer Wizard tab to display the Answer Wizard page.

3. Type **Command Bars** in the **What would you like to do?** text box. Click Search.

4. Read the information associated with each of the following topics from the **Select topic to display** list. Take notes so that you can better remember the information.

- Create a custom toolbar
- Add a button to a toolbar
- Troubleshoot toolbars and menus

- Delete a command from a menu
- Add a command to a menu
- Delete a custom toolbar
- Rename a menu command or toolbar button
- Change the image on a toolbar button or menu command
- Move a toolbar
- Hide all toolbars except the Web toolbar.

5. Close the Help window. Share what you learn with at least one other user. Leave PowerPoint running if you plan to complete additional exercises.

2. Customizing an Existing Toolbar

You work with PowerPoint regularly to develop business presentations, but you find that you don't use many of the buttons on PowerPoint's Standard toolbar. Additionally, there are many buttons that you use that are *not* included on the toolbar. You decide to customize the Standard toolbar to better fit the commands that you use most regularly. [L1]

1. In PowerPoint, right-click any visible toolbar to display the shortcut menu, and then choose Customize to display the Customize dialog box. Click the Toolbars tab, if necessary, to display a list of toolbars.

2. Make sure that the Standard toolbar is selected on the Toolbars list.

3. Click the Commands tab and select File on the Categories list. Drag the Close button from the Commands list to the right side of the Standard

toolbar. (*Hint:* Make sure that the I-beam displays before releasing the mouse button.)

4. Move the Close button to a new location on the Standard toolbar by dragging it to the left until you see the I-beam display between the Open and Save buttons. Release the mouse button.

5. Click View on the Categories list. In the Commands list, drag the Slide Sorter button to the right side of the Standard toolbar, and then release the mouse button.

6. Now remove some buttons from the Standard toolbar. Drag the Email button from the Standard toolbar into the PowerPoint window, and then release the mouse button. Repeat the process to remove the Insert Table, Expand All, and Grayscale Preview buttons from the toolbar. (*Hint:* To identify a toolbar button when the Customize dialog box is open, right-click the button to display the name in the shortcut menu.)

7. Close the Customize dialog box so you can test your modified Standard toolbar. Click the Close button, and then choose Cancel in the message box that displays.

8. Reset the Standard toolbar to include the default buttons. Choose <u>T</u>ools, <u>C</u>ustomize to display the Customize dialog box, and then click the Tool<u>b</u>ars tab.

9. Make sure that Standard is selected on the Toolbars list, and then click <u>R</u>eset. Choose OK in the message box that displays.

10. Close the Customize dialog box. Leave PowerPoint running if you plan to complete additional exercises.

3. Creating a New Custom Toolbar

You work for a museum and put together a lot of presentations for educational programs. You're excited because you recently discovered that you can create your own customized toolbars in PowerPoint—something that you think will make you more efficient when you work with PowerPoint. You decide to try your hand at creating a new custom toolbar. [L2]

1. Display the Customize dialog box, and then click the Tool<u>b</u>ars tab.

2. Click the <u>N</u>ew button, and then type **My Toolbar** in the New Toolbar dialog box before pressing (↵**Enter**).

3. Click the <u>C</u>ommands tab, and then select File on the Categories list. Drag the New, Close, and Print buttons from the Comman<u>d</u>s list to your new toolbar.

4. Click Format on the Categories list. Drag the Bold, Italic, and Underline buttons from the Comman<u>d</u>s list to your new toolbar.

5. Close the Customize dialog box to try out your new toolbar. First, create a new presentation by clicking the New button on your toolbar. Create a Blank presentation and use the Title Slide AutoLayout for your first slide.

6. Click in the title placeholder, and then click the Bold, Italic, and Underline buttons on your toolbar. Enter **Welcome to Our Museum!** in the placeholder.

7. Click the Print button on your toolbar to print the slide. Then click the Close button. Choose <u>N</u>o in the message box that displays.

8. Redisplay the Toolbars page of the Customize dialog box. Scroll down the list of toolbars, and then select My Toolbar.

9. Click <u>D</u>elete. Choose OK to confirm your action.

10. Close the Customize dialog box. Leave PowerPoint running if you plan to complete additional exercises.

Challenge

Challenge exercises expand on or are somewhat related to skills presented in the lessons. Each exercise provides a brief narrative introduction, followed by instructions in a numbered-step format that are not as detailed as those in the Skill Drill section.

1. Creating a Custom Toolbar

You work for your college's admissions department. Your boss, impressed with your computer skills, has asked you to develop a series of presentations—one for each college major. To be more efficient, you decide to create a custom toolbar to include the buttons you expect to use most frequently. [L2]

1. Display the Customize dialog box. Create a new toolbar using the name **College**.

2. Add the following commands from the File category: New, Open, Close, Save, and Page Setup.

3. Add the following commands from the Edit category: Undo, Copy, and Paste.

4. Add the following commands from the Format category: Font, Font Size, and Apply Design Template.

5. Add the following commands from the Table category: Draw Table and Eraser.

6. Close the Customize dialog box. Try out your College toolbar by creating a new presentation about a major at your college. Use each of the buttons on your toolbar.

7. After you've finished creating, saving, and closing your presentation, redisplay the Customize dialog box.

8. On the Toolbars page, click College on the list of Toolbars. Choose Delete, and then confirm your action by choosing OK.

9. Close the Customize dialog box. Leave PowerPoint running if you plan to complete additional exercises.

2. Customizing Menus

You work for the technical support staff at your college. Many of the professors use PowerPoint to give their classroom lectures. One professor, however, doesn't want to be bothered with extra menu commands and has asked you to help him customize the menus on his system. [L2]

1. In PowerPoint, display the Customize dialog box.

2. Click Menu Bar on the Toolbars page.

3. Click the File command on the menu bar. Point to the Properties command on the drop-down menu, and then drag it from the menu into the PowerPoint window before releasing the mouse button.

4. With the Customize dialog box still open, drag the following commands off of the File drop-down menu: Send To, Web Page Preview, and Save as Web Page.

5. Using the same method, remove the following commands from the Edit drop-down menu: Clear, Duplicate, and Go to Property.

6. Close the Customize dialog box. Open the File and Edit menus to see your customized menus.

7. Redisplay the Customize dialog box. Select Menu Bar on the Toolbars list, and then click Reset. Choose OK to confirm your action.

8. Close the Customize dialog box. Open the File and Edit menus to view the default menu commands. Leave PowerPoint running if you plan to complete additional exercises.

3. Changing and Resetting Default Options

You freelance as a computer consultant, helping individual users and small businesses get up and running with PowerPoint. You frequently find that users either want to customize PowerPoint but they don't know how, or they want to restore the default settings. You spend a few minutes brushing up on ways to perform both types of actions, so that you can better help your clients. [L3]

1. In PowerPoint, display the Customize dialog box, and then click the Options tab. Turn on the display of large icons. Also activate the Unfold menu animation.

2. Close the Customize dialog box. Open several menus to see the animation.

3. Redisplay the Options page of the Customize dialog box. Turn off the menu animation and the display of large icons. Then make other changes to the settings as follows: Uncheck the `List Font names in their font` check box, and check the `Show shortcut keys in ScreenTips` check box.

4. Create a new blank presentation. Rest your mouse pointer over several toolbar buttons to view toolbar shortcuts for each button.

5. Click the Font drop-down list arrow to note that all the fonts are shown using the same typeface.

6. Reset the options that you changed in Step 3, and then close the Customize dialog box. Click the Font drop-down list arrow to see that the fonts display by using their own typeface. Keep PowerPoint running if you plan to complete additional exercises.

Discovery Zone

Discovery Zone exercises require advanced knowledge of topics presented in *MOUS Essentials* lessons, application of skills from multiple lessons, or self-directed learning of new skills. Each exercise is independent of the others, so that you may complete the exercises in any order.

I. Using Help to Find Out About Toolbars

You work for a large computer training organization and you're scheduled to conduct a seminar on PowerPoint for advanced users. One of the main topics is about how to customize PowerPoint. Using Help and the Web, research the following subjects:

- How to add a custom menu to a toolbar
- How to change the image on a toolbar button
- How to display text, an icon, or both on a toolbar button
- How to display a button image on a menu command
- How to rename a menu command or toolbar button

Develop a presentation based on the information you find. Your presentation should be approximately 25–50 slides in length. Use clip art to help illustrate your presentation. Practice giving the presentation to another user or to your class. Save the presentation, and then close it. Leave PowerPoint running if you plan to complete the final exercise. [LI–3]

2. Customizing Menus and Toolbars

You work for the Information Technology Department of a company that manufactures high-end electrical motors. Many of the managers use PowerPoint to create presentations. To make it easier for the managers to quickly create presentations, your boss has asked you to customize toolbars and menus for several of them.

Using the commands and procedures that you learned in the preceding exercise, customize PowerPoint by making these changes:

- Remove the following commands from the File menu: Save as Web Page and Properties. Then add these commands from the File category: Online Meeting Participant, Genigraphics, and Routing Recipient.
- Change the button image for the Online Meeting Participant command to a bell icon.
- Change the button image for the Save command to an image of your choice.
- Turn on a menu animation of your choice.
- Create a new custom toolbar. Include at least 10 commands (of your choosing) on the toolbar.
- Display the toolbar as a floating and docked toolbar. Also practice resizing, hiding, and displaying the toolbar.
- Test your new menu commands and settings.

- Change the settings back to the defaults. Also, reset your menu bar to the original settings.
- Delete your customized toolbar.
- Reset your usage data.

When you are certain that you reset all settings, toolbars, and the menu bar, close any open presentations without saving them. Exit PowerPoint. [L1–3]

PinPoint Assessment

You have completed this project and its associated lessons, and have had an opportunity to assess your skills through the end-of-project questions and exercises. Now use the PinPoint software Evaluation Mode to further assess your comprehension of the specific exam activities you have just learned. You can also use the PinPoint Trainer Mode and the Show Me tutorials to practice these exam activities.

Appendix A

Using the MOUS PinPoint 2000 Training and Testing Software

Objectives

➤ Install and Start the PinPoint Launcher

➤ Start and Run PinPoint Trainers and Evaluation

➤ View Trainer and Evaluation Results

➤ Recover from a Crash

➤ Remove PinPoint from Your Computer

Introduction to PinPoint 2000

PinPoint 2000 is a software product that provides interactive training and testing in Microsoft Office 2000 programs. It is designed to supplement the projects in this book and will aid you in preparing for the MOUS certification exams. PinPoint 2000 is included on the CD-ROM in the back of this text. PinPoint 2000 Trainers and Evaluations currently run under Windows 95, Windows 98 and Windows NT 4.

The MOUS PinPoint software consists of Trainers and Evaluations. Trainers are used to hone your Office user skills. Evaluations are used to evaluate your performance of those skills.

PinPoint 2000 requires a full custom installation of Office 2000 to your computer. A full custom installation is an option you select at the time you install Microsoft Office 2000, and means that all components of the software are installed.

The PinPoint 2000 Launcher

Your PinPoint 2000 CD contains a selection of PinPoint 2000 Trainers and Evaluations that cover many of the skills that you may need for using Word 2000, Excel 2000, PowerPoint 2000 and Access 2000.

Concurrency

PinPoint 2000 Trainers and Evaluations are considered "concurrent." This means that a Trainer (or Evaluation) is run simultaneously with the Office 2000 application you are learning or being tested in. For example, when you run a Pinpoint Excel 2000 Trainer, the Microsoft Excel 2000 application is automatically started and runs at the same time. By working directly in the Office 2000 application, you master the real application, rather than just practice on a simulation of the application.

Today's more advanced applications (like those in Office 2000) often allow more than one way to perform a given task. Concurrency with the real application gives you the freedom to choose the method that you like or that you already know. This gives you the optimal training and testing environment.

Trainer/Evaluation Pairs

Trainers and Evaluations come in pairs. For example, there is a Trainer/Evaluation pair for Word 2000 called "Expert Creating a Newsletter." This means that there is both a Trainer and an Evaluation for "Expert Creating a Newsletter."

Pinpoint Word 2000, Excel 2000, PowerPoint 2000, and Access 2000 all have such sets of Trainers and Evaluations.

Tasks

Each Trainer/Evaluation pair, or *module*, is a set of tasks grouped according to level (Core or Expert) and skill set.

Trainers

If you need help to complete the task you can click the Show Me button and activate the Show Me feature The Show Me will run a demonstration of how to perform a similar task.

After you attempt the task, the program checks your work and tells you if you performed the task correctly or incorrectly. In either case you have three choices:

- Retry the task.
- Have the Trainer demonstrate with the task's Show Me an efficient method of completing the task.
- Move on to the next task.

After you have completed all of the tasks in the module, you can study your performance by looking at the report that appears when you click the Report tab on the Launcher. Reports are covered in Lesson 7.

You may take a Trainer as many times as you like. As you do so, the Launcher keeps track of how you perform, even over different days, so that when you run a Trainer another time, the Trainer is set up to run only those tasks that were performed incorrectly on all of your previous run(s).

Evaluations

Since an Evaluation is really a test, it does not give you immediate feedback. You also cannot go back to a previous task or watch a demonstration of how to do the current task. You simply move from task to task until you have attempted all of the tasks in the Evaluation.

When you have finished, you can look at the report in the Reports section to see how you performed.

You can take an Evaluation as many times as you like. While you do so, the Launcher program keeps a record of how you have performed. As a result, if you take a Trainer after the corresponding Evaluation has been taken, the Trainer will set up to run only those tasks that were performed incorrectly on the Evaluation.

System Requirements

Table A.1 shows the system requirements to run PinPoint 2000 software on your computer.

Table A.1 PinPoint 2000 System Requirements

Component	Requirement
CPU	Minimum: Pentium
	Recommended: 166 MHz Pentium or better
Operating System	Windows 95, Windows 98 or WindowsNT 4.0 sp5
Installed Applications	Full Custom Installation of Office 2000*
	Printer
RAM	Minimum: 16 MB
	Recommended: 32 MB or higher

*Office 2000 must be installed before installing PinPoint 2000. If a Full Custom Installation of Office 2000 has not been performed, some tasks will not be available, because the components required for those tasks will not have been installed. The tasks will not be counted as right or wrong but recorded as N/A.

Table A.1   PinPoint 2000 System Requirements   (continued)

Component	Requirement
Hard Drive Space	Minimum: Installing PinPoint 2000 software requires about 4 MB of hard drive space.
	Recommended: For efficient operation, however, you should make sure you have at least 100 MB of unused drive space after installing PinPoint 2000.
CD-ROM Drive	4X speed or faster
Video	Minimum: Color VGA video display running at 640x480 resolution with 16 colors.
	Recommended: Color VGA video display running at 800x600 (or higher) resolution with 16 colors.
	Note for Gateway computer users: If running a P5 90 (or less) Gateway computer, obtain the latest ATI "Mach 64" video driver from Gateway. This can be downloaded from Gateway's web site.

Running PinPoint 2000

Now that you know what PinPoint 2000 is and what is required to use it, you now see how to install and use the Launcher, and start and run Trainers and Evaluations. You also see how to view Trainer and Evaluation reports. Lastly, you find out how to recover from a crash of PinPoint 2000, should one occur.

Lesson 1: Installing the Launcher on Your Computer

To run the PinPoint 2000 Trainers or Evaluations, you must first install the Launcher program.

To Install the Launcher

1 **Start Windows on your computer.**

2 **Be sure that Office 2000 has already been installed to your computer with a Full Custom Install. If this is not the case, perform this installation before you continue with step 3.**

3 **Insert the PinPoint 2000 CD into your CD-ROM drive.**

4 **From the Start menu, select Run.**

5 **In the Run dialog box, enter the path to the SETUP.EXE file found in the root directory of the CD. For example, if your CD-ROM drive has been assigned the letter D, you would enter D:\setup.exe as shown in Figure A.1.**
Note: If your CD-ROM drive has been assigned a letter different from D, use that letter to begin the path in this dialog box. For example, if your CD-ROM drive has been assigned the drive letter E, enter E:\setup.exe in this dialog box.

6 **Click OK.**

7 **When the Setup Type screen appears, select Normal Single-User Installation.**

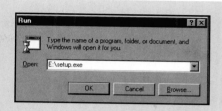

Figure A.1

8 **Click Next to continue.**

You are given a choice concerning the location of the PinPoint 2000 folder

The recommended location of the PinPoint 2000 folder is shown as the default. (*Note:* Two files that initially take up only 109 KB will be placed in this folder.)

If you prefer to use a different path or name for the PinPoint 2000 folder click the Browse button and navigate to the location you prefer, or rename the folder.

9 **Click Next to continue.**

After the installation is complete, the PinPoint 2000 program group window appears.

10 **Close the PinPoint 2000 program group window.**

If the installation has occurred correctly, the following changes have been made to your computer:

■ A PinPoint 2000 shortcut icon has been installed that will enable you to run the Launcher program via the Start menu.

■ A new folder called PinPoint 2000 has been created on the hard drive of your computer (see Figure A.2).

PinPoint 2000 folder →

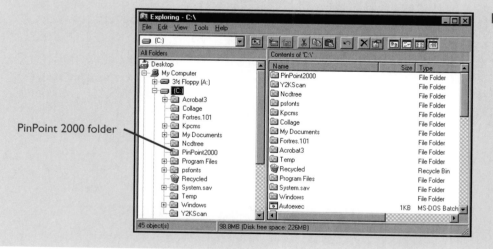

Figure A.2

The PinPoint 2000 folder contains:

■ An empty database file, CC_Admin.mdb. As you run Trainers and Evaluations, this file records your performance.

■ A small file, Uninst.isu, that is used for removing PinPoint 2000 from your computer.

Note: If your computer is configured so that file extensions are turned off, the CC_Admin.mdb file will appear without the .mdb extension.

Some files necessary for database access have been added to the Windows\System folder.

Lesson 2: Preparing to Run the PinPoint 2000 Launcher

Before running the PinPoint 2000 Launcher, it is necessary to initialize each of the Microsoft applications (Word 2000, Excel 2000, PowerPoint 2000, and Access 2000) at least one time. If you have already used each of these applications, you can ignore this section.

Initializing these applications enables PinPoint training and testing to run in a more stable environment. You will need to provide user information in the first application that you run.

Preparing to Run PinPoint 2000

❶ **Start Microsoft Word 2000.**

❷ **When the User Name dialog box appears type your Name and Initials.**

❸ **Click OK to confirm.**

❹ **When the Word window is completely set up and ready for use, you can close the application.**

❺ **Start Microsoft Excel 2000.**

❻ **When the Excel window is completely set up and ready for use, you can close the application.**

❼ **Start Microsoft PowerPoint 2000.**

❽ **When the PowerPoint window is completely set up and ready for use, you may close the application.**

❾ **Start Microsoft Access 2000.**

❿ **When the Access window is completely set up and ready for use, you can close the application.**

You are ready to run the Launcher program and begin Trainers and Evaluations.

Lesson 3: Starting the PinPoint 2000 Launcher

The Launcher program enables you to run Trainers and Evaluations. It also gives you a performance report after you have taken a Trainer or Evaluation.

To Start the PinPoint 2000 Launcher

1 Select Start, **P**rograms, PinPoint 2000, PinPoint 2000 (see Figure A.3).

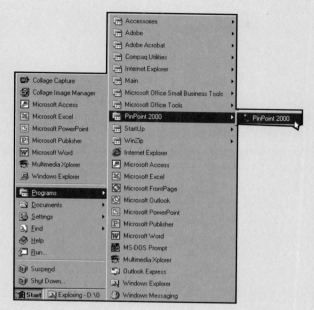

Figure A.3

2 Enter a user name and password (see Figure A.4).

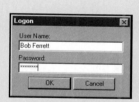

Figure A.4

The user name and password can consist of any characters, as long as neither of them exceeds 50 characters. They are NOT case sensitive: It doesn't matter if you use upper- or lowercase letters.

If more than one person will be running PinPoint 2000 from your computer, each person must enter a different user name. However, passwords can be the same.

3 **Click OK in the Logon dialog box.**
If you are logging on for the first time, you need to enter some information in the User Information dialog box.

4 **Enter the requested information and click OK.**
The PinPoint 2000 Launcher screen appears (see Figure A.5).

continues ▶

To Start the PinPoint 2000 Launcher (continued)

Figure A.5

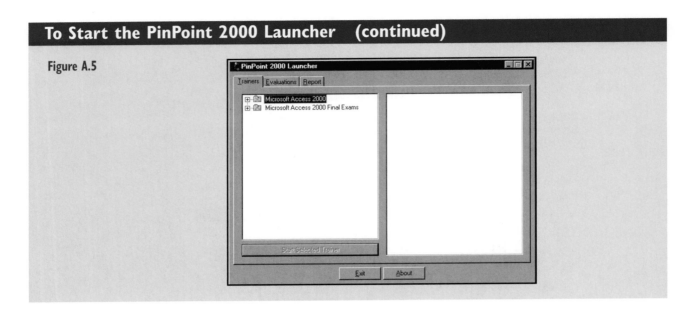

You are now ready to run PinPoint Trainers and Evaluations.

Lesson 4: Starting PinPoint 2000 Trainers and Evaluations

To Start Trainers and Evaluations

❶ **From the PinPoint Launcher, click the Trainers tab if you want to start a Trainer, or the Evaluations tab if you want to start an Evaluation (see Figure A.6).**

Figure A.6

Trainer tab

Evaluation tab

Report tab

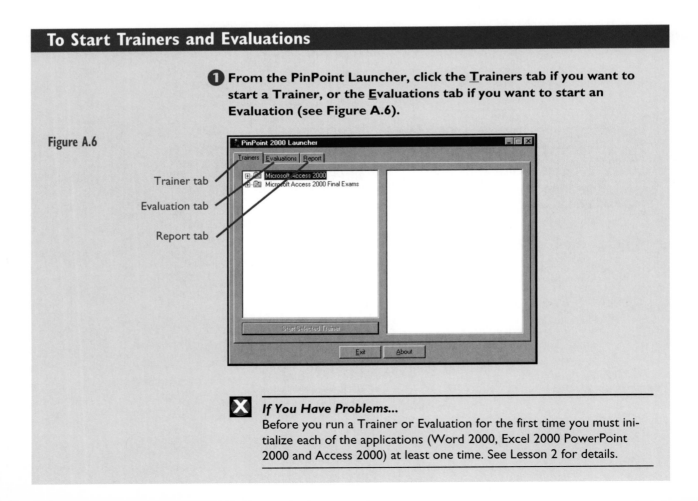

✖ If You Have Problems...
Before you run a Trainer or Evaluation for the first time you must initialize each of the applications (Word 2000, Excel 2000 PowerPoint 2000 and Access 2000) at least one time. See Lesson 2 for details.

2 **Click the plus sign (+) to open an application's modules and exams. The plus sign becomes a minus sign (–), as shown in Figure A.7.**

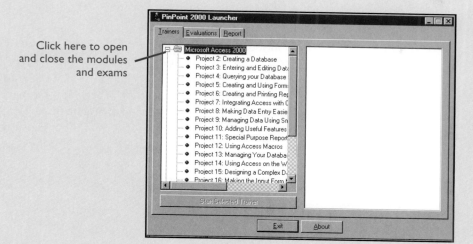

Click here to open
and close the modules
and exams

Figure A.7

3 **Select the module or exam that you want to run.**
The individual tasks that are part of the Trainer or Evaluation appear in the pane on the right.

4 **If you are running a Trainer without an Evaluation, you can select or deselect individual training tasks by clicking on the box beside the task name (see Figure A.8).**
The tasks that are deselected will not run during the Trainer. This enables you to adjust your training to include only those tasks that you do not already know how to do.

When running an Evaluation, however, you cannot deselect individual tasks. All tasks will run.

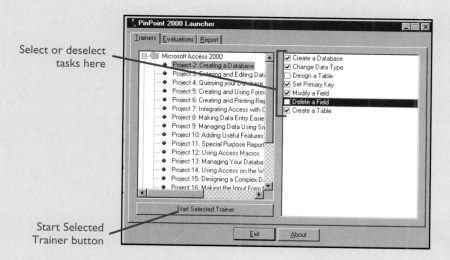

Select or deselect
tasks here

Start Selected
Trainer button

Figure A.8

continues ▶

To Start Trainers and Evaluations   (continued)

5 **Click** `Start Selected Trainer` **button if you are starting a Trainer. Click the** `Start Selected Evaluation` **button if you are starting an Evaluation.**

6 **When you start the Trainer, you might encounter a warning message instructing you to change your computer's Taskbar settings (see Figure A.9).**

If this message appears, follow its instructions before proceeding. Changing your taskbar settings in this way is necessary for proper functioning of a PinPoint Trainer. You can carry out the instructions given without canceling the box.

Figure A.9

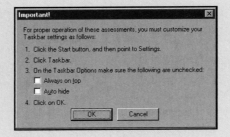

The PinPoint 2000 Launcher dialog box with your name and module selection appears (see Figure A.10).

Figure A.10

7 **Click Yes to continue.**

The Trainer or Evaluation starts.

Proceed to the next two sections to see how to run Trainers and Evaluations.

Lesson 5: Running a Trainer

This lesson shows you how to run a Trainer. It also details how to handle some of the situations you might encounter during a Trainer.

To Run a Trainer

1 **Once your name and the selected module are displayed, click OK to begin the Trainer.**

The PinPoint 2000 launcher dialog box appears before a Trainer runs (see Figure A.11).

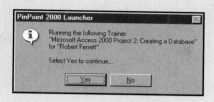

Figure A.11

2 Click Yes to continue.

The first thing you see is an introduction to how all PinPoint 2000 Trainers work. If you want to see the demonstration of how a PinPoint Trainer works and how to use the PinPoint 2000 controls, press any key or click the mouse to continue.

3 Skip through the introduction for now and go directly to a task.

After initializing, the Trainer opens the first selected task.

 Inside Stuff: Exiting the Introduction

You can exit the introduction at any time by pressing Esc and moving straight to the training.

The task instructions display in a moveable instruction box that hovers over the application (see Figure A.12).

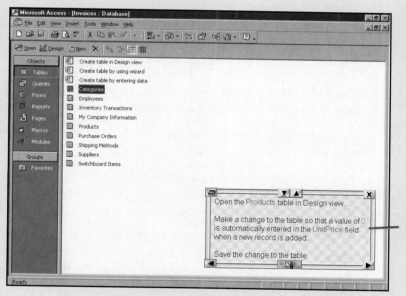

Figure A.12

The instruction box can be moved to different parts of the screen

 If You Have Problems...

If the instruction box is blocking your view of something, you can drag it to another part of the screen. To instantly move the box to the other side of the screen, right-click the instruction box.

Notice the PinPoint control buttons that appear on the perimeter of the instruction box. Use these buttons to interact with the Trainer according to your needs (see Figure A.13).

continues ▶

To Run a Trainer (continued)

Figure A.13

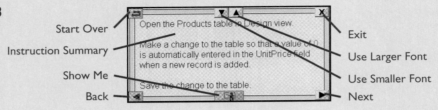

Start Over
Instruction Summary
Show Me
Back

Exit
Use Larger Font
Use Smaller Font
Next

The features of the instruction box in Figure A.13 and their descriptions are listed here:

■ The Instruction Summary displays the task to be completed. Instructions remain visible during the task.

■ The Start Over button starts the current task again.

■ The Back button returns you to the previous task.

■ The Show Me button gives you a step-by-step demonstration using a similar example.

■ The Use Larger Font and Use Smaller Font buttons enlarge or reduce the size of the box and text.

■ The Quit button ends the current training session and returns you to the Launcher.

■ The Next button checks a finished task for correct performance and moves you to the next task.

❹ Try to do the task exactly as instructed in the PinPoint instruction box.

❺ Click the Next button (refer to Figure A.13).
PinPoint 2000 gives you feedback in the Results dialog box.

Whether you performed the task correctly or not, you now have three choices:

■ Click the Show Me button to display a step-by-step demonstration using a similar example.

■ Click the Try Task Again button to set up the task so you can attempt it again.

■ Click the Next Task button to move on and attempt the next task.

If you click the Show Me button, a demonstration of how to perform a similar task is given. This demonstration, called a Show Me, begins with a summary of the steps required to perform the task.

❻ Press any key or click the mouse to advance the next Show Me box.
Usually the key concept behind the particular skill is explained during the Show Me.

After the instruction summary (and possibly a key concept), each of the instructions in the summary is explained and demonstrated in detail.

 Inside Stuff: **Exiting Show Me Demonstrations**
If you want to exit from the Show Me demonstration at any point, press Esc to return to the PinPoint task.

During the Show Me demonstration, the mouse pointer moves and text is entered automatically when appropriate to the demonstration, but whenever the description or action is completed the demonstration halts until the user prompts it to continue with either a mouse click or a key stroke.

After the demonstration is complete, you can perform the task yourself.

7 **Continue through the PinPoint Trainer at your own pace, attempting each task and watching Show Me demonstrations when you need help.**

When you have finished with the training session, the Trainers screen of the Launcher is visible again. You can see a report of your performance by clicking the Report tab in the Launcher (viewing reports is covered in Lesson 7).

 Inside Stuff: **Exiting Trainers**
You are free to exit from the training at any time by clicking the Exit button (refer to Figure A.13). When you attempt to exit a Trainer before it is finished, you are asked to confirm this decision (see Figure A.14).

Figure A.14

If you want to exit from the trainer at this point, click Yes.

Lesson 6: Running an Evaluation

This lesson shows you how to run an Evaluation. It also details how to handle some of the situations you might encounter during an Evaluation.

To Run an Evaluation

1 **When you start the Evaluation, you might encounter a warning message instructing you to change your computer's Taskbar settings (refer to Figure A.9).**

If this message appears, follow its instructions before proceeding. Changing your taskbar settings in this way is necessary for proper functioning of a PinPoint Trainer. You can carry out the instructions given without canceling the box.

2 **After you have carried out the steps listed, click OK to continue.**

The Pinpoint 2000 Launcher dialog box appears before an Evaluation runs (refer to Figure A.11).

3 **Click Yes to continue.**

The first thing you see is an introduction to how all PinPoint 2000 Evaluations work. If you want to see the demonstration of how an Evaluation works and how to use the PinPoint 2000 controls, press any key or click the mouse to continue past each screen. If you do not need to see the demonstration, press Esc to go straight to the testing.

continues ▶

To Run an Evaluation (continued)

Like a Trainer, an Evaluation presents you with a task to perform. In an Evaluation, however, the Start Over, Back, and Show Me buttons are all disabled. Therefore, you cannot restart a task, return to a previous task, or run a Show Me demonstration of how to perform the task.

4 **After attempting a task, click the Next button to continue to the next task.**
Normally, you would attempt all of the tasks in the Evaluation. But if you need to finish early and click the Exit button before you have attempted all of the tasks, the message box in Figure A.14 will display. Click the Yes button if you want to exit the Evaluation and go back to the Launcher program.

5 **You can view a report of your performance by clicking the Report tab in the Launcher.**
See the next section for details about viewing reports.

 Inside Stuff: **What to Avoid While Running Trainers and Evaluations**
Keep the following in mind for PinPoint 2000 Trainers and Evaluations to run properly:

- Only perform actions that the PinPoint task instructions ask you to perform.

- Do not exit from the Microsoft Office 2000 application in which you are training or testing unless you are told to do so.

- Do not close the example document (the document that PinPoint opens for you when you begin a task) unless you are told to do so.

- Do not run other programs (such as email, Internet browsers, virus shields, system monitors, and so on) at the same time as running PinPoint, unless you are asked to do so.

- Do not change views in one of the Office 2000 applications unless you are asked to do so.

- Do not change the way your Windows operating system or Office 2000 applications are configured by default.

- Do not turn off your computer in the middle of a PinPoint Trainer or Evaluation. Instead, first exit from the Trainer or Evaluation, and then turn off your computer.

Lesson 7: Viewing Reports in the Launcher

After you have taken at least one PinPoint 2000 Trainer or Evaluation, you can view detailed reports at any time concerning your performance on any of the modules that you have taken.

To View Reports in the Launcher

❶ If the Launcher is not running, click Start, Programs, PinPoint 2000, PinPoint 2000 to run it. Then log on.

❷ Click the Report tab.

The Report screen appears (see Figure A.15).

Click the Report tab to view a detailed report of your performance

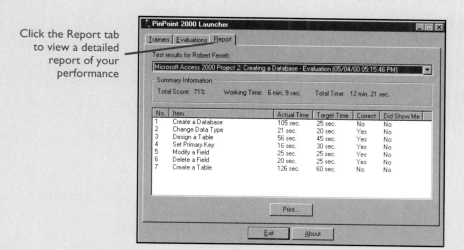

Figure A.15

The very last Trainer or Evaluation that you ran displays onscreen. The information displayed in the Report screen is as follows:

- *Total Score*—The percentage of the correctly performed tasks out of the total number of tasks set to run.

- *Working Time*—The total time you actually spent working on all of the tasks in the Trainer or Evaluation.

- *Total Time*—The total time you spent running the entire Trainer or Evaluation.

- *Item*—The name of the task.

- *Actual Time*—The time you took to perform the task.

- *Target Time*—A reasonable amount of time required to perform the task by an efficient method.

- *Correct*—Displays Yes if you performed the task correctly; No if you did not.

- *Did Show-Me*—Displays Yes if you ran a Show Me demonstration for that task; No if you did not.

Note: A blank or dotted line running through the task line, or N/A, indicate that the task was not taken.

❸ If you want to print a report, click the Print button.

❹ If you want to see a report for a Trainer or Evaluation that you took previously, select it from the Test results for <your name> drop-down list.

The reports are listed in the order in which they were taken.

Note: You will see only your own reports on the Reports screen and not the reports for anyone else using PinPoint on your computer.

 Inside Stuff: User History

An important feature of the PinPoint 2000 Launcher is its capability to keep track of your history of running Trainers and Evaluations. The Launcher uses your history to reconfigure a Trainer each successive time you run it. To "re-configure" means to change the tasks that will run.

The Launcher does not reconfigure an Evaluation the same way it does a Trainer. No matter which tasks you have performed correctly in the past (on either a Trainer or Evaluation), all tasks are automatically selected to be run when you attempt to take an Evaluation.

Lesson 8: Recovering from a Crash During a Trainer or Evaluation

If your computer crashes while you are running a Trainer or Evaluation, all the work you have already done is not wasted. You do not need to start the Trainer or Evaluation over again from the beginning. To recover from a crash during a Trainer or Evaluation, follow these simple instructions.

To Recover from a Crash

1 **Reboot your computer.**

2 **Start the Launcher again and log on as usual.**

3 **When a message like the one in Figure A.16 appears, close the Office application you were working on (if it's still running in the background) by clicking the Close button in the top right corner of the application window.**

Figure A.16

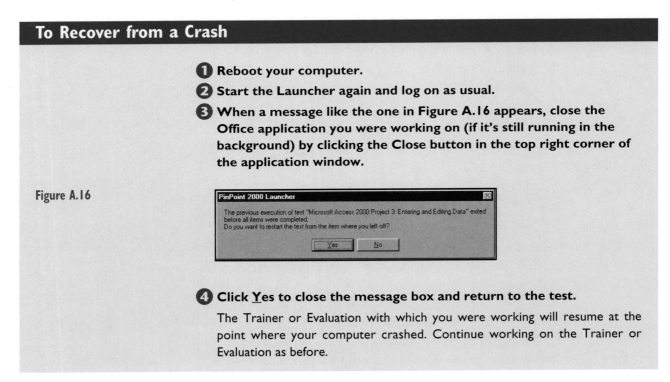

4 **Click Yes to close the message box and return to the test.**

The Trainer or Evaluation with which you were working will resume at the point where your computer crashed. Continue working on the Trainer or Evaluation as before.

Removing PinPoint 2000

When you have finished training and testing with PinPoint 2000, you may want to remove the Launcher program from your computer. PinPoint 2000 can be removed using the procedure for removing most other applications from your computer.

Lesson 9: Removing PinPoint 2000

To Remove PinPoint 2000

① From the Start menu, select <u>S</u>ettings, <u>C</u>ontrol Panel.

② Double-click the Add/Remove Programs icon.
The Add/Remove Programs Properties dialog box displays.

③ Select PinPoint 2000.

④ Click the Add/<u>R</u>emove button.

⑤ Confirm the removal of PinPoint 2000 by clicking <u>Y</u>es in the dialog box.

⑥ If the Remove Shared File? dialog box appears, click the Yes To <u>A</u>ll button (see Figure A.17).

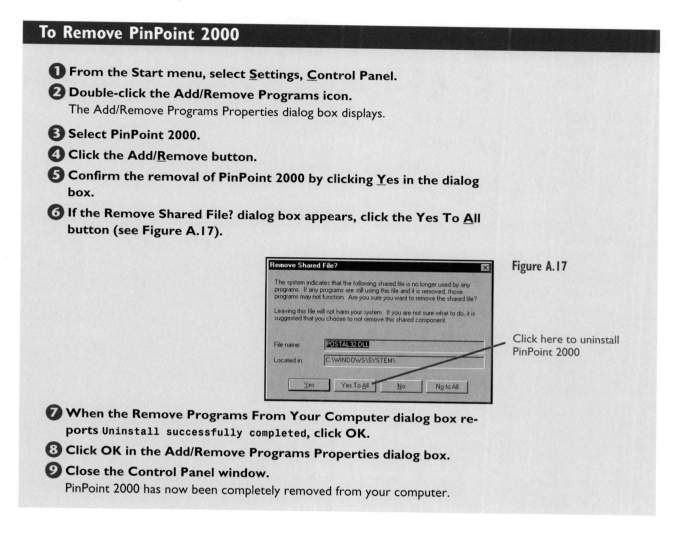

Figure A.17

Click here to uninstall PinPoint 2000

⑦ When the Remove Programs From Your Computer dialog box reports Uninstall successfully completed, click OK.

⑧ Click OK in the Add/Remove Programs Properties dialog box.

⑨ Close the Control Panel window.
PinPoint 2000 has now been completely removed from your computer.

Summary

PinPoint 2000 is a very valuable tool for preparing yourself for a MOUS Exam. You've learned how to install and start the PinPoint Launcher. You can now run Trainers and Evaluations, and view a report of their results. You also know what to avoid while running Trainers and Evaluations. You've seen how to recover if PinPoint crashes. And finally, you've learned how to uninstall PinPoint when you no longer need it. You are now equipped to take full advantage of the PinPoint 2000 training and testing software.

Preparing for MOUS Certification

This appendix gives you information that you need regarding the certification exams—how to register, what is covered in the tests, how the tests are administered, and so on. Because this information may change, be sure to visit www.mous.net for the latest updates.

What This Book Offers

This text is certified for both levels of certification:

- Core—You are able to manage a wide range of real world tasks efficiently.
- Expert—In addition to the everyday tasks at the Core level, you are able to handle complex assignments and have a thorough understanding of a program's advanced features.

In addition to the Core and Expert levels, Microsoft now offers a Master certification, which indicates that you have a comprehensive understanding of Microsoft Office 2000 and many of its advanced features. A Master certification requires students to successfully pass all five of the required exams: Word, Excel, PowerPoint, Access and Outlook.

Each exam includes a list of tasks you may be asked to perform. The lessons in this book identify these required tasks with an icon in the margin. You can also review the MOUS Skill Guide in the front of this book to become familiar with these required tasks.

In addition to these icons, this book contains various study aids that not only help you pass the test, but also teach you how the software functions. You can use this book in a classroom or lab setting, or you can work through each project on your own using the PinPoint CD-ROM. You don't have to move through the book from front to back as each project stands on its own. Each project is broken down into lessons, which are then broken down into step-by-step instructions.

The PinPoint CD-ROM includes Project Review Tests for each MOUS Exam skill set. The coverage has two parts: a Task and a Show Me. The Task requires you to do something, (for example, format a document) and the Show Me demonstrates how to perform that task. In addition, each PinPoint has a practice test that mirrors the actual MOUS exams.

Follow the steps within each of the lessons, and use the PinPoint software as an evaluation of your comprehension. If you get stuck, be sure to use the Show Me demonstration.

Registering for and Taking and the Exam

All MOUS exams are administered by a MOUS Authorized Testing Center (ATC). Most MOUS ATCs require pre-registration. To pre-register contact a local ATC directly. You can find a center near you by visiting the MOUS Web site at www.mous.net. Some ATCs accept walk-in examination candidates, allowing on-the-spot registration and examination. Be sure to check with a specific ACT to make certain of their registration policy.

The exam is not written and there are no multiple choice or true-false questions. You perform the required tasks on a computer running the live Microsoft application. A typical exam takes 45 to 60 minutes to complete. You must work through each task in the exam as quickly as you can.

All examination data is encrypted, and the examination process is closely monitored so your test scores are completely confidential. Examination results are provided only to the candidate and to Microsoft.

The Day of the Exam

Bring the following items with you to the testing center on exam day:

- Picture ID—driver's license or passport
- Your MOUS identification number (if you have take a previous MOUS certification exam)
- ATC Student ID, if applicable

At the exam center, you can expect to first complete the candidate information section, which provides the information necessary to complete your MOUS certificate.

After confirming your ID, the administrator will seat you at the test computer, log you onto the test system, and open your test module. You are now ready to begin.

To start the test, click the "Start Test" button and you're ready to begin your certification exam.

The Exam Itself

Instructions are displayed in a separate window on the screen. You can close the instruction window by clicking on it. You can restore it by clicking "Instructions" on the test information bar at the bottom of the screen. Read the test instructions carefully. Once you have started, a box in the bottom right corner of the screen indicates the question on which you are currently working. (For example, "question 3 of 50".)

If anything abnormal happens during the exam, or if the application "crashes," stop immediately and contact the administrator. The administrator will restart the test from where you left off. You will not be penalized any time for this.

When you have completed your exam, the computer will calculate your score. The scoring process takes a short time, and you will be notified onscreen whether you passed or failed. You may then ask the administrator to give you a printed report.

If you complete the exam successfully, your MOUS certificate will be delivered within 2-3 weeks.

General Tips

Unlike earlier MOUS exams, the results of the Office 2000 MOUS exams are expressed as a value on a 1000-point scale, rather than a percentage.

Each activity or question on the Office 2000 MOUS exams is comprised of several individually scored subtasks. A candidates's score is derived from the number of subtasks successfully completed and the "weight" or difficulty assigned to each.

Pay close attention to how each question is worded. Answers must be precise, resolving the question exactly as asked.

You can use any combination of menus, toolbars and shortcut keys to complete each assigned task. Answers are scored based on the result, not the method you use or the time taken to complete each required task. Extra keystrokes or mouse clicks will not count against your score as long as you achieve the correct result within the time limit given.

Remember that the overall test is timed. While spending a lot of time on an individual answer will not adversely affect the scoring of that particular question, taking too long may not leave you with enough time to complete the entire test.

Answers are either right or wrong. You do not get credit for partial answers.

Important! Check to make sure you have entirely completed each question before clicking the NEXT TASK button. Once you press the NEXT TASK button, you will not be able to return to that question. A question will be scored as wrong if it is not completed properly before moving to the next question.

Save your Results Page that prints at the end of the exam. It is your confirmation that you passed the exam.

Take note of these cautions:

- DON'T leave dialog boxes, Help menus, toolbars, or menus open.
- DON'T leave tables, boxes, or cells "active or highlighted" unless instructed to do so.
- DON'T click the NEXT TASK button until you have "completely" answered the current question.

Lastly, be sure to visit the mous.net Web site for specific information on the Office 2000 exams, more testing tips, and to download a free demo of the exams.

Glossary

All key terms in this book (in bold italic) are listed alphabetically in this Glossary for easy reference. If you'd like to learn more about the feature or concept, just turn to the page listed after the definition. You can also use the Index to find the term's other significant occurrences.

action buttons   Objects, such as an AutoShape or a drawn object, that you link to files or Web sites. [pg. 314]

action items   Items that you assign to people during a slide show or meeting. [pg. 178]

activating   Opening a peripheral program (such as Microsoft Graph) in memory by double-clicking the associated object. Activated objects typically have black selection handles and a rope-like border. [pg. 152]

adjustment handle   A diamond-shaped handle that you can use to change the appearance (not the size) of an AutoShape. [pg. 253]

animated GIF   A file that includes a series of Graphics Interchange Format (GIF) images. These images are played in rapid sequence to give the illusion of movement. GIF files usually have an extension of .gif. [pg. 238]

animating   Displaying objects in sequence to produce the illusion of movement or to control the flow of information. Use of animation in a slide show enables you to focus on important points or just add interest to your presentation (for example, to display bullet points one at a time). [pg. 163]

annotate   To write or draw directly on a slide during a slide show. [pg. 188]

annotation pen   A special mouse pointer that enables you to write or draw directly on a slide during a slide show. [pg. 188]

array   An arrangement in which duplicates of an object are evenly distributed on a slide. [pg. 260]

AutoContent Wizard   A wizard that helps you to create a presentation that includes a preset design and sample content. [pg. 31]

AutoLayout   A predefined layout option in PowerPoint. [pg. 5]

AutoShapes   Professionally designed shapes such as stars, banners, and bubble callouts that are supplied with all Office applications. [pg. 248]

broadcast   Using NetShow Services to communicate one-way meetings with others in remote locations via a computer network. [pg. 347]

building   (see **animating**)

bullets   Objects, such as circles or squares, used to set off items in a list. [pg. 78]

case   The mix of upper- and lowercase letters in a text string. [pg. 204]

cell   The intersection of a column and row in a datasheet. [pg. 149]

cell pointer   A darkened border around a datasheet cell, which indicates the location of the active cell. [pg. 150]

character attributes   Characteristics such as bold, italic, or underline applied to text for emphasis. [pg. 78]

chart   A pictorial representation of data. [pg. 146]

chart subtypes   Variations on the main chart types. For example, a pie chart has subtypes, such as exploded pie and 3-D pie. [pg. 147]

clip art   Electronic pictures, available from various sources, which you can add to PowerPoint slides. [pg. 35]

Clip Gallery   A peripheral program shared by all Office applications that you can use to find and insert clips into a presentation. [pg. 224]

Clip Gallery Live   A Microsoft Web site that includes a wealth of free clips. [pg. 224]

Clipboard   A temporary area of memory that holds material that is cut (or copied) to be pasted elsewhere. [pg. 66]

collaborate   To work interactively with others on projects. PowerPoint 2000 includes several collaboration features, many of which depend on being connected electronically through your company's intranet or the World Wide Web. [pg. 336]

color scheme   The underlying set of eight coordinated colors for a presentation. [pg. 130]

context sensitive   The way a menu displays the commands that relate to the area of the screen that you click. [pg. 41]

custom slide shows   Presentations that have several variations, based on which slides you choose. [pg. 314]

data charts   Charts that show numeric data in a pictorial manner. [pg. 146]

data series   A collection of values in a chart that pertains to a single subject. [pg. 160]

datasheet   A mini-worksheet that enables you to revise the information in a data chart. [pg. 149]

default   The original settings used in a program, which you can modify to change the way the program operates. [pg. 151]

demote Indenting text on a slide to show that it has less importance than the preceding text item. [pg. 65]

design templates (see **templates**)

destination program The program that accepts the data that you want to link or embed. (see also **Object Linking and Embedding**) [pg. 280]

docked Refers to a toolbar attached to one side of the application window. [pg. 286]

drag-and-drop A method in which you select an object, and then drag it to a new location before releasing the mouse button. [pg. 62]

drawn objects Objects such as rectangles, ovals, lines, or arrows that you can draw on a slide to jazz it up or emphasize specific information. [pg. 248]

editing mode A state in which you can enter or edit text in a placeholder. [pg. 6]

electronic slide show A predetermined list of slides displayed sequentially. You can show the slides on a monitor, or use an overhead projector to cast the image from your computer onto a large screen. [pg. 2]

electronic clips Electronic graphic or multimedia files (including pictures, sounds, and movies) that you can use in presentations. [pg. 224]

embedded object An item created by one program, but inserted into a document created by another program. [pg. 149]

field An area used especially for data that might change in a document[md]for example, the page number field used in a footer. [pg. 137]

fill effects Methods you can use to format objects, such as adding solid colors, shading styles, textures, or semi-transparent fills. [pg. 261]

floating toolbar An onscreen toolbar that displays in its own window. [pg. 286]

font Also called typeface, a font is a collection of characters (letters, numbers, and special symbols) that have a specific appearance. [pg. 78]

footer area The place at the bottom of each slide where you can add items such as your company name or a slide number. [pg. 32]

Format Painter A feature used to quickly copy text or object formatting from one area of text (or an object) to another. [pg. 262]

formatting The way that a presentation is set up to display (including text, alignment, bullets, margins, and so on). [pg. 78]

frame A border that surrounds a slide element. [pg. 106]

freehand shapes Objects such as lines, rectangles, and ovals that you draw from scratch with the mouse. [pg. 248]

full menu A menu that includes all of PowerPoint's commands. [pg. 10]

gradient fill A popular visual effect you can apply to an object or slide background where colors fade from one color to another. [pg. 132]

grayscale Shades of white, gray, and black on printed output. [pg. 46]

handouts Printed output that includes only the slides' contents, not the accompanying notes. [pg. 106]

home page The opening page of a Web site, which is usually devoted to the main topic for the site and includes hyperlinks to other areas in the site. [pg. 341]

horizontal text alignment The way that text displays horizontally in a placeholder. [pg. 83]

hyperlinks Text or objects in your presentation (or on a Web page) that provide a pathway (link) to another slide, presentation, graphic, file, intranet, or World Wide Web location. [pg. 15]

Hypertext Markup Language (HTML) A file format that controls the display of graphics, formatting, and hyperlinks for pages used on the World Wide Web. Others can view HTML documents if they have a Web browser. [pg. 336]

icon bar A special bar in Microsoft Organization Chart that displays box tools and its own menu bar so that you can use its commands. [pg. 166]

install on first use feature A feature that you're prompted to install the first time you try to use it. If the feature hasn't been used before on your system, PowerPoint displays a message box, prompting you to install it. [pg. 337]

integration Combining two or more software functions or program features to produce a result that is not possible otherwise. For example, you can link an Excel chart to a PowerPoint presentation to combine features from both programs. [pg. 280]

interactive slide shows Slide shows that perform an action in response to user input. Interactive slide shows are useful when you want to involve the users or require input from them (such as at a trade show). [pg. 314]

Internet A loose association of thousands of networks worldwide, through which you can access libraries, scientific, medical, and business information, and so on; originally designed as a way for government and university facilities to share information. [pg. 336]

intranet A private Web server used to post Web pages for internal use, commonly used in companies and schools. [pg. 314]

keyboard shortcuts The keys you can press on the keyboard to perform actions. [pg. 38]

keyword An item in a list of alphabetic Help topics that you can use to find all related topics. [pg. 17]
Also refers to a topical word that you use to find related clips in the Clip Gallery. [pg. 224]

landscape orientation The layout used where the width of the paper is greater than the height. [pg. 110]

linking The process of actively sharing information among different programs via an "electronic pipeline" (see also **Object Linking and Embedding**). [pg. 280]

motion clips Video or movie clips in a presentation that you insert via the Clip Gallery from a file on your hard disk or from the Web. [pg. 236]

mouse over action   A command that PowerPoint executes whenever you move your mouse pointer over a hyperlink. [pg. 326]

move bars   The double gray bars that appear at one end of a docked toolbar. They are used to move the toolbar to another location. [pg. 286]

multimedia   Special effects that you can add to a presentation, such as music, sound, and videos. Also refers to the computer's capability to integrate various ways of communicating with others. [pg. 188]

Navigation pane   The left pane of the Help window, which helps you navigate through various topics, by topic or by keyword. [pg. 15]

NetMeeting   A feature included with Office 2000 that enables you to set up an online meeting and share information with others in real-time (the actual time when events occur) over the Internet or your company's intranet. [pg. 347]

Normal view   A tri-pane view that includes a Slide pane, an Outline pane, and a Notes pane. Each of these three panes represents a way to work with your presentation. [pg. 5]

notes box   An area where you can enter your notes while in Notes Page view. [pg. 102]

Notes pane   An onscreen area that help you to develop speaker notes. [pg. 5]

object   An item placed on a slide (such as a chart). [pg. 149]

Object Linking and Embedding (OLE)   The capability Windows programs have to constantly share updated information with each other because they maintain an active connection. [pg. 280]

Office Assistant   PowerPoint's online Help system that supplies answers to your questions. [pg. 2]

Office Clipboard   Enables you to insert data from multiple sources all at once. For example, you can "collect" data from several Excel and Word files, and then paste it simultaneously into a PowerPoint presentation. [pg. 280]

organization chart   A chart that visually shows the structure of an organization. [pg. 148]

orientation   The rotation of a slide when viewing or printing it. [pg. 110]

Outline pane   An onscreen area that organizes the content of the entire presentation and enables you to get a feel for the overall flow. [pg. 5]

output   The product used in a presentation. In PowerPoint, you can choose among onscreen presentations, Web presentations, black-and-white overheads, color overheads, and 35mm slides. [pg. 32]

Pack and Go Wizard   A PowerPoint feature that enables you to package all presentation files (including linked files and fonts) on a disk so that you can run the presentation on another computer. [pg. 337]

palette   A drop-down list of colors from which you can choose the colors that coordinate with your presentation's color scheme. [pg. 81]

parent box   A selected box in an organization chart to which you want to attach a new box. [pg. 167]

peripheral program   A program that you activate from within another program. For example, Microsoft Graph is a peripheral program that you can access within Microsoft Office applications. [pg. 149]

personalized menus and toolbars   Menus and toolbars that PowerPoint continually adapts to an individual's work habits by displaying only the commands and buttons that you use most frequently. [pg. 11]

placeholder   An area on a slide that can accept different types of objects, such as graphics and text. [pg. 5]

points   A unit of measurement used to designate character height in a font. [pg. 79]

pop-up menu   A menu that displays when you click a clip in the Clip Gallery. [pg. 225]

portrait orientation   The layout used where the height of the page is greater than the width. [pg. 110]

presentation   A series of slides that contains visual information you can use to persuade an audience. [pg. 2]

PowerPoint Viewer   A program you can use to run slide shows on computers that don't have PowerPoint installed on them. [pg. 337]

Presentation Assistant   A special type of Office Assistant that checks a presentation for problems with style and offers help and tips on how to improve the presentation. [pg. 211]

presentation graphics program   A software package, such as PowerPoint, that helps you structure, design, and present information to an audience so that it is catchy and visually appealing. [pg. 2]

promote   Indenting text less, indicating the relative importance of the text. [pg. 65]

pure black and white   All gray areas are converted to black or white on printed output. [pg. 46]

Random Access Memory (RAM)   The temporary storage space that a computer uses for programs that it is currently running. [pg. 3]

real-time   The actual time in which online events occur. For example, the NetMeeting feature enables you to communicate in real-time with others; email does not. [pg. 347]

recoloring   The process of changing the colors in a clip, to make the image display more attractively with the template's colors or to emphasize information. [pg. 231]

reverse video   The computer's method of highlighting text on the display so that dark text is shown as bright characters on a dark background. [pg. 58]

rotate handles   Small green handles that appear around an object that you drag to rotate the object. [pg. 259]

ScreenTip   A small box that displays the name of a button or object when you rest the mouse pointer on that object. [pg. 8]

selecting Clicking an object (or dragging over text). When an object, such as a chart is selected, white square selection handles appear around its border. [pg. 152]

semi-transparent fill A fill effect, in which an object is not completely filled with color; used to create visual effects. [pg. 262]

sentence case The case in which the first letter of a sentence or phrase is capitalized. [pg. 204]

short menu An abbreviated list of commonly used commands. [pg. 10]

shortcut menu A list of context-sensitive commands that you display by right-clicking an object. [pg. 4]

slide image A small-scale version of a slide shown in Notes Page view. [pg. 102]

slide master A framework slide that controls the way presentation slides will look by governing characteristics such as font, background color, shadowing, and bullet style. [pg. 124]

Slide pane An onscreen area that shows how an individual slide appears. You can add text, graphics, and other objects to a slide in this window. [pg. 5]

slide transitions Visual effects that PowerPoint uses to change from one slide to the next slide in a screen show. [pg. 178]

source program The program in which the data you want to link or embed is originally created or modified (see also **Object Linking and Embedding**). [pg. 280]

speaker notes Supporting data, quotations, or illustrations that you can use when giving a presentation. [pg. 102]

style The way elements, such as text and graphics, are handled in a presentation (or any document). [pg. 209]

stylistic problems Incorrect capitalization, too much text on a slide, and so on. You can use the Presentation Assistant to help avoid these problems. [pg. 283]

summary slide Sometimes called an agenda slide, a summary slide is a presentation slide that converts the titles of selected slides into bulleted points on a single slide. You usually place this slide immediately after the title slide, so your audience can see at a glance what your presentation will cover. [pg. 215]

sweep An arrangement in which duplicates of an object slightly overlap. [pg. 260]

tab type button A button that appears on the left end of the ruler. You click the button to change between left-, center-, and right-aligned tabs. [pg. 85]

table A grid of columns and rows that you can use to display slide data in an organized manner. [pg. 285]

templates (also called **design templates**) "Blueprints" upon which you can base your presentation. Templates include the formatting, color, and graphics necessary to create a particular "look." [pg. 28]

thumbnail A miniature slide representation. [pg. 28]

title case The case in which the first letter of each word is capitalized. [pg. 284]

toggle To turn a feature on and off using the same button or command. [pg. 109]

TrueType fonts Scalable fonts (designated by the TT next to a font's name) that print the same as they display onscreen. [pg. 206]

typeface (see **font**)

upload To copy files to your Web server. For example, you can upload a PowerPoint presentation to a Web server so that others can view your presentation online from a remote location. [pg. 345]

usage data The list of commands that PowerPoint tracks to personalize your menus. You can reset the usage data to the original program settings at any time. [pg. 365]

views The various perspectives which PowerPoint provides to work with a presentation. You can switch between views to choose the most appropriate one for modifying or presenting your presentation. [pg. 28]

visual clarity The way in which text is used in a presentation (or any document), which includes appropriate font usage and the legibility of slide text. [pg. 209]

voice narration A soundtrack that you can add to a presentation, which plays when you run the slide show. [pg. 236]

watermark A faint image of a picture that displays beneath other text or images on a slide. [pg. 233]

Web browser The software program you use to view Web pages, such as Internet Explorer or Netscape Navigator. [pg. 336]

Web Page Preview A PowerPoint view that helps you see how your presentation will look as a Web page by opening it in your Web browser. [pg. 341]

Windows Clipboard An area in memory that temporarily stores data. Whenever you cut (or copy) information, it's placed in the Clipboard. You can then move to a different location[md]either in the same application or a different one[md]and use the Paste command to insert the data at the new location. [pg. 280]

wizard An interactive help utility that guides you through each step of a multistep operation. [pg. 31]

worksheet A spreadsheet file used in Microsoft Excel that can be imported into PowerPoint. [pg. 285]

World Wide Web (WWW) The graphical, user-friendly way to explore the Internet. Web pages typically include many hyperlinks that you can click to quickly jump to related information. [pg. 336]

Index

GLE PC LICENSE AGREEMENT AND LIMITED WARRANTY
AD THIS LICENSE CAREFULLY BEFORE USING THIS PACKAGE. BY USING THIS PACKAGE, YOU ARE
REEING TO THE TERMS AND CONDITIONS OF THIS LICENSE. IF YOU DO NOT AGREE, DO NOT USE THE PACK-
AGE. PROMPTLY RETURN THE UNUSED PACKAGE AND ALL ACCOMPANYING ITEMS TO THE PLACE YOU OBTAINED.
THESE TERMS APPLY TO ALL LICENSED SOFTWARE ON THE DISK EXCEPT THAT THE TERMS FOR USE OF ANY
SHAREWARE OR FREEWARE ON THE DISKETTES ARE AS SET FORTH IN THE ELECTRONIC LICENSE LOCATED ON
THE DISK:

1. GRANT OF LICENSE and OWNERSHIP: The enclosed computer programs and data ("Software") are licensed, not sold, to you by Prentice-Hall, Inc. ("We" or the "Company") and in consideration of your purchase or adoption of the accompanying Company textbooks and/or other materials, and your agreement to these terms. We reserve any rights not granted to you. You own only the disk(s) but we and/or our licensors own the Software itself. This license allows you to use and display your copy of the Software on a single computer (i.e., with a single CPU) at a single location for <u>academic</u> use only, so long as you comply with the terms of this Agreement. You may make one copy for back up, or transfer your copy to another CPU, provided that the Software is usable on only one computer.

2. RESTRICTIONS: You may <u>not</u> transfer or distribute the Software or documentation to anyone else. Except for backup, you may <u>not</u> copy the documentation or the Software. You may <u>not</u> network the Software or otherwise use it on more than one computer or computer terminal at the same time. You may <u>not</u> reverse engineer, disassemble, decompile, modify, adapt, translate, or create derivative works based on the Software or the Documentation. You may be held legally responsible for any copying or copyright infringement which is caused by your failure to abide by the terms of these restrictions.

3. TERMINATION: This license is effective until terminated. This license will terminate automatically without notice from the Company if you fail to comply with any provisions or limitations of this license. Upon termination, you shall destroy the Documentation and all copies of the Software. All provisions of this Agreement as to limitation and disclaimer of warranties, limitation of liability, remedies or damages, and our ownership rights shall survive termination.

4. LIMITED WARRANTY AND DISCLAIMER OF WARRANTY: Company warrants that for a period of 60 days from the date you purchase this SOFTWARE (or purchase or adopt the accompanying textbook), the Software, when properly installed and used in accordance with the Documentation, will operate in substantial conformity with the description of the Software set forth in the Documentation, and that for a period of 30 days the disk(s) on which the Software is delivered shall be free from defects in materials and workmanship under normal use. The Company does <u>not</u> warrant that the Software will meet your requirements or that the operation of the Software will be uninterrupted or error-free. Your only remedy and the Company's only obligation under these limited warranties is, at the Company's option, return of the disk for a refund of any amounts paid for it by you or replacement of the disk. THIS LIMITED WARRANTY IS THE ONLY WARRANTY PROVIDED BY THE COMPANY AND ITS LICENSORS, AND THE COMPANY AND ITS LICENSORS DISCLAIM ALL OTHER WARRANTIES, EXPRESS OR IMPLIED, INCLUDING WITHOUT LIMITATION, THE IMPLIED WARRANTIES OF MERCHANTABILITY AND FITNESS FOR A PARTICULAR PURPOSE. THE COMPANY DOES NOT WARRANT, GUARANTEE OR MAKE ANY REPRESENTATION REGARDING THE ACCURACY, RELIABILITY, CURRENTNESS, USE, OR RESULTS OF USE, OF THE SOFTWARE.

5. LIMITATION OF REMEDIES AND DAMAGES: IN NO EVENT, SHALL THE COMPANY OR ITS EMPLOYEES, AGENTS, LICENSORS, OR CONTRACTORS BE LIABLE FOR ANY INCIDENTAL, INDIRECT, SPECIAL, OR CONSEQUEN-TIAL DAMAGES ARISING OUT OF OR IN CONNECTION WITH THIS LICENSE OR THE SOFTWARE, INCLUDING FOR LOSS OF USE, LOSS OF DATA, LOSS OF INCOME OR PROFIT, OR OTHER LOSSES, SUSTAINED AS A RESULT OF INJURY TO ANY PERSON, OR LOSS OF OR DAMAGE TO PROPERTY, OR CLAIMS OF THIRD PARTIES, EVEN IF THE COMPANY OR AN AUTHORIZED REPRESENTATIVE OF THE COMPANY HAS BEEN ADVISED OF THE POSSIBILITY OF SUCH DAM-AGES. IN NO EVENT SHALL THE LIABILITY OF THE COMPANY FOR DAMAGES WITH RESPECT TO THE SOFTWARE EXCEED THE AMOUNTS ACTUALLY PAID BY YOU, IF ANY, FOR THE SOFTWARE OR THE ACCOMPANYING TEXT-BOOK. BECAUSE SOME JURISDICTIONS DO NOT ALLOW THE LIMITATION OF LIABILITY IN CERTAIN CIRCUM-STANCES, THE ABOVE LIMITATIONS MAY NOT ALWAYS APPLY TO YOU.

6. GENERAL: THIS AGREEMENT SHALL BE CONSTRUED IN ACCORDANCE WITH THE LAWS OF THE UNITED STATES OF AMERICA AND THE STATE OF NEW YORK, APPLICABLE TO CONTRACTS MADE IN NEW YORK, AND SHALL BENE-FIT THE COMPANY, ITS AFFILIATES AND ASSIGNEES. HIS AGREEMENT IS THE COMPLETE AND EXCLUSIVE STATEMENT OF THE AGREEMENT BETWEEN YOU AND THE COMPANY AND SUPERSEDES ALL PROPOSALS OR PRIOR AGREE-MENTS, ORAL, OR WRITTEN, AND ANY OTHER COMMUNICATIONS BETWEEN YOU AND THE COMPANY OR ANY REPRESENTATIVE OF THE COMPANY RELATING TO THE SUBJECT MATTER OF THIS AGREEMENT. If you are a U.S. Government user, this Software is licensed with "restricted rights" as set forth in subparagraphs (a)-(d) of the Commercial Computer-Restricted Rights clause at FAR 52.227-19 or in subparagraphs (c)(1)(ii) of the Rights in Technical Data and Computer Software clause at DFARS 252.227-7013, and similar clauses, as applicable.

Should you have any questions concerning this agreement or if you wish to contact the Company for any reason, please contact in writing:

Director, New Media
Prentice Hall
1 Lake Street
Upper Saddle River, New Jersey 07458